Understanding
QUANTITATIVE DATA
in EDUCATIONAL
RESEARCH

Sara Miller McCune founded SAGE Publishing in 1965 to support the dissemination of usable knowledge and educate a global community. SAGE publishes more than 1000 journals and over 800 new books each year, spanning a wide range of subject areas. Our growing selection of library products includes archives, data, case studies and video. SAGE remains majority owned by our founder and after her lifetime will become owned by a charitable trust that secures the company's continued independence.

Los Angeles | London | New Delhi | Singapore | Washington DC | Melbourne

Understanding
QUANTITATIVE DATA
in EDUCATIONAL
RESEARCH

Nicoleta Gaciu

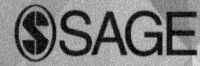

Los Angeles | London | New Delhi
Singapore | Washington DC | Melbourne

Los Angeles | London | New Delhi
Singapore | Washington DC | Melbourne

SAGE Publications Ltd
1 Oliver's Yard
55 City Road
London EC1Y 1SP

SAGE Publications Inc.
2455 Teller Road
Thousand Oaks, California 91320

SAGE Publications India Pvt Ltd
B 1/I 1 Mohan Cooperative Industrial Area
Mathura Road
New Delhi 110 044

SAGE Publications Asia-Pacific Pte Ltd
3 Church Street
#10-04 Samsung Hub
Singapore 049483

© Nicoleta Gaciu 2021

First published 2021

Editor: James Clark
Senior assistant editor: Diana Alves
Associate content development editor: Sunita Patel
Production editor: Nicola Carrier
Copyeditor: Richard Leigh
Proofreader: Sharon Cawood
Indexer: Gary Kirby
Marketing manager: Dilhara Attygalle
Cover design: Naomi Robinson
Typeset by: C&M Digitals (P) Ltd, Chennai, India
Printed in the UK

Library of Congress Control Number: 2020936578

British Library Cataloguing in Publication data

A catalogue record for this book is available from the British Library

ISBN 978-1-4739-8214-7
ISBN 978-1-4739-8215-4 (pbk)

At SAGE we take sustainability seriously. Most of our products are printed in the UK using responsibly sourced papers and boards. When we print overseas we ensure sustainable papers are used as measured by the PREPS grading system. We undertake an annual audit to monitor our sustainability.

To my wonderful mother, Paula Dora, for always loving and supporting me.
Thank you for everything.

CONTENTS

ABOUT THE AUTHOR

Dr Nicoleta Gaciu has followed Education as her professional path since the first years of her pedagogical college. Her academic and research specialisations in disciplines such as physics, statistics, computer sciences, research methods and business have given her the best opportunities to make connections across disciplines, to view real-life phenomena through different lenses and to take different perspectives, knowledge, logical and methodological approaches for interdisciplinary research. Nicoleta is Senior Lecturer in Education at Oxford Brookes University, UK.

ABOUT THE ONLINE RESOURCES

This book is supported by a set of online resources available at:

https://study.sagepub.com/gaciu

These include:

- Data files, linked to specific exercises in the book
- Text versions of R scripts from the book for you to use
- Links to open access data sets and other useful resources.

ACKNOWLEDGEMENTS

Special thanks to James Clark, Senior Commissioning Editor, for his encouragement and patience in publishing this book, and to Diana Alves, Education Assistant Editor, who supported me throughout the entire production process. I am also very grateful to Richard Leigh for his diligent copyediting and useful suggestions and remarks.

INTRODUCTION

Understanding quantitative data in educational research is not only about collecting and analysing quantitative data to find answers to a research question or to test a hypothesis, but also crucial for understanding and critiquing published research results in the form of research papers, projects, reports or dissertations with a focus on quantitative data and statistics. Often the analysis, interpretation and presentation of quantitative data is very stressful for undergraduate and postgraduate students, teachers and early-career researchers in education due to a fear of working with numbers and statistical tests. This book is designed to help students, researchers and teachers to overcome such fear and to become confident in analysing and interpreting quantitative data and selecting the appropriate statistical tests.

The primary aims of the book are to describe, in plain language, a variety of methods for analysing quantitative data in educational research, which are supported by practical examples of how to select and run these tests using R, the free software environment for statistical computing and graphics. Each chapter includes step-by-step instructions on how to run a specific statistic test in R, which are presented in boxed form throughout the book. No specific experience in statistics or knowledge of R is assumed. In addition, many practical tips are offered on how to interpret the test results correctly. All mathematical formulae can be found at the end of the chapter, followed by exercises and further readings.

Analysis of quantitative information typically requires the use of multiple statistical and computational techniques before reaching any conclusions. For example, descriptive statistics include measures of central tendency, such as the mean, median and mode, and measures of dispersal or variability, such as the range, variance and standard deviation, to summarise an entire distribution of data by a single measure. These techniques will be addressed in Chapter 3. To make predictions, estimates and generalisations of a population based on information obtained from a sample, inferential statistics can be used, and a variety of techniques belonging to this type of statistics will be presented in Chapters 4–14. However, using only these techniques is not enough; they just make calculations and do not interpret data. Statistical analysis goes hand-in-hand with the graphical display of data because it helps with the process of understanding and communicating results and conclusions in useful ways. Different types of scales of measurement require different types of visualisation and can be quickly done by the graphical representation of data before any computational assessment. For example, to get an overview of ordinal data, a bar chart can be used, and for a time series, to find relevant patterns in observed data, a line graph is useful. Besides, graphs help us not only to perceive some features of data but also to check if the assumptions made for a statistical test are correct.

0 1 Organisation of this book

This book is divided into six parts. Part I includes Chapter 1, an introduction to information, knowledge and quantitative data, and Chapter 2, an introduction to R and RStudio. Part II, consisting of Chapter 3, discusses how to visualise quantitative data. Part III includes three chapters on descriptive statistics (Chapter 4), measures of dispersion (Chapter 5) and the normal distribution and standardised scores (Chapter 6). Part IV, on making estimations and predictions from data, includes two chapters: the fundamentals of inferential statistics are discussed in Chapter 7, and the fundamentals of estimations and hypothesis testing are presented in Chapter 8. Part V includes the next four chapters, which describe various statistical tests suitable for making inferences from one sample (Chapter 9), analysing and interpreting the differences between two dependent or independent samples (Chapter 10), differences between more than two independent samples (Chapter 11) and differences between more than two dependent samples (Chapter 12). Finally, Part VI includes two chapters on relationships between variables (Chapter 13) and on making predictions for independent and dependent variables using regression analysis (Chapter 14).

PART ONE

Understanding quantitative data and R

1

Introduction to information, knowledge and quantitative data

Chapter Objectives

In this chapter, we will:

- define quantitative data
- discuss the difference between data, information and knowledge
- explore and exemplify the difference between discrete and continuous data
- define and exemplify scales (or levels) of measurement in education research
- describe, discuss and exemplify concepts, constructs and variables
- discover the relationship between concepts and research problems and hypotheses.

Educational research deals with complex information and variability in qualitative and quantitative data collected using various research methods, such as tests, observations, interventions, interviews or questionnaires. Analysing and interpreting educational data, especially quantitative data, which is often linked with statistical techniques, and learning the mathematical theory behind statistical concepts is not an easy task for most researchers, students, teachers or policy-makers. This book aims to keep the mathematical calculations to a minimum and emphasise the practical applications of the analysis of quantitative data and interpretation of various statistical test results in educational research.

Most educational research involves generating quantitative data, also called numerical data. Analysing, interpreting and presenting this type of data is becoming increasingly important as a tool in various investigations, not only in universities but also in schools. When the results of an intervention or series of observations have been recorded, the final aim is to interpret them and reach reliable conclusions. Standard procedures in an educational research design consist of collecting, organising and analysing data, followed by interpreting the results and presenting findings. Due to the variability within educational data, the results can be examined using descriptive and inferential statistics. The choice of statistics will be guided, in the first instance, by levels of measurement and distribution of data. In addition, theoretical stance and ethical factors can influence a researcher's choice of research methods to analyse quantitative data. For example, positivists are generally concerned with reliability and representativeness, and they will consider inferential statistics, which fulfil these requirements. The choice of statistical tests will be guided throughout the research process by the methodological approach adopted, which in turn depends on how the research question and hypotheses are formulated.

 **Quantitative data, information and knowledge in education**

Data is a rich source of information and might reveal essential aspects of knowledge in the education process. Quantitative data is used at different levels and in various settings, from teachers and researchers to local, national and international authorities, and is important in all areas of education, including the fields of policy, practice and research. For example, the various types of attitude and performance assessments create large sets of quantitative data on student performance at school, regional, national and international levels. Quantitative data is often referred to as evidence for decision-making and accountability or can provide a basis for investigating a research problem and/or generating the information used in policy-making and knowledge.

In recent years, a considerable amount of educational data has been created, and its availability is growing due to a new generation of technology. As a result, there is considerable and growing interest in and need for turning such data into useful information and knowledge from a broad range of perspectives: in theory, research and practice. However, data is just 'raw material', and the process of transforming data into information and knowledge has been seen as a linear and hierarchical process which can be represented by the data–information–knowledge–wisdom (DIKW) model. The presumption of this model is that data is transformed into wisdom using a stepwise process based on the six 'W' questions. The process starts with the collection of raw data, followed by data analysis to answer the 'who', 'what', 'when' and 'where' questions about that raw data, which at this stage becomes information. In the third step, the information is converted into knowledge by trying to answer the 'how' question about the information. And in the final step, the knowledge is applied and implemented to answer the 'why' question. Zins (2007) has documented over 100 definitions of data, information and knowledge, which reflect different theoretical and philosophical perspectives. For example, data is defined as 'facts and statistics that can be measured, counted and stored'. Information gives 'meaning, relevance and purpose' to quantified data. Knowledge is information that has been emerging from analysis, reflection upon and synthesis of information (Zins, 2007, p. 483).

In this book, we do not propose a new model or follow the DIKW model, because all processes of educational data collection and analysis follow a complex and nonlinear path. The exponential development of technology has made it possible to perform an advanced data analysis which involves introducing educational data mining to explore the multiple levels of hierarchy in educational data to transform information into knowledge. Before performing any types of analysis, data has to be organised and categorised, and, using data visualisation, a researcher can quickly get information (for example, on how students choose to use their electronic devices) and consider data at various levels (such as the session level, student level, classroom level, and university level). Furthermore, the transformation of information from concepts into constructs and variables and the use of descriptive and inferential statistical techniques will enable a better understanding of educational processes and phenomena.

1.1.1 What is quantitative data?

Quantitative data is numerical information that is measured or counted and recorded in a variety of forms, including counts, scores or ranks. There are two types of quantitative data. If data is acquired directly by the researcher, then it is classified as *primary* quantitative data. Typical examples of methods to collect primary quantitative data include interviews and questionnaires that employ closed-ended questions. Counting the number of pupils passing an exam or observing and making notes on the time spent by a group of children solving a problem are examples of primary quantitative data. If quantitative data is collected from published papers or government publications and unpublished research, it is classified as *secondary* quantitative data.

If the quantitative data, whether primary or secondary, can take a finite number of possible values, then it would be classified as *discrete* data. Typically, this type of data involves integer numbers (for example, the number of pupils taking a maths exam). If the numerical values fall on a continuum, and it is possible to have fractional or decimal values (such as height, age, and distance), this numerical data would be classified as *continuous* data. For example, we can divide this type of data into smaller and smaller portions; each portion's value continues to have a meaning.

1 2 Measurement and scales of measurement

1.2.1 What is a measurement? What is a scale?

The concepts of measurement and scales of measurement are often used interchangeably by practitioners and in some news articles and textbooks. However, they do not have the same meaning. Stevens (1946, p. 677) defines measurement, in general terms, as the 'assignment of numerals to objects or events according to rules'. There is an interlocking connection between the aspects of an object or event, the properties of numerals, and certain empirical operations performed, which will lead to certain types of scales, as shown in Table 1.1. The four scales of measurement are *nominal*, *ordinal*, *interval* and *ratio*. Also, these scales of measurement can serve as a guide to the statistical procedures that can be used with the data and the conclusions that can be drawn from them.

Table 1.1 Scales of measurement for different types of data

Scales of measurement	Types of data	
	Discrete	Continuous
Nominal	✓	
Ordinal	✓	
Interval		✓
Ratio		✓

Nominal measurement involves arranging data into named categories which are qualitatively rather than quantitatively different and do not have an implicit or natural order, rank or value. For example, pupils can be classified into gender groups (boys and girls), religious groups (Christian and non-Christian), and school groups (state, independent and grammar). The process of assigning numerical codes for categories is called quantitative coding. Numbers can be assigned as labels, but only arbitrarily, to identify the categories. For example, school groups may be given labels 1, 2 and 3. These numbers do not represent the absolute or relative amount of any characteristics; they only help to identify the members of a given group and cannot be arithmetically manipulated through mathematical calculations such as addition, subtraction, multiplication or division. The only mathematical operation permitted is counting the number of observations in each category, from which the frequency and the mode (Table 1.2) can be calculated.

Table 1.2 Mathematical operation allowed for different scales of measurement

Mathematical operation	Scales of measurement			
	Nominal	Ordinal	Interval	Ratio
Frequency	✓	✓	✓	✓
Mode	✓	✓	✓	✓
Median		✓	✓	✓
Mean			✓	✓
Percentile			✓	✓
Standard deviation			✓	✓

An *ordinal* measurement indicates the relative position of the individuals or objects concerning a specific attribute and a specific progression or ordering (increasing or decreasing). At this level, the intervals between adjacent groups, or the distances between the positions, are not assumed to be the same. Ordinal measurement requires that the elements of a category can be rank-ordered on an operationally defined characteristic or property. When a teacher ranks his students on individual characteristics such as their spelling ability on a scale from 1 to 5, an ordinal measurement occurs. At the ordinal level, data is ordered (for example, 5 is the best score and is better than 4, which is better than 3 and so on), but we cannot be sure that the distances between any two consecutive values are equal. In this case, the only information considered for analysis is their order.

Another example of the ordinal scale used extensively in educational research is the Likert scale. If numbers 1, 2, 3, 4, 5 are used to indicate degrees of agreement, from strongly agree to strongly disagree, with a given statement, there is a definite order in responses, but there is no evidence that the distance between an answer of 1 (strongly agree) and 2 (agree) is the same as the distance between 2 (agree) and 3 (neutral). There is just no evidence for interpreting the magnitude of the difference between numbers or the ratio of numbers. The number of mathematical operations is limited for ordinal scales because the intervals between categories are not equal. The frequency, mode and median (Table 1.2) are the only ones allowed for this type of measurement.

The *interval* scale is the next measurement scale, which not only classifies and orders data into categories but also has equal intervals between the units of measurement. For example, if we measured four test running times for four students on an interval scale and got the scores 100, 70, 40 and 10 seconds, we could say that the difference between the first and second is 30 seconds and third and fourth is 30 seconds. So, the difference between the first and second is equal to the difference between the third and fourth.

Thermometers are examples of objects that use an interval scale to measure the temperature on either or both temperature scales, Fahrenheit or Celsius, and the order and distance between numbers have the same meaning. For instance, the difference between 20°C and 10°C is the same as that between 25°C and 15°C. However, we cannot say that 20°C is twice as hot as 10°C. This is because the zero value on an interval scale is not a real zero point. It is an arbitrary zero point. All the mathematical operations, such as addition, subtraction, multiplication and division, and all the statistical tests which are based on these mathematical operations are allowed for data on an interval scale (Table 1.2).

The *ratio* scale is the uppermost level of measurement and has all the properties of the interval scale. Thus all types of arithmetical operations and statistical tests are appropriate for ratio scales (Table 1.2). In addition to the characteristics of the interval scale, the ratio scale has a zero point or value that means that the attribute is absent. This means that ratios can be calculated between any two given values on the scale and are meaningful. An example of a ratio scale is teachers' salaries; if there is a value of 0 in the data set, it means that a teacher has no salary. Other examples are physical measurements such as length, weight and volume. For example, a length of 0 means no length at all. Note, however, that in education or social science a zero value might not have any meaning. For instance, it is established by convention that the zero value in an educational measurement is arbitrary. It is not a fixed zero value and we cannot find or identify an individual with zero achievements.

1●3 From concepts to constructs and variables

In the context of educational research, whether it is empirical or theoretical, basic terms such as research problem, concepts, variables and hypothesis arise frequently. Educational researchers assume that the characteristics or attributes of a phenomenon, object or idea are measurable – in other words, they have a structure that can be quantified. We begin with the phenomena that we are interested in investigating empirically (Figure 1.1), and before we establish the research problem we must define a set of concepts.

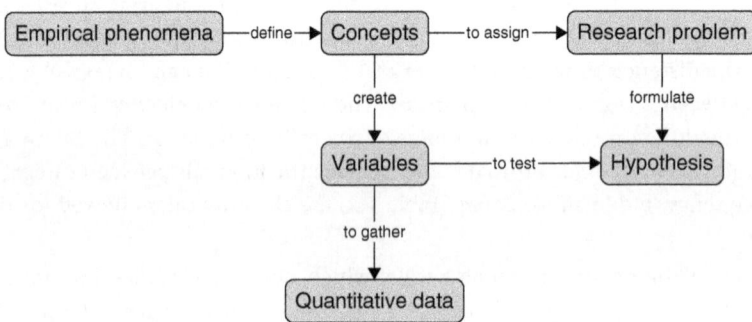

Figure 1.1 The research process

A *concept* is an objective (visual) or abstract representation of a phenomenon, idea, object, and so forth, which is the foundation of communication enabling information to be transmitted and related to some aspects of reality. Educational researchers categorise or order their observations or experiences in terms of the degree to which a concept does or does not have something objective to refer to. For example, the iPad is an *objective concept* because we all have a clear image of its characteristics in our mind. Personality, intelligence and attitudes are examples of *abstract concepts*, which are rather challenging to visualise.

A *construct* is a theoretical definition of an abstract concept and must be observable and mea-surable. In order to move from conceptual to empirical and measurement levels, concepts are operationalised or converted into *variables* which can take a set of values. A construct is often mistaken for a variable; care should be taken not to confuse the two. A variable should have at least two possible values. For example, if sex is a construct it is only represented by one value, sex; but as a variable representing the construct, it should have at least two values (for example, male and female).

When a specific form of relationship is made between certain variables, a *hypothesis* is expressed, which is a tentative answer to the *research problem* after analysing *quantitative data* collected using various research methods. Developing the right research questions and hypotheses is essential to the educational research process. A hypothesis is a statement of the assumed rela-tionship between types of variables to answer a research question and can be verified after they are tested experimentally. There are different types of hypothesis, depending on the form of the relationship. For example, the null hypothesis is a statement that expresses no relationship between variables, and the alternative hypothesis is contradictory to the null hypothesis. There are three types of alternative hypothesis, which are presented in Figure 1.2. A *relational hypoth-esis* is a statement that specifies a relationship between two variables. A *correlational hypothesis* states that the variables occur together in some specified manner without implying that one causes the other. If the implication is that one variable causes the other, we have a *causal* or *explanatory hypothesis*.

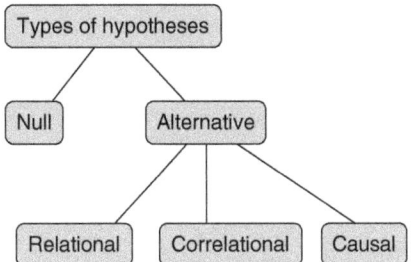

Figure 1.2 Types of hypotheses

Sometimes, students get confused about the distinction between a research question and a research hypothesis. A research problem is a general question about relationships among variables, while a hypothesis is concrete and is based on testable answers. Research questions can be operationalised into hypotheses.

1.4 Types of variables

There are different types of variables, and their classification relates very much to the purpose and objectives of research. It also depends on how the researcher decides to view them and on the complexity of the research. The opposite of a variable is a *constant*, and statistics draw on a type of constant called a *parameter*.

Manifest variables are directly observed variables which are directly measured, and *latent* variables are 'hidden' variables because they cannot be seen or directly measured (Figure 1.3). A latent variable can be measured indirectly by using an observed variable and inferring the unseen variable by using advanced statistical techniques such as factor, Rasch or latent class analysis. Manifest variables can be either *dependent* or *independent*.

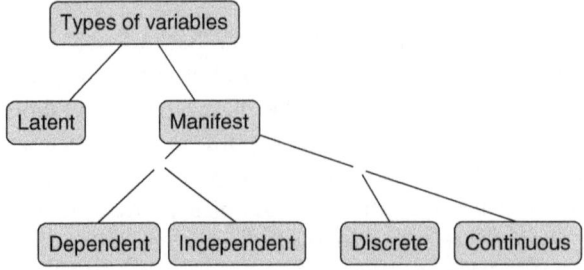

Figure 1.3 Types of variables

A *dependent* variable is a variable that the researcher wishes to explain; it is also called a *criterion* variable. A variable expected to explain a change in the dependent variable is called an *independent* variable, also referred to as a *predictor* variable. An essential characteristic of any variable, as mentioned above, is being either *continuous* or *discrete* (Section 1.1.1) or, if we refer to the levels of measurement, being *nominal*, *ordinal*, *interval* or *ratio* (Section 1.2.1). These characteristics strongly influence the measurement procedures, graphical representation and data analysis, as we shall see in the next chapters.

1.5 Quantitative data and R

In the past several years, the popularity of R has grown considerably among researchers, educators and students. It offers several advantages that could be extremely valuable for anyone collecting and analysing quantitative educational data and allows reducing the gap between quantitative data and information, which later can be turned into knowledge. R is a language and a repository of over 10,000 programs, called *packages*, that perform statistical analysis and support detailed data manipulations, data analysis and graphical displays.

1.5.1 Why use R?

There are several reasons why it is useful to use R:

- It is free and open-source, meaning that the software can be modified and distributed without restrictions, as long as the user complies with the licensing requirements.
- It provides thousands of statistical tests. For example, R provides free descriptive statistical tests, linear and nonlinear modelling, time-series analysis, classification, clustering and many more tests.

- It handles a variety of graphical methods to visualise data. R can also handle maps, and can therefore be used for geographical visualisations.
- It is a programming language.
- It uses simple text commands.
- It runs on different types of hardware and software; this means that R is available for Windows, Unix systems (such as Linux), and the Mac.
- It has vast documentation and a broad community of users.

Exercises

1.1 Define primary quantitative data and give an example in which it might be found.

1.2 How does the notion of concept help a researcher formulate a hypothesis?

1.3 (a) Define the terms 'measurement' and 'scales of measurement' in educational research.
    (b) What are the four scales of measurement?

1.4 (a) Define the term 'variable'.
    (b) What is the difference between a manifest and a latent variable?

1.5 Give an example from educational research for each type of variable.

1.6 Describe how researchers can influence the choice of variables.

Further reading

Ackoff, R. (1989) From data to wisdom. *Journal of Applied Systems Analysis*, 16, 3–9.

The author formulates a model as a pyramid between wisdom, understanding, knowledge, information, and data, which is now commonly called the data–information–knowledge–wisdom hierarchy.

Stevens, S. (1946) On the theory of scales of measurement. *Science*, 103(2684), 677–680.

This article presents a broad definition of measurement and a classification of the scales of measurement.

Zins, C. (2007) Conceptual approaches for defining data, information and knowledge. *Journal of the American Society for Information Science and Technology*, 58(4), 479–493.

This article details 130 definitions of data, information, and knowledge developed by 45 scholars, and draws key conceptual approaches for defining these three key concepts.

2

An introduction to R and RStudio

━━━━━━━━━━ **Chapter Objectives** ━━━━━━━━━━

In this chapter, we will:

- learn how to install R and RStudio
- understand how to create and use functions, packages and libraries in R
- explore basic data types and data structures
- examine how to import data in different formats from different systems in R.

R is an open-source integrated suite of software that is designed to create and manipulate *objects* for a variety of arithmetic functions, statistical analyses and graphical displays. These objects may be variables, arrays of numbers, characters, functions, or more complex structures, which can be saved and stored permanently in a file for later use. One of the many advantages of R is that it runs on Windows, Unix systems (such as Linux), and Mac.

RStudio is a standard editing tool, which makes R easier to use because it includes a code editor to execute R code, debugging and visualisation tools, and integrated R help and documentation. Furthermore, it simplifies the facilities of R.

2 ● 1 Installing R

R is available free to download from any Comprehensive R Archive Network (CRAN) mirror for all major platforms (Windows, Mac, and Linux). To install R, go to http://cran.r-project.org/mirrors.html and find a mirror site that is geographically near you. Choose your operating system and follow the installation instructions.

For Windows users the procedure is as follows:

1. Click on *Download R for Windows*.
2. This opens a new page; click on the *base* link.
3. When the next page appears, click on the link *Download R 3.6.2 for Windows*. The number 3.6.2 is associated with the latest version of R (at the time of writing).
4. Save the executable file *R-3.6.2-win.exe*.
5. Double-click on the executable file and follow the instructions.
6. If the installation has been successful, then R can be found in the *All Programs* area of the *Start Menu* or on the desktop, if we have selected a shortcut for desktop.
7. To run R, double-click on the R icon on the desktop.

2 ● 2 Upgrading R

If R has already been installed and you would like to upgrade it to the latest version, firstly you need to install the `installr` package by writing the following commands in the R Console:

1. Install the `installr` package in R with the function `install.packages()`:
   `install.packages("installr")`
2. Load the `installr` package in R with the function `library()`:
   `library(installr)`
3. Update R by writing the following command in the R Console:
   `updateR`
   or by selecting 'Update R' from the new `installr` menu in the R window, as shown in Figure 2.1.

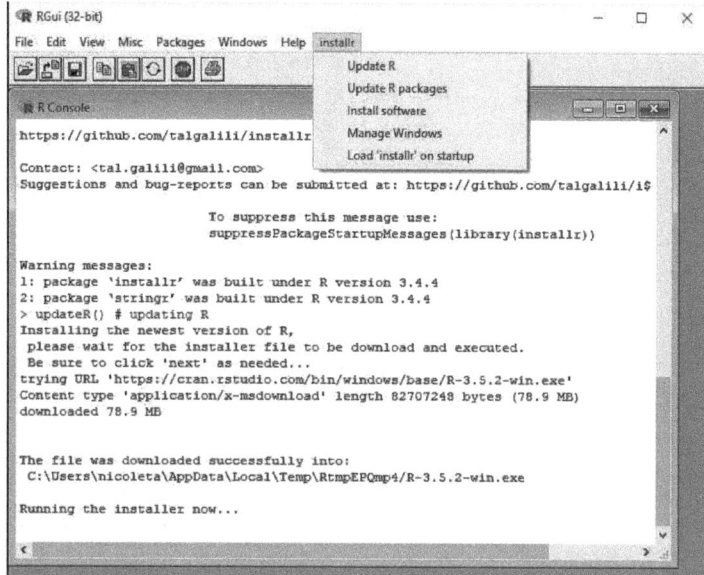

Figure 2.1   Updating R using 'Update R' from the new `installr` menu

2 3 Installing and using RStudio

RStudio is also open-source software, and it makes R more intuitive. It is available to download free from www.rstudio.com and runs on different platforms (Windows, Mac, and Linux).

Windows users should proceed through the following steps:

1. Click on *Download*.
2. When the next page appears, click on the *Download* link under *RStudio Desktop, Open Source License*.
3. Click on *RStudio 1.2.5033 for Windows 10/8/7* operating system. The number 1.2.5033 is associated with the latest version of RStudio (at the time of writing).
4. Save the executable file *RStudio-1.2.5033.exe*.
5. Double-click on the executable file and follow the instructions.

6. If the installation has been successful, then RStudio can be found in the *All Programs* area of the *Start Menu* or on the desktop, if you have selected a shortcut for desktop.

Once both R and RStudio are installed, R can either run using RStudio, using the shortcut on the desktop, or opening the Windows Start Menu bar to select the program. When you open RStudio for the first time, you will see the RStudio screen, as shown in Figure 2.2 if you are using Windows.

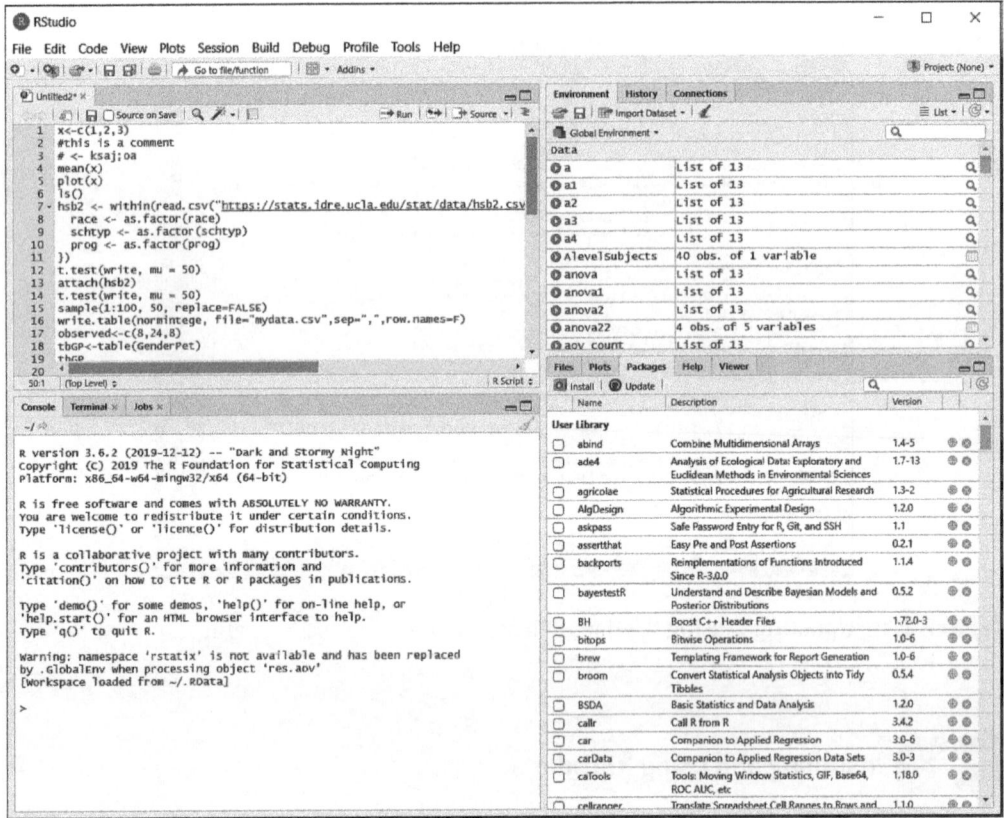

Figure 2.2 The RStudio screen when RStudio opens

The RStudio screen has *four quadrants* (or windows) and several tabs:

1. In the upper left-hand quadrant is the *Source* window (also called *Script* window). This is where you write, run and save your R code by clicking on the appropriate tab (Figure 2.3).

2. In the lower left-hand quadrant is the *Console* (also called *Command* window). This is where you can type commands and see the output. This quadrant is the same as the Console in R, and this is the place where interactive R work is done. The command line of the Console, after the greater-than symbol >, is where we write R commands (Figure 2.4). Any line starting with a > character

denotes R asking for input. Pressing the Enter (or return) key will send your input to R to be evaluated. For example, if we type q() after > and hit the Enter key, we will exit RStudio.

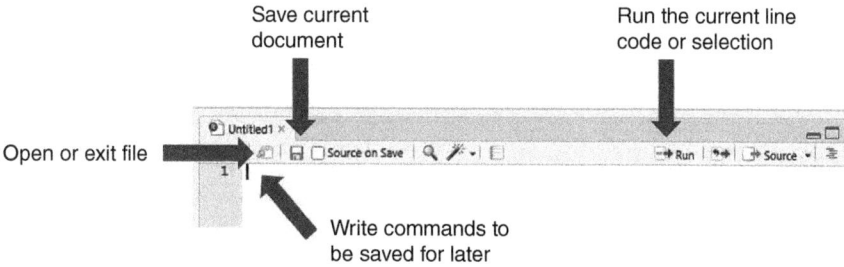

Figure 2.3 The Save, Search and Run tabs in the RStudio Source window

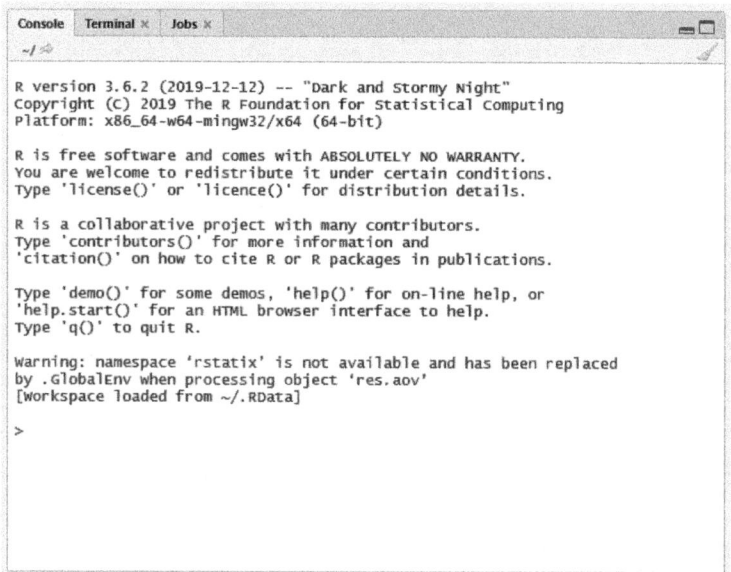

Figure 2.4 The Console in RStudio

The Terminal tab, which is next to the Console tab (Figure 2.4), creates a new terminal that provides, for example, remote logins or an interactive text editor.

3. In the upper right-hand quadrant are the *Environment*, *History* and *Connections* panes:

    - If we click on the *Environment* pane (Figure 2.5(a)), the window shows all the active objects, values, functions and anything else created during the R session and held in memory.
    - The *History* pane (Figure 2.5(b)) shows a list of commands used so far.
    - The *Connections* pane (Figure 2.5 (c)) helps us to connect to a variety of data sources.

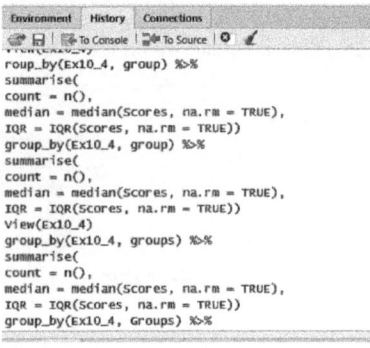

(a) Environment pane   (b) History pane

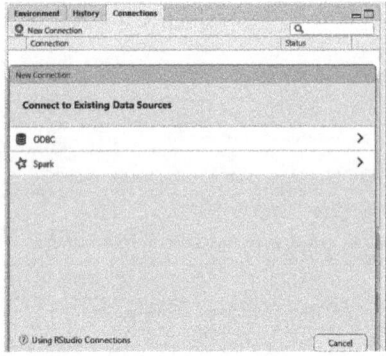

(c) Connections pane

Figure 2.5   (a) The Environment, (b) History and (c) Connections panes in RStudio

4. In the lower right-hand quadrant are the *Files*, *Plots*, *Packages*, *Help* and *Viewer* panes (Figure 2.6).

    If we click on the *Files* pane, the window shows all the files and folders in our default workspace. Here we can also open files.

    - The *Plots* pane will display graphs.
    - The *Package* pane will list a series of packages or add-ons needed to install, load and run individual packages.
    - The *Help* pane is for additional information and help on functions.
    - The *Viewer* pane is used to view local web content.

2.4 Functions, packages and libraries

In R, a *function* is a 'piece of code' or a set of statements or instructions that are organised together to perform a specific task, and its general format is:

```
function(argument list){code}
```

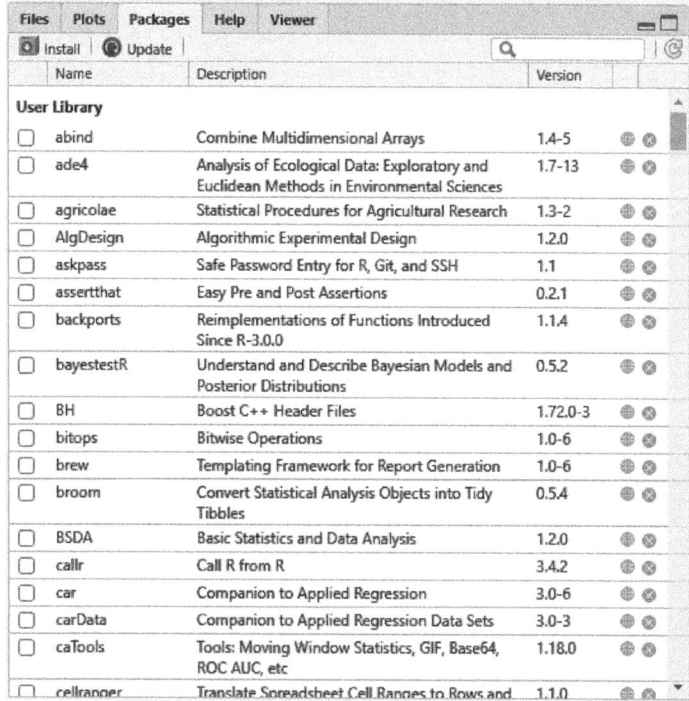

Figure 2.6   The Files, Plots, Packages, Help and Viewer panes in RStudio

where the code is written between the curly brackets and the arguments between the parentheses. Every existing or newly created function is stored in R as an object so the R interpreter can pass control to the function, along with arguments that may be necessary for the function to accomplish the actions. In turn, the function performs its task and returns control to the interpreter as well as any result which may be stored in other objects.

R has many in-built functions, as shown in Table 2.1, which are generic mathematical functions and can be directly called in the program without defining them first.

Table 2.1   Example of generic mathematical functions in R

Function name	Description	Examples
sum()	Calculate the sum of all the arguments	sum(2,5,6) [1] 13
min()	Gives the minimum value from the list of arguments	min(2,5,6) [1] 2
max()	Gives the maximum value from the list of arguments	max(2,5,6) [1] 6

(Continued)

Table 2.1 (Continued)

Function name	Description	Examples
median()	Calculates the median value	median(2,5,6) [1] 2
log()	Calculates the natural logarithm of an argument	log(2) [1] 0.6931472
log10()	Calculates the log to base 10 of the argument	log10(2) [1] 0.30103
exp()	Gives the exponential value of the argument	exp(2) [1] 7.389056
abs()	Gives the absolute value	abs(-2) [1] 2
sqrt()	Calculates the square root	sqrt(2) [1] 1.414214
round()	Returns the numeric value rounded off to the number of decimal places specified by the user	round(sqrt(2),digit=1) [1] 1.4
cos()	Returns the cosine	cos(30) [1] 0.1542514
sin()	Returns the sine	sin(30) [1] -0.9880316
tan()	Returns the tangent	tan(30) [1] -6.405331

We can also create and use our own functions, referred to as *user-defined functions*, which are defined using the following syntax:

```
function.name<-function(argument1,argument2,...){some functionality}
```

For example, R does not have a built-in function to calculate the mode; however, it can be created as shown below:

Computing the mode in R

```
getmode <- function(v) {uniqv <- unique(v)
+ uniqv[which.max(tabulate(match(v, uniqv)))]}
```

(Source: www.tutorialspoint.com/r/r_mean_median_mode.htm)

Packages are collections of additional functions in a well-defined format. A directory where packages are stored is called a *library*. There are many packages available for R. A list of packages can be found on the R website (https://cran.r-project.org/web/packages/available_packages_by_name.html).

With the standard installation of R, most common packages are installed. To get a list of all installed packages, select the Packages pane in the lower right-hand quadrant in RStudio (Figure 2.7) or type `library()` in the Console window. If the box in front of the package name is ticked, the package is loaded (activated) and can be used. If not, we can tick the box, and the package is loaded.

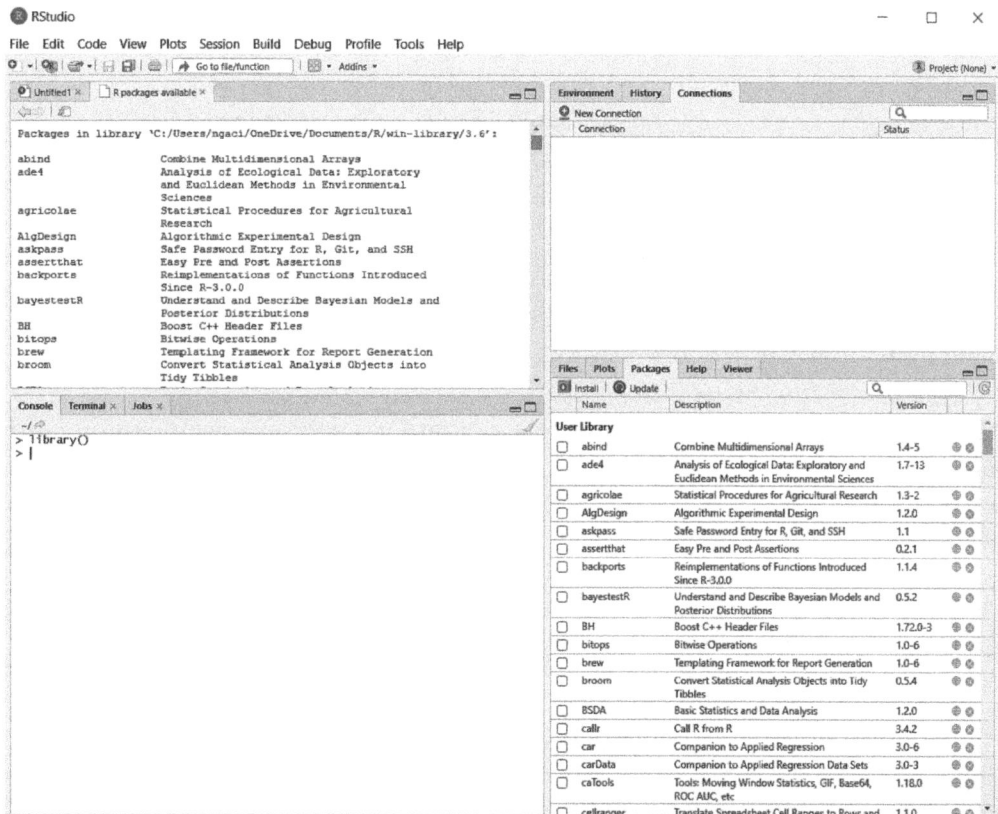

Figure 2.7 Visualising the list of packages installed in R by clicking on the Packages tab in RStudio

To install and use a package (for example, the package called abind), we will follow the steps described below:

1. Click on the 'Tools' tab on the RStudio menu bar.
2. Select 'Install Packages ...' and a new window with the same name will open (Figure 2.8).

3. Type the word 'abind' in the empty box below the line which says 'Packages (separate multiple with space or comma)'.
4. Click on 'Install', and the 'abind' package will be installed in R.

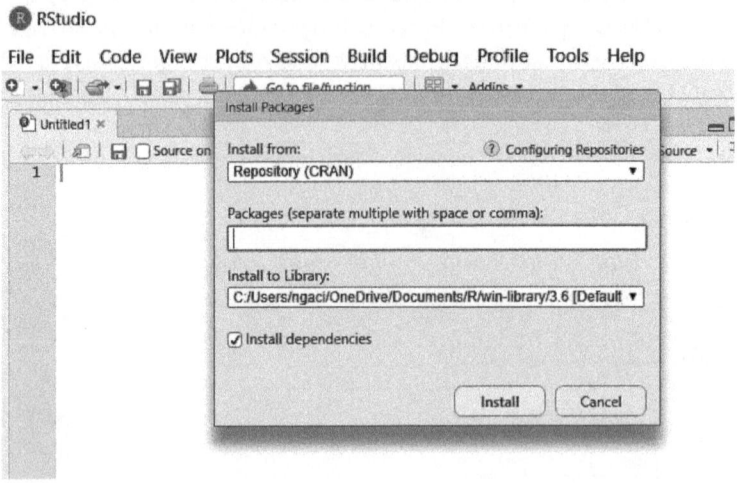

Figure 2.8 Installing a package in R

Alternatively, we can type the following command in the RStudio Command window to install the package:

```
install.packages("abind").
```

Before using any package in R, it is necessary to load it into R. This can be done in two different ways:

1. Check the box in front of the package to be installed in the RStudio Packages pane (Figure 2.7).
2. Alternatively, type `library(name of package)` in the Console window:

```
library(abind)
```

2.5 Working with data in R

Everything in R is an object, for example, data structures, functions, symbols and expressions. When creating an object, the first step is to give the object a name which is different from that of any existing function in R. The second step is to assign a value or a set of values to the object, for example:

```
x < -5
```

where

- *x* is the name of the object.
- <- is the assignment operator which assigns whatever is on the right-hand side to whatever is on the left-hand side and is equivalent to the equals ('=') sign. If we want to see the result, we type the variable name *x* and then press *Enter* to print out the variable.
- the number 5 is the numeric value assigned to the object *x*.

In addition, the R Console can be used as a simple calculator. We can simply type in a mathematical expression and then press Enter to print out the results:

```
2 + 3

[1]  5
```

The unary and binary operators, shown in Table 2.2, perform arithmetic, relational or logical operations on scalars or vectors (or objects). They are built-in operators in R and can be used on different data and value types.

Table 2.2 Descriptions of key R operators

Operator		Description
Type	**Symbol**	
Arithmetic	+	Addition
	-	Subtraction
	/	Division
	*	Multiplication
	^	Exponent
	%%	Modulus (remainder for division)
	%/%	Integer division
Relational	<	Less than
	>	Greater than
	<=	Less than or equal to
	>=	Greater than or equal to
	==	Equal to
	!=	Not equal to
Logical	!	Logical NOT
	&	Elementwise logical AND
	&&	Logical AND
	|	Elementwise logical OR
	||	Logical OR

(Continued)

Table 2.2   (Continued)

Type	Operator	Description
	Symbol	
Assignment	<-, <<-, =	Leftwards assignment
	->, ->>	Rightwards assignment

2.5.1 Data structures and value types in R

Data is organised in R in different structures (or types) including scalars, vectors, matrices, data frames and lists (Figure 2.9).

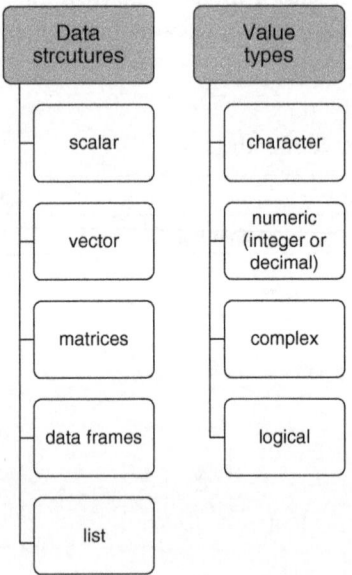

Figure 2.9   Data and value types in R

Scalars

In R the term *scalar* refers to the most basic data structure that can hold one value at a time and can be assigned a different set of data types. For example, if we want to assign a specific *value type* to a scalar (Figure 2.9), we use one of the following assignment operators: =, <-, ->, <<-. Traditionally in R <- is the preferred assignment operator because it can be used anywhere (see the second column of Table 2.3). Every object in R belongs to a class describing the type of value it represents. The fourth column of Table 2.3 shows examples of how the function class() is used to determine the object class.

Table 2.3 Examples of different types of scalars in R

Data type	Commands in R		
	Assigning a value to the object	Seeing the results	Determining the object class
Character	`a<-"alphabet"`	`a # then press Enter`	`class(a)`
		`[1] "alphabet"`	`[1] "character"`
Numeric	`m<-1`	`m`	`class(m)`
	`n<-2.5`	`[1] 1`	`[1] "numeric"`
	`o<-pi`	`n`	`class(n)`
		`[1] 2.5`	`[1] "numeric"`
		`o`	`class(o)`
		`[1] 3.141593`	`[1] "numeric"`
Complex*	`x<-2+1i`	`x`	`class(x)`
		`[1] 2+1i`	`[1] "complex"`
Logical	`z<-m<n # Is m smaller than n?`	`z`	`class(z)`
		`[1] TRUE`	`[1] "logical"`
	`t<-m>n #Is m greater than n?`	`t`	`class(t)`
		`[1] FALSE`	`[1] "logical"`

Note that anything after the hash symbol (#) is ignored by R. We can use this to insert any comments that we might find useful in our R code.

Vectors

A *vector* is a structure containing data elements of the same value type. This is built by using the function `c()` to combine multiple values into a single object, as shown in Table 2.4.

Table 2.4 Examples of different types of vectors in R

Data type	Commands in R		
	Assigning a value to the object	Seeing the results	Determining the object class
Character	`d<-c("school","university")`	`d`	`class(d)`
		`[1] "school" "university"`	`[1] "character"`
Numeric	`b<-c(1,3,-1,5.6)`	`b`	`class(b)`
		`[1] 1.0 3.0 -1.0 5.6`	`[1] "numeric"`
Complex	`vc<-c(2i,-1i)`	`vc`	`class(vc)`
		`[1] 0+2i 0-1i`	`[1] "complex"`
Logical	`vl<-c(b<=5)`	`vl`	`class(vl)`
		`[1] TRUE TRUE TRUE FALSE`	`[1] "logical"`

Matrices and data frames

A *matrix* object displays different types of value (character, numeric, logical), and it is much like tabular data with a given number of columns and rows. It can be constructed in two different ways, using either the function `matrix()` or the function `data.frame()`.

Example 2.1 Create a matrix object

Let us now look at an example of how to create a matrix object.

Create a 3 × 3 matrix object named 'mat' using the function `matrix()`.

```
mat<-matrix(1:9,nrow=3,ncol=3,byrow=TRUE)

mat

         [,1] [,2] [,3]
   [1,]     1    2    3
   [2,]     4    5    6
   [3,]     7    8    9
```

or

```
mat<-matrix(1:9,nrow=3,ncol=3,byrow=FALSE)
mat
         [,1] [,2] [,3]
   [1,]     1    4    7
   [2,]     2    5    8
   [3,]     3    6    9
```

In this example, the matrix has the following arguments:

- The first argument *1:9* is the collection of elements that R will arrange into the rows and columns (it is a shortcut for c(1,2,3,4,5,6,7,8,9)).
- The second argument *nrow=3* indicates that the collection of elements will be arranged into three rows.
- The third argument *ncol=3* indicates that the collection of elements will be arranged into three columns.
- The fourth argument *byrow=TRUE* indicates that the matrix is filled by row. If we want the matrix to be filled by column, we use *byrow = FALSE*.

The function `data.frame()` can be used to construct a matrix object where each column has a different data type and with data passed as a separate argument.

Example 2.2 Creating a matrix object using the function `data.frame()`

Create a vector for each data set, for example for the years when the National Curriculum assessments at Key Stage 2 in England took place (YearSATs) and three more vectors on attainment in the following Key Stage 2 assessments: reading test (SATR), maths test (SATM) and GPS test (SATGPS).

Creating vectors in R

```
YearSATs<-c(2016,2017,2018)      # Years of SATs exams
SATR<-c(66,72,75)                # Reading test results
SATM<-c(75,76,73)                # Maths test results
SATGPS<-c(73,77,78)              # GPS test results
```

Create the matrix named 'SAT' on attainment in the Key Stage 2 assessments:

Creating a matrix in R

```
SAT<-data.frame(YearSATs=YearSATs,SATR=SATR,SATM=SATM,SATGPS=GP)
SAT
  YearSATs SATR SATM SATGPS
1     2016   66   75   73
2     2017   72   76   77
3     2018   75   73   78
```

Source: www.gov.uk/government/publications/national-curriculum-assessments-key-stage-2-2018-interim/key-stage-2-2018-interim-results-text

The function `data.frame()` can also be used to assign a variable name (or heading) to a vector or to bring together more than one vector to form a matrix-like object. For example, we can assign the heading 'study' to vector *d*, described in Table 2.4.

```
d1<-data.frame(study=d)

d1

       study
1     school
2 university
```

Or if the variable 'rate' is assigned to vector *b*, described in Table 2.4:

```
b1<-data.frame(rate=b)
b1
  rate
1  1.0
2  3.0
3 -1.0
4  5.6
```

2.6 Importing and exporting data sets

R allows us to import and export data sets in a broader range of file formats, including the *comma-separated values* (CSV) and *tab-separated values* (TSV) formats.

Example 2.3 Creating a CSV file

A CSV file has the extension .csv and contains numbers and letters in the form of columns, separated by commas, with line breaks separating rows. This example demonstrates how line breaks distinguish the information (three fields: Country, Code, Scores) on five participant countries in the PISA 2015 Science test, which is recorded as a CSV file:

```
Country, Code, Scores
Albania, ALB,427
Algeria, DZA,376
Argentina, ARG,432
Australia, AUS,510
Austria, AUT,495
```

Example 2.4 Creating a TSV file

A TSV file is a simple text format for storing data in a tabular structure, for example a database table or spreadsheet data (Table 2.5). Each record in the table is one line of the text file. Each field value of a record is separated from the next by a tab character.

Table 2.5 Example of spreadsheet data

Country	Code	Scores
Albania	ALB	427
Algeria	DZA	376
Argentina	ARG	432
Australia	AUS	510
Austria	AUT	495

2.6.1 Importing data sets in R

R facilitates importing data from other systems and in different formats for analysis either in R itself or via packages available from CRAN or other websites. Text files are the most accessible form of data to import in R, and the function to import from this type of data is called `scan()`. For other formats, for example an Excel spreadsheet or an SPSS file, before importing a data set, the following steps must be followed:

1. Check the file format, for example, if it was created using Excel, SPSS, CSV, SAS, Minitab.
2. Find where the file is located in the computer system.
3. Check and set up the *working directory* in the location containing data.

The *working directory* is the folder on the computer in which we want to save a file or a figure, or to open an existing file. If we want to read or save files from and to a specific location, we will need to set the working directory in R. The following example shows how to check the current working directory of the R process. Type in the command `getwd()` in the RStudio Console and then press Enter.

Returning the file path for the current working directory

```
getwd()
[1] "C:/Users/Documents"
```

The output displayed [1] tells us that the working directory in R is found on the C drive within the folder "Documents".

To set the working directory in R to a different folder, for example "Data", within the "R" folder within "Documents" on the C drive (Users), we type the following commands and then press Enter.

Setting up the working directory

```
setwd("C:/Users/Documents/R/Data")
dir()
[1] "sample.tex"
```

If we are working with an Excel spreadsheet, first check:

- whether the data file has its first row reserved for the header, while the first column is used to identify the sampling unit;
- the names, values and fields do not contain blank spaces, otherwise each of these will be interpreted as a separate variable – if we want to concatenate words, insert a full stop in between words instead of a space;

- that there are no names that contain symbols such as ? $ % ^ & * ( ) - # ? , < > / | \ [ ] { };
- for any comments that we have made in the Excel file to avoid extra columns and delete them;
- whether there are any missing values in the data set and they are indicated by NA.

Example 2.5 Importing a .csv file

Go to www.stats.govt.nz/large-datasets/csv-files-for-download and download the file 'Well-being statistics: 2016 – well-being measures CSV' into the working directory, then check if the file is there by writing the following command into the RStudio Console.

Listing all the files in a directory

```
dir()
[1]  "sample.tex"
[2]  "well-being-gss16-social-identity-measures-tables-csv.csv"
[3]  "well-being-gss16-well-being-measures-tables-csv.csv"
```

To successfully load this file into R, we can use the `read.csv()` function.

Importing a .csv data file in R

```
read.csv("well-being-gss16-well-being-measures-tables-csv.csv")
```

	CACode	VaCode	Estimate	LowerCIB	UpperCIB	Flag
1	C01T	V01A	17.1	16.2	18.1	
2	C01T	V01B	18.0	17.1	18.9	
3	C01T	V01C	31.0	29.9	32.2	
4	C01T	V01D	15.8	14.8	16.8	
5	C01T	V01E	18.0	16.9	19.0	
6	C01T	V02A	12.5	11.7	13.4	
7	C01T	V02B	16.0	14.8	17.1	

Another way to do this is to use `read.csv(file.choose())`.

Example 2.6 Importing an Excel file

To import an Excel file (with extension .xls or .xlsx), we need to upload a new package into R, called `readxl`. To find out if this package is installed in R, we write the following function in the RStudio Console:

Checking if a package is installed in R

```
any(grepl("<name of your package>", installed.packages()))
```

If the answer is TRUE, then the package is installed, and if the answer is FALSE, it needs to be installed. Follow the next step to install the readxl package:

Installing a package in R

```
install.packages("readxl")
```

Go to https://data.gov.uk/dataset/b5b7b99b-2d16-4c64-8699-aa8fd33fcf2c/pupils-with-english-as-an-additional-language-eal-secondary-schools and download the file: "Secondary Pupils with English as an Additional Language (EAL) – May 2017.xlsx" into the working directory, then load the file into R.

Importing a .xlsx data file in R

```
df <- read_excel("Secondary Pupils with English as an Additional Language
(EAL) - May 2017.xlsx")
```

Alternatively, use:

```
df <- read_excel(file.choose())
```

Furthermore, to view the file, type df in the RStudio Console. The output is displayed below.

Viewing a data file in R

```
df
# A tibble: 18 x 6
   'Pupils with Engli~ X__1    X__2   X__3   X__4   X__5
   <chr>               <chr>   <chr>  <chr>  <chr>  <chr>
 1 <NA>                <NA>    <NA>   <NA>   <NA>   <NA>
 2 DfE No              School  Type ~ Total ~ No. o~ % of~
```

(Continued)

3	5406	Brighou~	Acade~	1399	36	2.57~
4	4022	Calder ~	LA ma~	1112	142	12.7~
5	5404	Lightcl~	Acade~	1415	40	2.82~
6	4001	Park La~	LA ma~	445	22	4.94~
7	5402	Rastric~	Acade~	1476	114	7.72~
8	7009	Ravensc~	LA ma~	163	33	20.2~
9	5408	Ryburn ~	Acade~	1420	70	4.92~
10	4024	Sowerby~	LA ma~	780	403	51.6~
11	5405	The Bro~	Acade~	1687	86	5.09~
12	5401	The Cro~	Acade~	1138	95	8.34~
13	4035	The Hal~	Acade~	937	844	90.0~
14	5400	The Nor~	Acade~	1106	72	6.50~
15	4026	Todmord~	LA ma~	722	37	5.12~
16	6905	Trinity~	Acade~	1730	107	6.18~
17	\<NA>	Calderd~	\<NA>	15530	2101	13.5~
18	\<NA>	Calderd~	\<NA>	15367	2068	13.4~

2.6.2 Exporting data sets from R

R allows us to export data sets to a broader range of file formats, including CSV and TSV.

Example 2.7 Exporting a .csv file

To export the data set named 'Assessment' to a csv file named Results_Assessment.csv in the working directory, we use the `write.csv()` function as follows:

Exporting a csv data file from R in the working directory

```
write.csv(dataset, "filename.csv")
write.csv(Assessment, "Results_Assessmnet.csv")
```

To save the file in a different folder than in the working directory, we should enter the full path for the file, as shown below.

Exporting a csv data file in R in a specific directory

```
write.csv(dataset, "filename.csv")
write.csv(Assessment, " C:/folder/Results_Assessmnet.csv")
```

Example 2.8 Exporting a .xls file

To export the 'Assessment' data set as an xls file named Results_Assessment.xls in the working directory, we use the `write.table()` function as follows:

Exporting a .xlsx data file from R in the working directory

```
write.table(dataset, "filename.xls)
write.table(Assessment, "Results_Assessmnet.xls")
```

or in a different folder:

Exporting an xlsx data file in R in a specific directory

```
write.table(Assessment, "C:/folder/Results_Assessmnet.xls")
```

2.7 Getting help on R and RStudio

There are several excellent resources available on the web for both R and RStudio. For example, the following websites are dedicated to R and RStudio: http://search.r-project.org and https://blog.rstudio.com.

To get help on any function in R, we can follow any of the following steps:

1. type `?` in the RStudio Console. For example, to get help on the `paste()` function, type `?paste` in the RStudio Console and press Enter. This code opens a Help window. In RStudio, the Help window is in the bottom-right corner of the RStudio main screen by default.
2. We can also type `help`, but remember to include parentheses around the search term: `help(paste)`

Exercises

2.1 What is R?
2.2 Which of the following editors is used as a code editor for R?

   (a) Studio
   (b) RStudio
   (c) Heck

(Continued)

2.3   How can we get help in R?

2.4   What are the key features of R?

2.5   What is the simplest data structure?

2.6   What are the main differences between data structures and data types?

2.7   Assignments can be made using the assignment operator <-. Can we make assignments in more than one direction?

2.8   What is the rule in R when there are missing values in a data set?

2.9   How many types of objects are there in R?

2.10 Is it possible to import a different format of data into R? How?

2.11 Set up the working directory to a new 'Uni' folder on your desktop.

2.12 List the objects in your current working space.

2.13 Create a new variable 'b' with value 252.

2.14 Convert 'b' from the previous exercise to character data type.

2.15 Create a matrix with 4 rows and 3 columns.

2.16 Try the commands:

    (a)   x <- c(2,6,9)

    (b)   x

    (c)   x/2

    (d)   x^2

    (e)   sqrt(x)

    (f)   y <- c(2,5,1)

    (g)   y

    (h)   x-y

    (i)   x*y

2.17 Import

    (a)   a CSV file into R.

    (b)   an Excel spreadsheet into R.

2.18 Export

    (a)   a CSV file from R into the working directory.

    (b)   an Excel spreadsheet from R.

Further reading

Manuals

R Installation and Administration, available at: https://cran.r-project.org/doc/manuals/R-admin.html

This is a guide to installation and administration for R.

An Introduction to R, available at: https://cran.r-project.org/doc/manuals/r-release/R-intro.pdf

The introductory session in Appendix A of this guide is recommended for R beginners.

Books

Crawley, M. (2013) *The R book* (2nd ed.). Chichester: John Wiley & Sons.

This is a good book for beginners to start using R.

Davies, T. (2018) *The book of R: A first course in programming and statistics*. San Francisco: No Starch Press.

The book is a beginner-friendly guide to R and provides lots of useful basic information on using R, including how to write data frames, create functions, and use variables.

McGrath, M. (2018) *R for data analysis in easy steps – R programming*. Leamington Spa: Easy Steps.

The first three chapters of the book describe in easy steps how to install R and RStudio, how to store different types of data and perform arithmetic operations.

PART TWO

Data visualisation

3

Graphical representation of data

═══ **Chapter Objectives** ═══

In this chapter, we will:

- introduce the concept of graphical representation of educational data
- present key principles for the graphical representation of data
- consider the essential features of different methods to visualise quantitative data
- understand how to create and work with tables and graphs in R correctly
- demonstrate examples from educational research to illustrate the use of graphs and tables for different types of variables and scales of measurement.

The *graphical representation of data* is the process of transformation of data into information through a wide range of graphical displays, including graphs, maps, pictograms and tables in a symbolic representation. This process is a vital part of data analysis that facilitates the process of identifying, interpreting and understanding patterns or trends, which may not be visible in the raw data. It is also a useful and accurate communication tool for a range of educational stakeholders. A proper understanding of graphical display is one of the most important aspects of data analysis for students, teachers and researchers, helping them to avoid mistakes when summarising large data sets and analysing relevant patterns in quantitative data. For anyone engaged in educational research, it is very helpful to find relevant patterns in the graphical representation of data before performing any statistical tests or transforming statistical values into more meaningful concepts. The graphical representation of data depends on the type of quantitative data. For example, to organise and summarise categorical data, a bar graph can be used. For a time series, a line graph is recommended. Small data sets are usually easier to interpret if data is displayed in tabular form. In conclusion, different types of data lead to different types of graphical displays, and not the other way around.

The essential graphical display principles are:

- Graphical displays should clearly and precisely communicate ideas and be tightly integrated with the statistical description of data.
- There are two types of graphical displays, *tables* and *figures*, which should accurately represent the data, and they do not act as a replacement for text.
- *Tables* show quantitative or qualitative data in a display of columns and rows. Each column must have a clear *heading* which should be centred over the column.
- All tables in the main body of the text should be labelled as 'Table', with a caption above the table, and numbered consecutively with arabic numerals as Table 1, Table 2 and so on, usually in the order in which they are first mentioned in the text. If all the data presented in the table is from a report or publication, which is a secondary source, then the information about the source must be included below the table, as shown in Table 3.1.
- Whenever a table or a figure is used, we must refer to it in the text (e.g. Table 1, Figure 1), followed by a brief and explanatory *caption*, which is a concise explanation of a specific point of interest or a critical domain.

Table 3.1 Caption[a]

Row descriptor	Column heading 1	Column heading 2	Column heading 3
Row heading 1			
Row heading 2			
Row heading 3			

Source (Name of the source)

[a] Footnote 1.

- Charts, graphs, photographs, drawings and any other illustrations are referred to as *figures*. The most common types of figures and their typical applications are shown in Figure 3.1. All figures in the main body of the text should be labelled as 'Figure', with a caption below the figure, and numbered consecutively with arabic numerals as Figure 1, Figure 2 and so on, usually in the order in which they are first mentioned in the text.

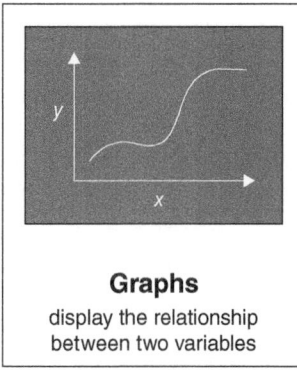

Graphs

display the relationship between two variables

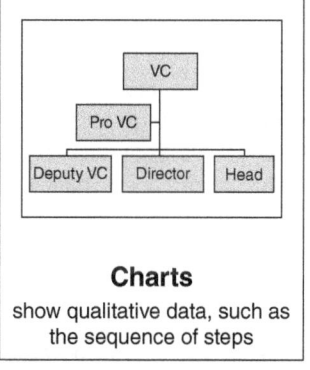

Charts

show qualitative data, such as the sequence of steps

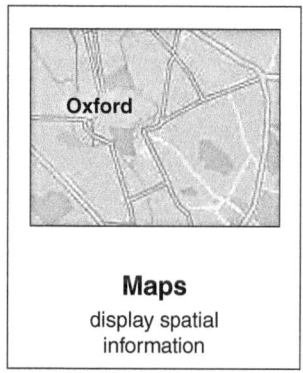

Maps

display spatial information

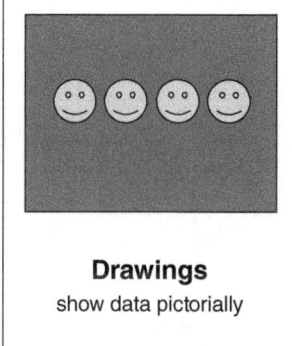

Drawings

show data pictorially

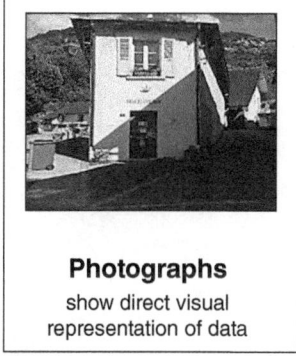

Photographs

show direct visual representation of data

Figure 3.1 Types of figures and their typical applications

- Discuss only the key points, and do not duplicate the information from the figure in the text.
- Data that only takes two values, such as 'yes' or 'no', should be presented in the text, not in a table or figure.
- Each data value should be plotted accurately.
- All graph axes, lines or bars should be labelled correctly, using appropriate scales for all *x*- and *y*-axes.
- All symbols used in a figure should be explained using a *legend* placed within the figure.

The graphical display of data facilitates key purposes:

- *perceiving* data (What does it show?)
- *interpreting* data (What does it explain?)
- *comprehending* data (What does it mean?).

3.1 Using tables

Tables are a very efficient and quick way to display and summarise both qualitative and quantitative data. There are different forms of tables, as shown in Figure 3.2.

1. *Reference tables* present a great deal of raw data as might be found in a database with the highest precision possible. The data in this form of table is arranged in an alphabetical or numerical code order and does not contain any derived information, such as percentages. Examples of such tables in education can be found in the OECD.stat database.
2. *Summary tables* present an extract of data from reference tables, with additional work done on the data, such as rounding, sorting or percentages. There are two types of summary tables within this category:
   (a) *Simple tables*, which are also known as *relational tables*, using a two-dimensional structure of rows and columns to store data.
   (b) *Multi-dimensional* or *multi-variate tables* contain data for more than two variables. A multidimensional table displays the distribution of variables in a matrix format. In many statistical books, this type of table is termed a *contingency table*, also known as *cross-tabulation* or *cross-tab*.

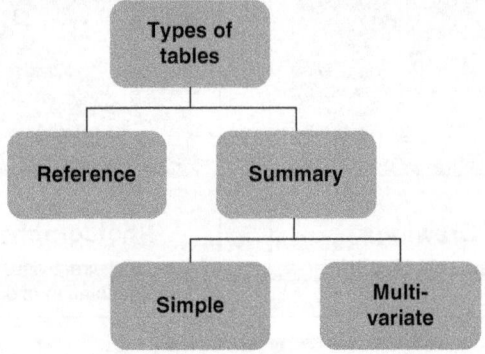

Figure 3.2 Different types of tables

Example 3.1 Creating reference and simple summary tables

Each school year, the head and deputy head teacher of a primary school ask parents to take part in an interview to find out what the school does well. Participants are asked for their consent before starting the interview. The answers to the question of consent are:

Yes, No, No, Yes, Yes, Yes, Yes, No, Yes, No

Creating a table in R using the function `table()`

Using the command `table()`, any form of a data sample, like a vector, matrix, list or data frame object, can be manipulated, altered and produced.

Create a character vector called 'Consent':

```
Consent<-c("Yes","No","No","Yes","Yes","Yes","Yes","No","Yes","No")
```

Create a simple table:

```
table(Consent)
Consent
 No Yes
  4   6
```

where `c()` is the function that assigns the vector 'Consent' to the string of letters.

Interpretation

The `table()` function performs categorical tabulation of data and displays the frequency distribution of the vector 'Consent' which summarises the number of 'Yes' and 'No' answers in tabular form; 4 is the frequency for 'No' and 6 for 'Yes'.

Example 3.2 Contingency table in R

A *contingency table* or *cross-tabulation* table shows the frequency of two or more variables and may be described according to the number of variables and the number of categories of each variable. For example, a 2 × 2 contingency table has two variables, each with two categories.

Grouping children by ability is increasingly common in nursery and primary schools in England. Setting is one way of grouping children for subjects such as maths and literacy. Suppose we collect data about children's gender and ability grouping and create a multi-dimensional table which displays the distribution of variables in a matrix format.

Creating a contingency table in R

First, we create two character vectors called 'Gender' and 'Ability':

```
Gender<-c("male","male","female","female","female","male","male",
"male","female","male")
Ability<-c("maths","maths", "maths", "literacy", "literacy", "literacy",
"maths", "literacy","maths","maths")
```

To create a contingency table of the counts, we use the function `table()` as follows:

```
crostab1<-table(Gender,Ability)
```

and the contingency table is displayed below the command line:

```
crostab1
       Ability
Gender  literacy maths
  female        2     2
  male          2     4
```

 **Using graphs**

There are two main components that we should consider when selecting a graph to present data:

1. *Scales of measurement.* For different types of variables and scales of measurement, a different type of graph is recommended (Table 3.2). For example, for nominal or ordinal scales of measurement, a bar or a pie graph is the best selection.

Table 3.2 Types of graph for different scales of measurement

Scales of measurement	Types of graph						
	Bar	Pie	Pareto	Scatter	Line	Histogram	Box and whisker
Nominal	✓	✓	✓				
Ordinal	✓	✓	✓				
Interval				✓	✓	✓	✓
Ratio				✓	✓	✓	✓

2. *Graph creation.* All graphs should have descriptive *titles*, *labels* for both axes (*x*- and *y*-axis), appropriate *units*, and *scales* that should be appropriate for the data displayed.

3.2.1 Bar graph

A *bar graph* consists of vertical or horizontal rectangular bars in which the length of each bar represents values, such as counts, amounts or percentages, of a nominal or ordinal variable. It is one of the most widely used graphical displays for the presentation of frequencies or percentages which are the most common attributes of nominal and ordinal values presented when data is analysed. For nominal data it compares different categories represented on the *x*-axis, and for ordinal data there is an order of categories represented on the horizontal axis.

Example 3.3 What is the spread of English exam grades in the first semester?

A first-semester English exam is marked using the GPA grading scale of A–E, where A is the highest grade and E is the lowest. Eighty-five students sat the exam and 12 A grades, 31 B grades, 28 C grades, 10 D grades and 4 E grades were awarded. This is an example of ordinal data. Nominal and ordinal data can be displayed in a bar graph with the `barplot()` function in R or with the `ggplot()` function from the library `ggplot2`.

Creating a bar graph in R with the function `barplot()`

Firstly, create two vectors: 'Grades' and 'Counts':

```
Grades<-c("A","B","C","D","E")
Counts<-c(12,31,28,10,4)
```

Create a bar graph:

```
barplot(Counts)
```

Add *x* and *y* labels to the graph:

```
barplot(Counts, xlab="Grades", ylab="Counts", names.arg=c("A", "B", "C",
"D", "E"))
```

where the argument `xlab=""` adds a title to the *x*-axis, `ylab=""` adds a title to the *y*-axis, and the function `names.arg=c()` adds labels to the *x*-axis.

The coordinate system for the graphics window can be set up by adding the function `ylim=c(,)`:

```
barplot(Counts, xlab="Grades", ylab="Counts", names.arg=c("A", "B", "C",
"D", "E"), ylim=c(0,35))
```

where `ylim=c(0,35)` sets up the *y*-value range from 0 to 35.

The results are displayed in Figure 3.3.

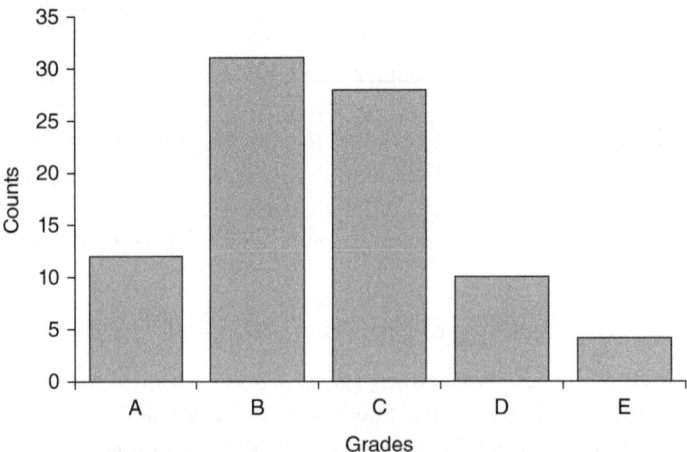

Figure 3.3 Bar graph created using the function `barplot()` for Example 3.3

Interpretation

The bar graph in Figure 3.3 displays the counts of grades, which is an ordinal variable, on the *y*-axis for five different categories of grades (A, B, C, D and E). Using counts instead of percentages matters for a small data set because the percentage is less stable. For example, if we take only those students with A and E grades, the percentages will be 12/16 = 75 per cent (grade A) and 4/16 = 25 per cent (grade E), which shows a huge change compared to the initial situation with five grades where it was 14 per cent for grade A and 5 per cent for grade B.

Alternatively, we can use the function `ggplot()` to create a bar chart (Figure 3.4). To use this function, it is necessary to install and load the `ggplot2` package which contains a variety of functions dedicated to improving the quality of data visualisation.

Creating a bar graph in R with the function `ggplot()`

Install and load the `ggplot2` package into R:

```
install.packages(ggplot2)
library(ggplot2)
```

Create a data frame named 'data' using the function `data.frame()`:

```
data=data.frame(Grades=c("A","B","C","D","E"),Counts=c(12,31,28,10,4))
```

Create a bar graph (Figure 3.4) using the function `ggplot()`:

```
ggplot(data, aes(x=Grades, y=Counts)) + geom_bar(stat = "identity")
```

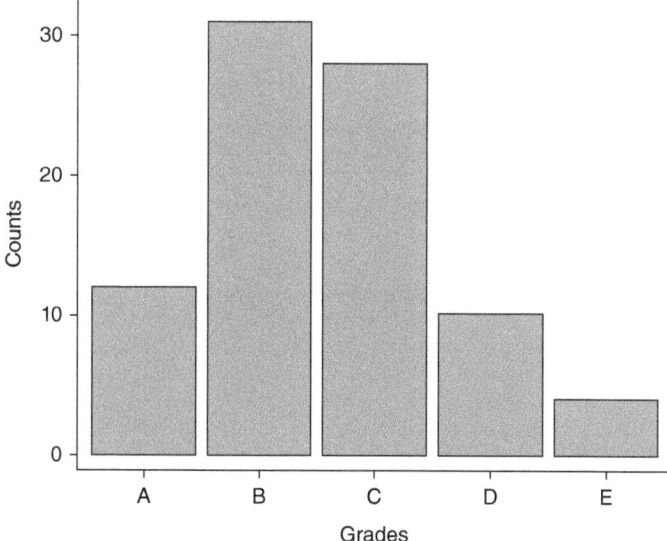

Figure 3.4 Bar graph created using the `ggplot()` function for Example 3.3

3.2.2 Pareto graph

A Pareto graph is a particular type of bar graph where each category is represented in a descending order from left to right on the *x*-axis, and contains a superimposed line that represents a cumulative running percentage. A Pareto graph enables us to focus on the most important categories by separating the 'vital few' from the 'trivial many' categories.

Example 3.4 How to increase students' satisfaction with an online course

A course leader explores which areas of students' satisfaction with his online course are most important for them. The feedback from students at the end of the course reveals the following underlying satisfaction components: assessment, content, convenience, design, feedback, flexibility, interaction, learning and resources. The results lead the course leader to hypothesise that students' satisfaction with the online course is influenced by constructs which were highly rated by students. The data is presented in the box below.

Creating a Pareto graph in R using the function `pareto.chart()`

The function `pareto.chart()` is part of the package `qcc` and we will need to install and load this package:

```
install.packages("qcc")
library(qcc)
```

(Continued)

Create the vector 'online':

```
online<-c(26,40,12,118,16,96,30,8,4)
```

Set the names of the object 'online':

```
names(online) <-c("Assessment", "Content", "Convenience", "Design",
"Feedback", "Flexibility", "Interaction", "Learning", "Resources")
```

The `names()` function will show us everything that is stored in R under that object name. Create the Pareto graph (Figure 3.5):

```
pareto.chart(online, xlab="Factors", ylab = "Counts")
```

```
Pareto chart analysis for online
```

	Frequency	Cum.Freq.	Percentage	Cum.Percent.
Design	118.000000	118.000000	33.714286	33.714286
Flexibility	96.000000	214.000000	27.428571	61.142857
Content	40.000000	254.000000	11.428571	72.571429
Interaction	30.000000	284.000000	8.571429	81.142857
Assessment	26.000000	310.000000	7.428571	88.571429
Feedback	16.000000	326.000000	4.571429	93.142857
Convenience	12.000000	338.000000	3.428571	96.571429
Learning	8.000000	346.000000	2.285714	98.857143
Resources	4.000000	350.000000	1.142857	100.000000

If the x-axis labels and title overlap, then, the standard argument `xlab=""` can be replaced with the argument `mtext("Factors", side=1, line=3)`, which will place the x-axis title at a distance of 3 lines from the x-axis.

```
pareto.chart(online, xlab="", ylab = "Counts")
pareto.chart(online, mtext("Factors", side=1, line=3),ylab = "Counts")
```

Interpretation

The lengths of the bars shown in Figure 3.5 represent the number of responses for the nominal variable – in our example the 'Factors' which correspond to the categories related to students' satisfaction with their online course experience. The bars are arranged with the longest bars on the left and the shortest on the right, which visually shows the areas in rank order from the most significant area of interest for students, down to the least. The line on the graph shows the cumulative relative frequency.

The course leader can find out which are the most important areas of students' satisfaction with the online course by using the Pareto graph and applying the so-called 80/20 Pareto rule (also called 'the vital few and useful many'). Of the contributions, the design, flexibility, online content and interaction are the ones (vital few) that account for about 80 per cent of the total. The remaining categories (useful many) will not significantly improve the students' experience with the online course.

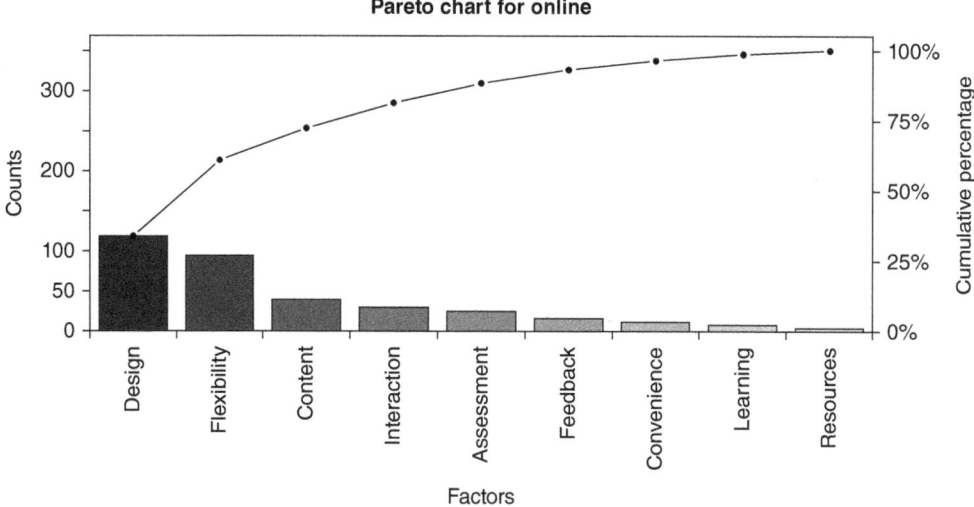

Figure 3.5 Pareto graph for Example 3.4 using the `pareto.chart()` function in R

3.2.3 Pie graph

A pie graph is a circle graph in which areas or pie slices represent the count, amount or percentage of each category. All the categories together account for the entire circle, that is, 100 per cent, which represents the total, and this enables us to see each category's proportion of the whole.

Example 3.5 What proportion of A grades has been obtained by students in an English exam in the first term?

For this example, we will use the same data as we used in Example 3.3.

Creating a pie graph in R using the function `pie()`

Create the vectors 'Counts' and 'Grades' for the English exam results, if you have not already done so:

```
Counts <- c(12, 31, 28, 10, 4)
Grades <- c("A", "B", "C", "D", "E")
```

(Continued)

Compute the frequencies (Counts/sum(Counts)*100) and round the results to the specified number of decimal places (default 0):

```
Counts/sum(Counts)*100
[1] 14.117647 36.470588 32.941176 11.764706 4.705882
pct <- round(Counts/sum(Counts)*100)
pct
[1] 14 36 33 12 5
```

Add per cent symbol to labels:

```
Grades <- paste(Grades, "=", pct) # the argument "=" adds an equals sign
between the letter of the grades and the percentage
Grades <- paste(Grades,"%",sep="") # the argument "%" adds % to labels
```

To create different shades of grey colour for each section, we use the argument col=grey.colors(length(Grades) which is part of the RColorBrewer package and needs to be installed in R:

```
install.packages("RColorBrewer")
library(RColorBrewer)
```

Create the pie graph (Figure 3.6):

```
pie(Counts,labels = Grades,
col=grey.colors(length(Grades)), main="Distribution of marks")
```

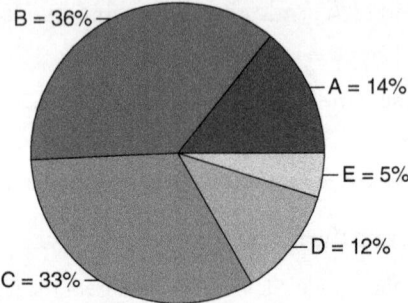

Figure 3.6 A pie graph created using the function pie() from base packages

If we want to have the pie chart in colour, we can replace the argument *grey.colors* with *rainbow*.

Interpretation

Percentages are encoded as pie slices, and it is straightforward for the user to compare categories when the number of slices is not large. As the number of categories increases, it becomes more difficult for the user to assimilate all the information. The maximum number of categories should be six for clarity. In Example 3.5 and Figure 3.6, there are five categories and we can easily compare them; for example, the number of students who obtained an A grade in the first-term maths exam is approximately half of the number of students who got a B, and three times as many as the number who got an E.

3.2.4 Histogram

A histogram is a type of bar graph, with no gaps between the bars, for interval data in which individual bars represent the frequencies or percentages (shown on the *y*-axis) in each group and the variable is plotted on the *x*-axis. The bars of histograms are sometimes referred to as 'bins'. A histogram reveals the overall shape of the frequencies in the groups, and it can give us information about the shape the population takes if the data is from a sample.

Example 3.6 What is the distribution of waiting time for students to get a coffee during their breaks between lectures?

A university cafeteria wants to reduce the serving time for students during the half-hour breaks between lectures. The manager of the cafeteria conducts a study of waiting times to get a better understanding of the problem. Twenty-eight students are asked how long they have to wait.

Creating a histogram in R using the function `hist()`

Create the vector 'coffeetime' for the waiting time:

```
coffeetime<-c(2,3,5,5,5,6,7,7,8,9,9,10,10,10,11,11,12,12,13,13,14,
+ 14,15,15,16,16,18,20)
```

Create the histogram (Figure 3.7):

```
hist(coffeetime, xlab = "Waiting time",col="gray", main="Distribution of
waiting time for students to get a coffee")
```

Interpretation

The histogram displayed in Figure 3.7 shows the distribution of interval data. There is no space between 'bins', which shows the continuous nature of the distribution of the variable (waiting time).

The height of each bar shows the number of data points that fall between the ranges. We see that students have to wait between 5 and 15 minutes to be served. The manager of the cafeteria concludes that it is necessary to invest in a new coffee machine which can make more than one coffee at a time.

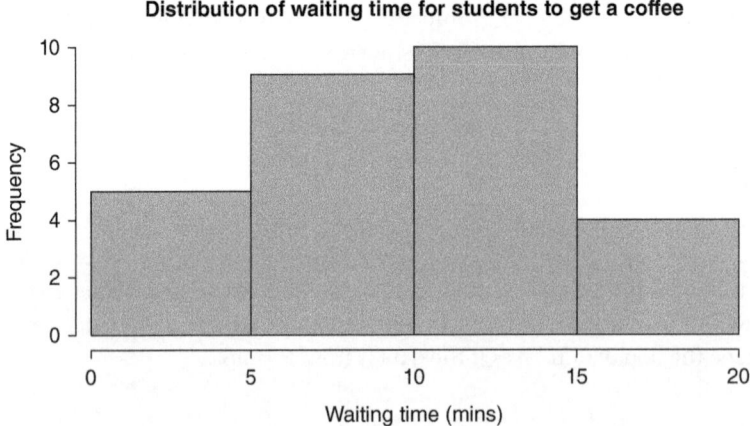

Figure 3.7 Histogram created using the `hist()` function in R for Example 3.6.

3.2.5 Box and whisker graph

The box and whisker graph, also known as a boxplot, is used to summarise data succinctly, to see if the data is symmetric and if there are outliers. This type of graph shows five statistics (the first quartile, median, third quartile, maximum (or 1.5 times the IQR of the data, whichever is smaller) and minimum (or −1.5 times the IQR of the data, whichever is smaller)), which we will discuss in detail in Chapter 4.

Creating a box and whisker graph in R using the function `boxplot()`

We will use the same vectors which were created in Example 3.6.

Create the box and whisker plot (Figure 3.8):

```
boxplot(coffeetime, col="lightgray", ylab=" Waiting time")
```

Interpretation

The box and whisker graph in Figure 3.8 summarises the data from Example 3.6. It consists of a box with a line at the bottom edge (the first quartile), a thicker line inside the box (the median), another line at the top edge (the third quantile), and whiskers which extend to the minimum and maximum. Thus, the boxplot allows us to check quickly for symmetry, which holds if the median is in the middle of the box and each quartile is about the same length. Our example clearly shows a symmetric distribution around 10 minutes' waiting time.

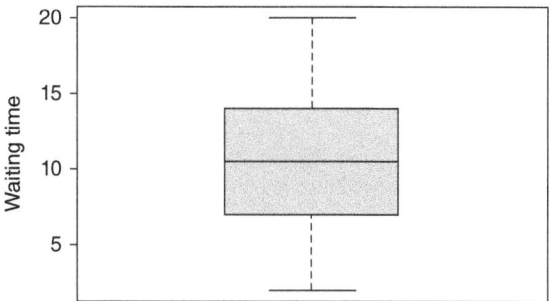

Figure 3.8 Box and whisker graph (or boxplot) created using the `boxplot()` function in R for Example 3.6.

Example 3.7 Plotting the histogram and boxplot on the same graph

Combining the histogram and the boxplot for the same data in the same figure helps the researcher to identify variances among data. For example, a histogram helps us to easily identify large or small variances among the observed frequencies, while a boxplot is used to analyse a moderate variance. The function `simple.hist.and.boxplot()` is part of the `UsingR` package and will plot both the histogram and the boxplot (Figure 3.9).

Comparing boxplot and histogram

Install and upload the `UsingR` package:

```
install.packages("UsingR")
library(UsingR)
```

Plot the histogram and boxplot in the same Figure 3.9:

```
simple.hist.and.boxplot(coffeetime)
```

3.2.6 Line graph

A line graph can be used to evaluate the relationship between variables, for example to reveal patterns over time when each point on the graph represents the value of an interval or ratio variable at a specific point in time, or to reveal how changes in one variable relate to changes in another variable. When any change in an independent variable produces the same constant change in the dependent variable, the relationship between the variables is described as linear and is represented by a straight line. If the variables move at a different rate of change, the relationship between them is nonlinear and is represented by a curved line.

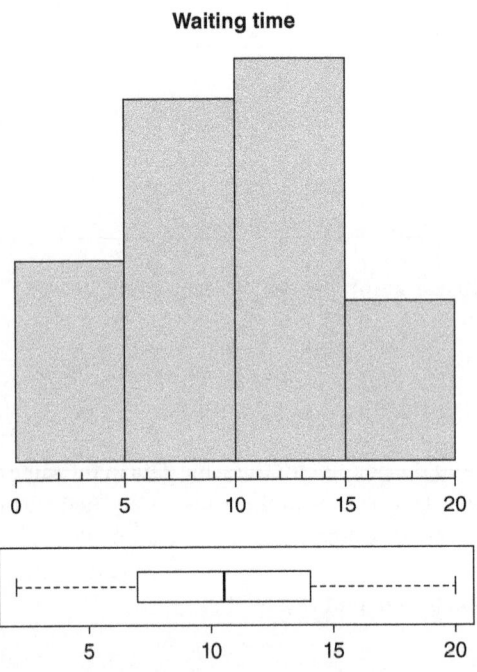

Figure 3.9 Histogram and boxplot created using the function `simple.hist.and.boxplot()` for Example 3.6

Example 3.7 How did Finland's average scores on the PISA Science assessment change from 2000 to 2015?

PISA is the Programme for International Student Assessment which measures 15-year-olds' ability to use their reading, mathematics and science knowledge and skills to meet real-life challenges. This global assessment is conducted every three years by the Organisation for Economic Co-operation and Development (OECD). PISA Science measures scientific literacy, which is defined as the ability to use scientific knowledge to identify questions, to acquire new knowledge, to explain scientific phenomena, and to draw evidence-based conclusions about science-related issues.

Finland has been among the top countries in the PISA assessment for several years. We would like to find out if that country's scores on PISA Science changed from 2000 to 2015.

Creating a line graph in R using the function `plot()`

Create two vectors named 'Year' for the years when the PISA Science test was held and 'Scores' for the average scores on the test for Finland from 2000 to 2015:

```
Year<-c(2000,2003,2006,2009,2012,2015)
Scores<-c(538,543,563,554,545,531)
```

Create a line plot (Figure 3.10):

```
plot(Year,Scores, type="o", pch=19, main="PISA Science performance scores
for Finland")
```

with the following arguments:

- *type="o"* creates both lines and points
- *pch=19* creates a solid circle for each point
- *main=" "* adds a title to the line graph.

Interpretation

Figure 3.10 shows the average PISA Science performance scores for Finland from 2000 to 2015. Time is shown on the *x*-axis, and the ratio variable 'Scores' is shown on the *y*-axis. The data shows some fluctuations over time, with the highest average in 2006 and the lowest in 2015.

3.2.7 Scatter graph

A scatter graph plots the values of two variables, with the dependent variable usually on the *y*-axis and the independent variable on the *x*-axis. This type of graph is useful when there are any patterns, for example linear correlation, in the relationship between two numerical variables.

Example 3.8 Is the mathematical literacy of a 15-year-old influenced by the ratio of students to teaching staff?

Data set: Ex3_8.csv

A research student investigates if there is a correlation between the two variables, mathematical literacy and the ratio of students to teaching staff, by analysing the 2015 PISA Mathematical performance scores and data on student–teacher ratio and average class size, extracted from OECD.stat.

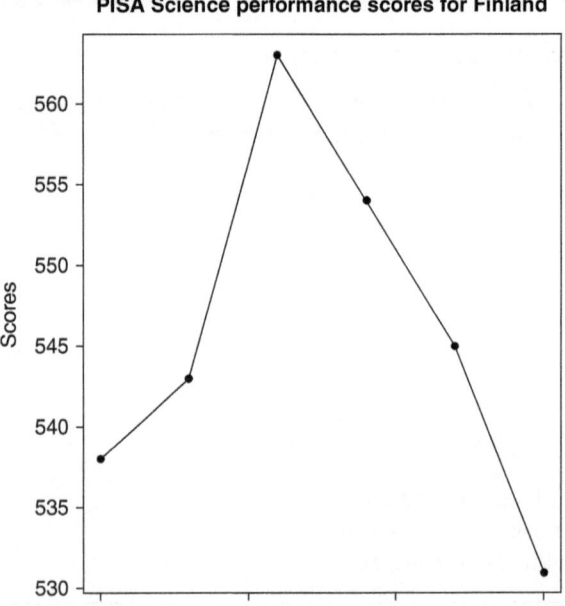

Figure 3.10 A line graph created using the function `plot()` for Example 3.7.

Creating a scatter graph in R using the function `plot()`

Save the file Ex3_8.csv in a folder of your choice, for example 'C:\Users\.'

Upload the .csv file to R and assign the name 'Scatter':

```
Scatter<-read.csv(file.choose(), header=TRUE)
```

To see the data set, type the name of the saved file and press Enter:

```
Scatter
```

	Country	Ratio	PISA2015Maths
1	Japan	11.961	532
2	Korea, Republic of	14.090	524
3	Estonia	15.229	520
4	Canada	12.966	516
5	Netherlands	18.033	512
6	Finland	16.474	511
7	Slovenia	13.435	510
8	Belgium	9.927	507

9	Germany	12.997	506
10	Poland	10.270	504
11	Norway	10.280	502
12	Austria	10.149	497
13	New Zealand	12.767	495
14	Czech Republic	11.135	494
15	Sweden	14.402	494
16	Australia	12.254	494
17	Portugal	9.698	492
18	United Kingdom	15.376	492
19	Italy	12.469	490
20	Luxembourg	10.754	486
21	Spain	11.124	486
22	Latvia	9.748	482
23	Lithuania	8.081	478
24	Hungary	11.472	477
25	Slovak Republic	13.537	475

Create the scatterplot (Figure 3.11):

```
plot(PISA2015Maths~Ratio, Scatter, pch=16, xlab="Scores")
```

where *pch=* is the argument used to select the shape of the points on the graph (*pch=16* gives a solid circle).

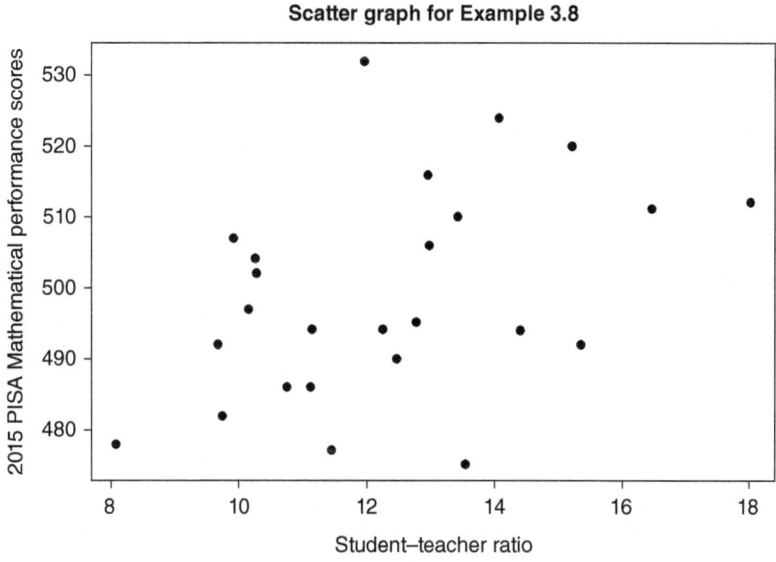

Figure 3.11 A scatter graph created using the function `plot()` for Example 3.8

Interpretation

Figure 3.11 displays the two ratio variables in a scatter graph; 'Ratio' is the independent variable (student–staff ratio) shown on the x-axis, while 'PISA2015Maths' is the dependent variable shown on the y-axis. The points do not show any pattern, it looks like there is no relationship between the two variables and the research might conclude that the mathematical literacy of a 15-year-old is not influenced by the ratio of students to teaching staff. However, this is only a first impression and further statistical tests, such as correlation coefficients, can be carried out to confirm the existence of correlation and its type and strength.

Exercises

3.1 What is the difference between a table and a figure?

3.2 List the key elements of a table.

3.3 How can we classify different forms of table?

3.4 List the key elements of a figure.

3.5 What is the difference between a graph and a chart?

3.6 How many types of graphs do you know?

3.7 If we have a nominal variable, which type of graph is it recommended to use?

    (a) Line

    (b) Bar

    (c) Scatter

    (d) Pareto

    (e) Histogram

    (f) Boxplot

3.8 Can we transform a scatter graph into a line graph by adding a joining line between the points? Why?

3.9 List all the R functions to create different types of graphs.

3.10 Can we find more than one function that is used to create a boxplot?

Further reading

Grant, R. (2019) *Data visualization: Charts, maps and interactive graphics*. Boca Raton, FL: CRC Press.

The book presents a brief overview of 125 visualisation techniques and tools, and it is accessible to anyone interested in how to make an excellent presentation of data.

Rahlf, T. (2019) *Data visualisation with R: 111 examples* (2nd ed.). Cham: Springer.

This book presents systematic explanations of 111 complete programming scripts in R and shows how to create various types of graphics, from simple graphs, such as barplots and boxplots, to more complex ones, such as mosaic and balloon charts.

Swires-Hennessey, E. (2014) *Presenting data: How to communicate your message effectively.* Chichester: John Wiley & Sons.

This is an excellent guide for anyone interested in finding out how to present and interpret statistical data in clear, concise, consistent and correct ways.

Tufte, E. (2004) *The visual display of quantitative information.* Cheshire, CT: Graphics Press.

This is a classic book on the visual presentation of data, with over 250 graphics accompanied by a detailed analysis of how to correctly display different types of data.

PART THREE

Providing information about data

Part Three Contents

4

Descriptive statistics

━━━━━━━━━━ **Chapter Objectives** ━━━━━━━━━━

In this chapter, we will:

- explain the meaning of the term 'statistics'
- define the statistics of location or central tendency
- describe different types of frequency distributions
- introduce the descriptive statistics techniques used to identify and characterise quantitative data
- demonstrate how to calculate the mean, mode and median using R.

Suppose we collect data on the length of time taken by students to solve a problem in mathematics and we would like to find out if there is a difference between boys and girls. We separate the data into two groups. The percentage of each group of students in a sample is a numerical measure that describes the two groups, and is an example of a sample *statistic*. There are two branches of statistics: the first one is descriptive statistics, which serves as a basis for inferential statistics; the second is a branch of statistics that analyses and discusses sample data to reach conclusions about that data. Data summaries and statistical techniques that are used to characterise and identify general or typical properties of the data and share the findings are called *descriptive statistics*. This chapter will introduce descriptive statistical techniques used to identify characteristics regarding *location* (or central tendency), while measures of *dispersion* of data, which are of great help in understanding the distribution of data, will be introduced in Chapter 5 (Figure 4.1). These techniques are easy to apply because they are easy to calculate manually or by using any statistical software or calculator.

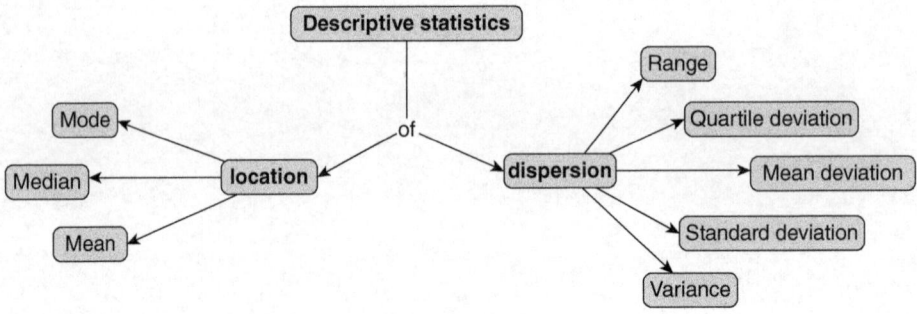

Figure 4.1 Descriptive statistical measures of location and dispersion

4●1 From raw data to frequency distributions

In Chapter 3, we showed how vital and useful the graphical displays are to find out what data tell us before deciding how to analyse it. For example, after collecting raw quantitative data in a given study, researchers start by arranging it in a form suitable for visualisation, computation and interpretation. A simple arrangement would be a *frequency distribution* of a variable, which reflects the distribution of the variable's values according to the magnitude of these values, and the data is grouped into *classes* and *frequencies*. A frequency distribution may be graphically displayed as a table, histogram, or boxplot and in different forms: as *a simple frequency distribution* which reflects the distribution of a single variable or as *a compound frequency distribution* for two or more variables (Figure 4.2). When we count the number of times a particular event or outcome occurs or the frequencies in a particular class, then we have a *simple frequency distribution*. If the frequencies are expressed as percentages of the total frequency, a *percentage frequency distribution* is created. When the frequencies are expressed as proportions of the total, then a *simple cumulative frequency distribution* is created.

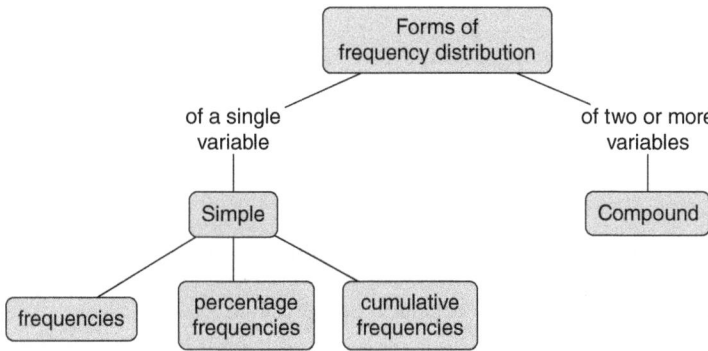

Figure 4.2 Forms of frequency distributions

Example 4.1 What are the characteristics of the data from a study which focuses on the time needed by a group of children to solve a problem in mathematics?

Suppose we have the set of values shown in Table 4.1, which were obtained by a classroom teacher by listing the length of time a group of children took to solve a problem in mathematics. Such a data set is referred to as *raw data*.

Table 4.1 Example of raw data

Student's name	John	Mary	Eve	Harry	Anna	Nazeefa	Caleb	Helen	Jo	Jane	Leon
Time (min)	10	12	10	8	11	8	15	11	9	10	13

Looking at this data set, it is difficult to detect whether there is a pattern in the data, how it is spread, or if there are any values around which the data is concentrated. If the raw data is rearranged from the smallest to the largest value, an *array* is created (Table 4.2).

Table 4.2 Example of an array

Student's name	Harry	Nazeefa	Jo	John	Eve	Jane	Anna	Helen	Mary	Leon	Caleb
Time (min)	8	8	9	10	10	10	11	11	12	13	15

Further examination of this array suggests that some values repeat; for example, the value 8 appears twice, 10 appears three times and 11 appears twice. The number of occurrences is called the *frequency*, and, for our example, this is the number of times each time length value occurs. Table 4.3 gives the *distribution* of frequencies of the time variable, in this case an *ungrouped frequency distribution*. The most important thing about a frequency distribution is that it allows the researcher to see meaningful patterns and characteristics of a variable, such as symmetry, spread or unusual values.

Table 4.3 Ungrouped frequency distribution

Value	8	9	10	11	12	13	15
Frequency	2	1	3	2	1	1	1

Creating a table and an ungrouped frequency table in R

Create the data set:

```
x<-c(10, 12, 10, 8, 11, 8, 15, 11, 9, 10, 13)
```

Create a table with frequencies using the function `table()`:

```
table(x)
x
 8  9 10 11 12 13 15
 2  1  3  2  1  1  1
```

Create a table with percentages using the function `prop.table()`:

```
prop.table(table(x))
x
        8         9        10        11        12        13        15
0.1818181 0.0909090 0.2727272 0.1818181 0.0909090 0.0909090 0.0909090
```

However, we can simplify even more by grouping the values into *classes*. In our example, we can group the occurrences between 6 and 8 into one class, then do the same for the next four categories, 8 to 10, and so on. A class interval defines each of these classes and, for example, the class interval between 6 and 8 is written as (6, 8]. The interval notation $(a, b]$ is used to display the limits of the classes and represents the set of all numbers between a and b, excluding a and including b. So the interval (6, 8] represents all numbers between 6 and 8, excluding 6 and including 8. The smallest and largest values in each class interval are known as *class limits*. For the class (8, 10], the lower limit is 8 and the upper limit is 10. The number of values falling within each class interval is called the *class frequency*. Thus, the data values for the variable time presented in Table 4.3 can be converted into classes with their corresponding frequencies, which is called a *grouped frequency distribution* and is shown in Table 4.4. Creating a *grouped frequency table* is a method of presenting the data in a summarised form, helping the researcher to detect possible patterns in the data. However, depending on the class interval, some information might be lost.

Table 4.4 Grouped frequency distribution

Classes	(6, 8]	(8, 10]	(10, 12]	(12, 14]	(14, 16]
Frequency	2	4	3	1	1

Creating a grouped frequency table in R

Create a list of class boundaries named 'bins' using the function `seq()`:

```
bins<-seq(6,16, by=2)
```

where `seq(6,16, by=2)` generates regular sequences starting at 2 and finishing at 16 with an increment of 2.

The data is then grouped into bins using the function `cut()`:

```
xbins<-cut(x,bins)
```

where *x* is a numeric vector which is to be converted to a factor by cutting.

Produce the table in a default format using the function `table()`:

```
table(xbins)
xbins
 (6,8]   (8,10]  (10,12]  (12,14]  (14,16]
    2        4        3        1        1
```

Produce the same table in a different format using the function `transform()`:

```
transform(table(xbins))
     xbins Freq
1    (6,8]    2
2   (8,10]    4
```

(Continued)

```
3 (10,12]    3
4 (12,14]    1
5 (14,16]    1
```

Produce a cumulative frequency distribution using the function `cumsum()`:

```
cumsum(table(xbins))
  (6,8]   (8,10]  (10,12]  (12,14]  (14,16]
     2       6        9       10       11
```

The `cumsum()` function returns a vector whose elements are the cumulative sums.

The *cumulative frequency* for each class interval is the sum of all previous frequencies up to the current point. The cumulative frequency is obtained by adding the frequency of a class interval and the frequencies of the preceding intervals up to that class interval. Table 4.5 shows the cumulative frequencies for the data values from Example 4.1. For the second class, (8, 10], the cumulative frequency is found by adding the frequency for class (6, 8] (2) to the frequency for class (8, 10] (4), which gives us a total of 6. For class (10, 12], we take the cumulative frequency for the previous class (6) and add 3, which equals 9; for class (12, 14] the total is 10; and for the last class it is 11. The cumulative frequency for class (10, 12] tells us how many students took 12 minutes or less to solve the maths problem.

Table 4.5 Cumulative frequency distribution

Classes	(6, 8]	(8, 10]	(10, 12]	(12, 14]	(14, 16]
Cumulative frequencies	2	6	9	10	11

Creating an ogive in R

Plot the cumulative frequency using the function `plot()`:

```
plot(cumsum(table(xbins)), ylab="Cumulative frequencies", pch=19)
```

Create the cumulative frequency curve using the function `lines()`:

```
lines(cumsum(table(xbins)), lty='dashed')
```

where the argument *pch=19* is used to specify point shapes ('solid circle') and `lty='dashed'` is used to specify the line type (dashed line).

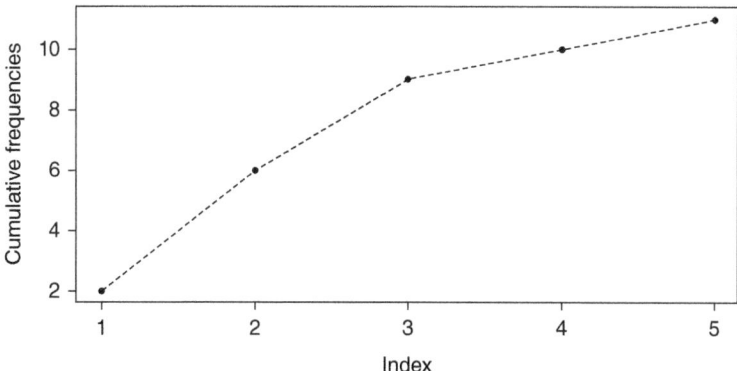

Figure 4.3   Ogive graph for cumulative frequency distribution

Cumulative frequencies are often represented by a graph called an *ogive*, in which each scattered point is connected by a line, and the *y*-axis represents the cumulative frequency and the *x*-axis the classes. The cumulative frequency curve, shown as a dashed curve in Figure 4.3, is useful for comparing different frequency distributions. When the class frequencies reach the maximum at one end of the range, they form a J-shaped curve.

Another convenient and appropriate way to visualise the characteristics of a variable and its frequency distribution is to use a histogram, as shown in Figure 4.4. The observed distribution of the times (in minutes) a group of students took to solve a problem in mathematics is exhibited in the form of a histogram (rectangles) together with a superimposed *frequency curve* (smooth curve). The area of each rectangle equals the observed frequency of times whose length falls into the corresponding group, and the area of all the rectangles together must be equal to the area under the frequency curve. In our case, all the groups are of the same width, but a new histogram can be easily created for the case when the intervals are unequal. However, if we had a large number of values, the final shape of the distribution of data would be like the continuous line shown in Figure 4.4. To find out the essential characteristics of a histogram or a frequency curve, we need to calculate statistical measures of central tendency, such as the mean, median and standard deviation, which will be described later in this chapter.

Creating a histogram in R

Create the histogram using the function `hist()`:

```
hist(x,bins, freq = FALSE)
```

where *x* is a vector of values for which the histogram is desired. If *freq=TRUE*, the histogram shows the frequencies or the counts on the y-axis; if *freq= FALSE*, the y-axis shows the probability densities, and the histogram has a total area of 1.

(Continued)

Create the line density using the function `lines()`:

```
lines(density(x))
```

where the `density()` function splits our data *x* into several small intervals and calculates the density for the midpoint of each interval.

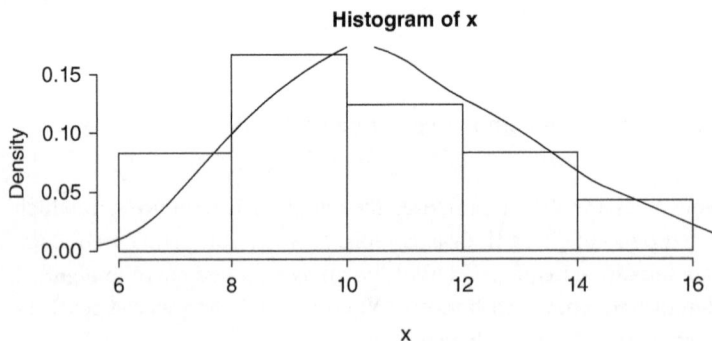

Figure 4.4 The histogram and frequency curve for the grouped frequency data from Example 4.1

 Measures of location or central tendency

Quantitative data show a tendency to group around specific values, and *measures of location*, also known as *measures of central tendency*, help us to identify the characteristics of data sets and describe the positions of the data values. Commonly used measures are the mode, median and mean. Use of these measures depends on both scales of measurement (Table 4.6) and the intended analysis. For example, for nominal variables, the only measure allowed is the mode, and for ordinal variables, the median and mode are appropriate. Only for interval and ratio variables can the mean be a measure of central tendency.

Table 4.6 Measures of location for different scales of measurement

Measures of location	Scales of measurement			
	Nominal	**Ordinal**	**Interval**	**Ratio**
Mode	✓	✓	✓	✓
Median		✓	✓	✓
Mean			✓	✓

4.2.1 Mode

The mode is the value or values in a data set that appears most frequently, and it is commonly used to describe nominal or ordinal variables, such as religion, social class or ethnicity. For example, for a survey question asked about nationality, the mode will tell us the most frequently occurring nationality on that survey. Sometimes a variable might have more than one mode or no single mode.

Example 4.2 What length of time occurs most often in the set of values from Example 4.1?

The mode is calculated by counting the number of times each value occurs in a data set. In this example, the value that appears more frequently (or often) in the data set is value 10. In this case, the mode tells us only that more students took 10 minutes to solve the maths problem than any other time between 8 and 15 minutes.

Computing mode in R for interval variable

In base R there is no function called mode () for computing the mode. Instead, enter the following code in the RStudio Console:

Create the vector x with numerical values from Example 4.1:

```
X<-c(10,12,10,8,11,8,15,11,9,10,13)
```

Create a table called 'temp':

```
temp<-table(as.vector(x))
```

See how often each value occurs:

```
temp
 8  9 10 11 12 13 14 15
 2  1  3  2  1  1  1  1
```

Find the mode:

```
names(temp)[temp==max(temp)]
[1] "10"
```

The last input in R returns in temp's second row the actual value, in our 10, that has the highest count (3).

Computing the mode in R for nominal data

Create a character vector named 'subjects' representing the top five after-school subjects for a small group of primary school children:

```
subjects<-c("Maths","Science","Maths","History","Art","Art","Music","Art")
```

Before calculating the mode, we need to convert the vector 'subject' into a non-distributed vector using the function `as.vector()` to then create a table of count:

```
temp<-table(as.vector(subjects))
temp

 Art History Maths Music Science
   3       1     2     1       1
```

Find the mode:

```
names(temp)[temp==max(temp)]
[1] "Art"
```

4.2.2 Median

The median is the middle value in a data set arranged in ascending order; as such, it has an equal number of items on either side of it. Depending on the number of observations, the median is:

- the middle value, when the number of observations is odd;
- the mean of the two middle values, when the number of observations is even.

The median is also known as the 50th percentile, because 50 per cent of the observations are smaller than the median.

Example 4.3 What is the value of the variable in Example 4.1 that divides the observations into two equal groups?

The first step to calculate the median is to arrange the data in ascending order:

8, 8, 9, 10, 10, 10, 11, 11, 12, 13, 15

↑

6th

In this example, there are 11 observations and this number of observations is *odd*. The middle observation is the sixth observation, so the median is 10. Half of the children took less than 10 minutes to solve a problem in mathematics and half of them more than 10 minutes.

Suppose we have one more observation, 14, to add to our data set. We now have 12 observations, an even number, and the new ordered data set is:

8, 8, 9, 10, 10, 10, 11, 11, 12, 13, 14, 15

↑ ↑

6th 7th

In this case, the median is halfway between the two middle observations, the sixth and seventh. To calculate the median, add the two values of these observations and divide them by 2:

$$Median = \frac{10 + 11}{2} = 10.5$$

Computing the median in R

Create the vector *x*:

```
x<-c(10,12,10,8,11,8,15,11,9,10,13,14)
```

Calculate the median using the build-in function `median()`:

```
median(x)
[1] 10.5
```

4.2.3 Mean

In educational research, 'means', which is a synonym for 'averages', are often used to answer questions such as:

- What are the test scores in special education assessments?
- What is the average UK starting salary for graduates?
- What is the average number of years of total schooling across all education levels, for the population aged 15-64?

However, it is essential to notice that there are several types of means in statistics, such as the arithmetic, geometric and harmonic mean. In this book, we only focus on the arithmetic mean because it is the most common type of mean used in education research. We will also use an example to present two other forms of the arithmetic mean, the trimmed and weighted mean.

Arithmetic mean

The *arithmetic mean* is the most frequently used measure of central tendency for interval and ratio variables. It is a good measure of the average when a data set contains values that are relatively evenly spread, with no exceptionally high or low values. Arithmetic means also serve as a basis for some measures of dispersion, such as the variance and standard deviation.

Example 4.4 What is the mean time to solve the maths problem in Example 4.1?

To find the arithmetic mean, we add up all the data values from Example 4.1 and then divide the sum by the total number of observations:

$$Arithmetic\ mean = \frac{8 + 12 + 10 + 8 + 11 + 10 + 10 + 11 + 9 + 13 + 15}{11} = 10.64$$

Computing the arithmetic mean in R

To calculate the arithmetic mean in R, we use the built-in function `mean()`:

```
mean(x)
[1] 10.63636
```

If there are missing values in the data set, then the argument *na.rm* is used to remove the missing values from the input vector, and the function will be:

```
mean(x,na.rm=FALSE)
```

Interpretation

The mean arithmetic time is 10.64 minutes, and this gives us an idea about where the data values seem to cluster. For example, we know Mary solved the maths problem in 12 minutes, a value which is above the mean. Thus, comparing this value with the arithmetic mean suggests that the test might have been difficult for her. Therefore, she needed more time, something that on its own a value will not be able to tell.

Weighted arithmetic mean

Sometimes each value in a set may be associated with a weight. The weight reflects the significance or frequency of occurrence attached to the respective value. The *weighted arithmetic mean* is the sum of all values, multiplied by the appropriate weight, divided by the sum of the weights.

$$Weighted\ arithmetic\ mean = \frac{8 \times 2 + 9 \times 1 + 10 \times 3 + 11 \times 2 + 12 \times 1 + 13 \times 1 + 15 \times 1}{11} = 10.64$$

Computing the weighted arithmetic mean in R

Create the vector *x*:

```
x<-c(10,12,10,8,11,8,15,11,9,10,13,14)
```

Create a vector *x1* using the function `sort()` which will list the values in the data set in ascending order:

```
x1<-sort(x)
x1
 [1]  8  8  9 10 10 10 11 11 12 13 15
```

Create a vector named *x2* containing the values whose weighted mean is to be computed:

```
x2<-c(8,9,10,11,12,13,15)
```

Create a vector for the weights (*wt*) and divide by the total number of values:

```
wt<-c(2,1,3,2,1,1,1)/11
```

Calculate the weighted mean using the function `weighted.mean()`:

```
weighted.mean(x2, wt)
[1] 10.63636
```

Trimmed arithmetic mean

The *trimmed arithmetic mean* is the arithmetic mean obtained after a small percentage of the largest and smallest values have been removed. This type of arithmetic mean can be used for data sets that contain *outliers*, which are not just the extreme values (lowest and highest), but values that are very different from the pattern established by the data set. The best way to identify outliers, for any size of data set, is to use a boxplot. We will demonstrate the use of a boxplot (Figure 4.5) to identify the outliers for the data in Example 4.1.

Visualising the outliers

Create the vector *x*:

```
x<-c(10,12,10,8,11,8,15,11,9,10,13)
```

Create a box and whisker plot (Figure 4.5) using the function `boxplot()` to check for outliers:

```
boxplot(x)
```

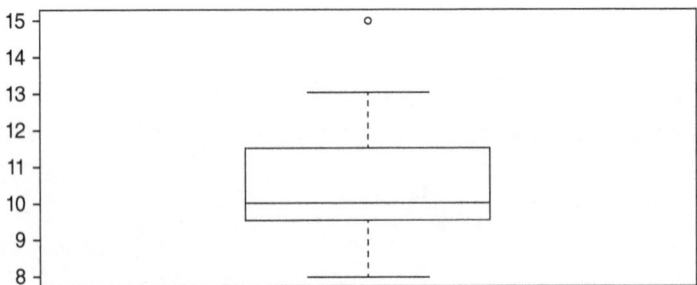

Figure 4.5   Visualising the outliers in a boxplot

Interpretation

In Figure 4.5, the point at 15 (black circle) lies at a distance that is more than one and a half times the length of the box, that is, more than 1.5 times the value of the interquartile range. In Chapter 5 we will go into detail about the interquartile range. If we remove this outlier from the data set, we then calculate the trimmed mean which, in our case, is 10.2, much lower than the case when the outlier was included.

 **Advantages and disadvantages of using the mode, median and mean**

Let us now look at the advantages of using the mode, median and mean. The mode:

- can be used for any variable, both numeric and character data and any levels of measurement;
- is not affected by extreme values; however, the mode varies much more from sample to sample;
- is easy to find from a graph or a table.

The median:

- is straightforward to calculate;
- is not sensitive to extreme observations.

The mean:

- is the most frequently used descriptive statistic;
- uses the numerical values of each observation;
- is used in many statistical analyses as a standard measure of the centre of the distribution of the data.

Now let us look at the disadvantages. The mode:

- does not explain very much about the entire data set;
- is not calculated by many statistical software programs.

The median:

- does not make use of all the information in the data, for example when there are extreme values, also called outliers, and this can be a disadvantage if a researcher wants to find out if and why there are extreme values;
- can be quite gross on an ordinal variable with only a small number of response options (i.e. perhaps less than 20).

The mean:

- is sensitive to unusual or extreme values of the observation; in this situation, we can compare the mean and the median to decide which is the better measure to use.

 ## Measures of location and graphical display

Making graphs and tables alongside computing statistics makes for a better understanding of quantitative data and seeing patterns that are not directly obvious, or when some of the detail in the original data might be lost if only one of the methods is used. The next example will show how to use mathematical calculations alongside a visual display for a large data set, the average score of 15-year-old students on the PISA 2015 Science assessment. Consult the PISA website for more detailed information: www.oecd.org/pisa.

Example 4.5 Measures of location for the 2015 PISA Science scores

Data file: Ex4_5.csv

PISA Science Performance is the OECD's international programme of assessment of 15-year-old students' science literacy. Suppose we would like to compare the 2015 PISA Science Performance scores for different countries, or how some countries performed against the average score and so forth (Table 4.6). The interval data in the third column are the scores from the PISA Science assessment in 2015 for the participant countries. What can we learn from these scores? It is quite challenging to make any comparisons or find the value that occurs most often when looking at the raw data. The information, which can be easily obtained, is the sample size, n, which is 70.

We start by calculating in R the mean, mode and median using the functions described in the previous sections, and then we will show these results on a histogram, which is a useful graphical display for interval data and the corresponding measures of central tendency.

Table 4.7 2015 PISA Science Performance scores

Country	Code	Scores	Country	Code	Scores
Albania	ALB	427	Lebanon	LBN	386
Algeria	DZA	376	Lithuania	LTU	475
Argentina	ARG	432	Luxembourg	LUX	483
Australia	AUS	510	Macao	MAC	529
Austria	AUT	495	Macedonia	MKD	384
Belgium	BEL	502	Malaysia	MYS	443
Brazil	BRA	401	Malta	MLT	465
Bulgaria	BGR	446	Mexico	MEX	416
Canada	CAN	528	Moldova	MDA	428
Chile	CHL	447	Montenegro	MNE	411
China	CHN	518	Netherlands	NLD	509
Colombia	COL	416	New Zealand	NZL	513
Costa Rica	CRI	420	Norway	NOR	498
Croatia	HRV	475	Peru	PER	397
Cyprus	CYP	433	Poland	POL	501
Czech Republic	CZE	493	Portugal	PRT	501
Denmark	DNK	502	Qatar	QAT	418
Dominican Republic	DOM	332	Romania	ROU	435
Estonia	EST	534	Russia	RUS	487
Finland	FIN	531	Singapore	SGP	556
France	FRA	495	Slovakia	SVK	461
Georgia	GEO	411	Slovenia	SVN	513
Germany	DEU	509	South Korea	KOR	516
Greece	GRC	455	Spain	ESP	493
Hong Kong	HKG	523	Sweden	SWE	493
Hungary	HUN	477	Switzerland	CHE	506
Iceland	ISL	473	Thailand	THA	421
Indonesia	IDN	403	Trinidad and Tobago	TTO	425
Ireland	IRL	503	Tunisia	TUN	386
Israel	ISR	467	Turkey	TUR	425
Italy	ITA	481	United Arab Emirates	ARE	437

Country	Code	Scores	Country	Code	Scores
Japan	JPN	538	United Kingdom	GBR	509
Jordan	JOR	409	United States	USA	496
Kazakhstan	KAZ	456	Uruguay	URY	435
Kosovo	OWID_KOS	378	Vietnam	VNM	525

As we know from Chapter 3, interval data can be visualised by using a histogram, and we can create it in R by using the function `hist()`. We proceed by importing the data into R, checking on how the 'object' is stored in R virtual memory (numeric, character, list and function), and then create the histogram. These steps are described below:

Step 1: Save the data file Ex4_5.csv on the computer.

Step 2: Upload the .csv file to R and assign it the name 'PISA2015Science' (or you can choose any preferred name):

```
PISA2015Science<-read.csv(file.choose())
```

The function `file.choose()` allows you to choose a file interactively. A window opens to allow you to select the .csv file (Ex4_5.csv) from the folder where it is saved and to be used by R, then reads the contents into PISA2015Science.

Step 3: Check how the .csv file is stored in R virtual memory:

```
class(PISA2015Science)
[1] "data.frame"
```

Step 4: Calculate the mode:

```
ScoreMode<-table(as.vector(PISA2015Science$Scores))
names(ScoreMode)[ScoreMode==max(ScoreMode)]
[1] "493" "509"
```

Step 5: Calculate the median:

```
median(PISA2015Science$Scores)
[1] 475
```

Step 6: Calculate the arithmetic mean:

```
mean(PISA2015Science$Scores)
[1] 464.2535
```

Step 7: Create the histogram for the interval variable 'Scores':

```
hist(PISA2015Science$Scores, freq = FALSE, xlab="Scores", main =
"2015 PISA Science Scores")
```

Step 8: Create the frequency line for the interval variable 'Scores':

```
lines(density(PISA2015Science$Scores))
```

Step 9: Create the vertical lines for the mean (dashed line) and median (dotted line):

```
abline(v=mean(PISA2015Science$Scores), lty=2)
abline(v=median(PISA2015Science$Scores), lty=3)
```

Step 10: Create the legend:

```
legend("topleft", inset=0.05, legend=c("Mean", "Median"),
+      lty = c(2,3), box.lty=0)
```

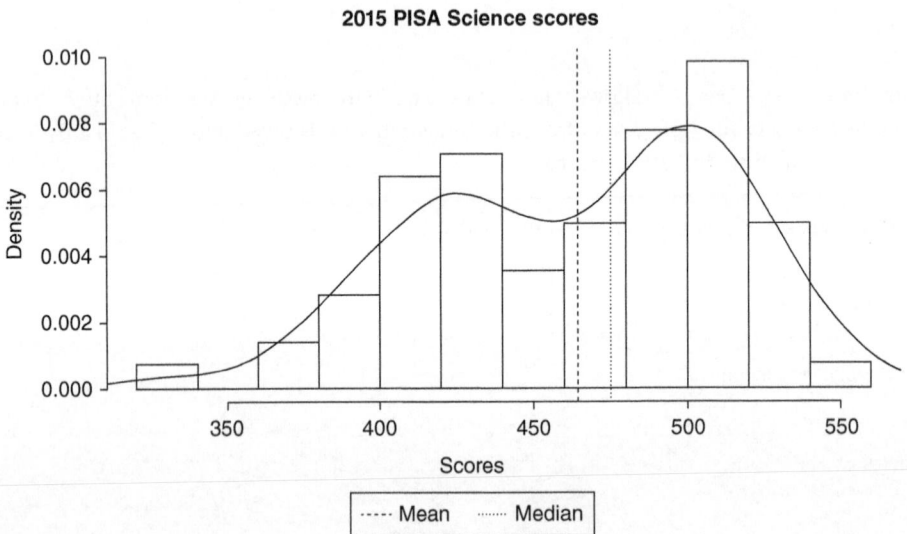

Figure 4.6 Histogram for the data stored in the data file Ex4_5.csv

Interpretation

The summary computations (steps 1–6) on the interval variable 'Scores' show that the score that occurs most often in 2015 PISA Science assessment is 493 (mode), that half of the scores are smaller than 475 (median) and half are larger than this value, and that the mean value of the scores is 464.2535 (mean). We have three different values for each measure, which gives us an indication that the data is not distributed normally or symmetrically, an important aspect that has to be taken into consideration when selecting statistical tests for further data analysis, which we will address later in the following chapters.

Distributions usually have a single mode; however, a variable might have two or more values that occur most frequently, and we would say that it has two or more modes. The frequency distribution in our example is said to be *bimodal*, and this might indicate that we have two different groups, for example boys and girls, or it might be due to other ways of grouping the data. However, the position of the modes might shift whenever the size of the categories (or bins) changes. Therefore, it is not a very stable measure of tendency.

Formulas

The symbol for a variable is a letter from the alphabet, where x is often used in mathematical formulas. Lower case n represents the total number of observed values of the variable x:

$$x_1, x_2, ..., x_n$$

When the observations are ranked from the smallest to the largest, this is shown by adding parentheses around the subscripts:

$$x_{(1)}, x_{(2)}, ..., x_{(n)}$$

Median

When n is an odd number, the median is found as the middle observation in the ranked observations. As a formula, this can be written as:

$$Median = x_{((n+1)/2)}$$

When n is an even number, the median is found by calculating the midpoint between the two middle observations:

$$Median = \frac{x_{(n/2)} + x_{((n/2)+1)}}{2}$$

Mean

The symbol for the mean is a $\bar{x}$ (pronounced 'x-bar') and the mean value is the sum of all the observation divided by the number of observations:

$$\bar{x} = \frac{x_1 + x_2 + ... + x_n}{n} = \frac{\sum x}{n}$$

where the Greek capital letter sigma Σ stands for the sum of all the x-values.

━━━━━━━━━━━ **Exercises** ━━━━━━━━━━━

4.1 Define descriptive statistics.

4.2 What is a frequency distribution? Give examples of different forms of frequency distribution.

4.3 Define the measures of central tendency.

4.4 Give an example of a variable in which the mode, median and mean would be a better choice to summarise the location of the variable.

4.5 Explain why we can or cannot use the mean to describe nominal data. What about ordinal data?

4.6 Find a magazine or newspaper article that makes use of measures of location. Try to find out what measures the author(s) uses and if they were used correctly.

4.7 Go to the Sage website and open the data file called PrimaryClassSizeP7Sctoland2017.csv. The file contains the data set on primary school P7 (10–12 years old) class sizes for September 2018:

(a) Create a simple and a grouped frequency distribution.

(b) Create an ogive curve for the cumulative frequency distribution.

4.8 List the main advantages and disadvantages of using the measures of central tendency to describe quantitative data.

4.9 Give an example of a graphical display that can be used to describe quantitative data and to visualise the measures of location.

4.10 Go to the Sage website and open the data file called PISAScience2012. The file contains the data set on PISA 2012 Science assessment scores from 2012:

(a) Find the mean, median and mode.

(b) Create a histogram and a frequency curve.

(c) Based on the histogram, which measure of central tendency is the best choice?

Further reading

Cramer, D. and Howitt, D. (2004) *The Sage dictionary of statistics: A practical resource for students in the social sciences*. London: Sage.

This is a practical reference for education students and researchers new to statistics and research in social sciences.

Holcomb, Z. (2017) *Fundamentals of descriptive statistics*. London: Routledge.

Several formulas are discussed throughout this book, which requires a very elementary knowledge of mathematics, and the calculations are illustrated with step-by-step, easy-to-follow examples.

Rowntree, D. (2018) *Statistics without tears: An introduction for non-mathematicians*. London: Penguin.

This is an excellent and very accessible book on the basic statistical concepts, offering a variety of examples and accessible explanations in Chapter 3 about central tendency and measures of dispersion.

5

Measures of dispersion and distributions

Chapter Objectives

In this chapter, we will:

- explain the statistics of dispersion
- give examples of the most common measures of dispersion used in educational research
- compute the range, percentiles, quartiles, interquartile range, mean deviation and standard deviation using R
- describe how a distribution can be divided into different parts
- understand the link between a distribution and the direction and degree of skewness.

The measures of central tendency described in the previous chapter identify the most representative values of the actual observations, but these measures alone are not sufficient to describe the numerical values. For example, there are situations when two variables might have identical means and medians, yet the distributions of their values around the mean might differ considerably. The *dispersion* or *variance* of data about the central value is the degree to which numerical data tend to spread in a distribution, and is obtained by several measures of dispersion, including the range, the mean deviation or the standard deviation.

5.1 Range

The range is the difference between the smallest and the largest values and measures the total width of the data set. Because this difference is based only on two numerical values in the entire data set, the range will be considerably influenced by extreme values (outliers).

Example 5.1 What is the range of the mathematics test scores?

Data file: Ex5_1.csv

We recorded 25 maths test scores in a spreadsheet named Ex5_1.csv. This is interval data. The range is calculated in two steps. Firstly, all the scores are arranged in ascending order, as shown in Table 5.1. Secondly, the lowest and the largest scores in the data set are identified. The range is:

$$Range = largest\ value - smallest\ value = 97 - 28 - 69$$

Table 5.1 Raw data – students' scores from a mathematics test

IDStudent	Score	IDStudent	Score
9	28	12	57
4	30	15	64
6	35	25	64

IDStudent	Score	IDStudent	Score
24	39	18	66
21	42	16	68
3	47	23	68
8	47	20	75
1	52	5	76
22	53	7	79
11	55	13	80
17	56	2	89
19	56	14	89
		10	97

Computing the range in R

Upload the Ex5_1.csv file into R and name the object 'MathTest':

```
MathTest<-read.csv(file.choose())
```

Compute the range for the scores using the function `range()`:

```
range(MathTest$Scores)
[1] 28 97
```

where the `range()` function lists the minimum and the maximum values. Subtract the lower from the higher value.

Interpretation

The simplest way to assess the spread of data is to find the range. In this example, the range is the difference between the maximum (97) and the minimum value (28), which is 69. However, the range is too much influenced by extreme values. If, for example, one more student got a zero score, the range would be 97 – 0 = 97, which is almost one and a half times as large as the previous range, although the dispersion of the other 25 students would have remained unchanged.

Creating a one–dimensional plot in R to visualise the range

Create a one-dimensional plot (Figure 5.1) using the function `plot()`:

```
plot(c(1,1),range(MathTest$Scores),type="l",col="lightgrey",xlab="",xaxt="n",
ylab = "Scores", ylim = c(0,100))
```

with the following arguments:

- *type=* indicates what type of plot should be drawn, in our case is set to `"l"` for line
- *xlab=* creates the title for the *x*-axis
- *ylab=* creates the title for the *y*-axis
- *xaxt="n"* removes the *x-axis* from the image plot
- *ylim=c(0,100)* set the *y*-axis from 0 to 100.

Add the data points to the plot:

```
points(rep(1,length(MathTest$Scores)), MathTest$Scores)
```

Add text ('minimum', 'maximum') to the minimum and maximum points:

```
text(rep(1,1),c(min(MathTest$Scores),max(MathTest$Scores)),c("minimum",
"maximum"),pos=4,xpd=T)
```

The result is displayed in Figure 5.1.

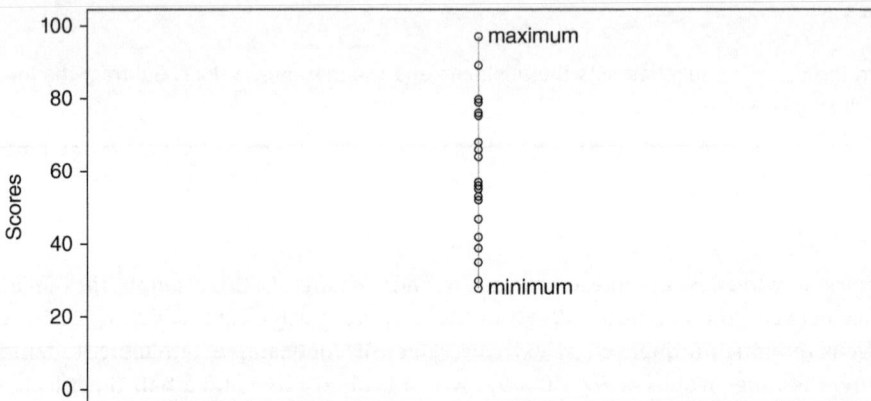

Figure 5.1 One-dimensional plot for the MathScores.csv data set, which shows the range

5.2 Percentiles, deciles and quartiles

Percentiles are values which divide a set of data into 100 equal intervals; each interval contains 1% of the elements in the data set. There are thus a total of 99 percentiles, and they are a useful and convenient way of ranking data sets with many observations or data values. *Deciles* are values which divide the data set into 10 intervals, and each interval contains 10% of the elements. A *percentile or decile range* can also be calculated, and this is the difference between two specified percentiles. The most common decile range is the 10–90, which is a robust estimator of spread and can be found by calculating the difference between the 90th percentile and the 10th percentile.

The *quartiles* are the values of the variable one-quarter, two-quarters and three-quarters of the way through the distribution. The value of the variable one-quarter or 25% of the way through the distribution is called the *lower* or *first quartile* (Q_1), and the one which is three-quarters or 75% of the way through the distribution is called the *upper* or *third quartile* (Q_3). The second quartile (Q_2), which is 50% of the way through the distribution is the *median*. Since a quarter of the distribution lies below the lower quartile and a quarter of the distribution lies above the upper quartile, half of the distribution lies between these two quartiles. Note that percentile, decile or quartile is not a percentage; it is a value in the data set that marks a certain percentage of the way through the data.

There are different ways (or algorithms) to estimate the percentile, deciles and quartiles because there are situations when there is no score that *is* the quartile. These methods may give slightly different values when the data sets are small. For large data sets, the differences among the results become less noticeable. The method we will demonstrate has the advantage of simplicity, and we will refer to the same data set as in Example 5.1. The following steps must be followed to find quartiles and percentiles:

1. The data must be ordered from the smallest to largest value.
2. Count the number of values (*n*). In this example *n* equals 25.
3. Find the observation in the first quartile (25th percentile) position by multiplying 25/100 by the total number of values plus 1:

$$Q_1 = \frac{25}{100} \times (n+1) = \frac{25}{100} \times 26 = 6.5\text{th observation}$$

This result is called the *index*. If the index is not a whole number, it is rounded off to the nearest whole number, which in this example is 7. Use the integer value to find the score corresponding to this value. Thus, count the values in the data set from the smallest to the largest value until the number indicated by the index is reached. The first quartile is the score 47, and this means that 25% of students scored 47 or less on the maths test.

4. The 90th decile can be found as follows:

$$\frac{90}{100} \times (n+1) = \frac{90}{100} \times 26 = 23.4\text{th observation}$$

Use the integer value, which is 23, and then find the score which corresponds to this value, which is 89.

Computing the deciles and quartiles in R

Upload the Ex5_1.csv file into R and name it MathTest

```
MathTest<-read.csv(file.choose())
```

Compute the quartiles:

```
quantile(MathTest$Scores)
  0%  25%  50%  75% 100%
  28   47   57   75   97
quantile(MathTest$Scores, probs = c(0.90), type=5)
90%
 89
```

where the *probs=c()* argument is the position to be measured and *type=* indicates the number of the algorithm used to calculate the quartiles or deciles. In R, there are nine different algorithms, from *type=1* to *type=9*, to calculate the quartile. The differences among algorithms become less noticeable when the data sets are significantly larger, for example 1000 or more. The appropriate algorithm for deciles is type 5, while the quartile is type 7, which is the default.

Interpretation

The percentile is the dispersion measure that is commonly used by teachers or lecturers to report test results because it does not require any assumptions about the distribution of data, which can have any shape, and it has the same interpretation when comparing different scores. For example, the Graduate Management Admission Test (GMAT) score report shows both the scores and the associated percentile ranking. If a student's result is in the 90th percentile, then it means that the student scored better than 90% of students who took the test, and if the score is in the 10th percentile, the student did very poorly. The percentile values, as for the mean, fluctuate because they are based on the performance of the test-takers and the distribution of data changes. The main advantage of using percentiles is that they represent the relative position of a particular score within a data set and that outliers are not included in the calculation.

Another use of percentiles is for describing income distributions. As an example, we will use the median salaries in the UK civil service.

Example 5.2 Describing income distributions using percentiles

Data file: Ex5_2.csv

Table 5.2 shows the median salaries of all employees in the UK civil service organisations as of 31 March 2018. Which employer pays the most, and which one pays the least? What median salary do employees earn in civil service organisations?

Table 5.2 Median salaries of all employees in UK civil service organisations as of 31 March 2018. (Source: www.ons.gov.uk/employmentandlabourmarket/peopleinwork/ publicsectorpersonnel/datasets/medianpayannexb)

Employee	Highest	Median
Attorney-General's Office	132,500	50,230
Crown Prosecution Service	207,500	32,960
Crown Prosecution Service Inspectorate	117,500	56,700
Government Legal Department	162,500	51,000
Serious Fraud Office	177,500	38,430
Department for Business, Energy and Industrial Strategy (excl. agencies)	177,500	43,430
Advisory Conciliation and Arbitration Service	137,500	32,920
Companies House	97,500	22,500
Insolvency Service	102,500	28,560
Met Office	137,500	35,750
UK Intellectual Property Office	117,500	29,370
UK Space Agency	87,500	38,560
Cabinet Office (excl. agencies)	247,500	32,000
Crown Commercial Service	197,500	35,000
Government in Parliament	142,500	62,100
Government Actuary's Department	187,500	51,300
National Savings and Investments	177,500	43,350
Charity Commission	127,500	30,000
Ministry of Housing, Communities and Local Government	162,500	37,630
Planning Inspectorate	142,500	41,020
Queen Elizabeth II Centre	117,500	32,620
Competition and Markets Authority	197,500	54,960
Department for Digital, Culture, Media and Sport	162,500	40,080
Ministry of Defence	182,500	26,430
Defence Science and Technology Laboratory	137,500	36,400
Defence Equipment and Support	247,500	31,600

(Continued)

Table 5.2 (Continued)

Employee	Highest	Median
Royal Fleet Auxiliary	87,500	32,350
UK Hydrographic Office	117,500	31,020
Department for Exiting the European Union	157,500	37,850
Department for International Trade	262,500	37,060
Department for Education	162,500	38,660
Education and Skills Funding Agency	152,500	38,760
Standards and Testing Agency	87,500	35,080
The National College for Teaching and Leadership	92,500	35,060
Department for Environment, Food and Rural Affairs	162,500	35,180
Animal and Plant Health Agency	132,500	26,120
Centre for Environment, Fisheries and Aquaculture Science	122,500	27,780
Rural Payments Agency	102,500	24,760
Veterinary Medicines Directorate	117,500	34,740
ESTYN	112,500	66,650
Food Standards Agency	137,500	29,160
Foreign and Commonwealth Office	182,500	31,910
FCO Services	112,500	28,880
Wilton Park Executive Agency	97,500	25,580
Department of Health and Social Care	212,500	38,790
Medicines and Healthcare Products Regulatory Agency	152,500	38,990
Public Health England	217,500	37,780
HM Land Registry	197,500	24,900
HM Revenue and Customs	187,500	24,030
Valuation Office Agency	132,500	28,040
HM Treasury	187,500	32,280
Debt Management Office	147,500	50,820
Government Internal Audit Agency	117,500	40,850
National Infrastructure Commission	102,500	48,000
Office for Budget Responsibility	87,500	48,000

Employee	Highest	Median
Home Office	182,500	26,830
Department for International Development	157,500	51,660
Ministry of Justice	182,500	35,900
Criminal Injuries Compensation Authority	92,500	21,800
Her Majesty's Courts and Tribunals Service	162,500	20,200
Legal Aid Agency	142,500	21,800
Her Majesty's Prison and Probation Service	147,500	27,840
Office of the Public Guardian	112,500	19,250
The National Archives	122,500	30,270
National Crime Agency	217,500	35,110
Northern Ireland Office	157,500	34,140
Office for Standards in Education, Children's Services and Skills	177,500	37,560
Office of Gas and Electricity Markets	197,500	41,200
Office of Rail and Road	157,500	52,280
Ofqual	132,500	38,380
Office of Water Services	162,500	48,000
Scotland Office (incl. Office of the Advocate General for Scotland)	92,500	46,890
Scottish Government	167,500	34,510
Accountant in Bankruptcy	72,500	25,680
Crown Office and Procurator Fiscal Service	117,500	26,580
Disclosure Scotland	72,500	19,980
Education Scotland	117,500	51,360
Food Standards Scotland	107,500	28,030
National Records of Scotland	77,500	27,620
Office of the Scottish Charity Regulator	72,500	32,130
Registers of Scotland	77,500	27,530
Revenue Scotland	92,500	34,330
Scottish Courts and Tribunals Service	97,500	20,620
Scottish Fiscal Commission	72,500	37,730

(Continued)

Table 5.2 (Continued)

Employee	Highest	Median
Scottish Housing Regulator	72,500	42,640
Scottish Prison Service	117,500	29,470
Scottish Public Pensions Agency	82,500	19,980
Student Awards Agency for Scotland	72,500	19,980
Transport Scotland	107,500	40,190
Department for Transport	257,500	42,680
Driver and Vehicle Licensing Agency	127,500	20,860
Driver and Vehicle Standards Agency	132,500	26,120
Maritime and Coastguard Agency	122,500	30,510
Vehicle Certification Agency	102,500	33,590
United Kingdom Statistics Authority	152,500	26,210
UK Export Finance	247,500	41,040
UK Supreme Court	97,500	31,000
Wales Office	87,500	32,060
Welsh Government	192,500	35,750
Department for Work and Pensions	202,500	24,480
The Health and Safety Executive	167,500	38,020

Calculating and displaying the percentile values on a histogram

Upload the file Ex5_2.csv and name it, for example 'MedianSalary':

```
MedianSalary<-read.csv(file.choose())
```

Create a histogram using the function `hist()`:

```
hist(MedianSalary$Median, xlab = "Median Salaries (£)", main="", ylim =
c(0,30), xlim = c(0,70000))
```

Find the 90th, 10th and 99th percentiles:

```
q90Salaries<-quantile(MedianSalary$Median, probs = c(0.90))
q90Salaries
```

```
  90%
50230
q10Salaries<-quantile(MedianSalary$Median, probs = c(0.10))
q10Salaries
  10%
24030
q99Salaries<-quantile(MedianSalary$Median, probs = c(0.99))
q99Salaries
  99%
62100
```

Draw a vertical solid line on the histogram for the 90th percentile, a dashed vertical line for the 10th percentile and a dotted vertical line for the 99th percentile:

```
lines(c(q90Salaries,q90Salaries), c(0,25), lty=1,lwd=2)
lines(c(q10Salaries,q10Salaries), c(0,25), lty=2,lwd=2)
lines(c(q99Salaries,q99Salaries), c(0,25), lty=3,lwd=2)
```

where *lty=* specifies the line type (1 is for solid line, 2 for dashed line and 3 for dotted line) and *lwd=* specifies the line width.

Add the values of the 90th, 10th and 99th percentiles to the histogram:

```
text(q90Salaries, c(28), round(q90Salaries,0))
text(q10Salaries, c(28), round(q10Salaries,0))
text(q99Salaries, c(28), round(q99Salaries,0))
```

The results of the above computations are shown in Figure 5.2.

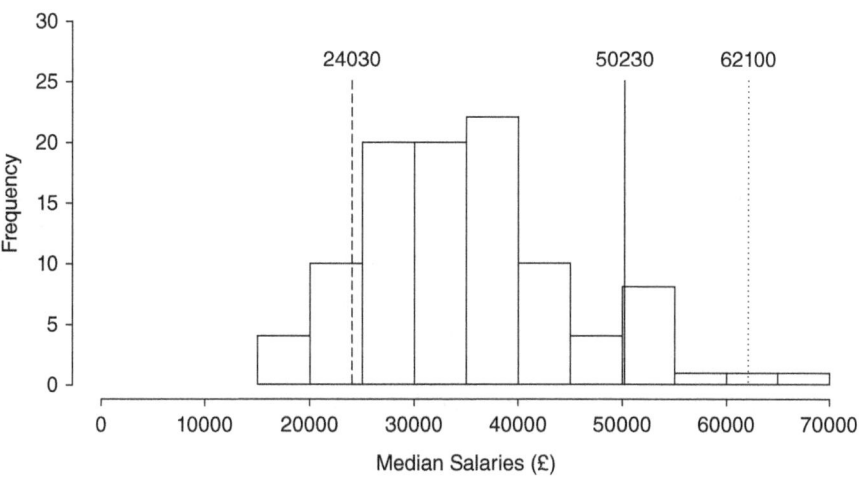

Figure 5.2 The 10th, 90th and 99th percentile values for the data file Ex5_2.csv

Interpretation

As we can see in Figure 5.2, the 90th percentile is £50,230, which means that 90% of median annual salaries for the civil service employee in the UK at the end of March 2018 are £50,230 or less. Only a civil service employee in the Department for International Development can get a salary above this cut-off value. If, for example, your annual salary is £62,100, then you have an excellent salary because only 1% of the median salaries are better than yours.

5.3 Interquartile range

The *interquartile range* (IQR) is the difference between the upper (Q_3) and lower (Q_1) quartiles, and measures the spread in the middle half of the distribution. It does not take into consideration the extreme observations.

$$IQR = Q_3 - Q_1$$

Computing the interquartile range in R

Upload the Ex5_1.csv file into R and name it 'MathTest':

```
MathTest<-read.csv(file.choose())
```

Compute the interquartile range using the function IQR():

```
IQR(MathTest$Scores)
[1] 28
```

Interpretation

Because the interquartile range is based only on the middle half of the distribution, or middle 50% of the values, it reflects only the dispersion in this defined section of the distribution; the outliers do not impact it. We should always also report the first and third quartiles because a quarter of scores were smaller than the lower quartile, and a quarter higher than the upper quartile. In Example 5.1, the interquartile range is as follows:

$$IQR = Q_3 - Q_1 = 75 - 47 = 28$$

which means 50% of the values lie within an interval of length 28, whereas the range is a much higher value, 69. The interquartile range is best used with measurements such as the median and total range to give a complete picture of the distribution of data around the median. For example, the higher the interquartile range, the more spread out the data values are around the mean.

Displaying the quartiles and the interquartile range in R using the boxplot

Create the boxplot for the data set from Example 5.1:

```
boxplot(MathTest$Scores, horizontal=TRUE, xlab="Scores")
```

Add the quartiles, maximum and minimum values to the graph:

```
text(x = boxplot.stats(MathTest$Scores)$stats, labels = boxplot.
stats(MathTest$Scores)$stats, y = 1.25)
```

Add appropriate text to the graph above each quartile and the maximum and minimum values:

```
text(x=boxplot.stats(MathTest$Scores)$stats, labels = c("Min", "Q1", "Q2",
"Q3", "Max"), y = 1.3)
```

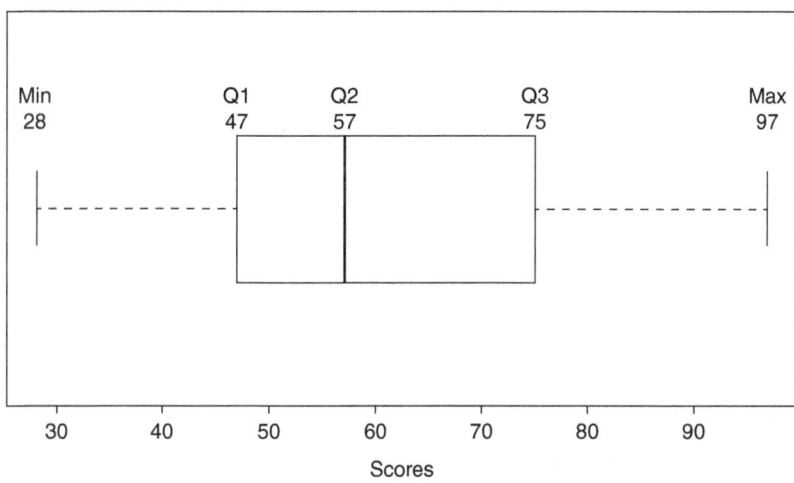

Figure 5.3 Boxplot for Example 5.1

Figure 5.3 shows the values of each quartile on the boxplot. The box represents the distance between the first quartile ($Q_1 = 47$) and the third quartile ($Q_3 = 75$), which is the interquartile range (IQR = $Q_3 - Q_1$ = 75 – 47 = 28). The second quartile ($Q_2 = 57$) is the median. The whiskers extend to the smallest and largest data values that are not outliers, in this example to the minimum and maximum values, 28 and 97, respectively.

Interpretation of boxplots and quartiles

In Example 5.1, knowing that the median (Q_2) is 57, shown in Figure 5.3 as the thickest line inside the box, gives no indication of how the scores are spread. In addition, if we calculate the first quartile (Q_1), which is 47, and the third quartile (Q_3), which is 75, then we know that half of the students obtained a score between these two values and the interquartile range is 28, which indicates how the middle 50% of the scores are spread out.

If the interquartile range is divided by 2, the figure obtained is called the *quartile deviation*, which is a better measure of variation than the range because it is not affected by the extreme values.

$$Quartile\ deviation = \frac{IQR}{2}$$

However, for example, if two different samples are selected from the same population, the quartile deviations are quite likely to be significantly different from each other. The difference between the quartile deviations will result in a sampling fluctuation, an aspect which would be better to avoid when conclusions are drawn for the population from which the samples have been selected.

Coefficient of quartile deviation

A better measure of dispersion based on the quartile deviation is the *coefficient of quartile deviation*, which is defined as the ratio between the difference and the sum of the third and first quartiles. The mathematical formula for this coefficient is:

$$Coefficient\ of\ quartile\ deviation = \frac{Q_3 - Q_1}{Q_3 + Q_1}$$

This coefficient has no units of measurement, and it can be used to compare the dispersion of two or more different sets of data.

5.4 Mean deviation

The *mean deviation* or *mean absolute deviation* (MAD) is simply the average deviation of all the values from the distribution mean. It is a useful measure of dispersion involved in deciding how good the mean is as a representative statistical measure. For example, when the mean deviation is larger than the mean, the mean is not a very representative measure of location for the whole set of data because the location of the data values varies widely. If the mean deviation is smaller than the mean, then the mean is a good representative of the whole set of values. When the mean deviation equals zero, there is no variability, and all data values are equal to the mean.

The MAD is the preferred statistical method for new researchers because it is more efficient in practice, mainly because it does not require a lot of mathematical calculations. As a measure of dispersion for any form of distribution, the mean deviation is a better alternative to the more common standard deviation, which is a good measure only under ideal conditions, working with a perfectly symmetrical distribution and no errors or missing data.

Example 5.3 What is the mean deviation of the values in Example 5.1?

The following four steps are required to calculate the mean deviation:

1. Compute the mean:

$$Mean = \frac{28+30+...+97}{25} = 60.48$$

2. Calculate all the absolute differences between each value and the mean. For example, for the first value:

$$|28-60.48|=|-32.48|= 32.48$$

where the bars $|\cdot|$ indicate that we take the absolute value, which means that if the value is negative, we take the positive value. All the calculations for the Ex5_1.csv data set (also named MathTest) are shown in Table 5.3.

Table 5.3   Mean absolute deviation calculation for Example 5.1

IDStudent	Score	Mean	Absolute difference
9	28	60.48	|28-60.48|
4	30	60.48	|30-60.48|
6	35	60.48	|35-60.48|
24	39	60.48	|35-60.48|
21	42	60.48	|35-60.48|
3	47	60.48	|47-60.48|
8	47	60.48	|47-60.48|
1	52	60.48	|52-60.48|
22	53	60.48	|53-60.48|
11	55	60.48	|55-60.48|
17	56	60.48	|56-60.48|
19	56	60.48	|56-60.48|
12	57	60.48	|57-60.48|
15	64	60.48	|64-60.48|

(Continued)

Table 5.3 (Continued)

IDStudent	Score	Mean	Absolute difference
25	64	60.48	|64-60.48|
18	66	60.48	|66-60.48|
16	68	60.48	|68-60.48|
23	68	60.48	|68-60.48|
20	75	60.48	|75-60.48|
5	76	60.48	|76-60.48|
7	79	60.48	|79-60.48|
13	80	60.48	|80-60.48|
2	89	60.48	|89-60.48|
14	89	60.48	|89-60.48|
10	97	60.48	|97-60.48|
Sum			378.48
Sum divided by n			15.1392

3. Sum all differences calculated in step 2. The sum is 378.48.
4. Divide the sum calculated in step 3 by the sample size (in our case 25). The MAD is equal to 15.1392.

The mean deviation is expressed in the formula:

$$MAD = \frac{\textit{sum of absolute differences between the mean and each data value}}{\textit{sample size}}$$

Computing the mean deviation in R

Install and load the `DescTools` package:

```
install.packages("DescTools")
library(DescTools)
```

Calculate the mean deviation using the function `MeanAD()`:

```
MeanAD(MathTest$Scores)
[1] 15.1392
```

Interpretation

For the data set from Example 5.1, because the mean deviation is 15.1392, and it is smaller than the mean (60.48), the mean is a good representative measure of the whole set of data.

5●5 Standard deviation

The *standard deviation* considers every value in the data set. It tells us about the amount of spread of data values around the mean of the variable and is usually used when the data is not too skewed, a distribution characteristic which will be discussed later, in Section 5.6. The two measures, the mean and the standard deviation, help to determine the range in which the majority of data values lie because the standard deviation measures the average amount by which all the data set values deviate from the mean. In other words, the standard deviation tells us about the difference between a particular observation and the mean, which is the residual, defined in the previous section. The larger is the standard deviation, the greater is the spread of data.

Example 5.4 What is the average distance from the mean of scores in the math test from Example 5.1?

Data set: Ex5_1.csv

There are four steps in computing the standard deviation:

1. Calculate the residual for each observation, which is the difference between that observation and the mean, as shown in the fourth column of Table 5.4.

Table 5.4 Residuals and squared residuals for the data set from Example 5.1

IDStudent	Score	Mean	Residuals	Squared residuals
9	28	60.48	28 - 60.48	$(28 - 60.48)^2$
4	30	60.48	30 - 60.48	$(30 - 60.48)^2$
6	35	60.48	35 - 60.48	$(35 - 60.48)^2$
24	39	60.48	35 - 60.48	$(35 - 60.48)^2$
21	42	60.48	35 - 60.48	$(35 - 60.48)^2$
3	47	60.48	47 - 60.48	$(47 - 60.48)^2$
8	47	60.48	47 - 60.48	$(47 - 60.48)^2$
1	52	60.48	52 - 60.48	$(52 - 60.48)^2$
22	53	60.48	53 - 60.48	$(53 - 60.48)^2$
11	55	60.48	55 - 60.48	$(55 - 60.48)^2$
17	56	60.48	56 - 60.48	$(56 - 60.48)^2$

(Continued)

Table 5.4 (Continued)

IDStudent	Score	Mean	Residuals	Squared residuals
19	56	60.48	56 - 60.48	$(56 - 60.48)^2$
12	57	60.48	57 - 60.48	$(57 - 60.48)^2$
15	64	60.48	64 - 60.48	$(64 - 60.48)^2$
25	64	60.48	64 - 60.48	$(64 - 60.48)^2$
18	66	60.48	66 - 60.48	$(66 - 60.48)^2$
16	68	60.48	68 - 60.48	$(68 - 60.48)^2$
23	68	60.48	68 - 60.48	$(68 - 60.48)^2$
20	75	60.48	75 - 60.48	$(75 - 60.48)^2$
5	76	60.48	76 - 60.48	$(76 - 60.48)^2$
7	79	60.48	79 - 60.48	$(79 - 60.48)^2$
13	80	60.48	80 - 60.48	$(80 - 60.48)^2$
2	89	60.48	89 - 60.48	$(89 - 60.48)^2$
14	89	60.48	89 - 60.48	$(89 - 60.48)^2$
10	97	60.48	97 - 60.48	$(97 - 60.48)^2$
		Sum		8314.24
		Square root of the sum divided by $n-1$		$\sqrt{8314.24 / 24} = 18.61254$

2. Square each residual, as shown in the fifth column of Table 5.4.
3. Add together all the squared residuals (8314.24), then divide the resulting sum by one less than the total number of observations (i.e. $n-1$) in the sample (8314.24/24=346.42666). Dividing by $n-1$ gives a better (unbiased) estimate of the sample standard deviation than dividing n, although when calculating the standard deviation for a population, n is used. If the sample mean is an unbiased estimate, there is an equal likelihood that it will fall above or below the population mean. If it is biased, it will always tend to fall below the population mean. As the sample gets larger, the difference between the size of the sample and the size of the population becomes negligible.
4. The square root of the results calculated in step 3 is the standard deviation, which equals 18.61254.

Any rounding error in the mean is compounded in every square computed. Using R to calculate the standard deviation gives a precise result.

Computing the standard deviation in R using the function sd ()

Calculate the standard deviation for the Example 5.1 data set:

```
sd(MathTest$Scores)
[1] 18.61254
```

Interpretation

The bigger the standard deviation, the greater the spread of the scores; the smaller the standard deviation, the smaller the spread of the scores. Like the mean, the standard deviation should be used with caution with highly skewed data, since the squaring of an extreme score would carry disproportionate weight.

Adding a constant to every score does not change the value of standard deviation because each score will remain at the same distance from other scores as it did before, and the mean increases by the constant too. However, multiplying each score by a constant caused the standard deviation to be multiplied by the constant. The examples below demonstrate the effect of the addition or multiplication of a constant on standard deviation:

- Add a constant 3 to each data value in Example 5.1:

```
MathTest$Scores+3
```

```
[1] 55 92 50 33 79 38 82 50 31 100 58 60 83 92 67 71 59 69 59 78 45 56
71 42 67
```

- Calculate the standard deviation:

```
sd(MathTest$Scores+3)
[1] 18.61254
```

The value of the standard deviation is unchanged after adding constant 3 to the initial values.

- Triple each data set value and calculate the standard deviation:

```
sd(MathTest$Scores*3)
[1] 55.83762
```

The value of the standard deviation is tripled after the initial values have been multiplied by 3.

Graphical display of standard deviation in R

Create the density plot for the distribution of scores from Example 5.1:

```
plot(density(MathTest$Scores), main="", xlab="Scores")
```

The result is shown in Figure 5.4.

(Continued)

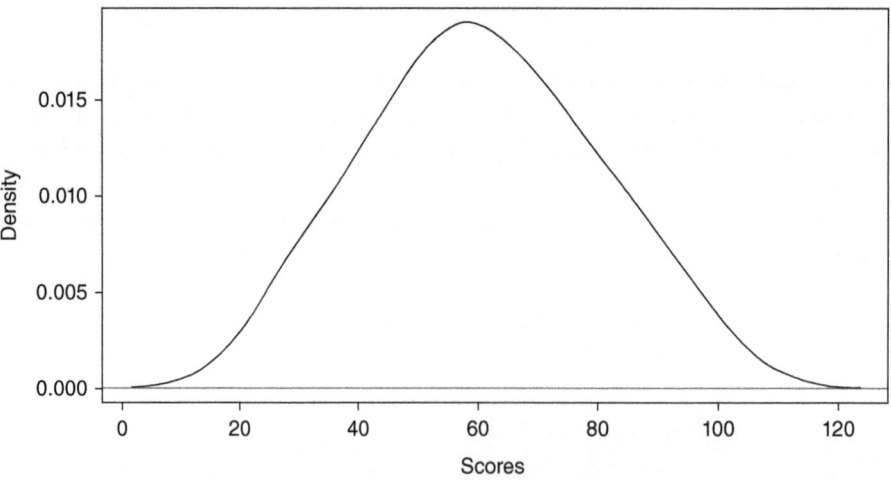

Figure 5.4 The density plot for the distribution of scores from Example 5.1

Compute the mean using the function `mean()` and name it 'meanMathTest':

```
meanMathTest<-mean(MathTest$Scores)
meanMathTest
[1] 60.48
```

Compute the standard deviation using the function `sd()` and name it 'sdMathTest':

```
sdMathTest<-sd(MathTest$Scores)
sdMathTest
[1] 18.61254
```

Compute the sum of the mean and one standard deviation and call it 'meansd':

```
meansd<-meanMathTest+sdMathTest
meansd
[1] 79.09254
```

Compute the sum of the mean and two standard deviations and call it 'plus2sd':

```
plus2sd<-meanMathTest+2*sdMathTest
plus2sd
[1] 97.70508
```

Compute the sum of the mean and three standard deviations and call it 'plus3sd':

```
plus3sd<-meanMathTest+3*sdMathTest
plus3sd
[1] 116.3176
```

Compute the difference between the mean and one standard deviation and name it 'mmeansd':

```
mmeansd<-meanMathTest-sdMathTest
mmeansd
[1] 41.86746
```

Compute the difference between the mean and two standard deviations and name it 'minus2sd':

```
minus2sd <-meanMathTest-2*sdMathTest
minus2sd
[1] 23.25492
```

Compute the difference between the mean and three standard deviations and name it 'minus3d':

```
minus3d<-meanMathTest-3*sdMathTest
minus3d
[1] 4.642378
```

Draw a solid vertical line for the mean:

```
lines(c(meanMathTest, meanMathTest), c(0,0.020), lty=1, lwd=2)
```

with the following arguments:

- *c(meanMathTest, meanMathTest)* sets up the vertical line for the corresponding value of the mean
- *c(0,0.020)* sets up the length of the solid line
- *lty=1* sets up the type of line (solid)
- *lwd=2* gives the width of the line.

Draw a dashed vertical line for the mean plus or minus one standard deviation:

```
lines(c(meansd,meansd), c(0,0.013), lty=2,lwd=2)
lines(c(mmeansd,mmeansd), c(0,0.013), lty=2,lwd=2)
```

Draw a dotted vertical line for the mean plus or minus two standard deviations:

```
lines(c(plus2sd,plus2sd), c(0,0.005), lty=3,lwd=2)
lines(c(minus2sd,minus2sd), c(0,0.005), lty=3,lwd=2)
```

Draw a dot-dashed vertical line for the mean plus or minus three standard deviations:

```
lines(c(plus3sd,plus3sd), c(0,0.001), lty=4,lwd=2)
lines(c(minus3d,minus3d), c(0,0.001), lty=4,lwd=2)
```

The results are shown in Figure 5.5.

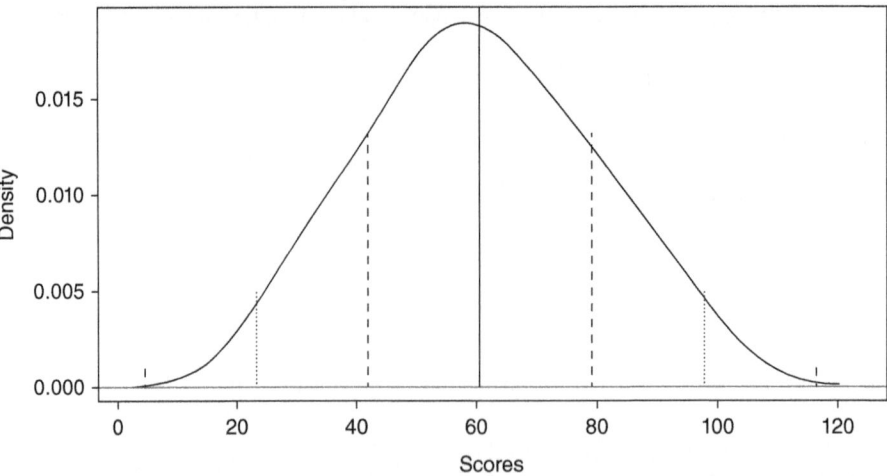

Figure 5.5 The mean (solid line), one standard division above and below the mean (dashed lines), two standard deviations above and below the mean (dotted lines) and three standard deviations above and below the mean (dot-dashed lines) for the Ex5_1.csv data (Example 5.1)

Interpretation

The percentages of scores which lie between the mean (the solid line in Figure 5.5) and a given number of standard deviations above and below the mean are fixed properties for any normal distribution of variables. These fixed properties are:

- 68.27% of all scores lie within one standard deviation of the mean, depicted by the two dashed vertical lines in Figure 5.5
- 95.45% of all scores lie within two standard deviations of the mean, depicted by the two dotted vertical lines
- 99.73% of all values lie within three standard deviations of the mean, depicted by the two dot-dashed vertical lines.

Figure 5.5 illustrates how this works with the data obtained from Example 5.1, where the calculated standard deviation is 18.61254. As the mean value is 60.48, about 68.26% of the scores lie between 70.10 and 41.87.

5.6 Coefficient of variation

Often, it is essential to compare the variability of two or more variables; these variables may be measured in different units, may differ in size, or have very different mean values. Using the standard deviations alone will not usually be sufficient to compare the variability. A better indication of the degree of variability is provided by the standard deviation as a percentage of the mean. This measure is called the *coefficient of variation*, also known as 'relative variability', and the formula is:

$$Coefficient\ of\ varatiation = 100 \times \frac{standard\ deviation}{mean}$$

The variable with the smaller coefficient of variation is less dispersed than the variable with the larger one. Also, if the coefficient of variation is less than 1, the values of the variable are considered to show low variance. The coefficient of variation can only be used for data measured on a ratio scale.

Example 5.5 Comparing the variability of the results from two different skills tests

A lecturer wants to compare the results from two different skills tests, but it is difficult to compare the results using the means or standard deviations because the tests have different measures due to the scoring mechanism (Table 5.5).

Table 5.5 The means and standard deviations of two skills tests

	Test A	Test B
Mean	49.8	34.6
Standard deviation	12.1	11.6

To assess which of the test results is more variable, we will find the coefficients of variation as follows:

1. Compute the sample mean. (See Chapter 4 on how to calculate the arithmetic mean, manually or using R.)
2. Compute the standard deviation. (See Section 5.5 on how to calculate the standard deviation, manually or using R.)
3. Divide the standard deviation by the mean and multiply by 100.

$$Coefficient\ of\ variation\ (test\ A) = \frac{12.1}{59.8} \times 100 = 24.30$$

$$Coefficient\ of\ variation\ (test\ B) = \frac{11.6}{35.6} \times 100 = 32.58$$

Interpretation

Looking at both standard deviations of 12.1 and 11.6, we might consider that the results for both tests are similarly spread. However, the means are different, and the coefficients of variation are also different: 24.30% for test A and 32.58% for test B. These results guide us to the conclusion that the results in test B are rather more variable than those in test A.

Computing the coefficient of variation in R for a single variable

Create a vector *x* with raw data:

```
x<-c(10, 12, 10, 8, 11, 8, 15, 11, 9, 10, 13)
```

Calculate the coefficient of variation for the variable *x*:

```
sd(x)/mean(x)
[1]  0.1984305
```

The coefficient of variations as a percentage is:

```
sd(x)/mean(x)*100
[1]  19.84305
```

5.7 Shape of distributions and skewness

Finally, we consider the last descriptive measure of the variation of a given distribution, the *skewness*, which is a measure of symmetry, or lack of symmetry, and can be measured as regards:

- the direction of the skew;
- the degree of skew.

We can get a general impression of the skewness by displaying the frequency distribution graphically, for example by drawing a histogram. If the peak of the distribution is in the centre of the histogram, and the frequencies are symmetrical on either side, the distribution is said to be *symmetrical* or to follow a 'bell-shaped' pattern (Figure 5.6). We say that the data values follow a *normal distribution*. It is worth noting the relationship between the mean, mode and median of a symmetrical distribution: all are equal and lie at the same point, at the centre of the distribution.

If the peak lies to one or other side of the centre of the histogram, the distribution is *skewed*. The mode will always be at the peak of the distribution and separated from the mean, which will lie on the side of the long tail, by a distance depending on the degree of skewness. The median usually lies between the mode and the mean, though it could lie on the mode.

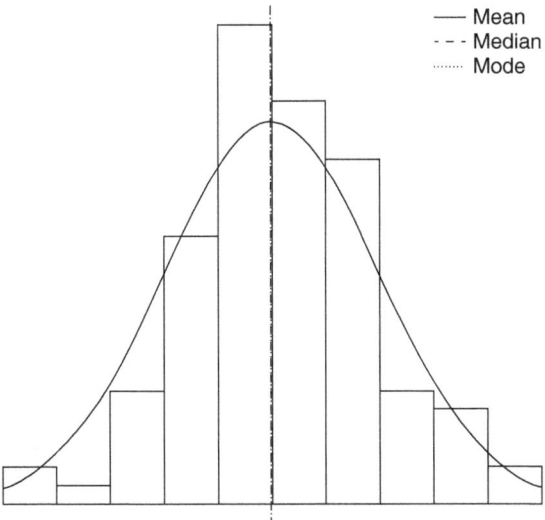

Figure 5.6   Symmetrical distribution of a data set

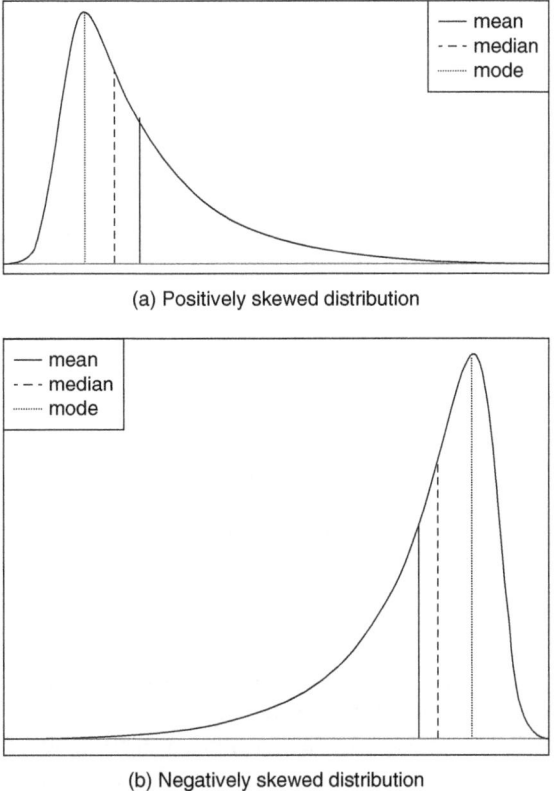

Figure 5.7   Positively and negatively skewed distributions

Look at the two graphs in Figure 5.7. The first distribution (Figure 5.7(a)) has a longer right tail, and most of the data is concentrated on the left, and we say that the distribution is right or positively skewed. The mean is greater than the median. By contrast, the second distribution (Figure 5.7(b)) has its long tail on the left and the data is concentrated on the right, at the higher end of the range. This distribution is called left or negatively skewed, and for this type of distribution, the mean is lower than the median.

A histogram's appearance varies if we alter the bin limits, and it might not give a definitive view of the distribution shape. There are also situations when we might not see a big difference between the mean and median so cannot say that the distribution of the data is skewed. The *degree of skew* gives a clear indication of whether the distribution of the data is skewed and is calculated either by using the Fisher–Pearson standardised third-moment coefficient or the Pearson coefficient of skewness. Many statistical textbooks and software packages, including R, report the *Fisher–Pearson coefficient of skewness* which is computed by the formula:

$$g_1 = \frac{sum(x - mean)^3 / n}{sum(x - mean)^2 / n}$$

where n is the sample size and x the raw data. This formula only works if we have raw data. The formula for the *Pearson coefficient of skewness* is:

$$Skew = \frac{mean - mode}{standard\ deviation}$$

The relation between mean, median and mode is expressed by the equation:

$$mode = mean - 3\left(mean - median\right)$$

Replacing the mode in the formula above will give us a new formula for the Pearson coefficient of skewness:

$$Skew = \frac{3\left(mean - median\right)}{standard\ deviation}$$

which only takes into consideration the mean, median and standard deviation, and lies between –3 and +3.

Regardless of which coefficient we use to assess skewness, we should understand that the larger the coefficient is, the greater the skew. If the skewness lies above +1 or below –1, the distribution is said to be highly skewed. If it is between –1 and –0.5 or between +0.5 and +1, it is said to be moderately skewed. If it is between –0.5 and +0.5, it is said to be approximately symmetric. A symmetric distribution has a zero skewness. Concerning the direction of skew, if the value is positive, the distribution is right or positively skewed, and if negative, the distribution is left or negatively skewed.

The *coefficient of kurtosis* is a measure of the height and sharpness or pointiness of a peak relative to the rest of the data in a variable distribution. The reference standard is the normal distribution, which has a kurtosis of 3. Any distribution with kurtosis approximately equal to this value is called *mesokurtic* (Figure 5.8, solid line). If the kurtosis is less than 3, the distribution is called *platykurtic* (Figure 5.8, dashed line); compared to a normal distribution, its central peak is lower and broader. If the kurtosis is greater than 3, the distribution is called *leptokurtic* (Figure 5.8, dotted line), compared to a normal distribution, and its central peak is higher and sharper.

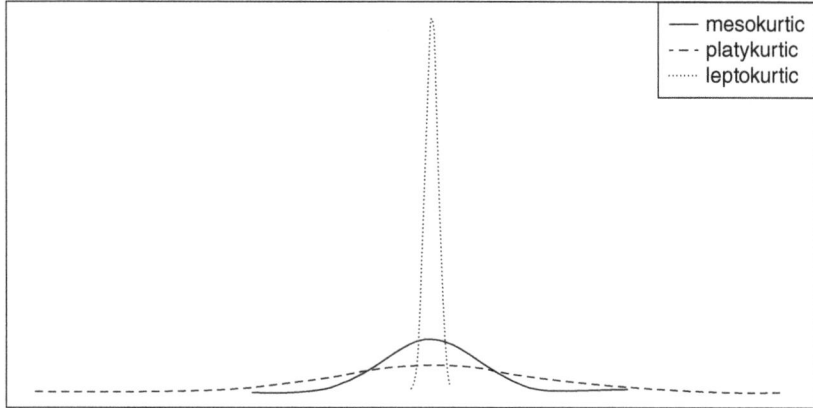

Figure 5.8 The shapes of distribution described by kurtosis: leptokurtic distribution (kurtosis is greater than 3), mesokurtic (kurtosis equals 3) and platykurtic (kurtosis is less than 3)

The coefficient of kurtosis is computed similarly to the Fisher–Pearson skewness coefficient of a data set, by the formula:

$$kurtosis = \frac{sum(x-mean)^4 / n}{sum(x-mean)^2 / n}$$

where n is the sample size and x the raw data.

Computing the skewness and kurtosis in R

Install and load the `moments` package which contains functions to calculate the Fisher-Pearson coefficient of skewness:

```
install.packages("moments")
library(moments)
```

(Continued)

To compute the skewness and kurtosis, we use the functions `skewness()` and `kurtosis()`, respectively.

Create a normally distributed set of data *x* using the function `rnorm()`:

```
x<-rnorm(1000)
```

Compute the skewness:

```
skewness(x)
[1] 0.05299824
```

Compute the kurtosis:

```
kurtosis(x)
[1] 2.923303
```

 ## Advantages and disadvantages of using the range, mean deviation and standard deviation

Let us now have a look at the advantages of using the range, mean deviation and standard deviation. The range:

• is very simple to calculate and understand.

The mean deviation:

• gives some indication of the extent of the dispersion of all the values in the distribution;
• indicates the average dispersion of values from the mean;
• uses all the values.

The standard deviation:

• makes the distribution of data easier to understand;
• is of great importance for later statistical tests.

Let us now have a look at the disadvantages. The range:

• is influenced by the extreme values;
• does not consider all values.

The mean deviation:

• has no further application in other statistical tests.

The standard deviation:

- is difficult to comprehend;
- gives more weight to extreme values because it squares the deviations from these values.

5 ● 9   Measures of dispersion and graphical display

When a sample is small, we can evaluate the symmetry and skewness of its distribution easily, using a histogram or box and whisker plots. Let us take the example of PISA Science Performance test scores from 2015 of 15-year-old boys and girls.

Example 5.6 2015 PISA Science Assessment Scores for Boys and Girls

Data file: Ex5_6.xlsx

To import an Excel file (.xls or .xlsx format) in R, we must first install and load the readxl package: `install.packages("readxl")`

```
library("readxl")
```

Import the data from the first sheet of the Excel file and name it 'PISABoys':

```
PISABoys<-read_excel(file.choose(),1)
PISABoys
# A tibble: 45 x 3
   LOCATION SUBJECT Value
   <chr>    <chr>     <dbl>
 1 AUS      BOY         511
 2 AUT      BOY         504
 3 BEL      BOY         508
 4 CAN      BOY         528
 5 CZE      BOY         497
 6 DNK      BOY         505
 7 FIN      BOY         521
 8 FRA      BOY         496
 9 DEU      BOY         514
10 GRC      BOY         451
# ... with 35 more rows
```

Read the data from the second sheet of the xlsx file and name it 'PISAGirls':

```
PISAGirls<-read_excel(file.choose(),2)
PISAGirls
```

```
# A tibble: 45 x 3
   LOCATION SUBJECT   Value
   <chr>    <chr>     <dbl>
 1 AUS      GIRL        509
 2 AUT      GIRL        486
 3 BEL      GIRL        496
 4 CAN      GIRL        527
 5 CZE      GIRL        488
 6 DNK      GIRL        499
 7 FIN      GIRL        541
 8 FRA      GIRL        494
 9 DEU      GIRL        504
10 GRC      GIRL        459
# ... with 35 more rows
```

Generating the box and whisker plots for boys and girls

The box and whisker plots in Figure 5.9 are generated as follows:

```
genders<-c("Boys","Girls")
boxplot(PISABoys$Value, PISAGirls$Value, names=genders, horizontal = TRUE,
xlab="Scores")
```

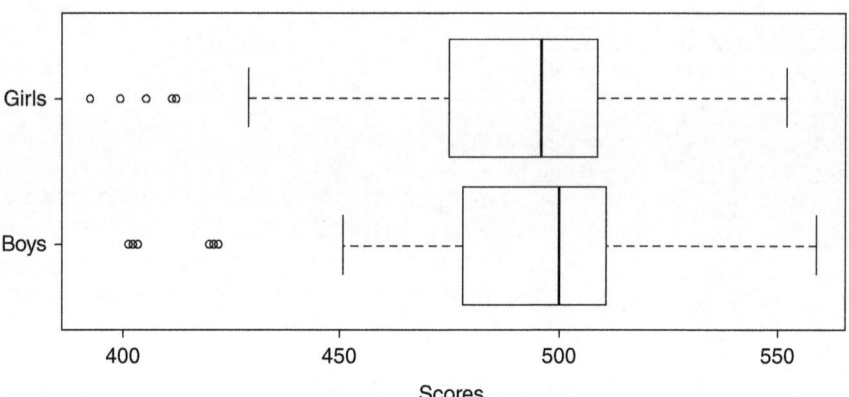

Figure 5.9 Box and whisker plots of 2015 PISA Science Performance scores for boys and girls

Add the first quartile, median, third quartile, maximum and minimum values for both data sets to the plot (Figure 5.10):

```
text(x = boxplot.stats(PISAGirls$Value)$stats, labels =
boxplot.stats(PISAGirls$Value)$stats, y = 2.50)
text(x = boxplot.stats(PISABoys$Value)$stats, labels =
boxplot.stats(PISABoys$Value)$stats, y = 1.50)
```

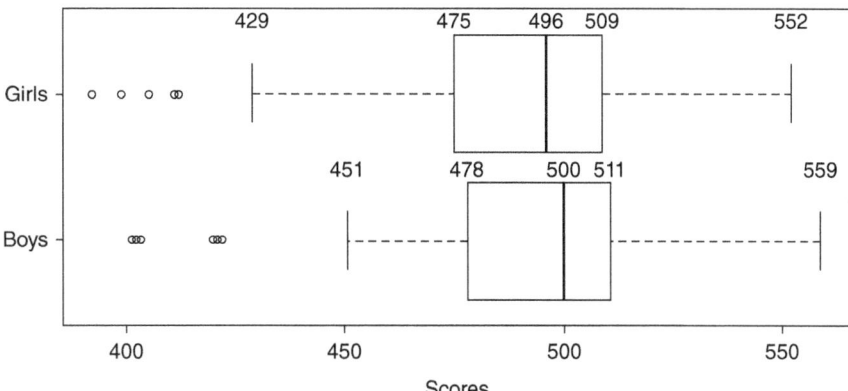

Figure 5.10 Box and whisker plots of 2015 PISA Science Performance scores for boys and girls, with various statistics added

Summary statistics

Compute the mean, median, first quartile, third quartile, minimum and maximum values for both data sets:

```
summary(PISABoys$Value)
   Min. 1st Qu.  Median   Mean 3rd Qu.   Max.
  401.0   478.0   500.0  490.6   511.0  559.0

summary(PISAGirls$Value)
   Min. 1st Qu.  Median   Mean 3rd Qu.   Max.
  392.0   475.0   496.0  487.2   509.0  552.0
```

Compute the standard deviations for both data sets:

```
sd(PISAGirls$Value)
[1] 38.87953
sd(PISABoys$Value)
[1] 38.25126
```

(Continued)

Compute the skewness (Pearson coefficient):

```
3*(mean(PISAGirls$Value)-median(PISAGirls$Value))/sd(PISAGirls$Value)
[1] -0.6790205
3*(mean(PISABoys$Value)-median(PISABoys$Value))/sd(PISABoys$Value)
[1] -0.7389736
```

Compute the mean absolute deviation:

```
library(DescTools)
MeanAD(PISABoys$Value)
[1] 28.72198
MeanAD(PISAGirls$Value)
[1] 28.94222
```

Interpretation

Figure 5.10 shows that both distributions are moderately left-skewed because the left-hand side of each box is longer than the right-hand side. The skewness of the distribution of data is also confirmed by comparing the difference between the median (Q_2) and the first quartile (Q_1) and the difference between the third quartile (Q_3) and the median. For example, for the boys' group, the difference between the median and the first quartile is:

$$Q_2 - Q_1 = 496 - 475 = 21$$

which is bigger than the difference between the third quartile and the median:

$$Q_3 - Q_2 = 509 - 496 = 13$$

The distributions are moderately left-skewed because the skewness is –0.679 for the girls' group and –0.739 for the boys' group, which is between –1 and –0.5. The mean is less than the median in both cases, due, to some extent, to some low-value outliers. The median will be a more useful measure of dispersion when the distribution is negatively or positively skewed because the outliers do not affect the median.

Box and whisker plots also give us an indication of the existence of extreme values or outliers. In this example, five data values are labelled as outliers for the girls' group and six for the boys' group. Furthermore, their detection can also be done by using three methods. The first method is based on setting a threshold of the mean plus or minus three standard deviations, a method which is based on the assumption that the data is symmetrically distributed. However, using this method is very unlikely to detect outliers in small samples or skewed distributions. The second method is to use the mean absolute deviation (MAD) which is insensitive to the sample size or the distribution of data, and if the values strongly deviate from the threshold of the mean plus or minus three times the MAD, then we can be confident that these values are outliers. The third method involves the IQR, with anything more than 1.5 times the IQR away from the median considered an outlier. To make decisions about these outliers, for example whether or not to exclude them from the data set, further investigations must be performed, taking into consideration other variables such as the response time or the time spent studying in school.

Formulas

The symbol for a variable is a letter from the alphabet, where x is often used in mathematical formulas. Lower-case n represents the total number of observed values of the variable x:

$$x_1, x_2, ..., x_n$$

When the observations are ranked from the smallest to the largest, this is shown by adding parentheses around the subscripts:

$$x_{(1)}, x_{(2)}, ..., x_{(n)}$$

Mean deviation

$$MAD = \frac{\sum_i \left| x_i - \bar{x} \right|}{n}$$

Quartile deviation

$$Quartile\ deviation = \frac{IQR}{2}$$

Standard deviation

$$s = \sqrt{\frac{\sum \left(x - \bar{x} \right)^2}{n-1}}$$

Coefficient of variation

$$Coefficient\ of\ variation = 100\ \frac{s}{\bar{x}}$$

(Continued)

Degree of skewness

$$\text{Pearson coefficient of skewness} = \frac{3(\bar{x} - median)}{s}$$

Exercises

5.1   Identify one measure of dispersion and explain how to calculate it for a given data set.

5.2   Explain the advantages and limitations of using the interquartile range to find the dispersion of a data set.

5.3   Why might it be better to know the standard deviation of a data set rather than the range?

5.4   Explain why the mean is always lower than the mode in a negatively skewed distribution of data.

5.5   A researcher carried out a study to look at the number of times per month two students accessed the library website, and collected the following raw data for each student:

A: 2,2,3,4,5,9,11,14,18,20,21,22,25
B: 2,5,8,9,9,10,11,12,14,15,16,20,25

(a)   Which measure of dispersion would be most suitable to use and why?

(b)   Name an appropriate graphical display for visualising the two data sets.

(c)   For each data set, what are the first, second and third quartiles?

(d)   Are there any outliers? How do we identify the outliers?

(e)   What conclusion can we draw about these two data sets?

Further reading

Doane, D. and Seward, L. (2011) Measuring skewness: A forgotten statistic? *Journal of Statistics Education*, 19(2).

This paper discusses common approaches to calculating skewness and explains why students need to know how to measure it.

Gorard, S. (2015) Introducing the mean absolute deviation 'effect' size. *International Journal of Research & Method in Education*, 38(2), 105–114.

This article explains the use of the mean absolute deviation as a measure of variation, as opposed to standard deviation.

van Blerkom, M. (2009) *Measurement and statistics for teachers*. New York: Routledge.

This is a book designed to give teachers a fundamental understating of measurement principles of educational data using a statistical test. Chapter 21 describes and discusses several measures of variability.

6

Normal distribution and standardised scores

Chapter Objectives

In this chapter, we will:

- explore the difference between a frequency histogram, a relative frequency histogram and a density curve
- define the density curve and the normal density curve
- explain the link between the normal distribution and the mean and standard deviation
- learn how to calculate and compute the z-score in R
- assess and test whether a data distribution is normally distributed
- give an outline of probability.

The distribution of a variable is of considerable interest in educational research because there are several characteristics, such as shape and symmetry, which show if the data is centred around the mean or if the distribution has one or more peaks. We often present the distribution using discrete or continuous frequency distributions. For a discrete distribution, we employ a bar graph because the bars do not touch each other, which indicates that the variable is nominal or ordinal. If the variable is interval or ratio, its frequency distribution is graphically presented as a histogram. This chapter deals more with the normal frequency distributions, the density curve and the connection between the distribution and standardised scores.

From histogram to normal distribution curve

We have already presented in previous chapters different forms of distribution of data and descriptive measures reflecting central tendency and dispersion. One type of distribution which has great significance in the analysis of quantitative data is the normal distribution, also called the Gaussian or 'bell-shaped' distribution. The normal distribution is useful in educational research because many variables or raw scores in this field, for example exam scores or the height of school children, are approximately normally distributed. For this type of distribution, most of the values of a continuous variable are concentrated in the centre of the distribution, with few very low or very high values. For example, most school children are of medium height, and few are very short or very tall. The simplest way to describe any type of distribution is by visual representation. Histograms are the most common visualisation technique for obtaining initial information about the shape and spread of the distribution.

Example 6.1 Creating a frequency histogram

Data file: Ex6_1.csv

Suppose that a medical survey of a regional community has provided us with a sample of 40 school children aged 11–13 years, whose heights are distributed as shown in Table 6.1.

Table 6.1 Height (in centimetres) of 40 school children aged 11–13

169	152	146	140
164	151	146	138
164	150	146	138
158	150	145	137
157	149	143	136
156	149	143	133
156	148	142	132
153	148	142	131
154	147	141	126
154	146	141	125

A histogram is constructed by organising the data into small groups (or bins) and counting the number of observations (or frequencies) in each bin. Since the histogram displayed in Figure 6.1 shows the frequencies, it is also called a *frequency histogram*.

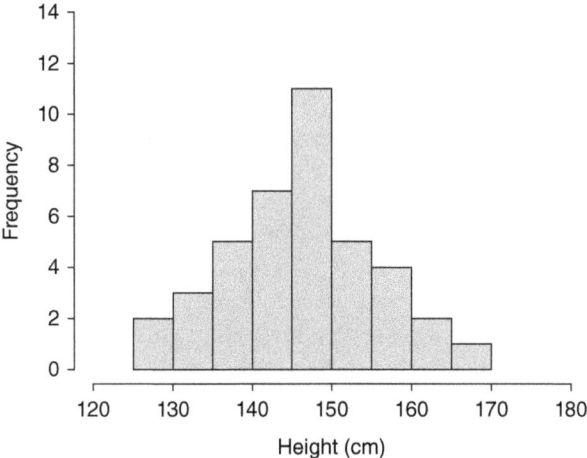

Figure 6.1 Frequency distribution of the heights of 40 school children aged 11–13

We can also make a *relative frequency histogram* (Figure 6.2), which is similar to a frequency histogram, except that the frequency of each category is displayed as a proportion of the total amount of data. The *relative frequency* is the result of dividing the frequency by the sample size. The area of each rectangle is equal to the observed proportion of children whose height falls in the corresponding group (or bin). The total area covered by all the rectangles adds up to 1 or 100 per cent. It is better to use a relative frequency histogram rather than a simple histogram, as different histograms can then be easily compared.

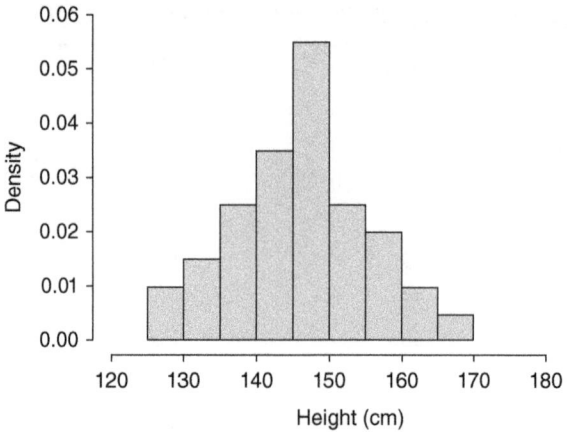

Figure 6.2   Relative frequency histogram

However, histograms are problematic when it comes to assessing the normality of a distribution when there are fewer than 50 observations because the appearance of the histogram depends on the number of data points and the number of bars. When we have few values, the bars on the histogram do not adequately display the distribution. With a large number of values, we will have more small-width rectangles, which would be more like a smooth curve.

Instead of counting the frequencies relative to the sample size, we can change the frequency histogram into a *density curve*, which is a useful display for comparing any distribution of data with a theoretical normal distribution. By 'density' we mean the relative concentration of the variable along the vertical axis. The density curve is a continuous smooth curve that estimates the bars in a histogram and displays the overall shape of the distribution. The total area underneath the density curve is equal to 1. For the same data presented above, the density curve is illustrated in Figure 6.3 by the solid black line, and the *probability density function* between the two class limits (two adjacent vertical lines) is the area between these limits and the curve. The *y*-axis in the density plot displays the probability density function. However, we need to be careful when we refer to the probability density because this is, in fact, not a probability as the probability density is the probability per unit on the *x*-axis. To convert the probability density to a probability, we simply find the area under the curve for a specific interval on the *x*-axis, which in our example can be found by multiplying the probability density values (*y*-axis) by the heights range on the *x*-axis.

There are a couple of important properties about the density curve to take into consideration:

- The *y*-axis (which represents the probability density) is scaled to be able to compare the density curve with the histogram.
- The total area under the density curve, which is always on and above the horizontal axis, is equal to 1. The area under this curve for a range of values (or bins) indicates the proportions of values on that range.
- Density curves come in a variety of shapes. A density curve is only an approximation to the histogram and can be thought of as a plot of a 'smoothed' histogram.

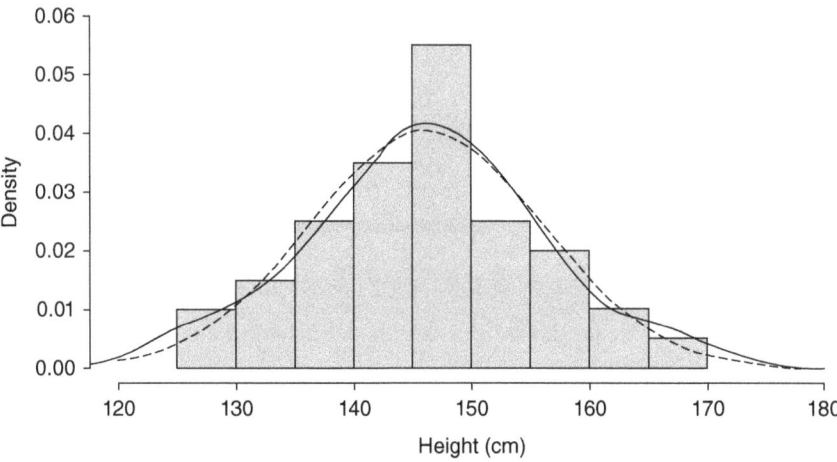

Figure 6.3 Relative frequency histogram together with an empirical density curve (solid line) and normal curve (dashed line)

The *normal density curve* is the ideal curve we are expecting to obtain because this normal curve often describes with sufficient accuracy the shape of histograms based on a large number of observations. In the next chapters, we will demonstrate how specific characteristics of the population can be inferred from calculations performed on samples. Moreover, this curve is the one most commonly used in statistical analysis, and it is easy to handle theoretically. The normal curve is illustrated in Figure 6.3 by the dashed line and represents the frequency distribution of children's stature for the ideal and infinitely large population of children aged 11–13. Its principal properties are as follows:

1. It is bell-shaped and symmetrical.
2. The mode, median and mean coincide at the centre of the distribution.
3. The curve is based on an infinite number of observations.
4. A fixed proportion of the observations lies between the mean and a fixed number of standard deviations.

The dashed curve in Figure 6.3 describes the variations in the height of all school children aged 11–13. Suppose we randomly select a child within this age range. Then the probability that this child has a height between, say, 145 and 150 cm is the area lying under the dashed curve and above the *x*-axis and between two vertical lines through the two points ($x = 145$ and $x = 150$). This area, in our example 0.04×5, represents the relative frequency or probability (0.2 or 20%) that any child aged 11–13 is 145–150 cm tall.

6 2 Other visual methods for assessing normality of data

If the shape of the histogram and the density curve does not resemble a bell-shaped curve, other visual approaches may be used instead to assess the normality. The boxplot and quantile–quantile

(QQ) plot are examples of graphs which are simple to use for visually assessing the normality of data. Figure 6.4 shows a boxplot of the same data values as those presented in Figure 6.1.

6.2.1 The boxplot and the normal distribution

Visual assessment of the normality of data using a box and whisker plot

By using the `simple.hist.and.boxplot()` function, we can create a box and whisker plot alongside a histogram (Figure 6.4):

```
install.packages("UsingR")
library(UsingR)
simple.hist.and.boxplot(Ex6_1$Height)
```

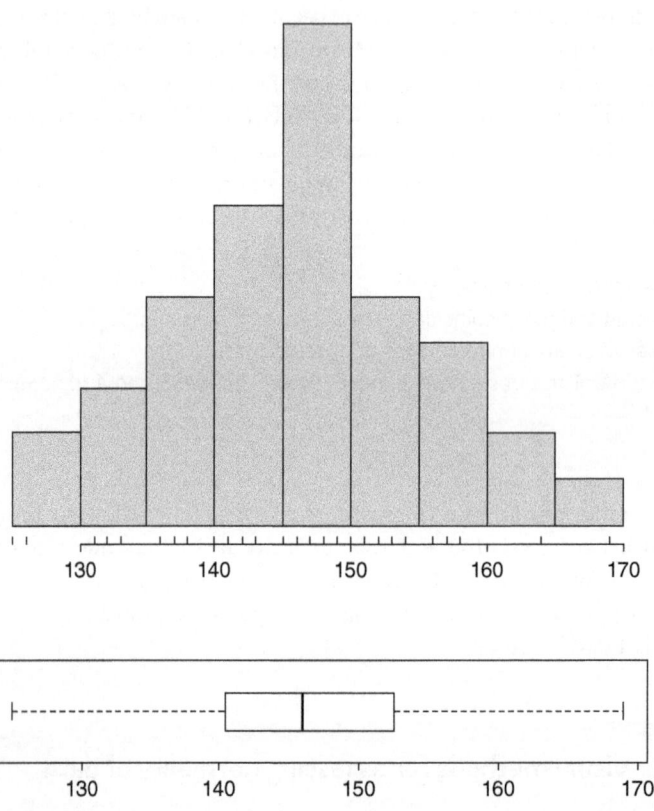

Figure 6.4 A boxplot and a histogram of the heights of 40 children aged 11–13 (Example 6.1)

Interpretation

The median line is approximately at the centre of the box, and the whiskers are symmetrical and slightly longer than the subsection of the centre box, which suggests that the data is normally distributed.

6.2.2 The QQ plot and the normal distribution

Instead of using a boxplot, we can use a normal quantile–quantile plot, which is a one-dimensional scatterplot of data, and the idea is to see whether the data fall on a straight line (the solid line in Figure 6.5). A normal QQ plot plots a vector of data in a sorted order (on the *y*-axis) against theoretical quartiles from a standard normal distribution (on the *x*-axis). For any type of distribution, a QQ plot can be created by plotting theoretical quantiles on the *x*-axis against sample quantiles on the *y*-axis. The theoretical quantiles are computed from the standard normal distribution with mean 0 and standard deviation 1. If all the data values are close to a straight line, then the data is normally distributed. Outliers appear as points that are far away from the straight line. Systematic deviations from the straight line indicate a non-normal distribution. In the next chapter, when we discuss regression analysis, this type of graph will help us to determine if residuals from regression analysis are also normally distributed.

Creating a normal QQ plot with the `qqnorm()` function

The `qqnorm()` function creates a normal QQ plot for our vector of data which represents the heights of 40 school children aged 11-13 (data set Ex6_1.csv):

```
qqnorm(Ex6_1$Height)
```

Add a solid straight line to the plot using the `qqline()` function:

```
qqline(Ex6_1$Height, ltw=2)
```

This gives the plot in Figure 6.5.

Interpretation

All the points seem to fall close to the straight line, and we can assume that our sample of children's heights comes from a population that is normally distributed.

6●3 Normal distribution and standard deviation

A normal distribution is determined by two parameters, the mean and standard deviation. The mean is simply the highest and central point of the normal density curve, which divides the distribution of the observations into two halves. Half of the area lies above the mean and the other half below the mean. This is shown in Figure 6.6. In term of probability, we can say that the *probability* of an observation being greater (or lower) than the mean is 0.5.

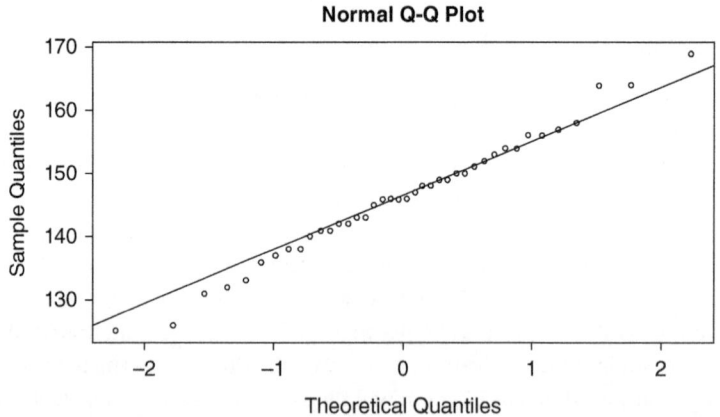

Figure 6.5   A QQ plot of the heights of 40 children aged 11–13 (Example 6.1)

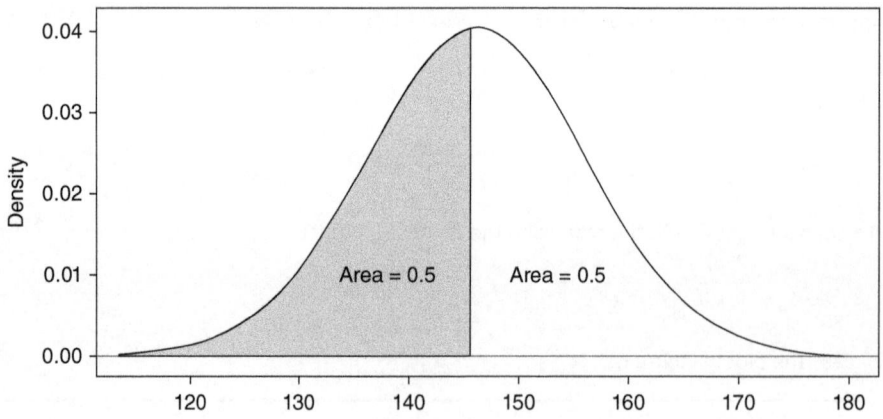

Figure 6.6   The total area under the density curve equals 1. Half of the area lies above the mean and half of it below the mean

The standard deviation is the measure of the dispersion about the mean, and its value determines the spread; the larger its value, the more spread out is the data. Different areas below the normal density curve, whether the curve is tall and thin or short and fat, can be described in terms of standard deviations away from the mean. Their areas are shown in Figure 6.7 which shows, for example, that:

- 0.6827 or 68.27% of the observations lie within one standard deviation either side of the mean
- 0.9545 or 95.45% of the observations lie within two standard deviations
- 0.9973 or 99.73% of the observations lie within three standard deviations.

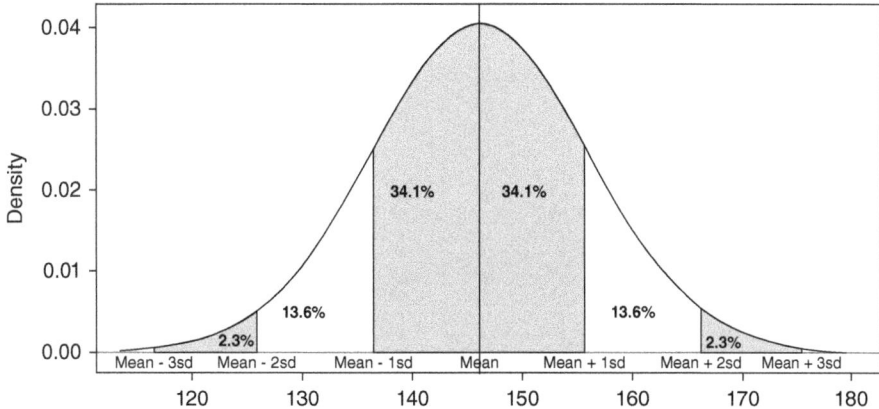

Figure 6.7 Areas under the normal density curve and the proportion of the total area lying between the mean and one (1sd), two (2sd) and three (3sd) standard deviations

About 34.13% of the total probability extends one standard deviation either side of the mean. Therefore, 68.27% of children's heights lie between the mean minus one standard deviation (Mean – 1sd = 136 cm) and the mean plus one standard deviation (Mean + 1sd = 156 cm). Only 4.6% of children have a height less than 126 cm or more than 166 cm.

6 4 Statistical tests for normality

There are many statistical tests which complement well the graphical techniques to assess the normality of a distribution. The main tests are the Kolmogorov–Smirnov test, Lilliefors' corrected Kolmogorov–Smirnov test, and the Shapiro–Wilk test. All these tests compare the values of a variable to a normal distribution with the same mean and standard deviation as the data to be tested. For samples of size less than 50, the Kolmogorov–Smirnov and Shapiro–Wilk tests are recommended. Note, however, that the Kolmogorov–Smirnov test is highly sensitive to extreme values, and it has less power to detect whether a sample comes from a normal distribution. The Shapiro–Wilk test is the best choice for testing the normality of data. R provides functions for both tests, and if the test is significant, the distribution is non-normal. The results of the Shapiro–Wilk normality test for our opening example referring to the heights of children aged 11–13, are shown below.

Computing the Shapiro–Wilk normality test in R using the function `shapiro.test()`

```
shapiro.test(Ex6_1$Height)
        Shapiro-Wilk normality test
data:   Ex6_1$Height
W = 0.9901, p-value = 0.9759
```

For the heights of children aged 11–13, the *p*-value of 0.9759 is greater than 0.05, which indicates that the data is normally distributed. A *p*-value less than 0.05 would mean that the distribution is not normal.

Example 6.2 Are the 2015 PISA Science scores normally distributed?

Data file: Ex4_5.csv

We begin by creating a histogram to visualise how the 2015 PISA Science scores are distributed (Figure 6.8). It can be seen that the variable 'Scores' takes a continuous range of values between 360 and 560, as plotted on the *x*-axis. Each bar shows the frequency of each bin on the *y*-axis.

Create a histogram in R for data file Ex4_5.csv

Upload the Ex4_5.csv file and name it 'PISA2015Science':

```
PISA2015Science<-read.csv(file.choose())
```

Create the vector 'PISA2015S' data with the Scores variable:

```
PISA2015S<-PISA2015Science$Scores
```

Create the histogram for the data 'PISA2015s':

```
hist(PISA2015S, xlab="Scores")
```

To find out how many countries have obtained average scores in the 2015 PISA Science test within a specific range (or within a given bin), we look to the length of the bar for the corresponding bin and read the value on the *y*-axis.

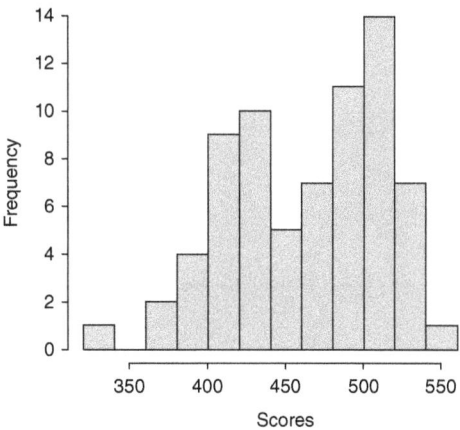

Figure 6.8 A histogram for the PISA2015S data set

Creating a density curve in R for data file Ex4_5.csv

```
PISA2015S<-Ex4_5$Scores
```

Create the histogram and scale the y-axis by setting the frequency to FALSE:

```
hist(PISA2015S, xlab="Scores", col="grey", freq = FALSE)
```

Create the density curve (Figure 6.9):

```
lines(density(PISA2015S), lty=2, lwd=2)
```

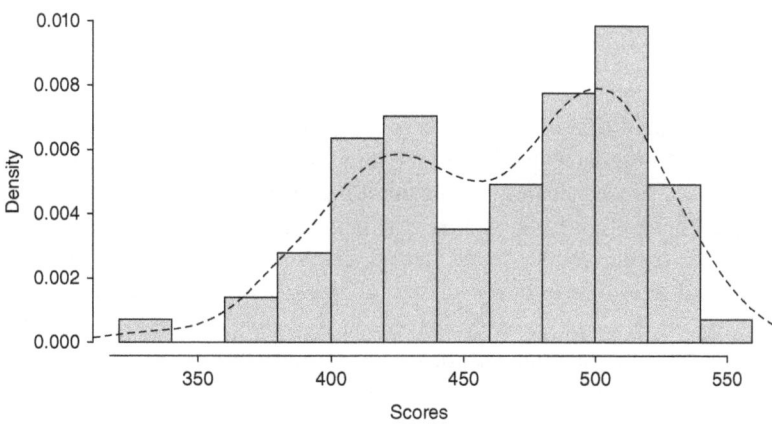

Figure 6.9 Density curve (shown as a dashed line) for PISA 2015 Science scores

Plotting a normal density curve in R

Plot the normal density curve with the same standard deviation and mean as calculated for the PISA2015Science variable:

```
curve(dnorm(x, mean=mean(PISA2015S), sd=sd(PISA2015S)), add=TRUE, lty=1,
lwd=2)
```

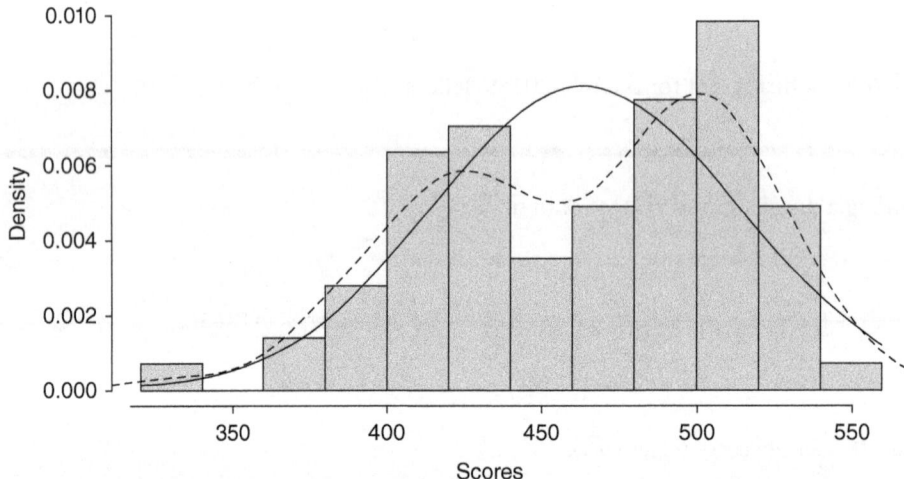

Figure 6.10 Empirical density curve (dashed line) and normal density curve with the same mean and standard deviation as the original data (solid line)

Interpretation

The function `curve()` plots the normal density of the distribution with the same mean and standard deviation as for our original data (PISA2015S), and the normal distribution is computed using the function `dnorm()`. This is illustrated in Figure 6.10, where the solid line represents a normal density curve. The density plot (dashed line) is completely different from the standard normal density, which indicates that the 2015 PISA Science scores are not normally distributed. Besides, the Shapiro–Wilk test (`Shapiro.test(PISA2015S)`) gives a p-value of 0.0009889, which indicates that the distribution is not normally distributed, and the QQ plot (`qqnorm(PISA2015S); qqline(PISA2015S)`) shows an apparent deviation of the scores from the normal line for the smaller scores (Figure 6.11). This deviation might be explained by the presence of outliers, which can be easily identified by displaying the data using a box and whisker plot (`boxplot(PISA2015S)`), as shown in Figure 6.12.

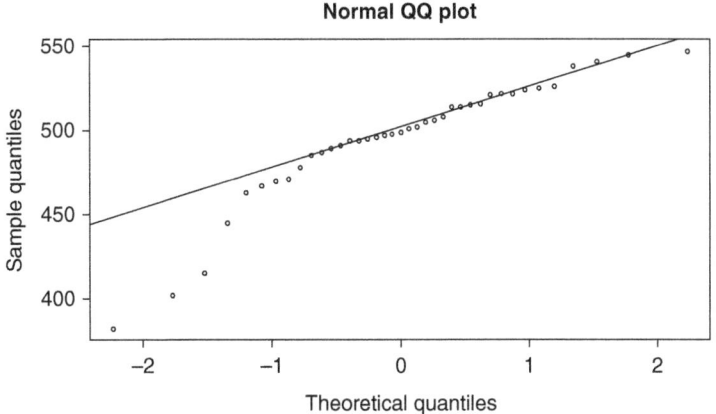

Figure 6.11 QQ plot of the PISA2015Science data

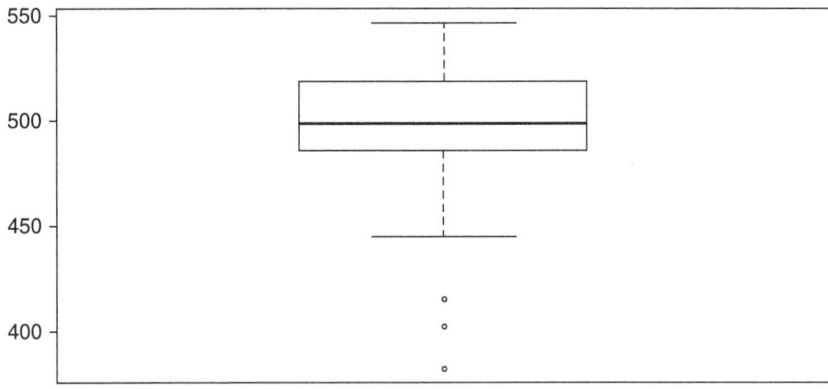

Figure 6.12 Boxplot of the PISA2015Science data

6 5 Standard normal distribution and z-scores

Sometimes we would like to make a comparison between distributions which have different units of measurement or have a set of measurement scores on different measures or highlight differences in the same distribution without considering the actual numbers. There are several ways of finding the relative position of a specific value of a set. One method is using ranking, where values are arranged in order, and the rank of each value gives information about their position in the order. The percentile ranking is another method on which educators rely to interpret exam scores to parents and students by calculating the percentage of values that are below a certain score. However, these two methods indicate the value's position within a specified group and the percentiles are not necessarily equal in size. By using a standardised value, it is possible to tell how the values are placed in their distributions, and then compare them.

The *standard score* is the distance (positive or negative) between the value of a variable and its mean in standard deviation units when the variable follows the *standard normal distribution*, that is, when the variable is normally distributed with mean 0 and standard deviation 1. Any variable for which the observations have been converted into one of these scores is known as a *standardised variable*.

There are many different kinds of standardised scores which are derived from raw values and based on standard deviations and means. One of the standardised scores is the *z-score* or sigma score, which is the number of standard deviations a given value is away from its mean. Once the standard score is known, then it is possible to calculate the proportions of individual observations between the standard score and the mean, by using the formula:

$$z\text{-}score = \frac{observation - mean}{standard\ deviation}$$

The difference between each observation and the mean, which is the deviation from the mean, will be positive when the observation is larger than the mean and negative when it is less than the mean. Since the standard deviation is always positive, the *z*-score will be either positive or negative in line with the deviation from the mean. The *z*-values are dimensionless, and they are represented along the horizontal axis, and there will be as many positive *z*-scores as there are negative *z*-scores. The maximum achievable value for the largest positive *z*-score is:

$$z_{max,positive} = \frac{n-1}{\sqrt{n}}$$

where *n* is the sample size. The maximum value for the largest negative score is:

$$z_{max,negative} = -\frac{n-1}{\sqrt{n}}$$

Since *z*-scores are measured in standard deviations from the mean, all observations will use the same scale and represent equal units of individual differences (Figure 6.13). The area under the curve represents the proportion or percentage of values (99.73%), which help us to describe the percentages of values between different data points. The *probability* of selecting a value from a given interval is equal to the area under the curve above that interval.

In conclusion, *z*-scores allow us to compare any one score to any other score in a distribution, or across distributions, because they are standardised based on the mean(s) and standard deviation(s). However, an important assumption when computing *z*-scores is that the distribution of the raw scores is approximately normal. If the raw values do not satisfy this assumption, they should not be converted into *z*-scores until the distribution is normalised.

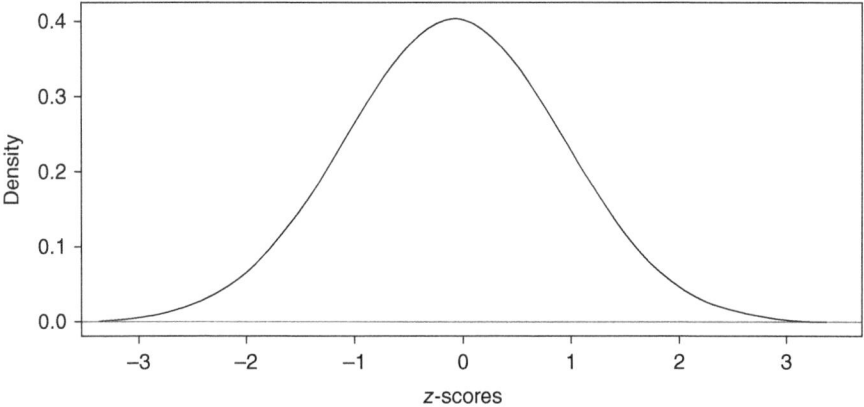

Figure 6.13 Density curve with z-scores

6 ● 6 Transforming data values into z-scores

To transform normally distributed data values into z-scores, we must find out how many standard deviations these values are from the mean, and this can be done by subtracting the mean of all the data values from each value, and then dividing each of these differences by the standard deviation of all data values. As an example, we will consider the values of the height variable from Example 6.1, which are normally distributed with a mean of 146.15 and a standard deviation of 9.89. To transform these raw values in to z-scores, we first subtract the mean from each value, then we divide the result by the standard deviation. For example, let us find out the z-score for the height of the first child listed in the data set (157 cm):

$$z = \frac{157 - 146.15}{9.89} = 1.10$$

The first child's height is 1.10 standard deviations above the mean.

Generate z-scores for a variable in R

In R, the calculation of all the z-scores can be accomplished by using the function `scale()`. We will demonstrate how to generate the z-scores for the variable 'Height' from Example 6.1:

```
scale(Ex6_1$Height, center = TRUE, scale = TRUE)
             [,1]
[1,]  2.31028493
[2,]  1.80475212
[3,]  1.80475212
```

(Continued)

```
 [4,]  1.19811275
 [5,]  1.09700619
 [6,]  0.99589963
 [7,]  0.99589963
 [8,]  0.69257995
 [9,]  0.79368651
[10,]  0.79368651
[11,]  0.59147338
[12,]  0.49036682
[13,]  0.38926026
[14,]  0.38926026
[15,]  0.28815370
[16,]  0.28815370
[17,]  0.18704714
[18,]  0.18704714
[19,]  0.08594058
[20,] -0.01516598
[21,] -0.01516598
[22,] -0.01516598
[23,] -0.01516598
[24,] -0.11627255
[25,] -0.31848567
[26,] -0.31848567
[27,] -0.41959223
[28,] -0.41959223
[29,] -0.52069879
[30,] -0.52069879
[31,] -0.62180535
[32,] -0.82401848
[33,] -0.82401848
[34,] -0.92512504
[35,] -1.02623160
[36,] -1.32955128
[37,] -1.43065784
[38,] -1.53176441
[39,] -2.03729721
[40,] -2.13840377
attr(,"scaled:center")
[1] 146.15
attr(,"scaled:scale")
[1] 9.890555
```

Plotting a standard normal distribution in R

Create a numerical vector 'zheight' with all the *z*-scores:

```
zheight<- scale(Ex6_1$Height, center = TRUE, scale = TRUE)
```

Plot the density curve:

```
plot(density(zheight), main="", xlab="", lwd=2)
```

Add the secondary x-axis ('raw scores'):

```
axis(1,-3:3,labels=c(116, 126, 136, 146, 156, 166,176),line=3)
```

Add text to the first x-axis:

```
mtext("z scores",1,line=1,at=-3.3)
```

Add text to the secondary x-axis (blue axis):

```
mtext("raw scores",1,line=3,at=-3.3)
```

The final plot is shown in Figure 6.14.

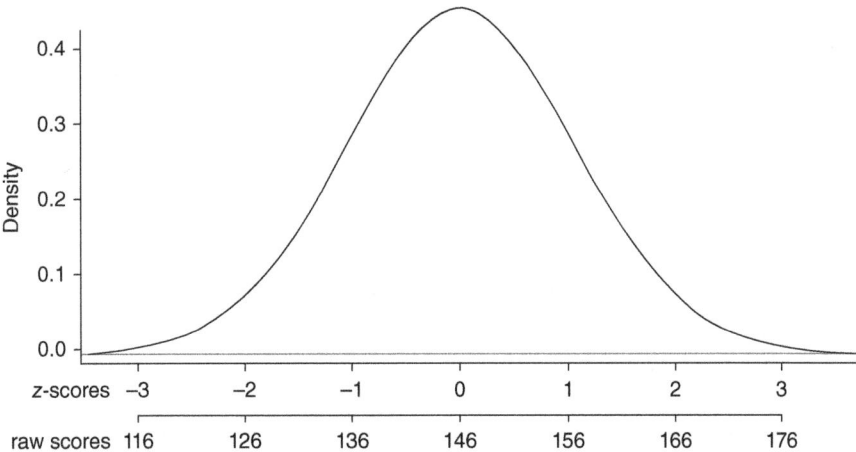

Figure 6.14 Distribution of heights of children (Example 6.1) and z-scores

In Figure 6.14, both distributions of raw data (heights of children) and z-scores are represented. The distribution of children's heights was transformed into a z-distribution, and because this is a linear transformation of data, the shape of the distribution is the same because all the values remain in the same relative position to each other. The z-score indicates how many standard deviations a value is above or below the mean; for example, a z-score of +1 indicates one standard deviation above the mean.

The area under the density curve between the mean and any z-score represents the percentage or proportion of data values in this interval and also equals the probability of selecting values from this interval. It is important to remember here that the whole area under the density curve equals 1 or 100%. The percentage of the area under the density curve and between a z-score of 0 (or the mean, 146 cm) and a z-score of 1 (156 cm is the corresponding height value) is 34%, and the probability of selecting a value (height) in this interval is 0.34 (Figure 6.15). It is important to remember that the z-scores are represented as points on the horizontal axis, and the areas represent proportions or probabilities.

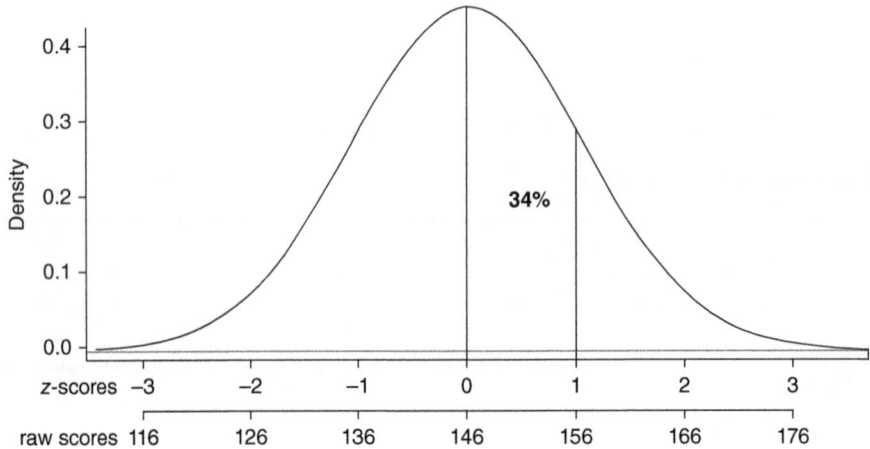

Figure 6.15   Area under the curve between the mean and a standard score of +1

To find the proportion of children who are taller than the child with height 169 cm, we can either look at a z-score table to find the probability or use a density plot where both the raw values and z-scores are represented.

You saw when generating the z-scores for the height variable earlier that they do not always take integer values like +1 or +2, and we might have values with several decimal places. To find the area between the mean and any z-score, we must use a table of standard z-scores. As an example, a portion of such a table is shown in Table 6.2. The values in this table give the proportion of the area of the curve between the mean and certain values of z. The first column gives the z-scores to one decimal place, and the top row gives the second decimal place of the z-score we want to find. For example, for the z-score z = 1.10, we look down the first column till we reach 1.1, then we look across that row till we get to the column with 0.00 at the top (in this case, it's just the next column). The area below the curve to the left of z = 1.10 is 0.86433 (or 86.4%). Knowing also that the total area under the curve equals 1, we can calculate the proportion of z-scores that exceed 1.10 by calculating the difference between 1 and 0.86433, which equals 0.13567. This result indicates that the percentage of z-scores that exceed 1.10 is 13.6%.

Table 6.2 A portion of standard normal distribution values ($z \geq 0$)

+ z	0.00	0.01	0.02	0.03	0.04	0.05	0.06	0.07	0.08	0.09
0.0	0.50000	0.50399	0.50798	0.51197	0.51595	0.51994	0.52392	0.52790	0.53188	0.53586
0.1	0.53983	0.54380	0.54776	0.55172	0.55567	0.55962	0.56356	0.56749	0.57142	0.57535
0.2	0.57926	0.58317	0.58706	0.59095	0.59483	0.59871	0.60257	0.60642	0.61026	0.61409
0.3	0.61791	0.62172	0.62552	0.62930	0.63307	0.63683	0.64058	0.64431	0.64803	0.65173
0.4	0.65542	0.65910	0.66276	0.66640	0.67003	0.67364	0.67724	0.68082	0.68439	0.68793
0.5	0.69146	0.69497	0.69847	0.70194	0.70540	0.70884	0.71226	0.71566	0.71904	0.72240
0.6	0.72575	0.72907	0.73237	0.73565	0.73891	0.74215	0.74537	0.74857	0.75175	0.75490
0.7	0.75804	0.76115	0.76424	0.76730	0.77035	0.77337	0.77637	0.77935	0.78230	0.78524
0.8	0.78814	0.79103	0.79389	0.79673	0.79955	0.80234	0.80511	0.80785	0.81057	0.81327
0.9	0.81594	0.81859	0.82121	0.82381	0.82639	0.82894	0.83147	0.83398	0.83646	0.83891
1.0	0.84134	0.84375	0.84614	0.84849	0.85083	0.85314	0.85543	0.85769	0.85993	0.86214
1.1	0.86433	0.86650	0.86864	0.87076	0.87286	0.87493	0.87698	0.87900	0.88100	0.88298

To transform the z-scores back in to raw values, we can look back to the calculations made for z-scores and find observation which corresponds to a specific z-score, or we can use the following simple equation:

$$observation = mean + z\text{-}score \times standard\ deviation$$

In our example, the corresponding height for $z = 1.10$ equals 157 cm. This value indicates that 86.4% of children in our sample have a height of less than 157 cm.

Formulas

The symbol for a variable is a letter from the alphabet, where x is often used in mathematical formulas. Lower-case n represents the total number of observed values of the variable x:

$$x_1, x_2, ..., x_n$$

When the observations are ranked from the smallest to the largest, this is shown by adding parentheses around the subscripts:

$$x_{(1)}, x_{(2)}, ..., x_{(n)}$$

(Continued)

Density curve

$$f(x) = \frac{1}{\sqrt{2\pi s^2}} e^{-\frac{1}{2s^2}(x-\bar{x})^2}$$

where x is the value of the observation, $\bar{x}$ is the mean, s is the standard deviation, $\pi = 3.1415$ is the number 'pi', and the number e is a constant which is approximately equal to 2.71828.

Standard score (z-score)

$$z = \frac{x - \bar{x}}{s}$$

where x is the value of the observation, $\bar{x}$ is the mean and s is the standard deviation.

Value of observation when z-score is known

$$x = \bar{x} + z \times s$$

Exercises

6.1 What is the difference between a density curve and a normal density curve?

6.2 Give an example of a normally distributed variable.

6.3 Which measures of central tendency and dispersion are most appropriate to describe a normal distribution and why?

6.4 Table 6.3 describes the attainment of girls in Key Stage 2 Mathematics tests in 2018 by region and local authority.

Table 6.3 Attainment of girls in Key Stage 2 tests in 2018 in London local authorities

Local authority	Region	Mathematics average scaled score
London	Camden	105
London	Hackney	105
London	Hammersmith and Fulham	106
London	Haringey	105
London	Islington	105
London	Kensington and Chelsea	107
London	Lambeth	105
London	Lewisham	105
London	Newham	107

Local authority	Region	Mathematics average scaled score
London	Southwark	105
London	Tower Hamlets	106
London	Wandsworth	105
London	Westminster	106
London	Barking and Dagenham	105
London	Barnet	106
London	Bexley	105
London	Brent	105
London	Bromley	106
London	Croydon	105
London	Ealing	105
London	Enfield	104
London	Greenwich	105
London	Harrow	106
London	Havering	106
London	Hillingdon	105
London	Hounslow	106
London	Kingston upon Thames	106
London	Merton	105
London	Redbridge	106
London	Richmond upon Thames	108
London	Sutton	106
London	Waltham Forest	105

Source: www.gov.uk/government/collections/statistics-key-stage-2

(a) Create a .csv file which contains the information displayed in Table 6.3.

(b) Create a histogram, a density curve and a normal density curve. Is the data normal distributed?

(c) Compute the mean and standard deviation.

(d) What does the standard deviation tell us about the spread of scores in the distribution?

6.5 (a) What is a standard score?

(b) Calculate the *z*-scores for the data shown in Table 6.3.

(c) Transform the distribution of scores displayed in Table 6.3 into a *z*-score distribution.

(d) Discuss the characteristics of a *z*-score distribution.

6.6 (a) Choose a *z*-score value from the calculations done for Exercise 5.5(b), and find the area beyond that value. What does this tell us about this value?

(b) What is the area between the mean and that *z*-score?

Further reading

Hinton, P. (2014) *Statistics explained* (3rd ed.). London: Routledge.

In Chapter 5, the author explains the difference between the normal and standard normal distributions and how to compare two scores that come from different distributions.

Pandya, K., Joshi, P. and Bulsari, S. (2018) *Statistical analysis in simple steps using R*. New Delhi: Sage.

Section 4.4 equips the reader with the commands and functions in R that are used to test normality, with the help of the Kolmogorov–Smirnov and Shapiro–Wilk statistics.

Pyrczak, F. and Oh, D. M. (2018) *Making sense of statistics: A conceptual overview* (7th ed.). New York: Routledge.

In Chapter 15, the authors show how to use z-scores as standardised values for comparisons of different data and how to determine the percentile of a score from given data.

PART FOUR

Making estimations and predictions from data

Part Four Contents

7

Fundamentals of inferential statistics

━━━━━ **Chapter Objectives** ━━━━━

In this chapter, we will:

- define the population and sample
- explain the role of inferential statistics
- describe statistics and parameters and explain the conventions used in statistical notation
- clarify how a target population differs from an accessible population
- learn to use different sampling procedures.

In the previous chapters, we have calculated statistics of location and dispersion only as descriptive summaries of samples. However, in many situations in education research, it is imperative to also get information about the populations from which samples are drawn. For example, we would like to know the mean of a Science test for the whole population of children aged 11–13 from which our sample was drawn. However, population parameters are generally unknown, and we need to use sample statistics to estimate them. If an estimate is *unbiased*, then a sample statistic, regardless of the sample size, will give the population parameter; otherwise the estimate is *biased*. For example, the sample variance can be a biased estimator of the population variance because it will underestimate the magnitude of the population variance. To overcome this bias, when computing a variance or a standard deviation, the sum of squares is divided by the quantity $n - 1$, which is generally referred to as the degrees of freedom, where n is the sample size.

7.1 What is inferential statistics and how does it work?

Before we discuss in detail different inferential tests, we start by explaining what inferential statistics is and how it works. When we want, for example, to evaluate the effectiveness of a teaching strategy, we usually collect data from one or more samples of students and then, using *inferential statistics* based on the sample data, we can make an inference about the population of students. This chapter is the first of two that elaborate on *statistical inference*, which is an essential process applied to either estimation or hypothesis testing to connect populations and samples. The first use of inferential statistics is to evaluate the accuracy of estimates of population parameters based on sample statistics, which is called inferential statistics for *estimation*. The second use of inferential statistics, which is called *hypothesis testing*, is to assess the probability of specific sample results under certain population conditions. With hypothesis testing, the assumptions about the population parameter are made in advance, and the sample is tested to confirm or to contradict these assumptions. The two aspects of statistical inference mentioned above can be formulated by asking 'What is the value of a population parameter?' and 'What is the probability that the population parameter is equal to a specified value?', and followed by a test of significance which is used to assess the strength of evidence against the hypothesis.

7●2 From sample to population

A *population* refers to a complete set of elements (people, objects, values or events) that have some common characteristics which are established by the researcher. There are two kinds of populations: target and accessible. The *target* population is the entire group of elements to which the researcher will generalise the findings, and the *accessible* population is that proportion of the target population to which the researcher has access. The characteristics or measures of a population are called *parameters*. Common examples of population parameters include the population mean (μ, lower-case Greek letter 'mu'), the population standard deviation (σ, lower-case Greek 'sigma') and the population proportion (π, lower-case Greek 'pi'). By convention, population parameters are typically denoted using lower-case Greek letters.

In educational research, it is rarely feasible or necessary to collect data on the entire accessible population, so a sample is used instead. A *sample* is a finite collection of subjects, values or events and represents a subgroup of the accessible population, which has been selected using different *sampling strategies* and based on a *sampling frame* to infer properties of the population from which the sample is drawn. These ideas are illustrated in Figure 7.1 and Example 7.1. The characteristics or measures of samples are called *statistics*; by convention they are denoted by Latin letters, for example the sample mean ($\bar{x}$), the sample standard deviation (s), and proportions (P). Because sample statistics are estimators of the corresponding population parameters, they behave in a probabilistic way, and we can use inferential statistics to draw conclusions on the population of interest. All possible samples from a population will fall into a predictable pattern specified by the distribution of sample means.

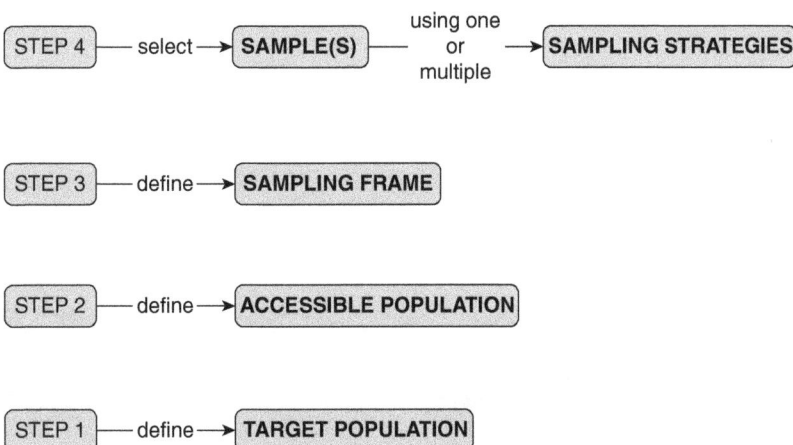

Figure 7.1 Steps to follow in the selection of a sample

Example 7.1 Defining the population and sampling frame

A research student is interested in investigating provisions and practices for dyslexic undergraduate students in UK universities, and the purpose of the study is to use a survey methodology to find out the average number of days undergraduate students have to wait to attend the Study Needs Assessment for the Disabled Students' Allowance process. A vital part of any survey is to define the population and select a sample. All dyslexic undergraduate students who are currently studying at UK universities are the target population, while all dyslexic undergraduate students who are currently studying at London's universities are an example of the accessible population. The sampling frame is the list of all dyslexic undergraduate students at London's universities who applied for the Disabled Students' Allowance. It would be possible to select thousands of different samples from this population, but it is almost impossible to formulate any rules to determine the similarities between these samples and the population. However, the means of a large number of random samples tend to be normally distributed. This distribution is called the *distribution of sample means*, also called the sampling distribution of the means, which will be discussed in more detail in Chapter 8, after we present different sampling strategies.

7 3 Sampling strategies

There are several ways of drawing a sample from a target population, each of them with specific characteristics, advantages and disadvantages. There are two primary forms of sampling, as shown in Figure 7.2: *random* (sometimes called *probability*) and *non-random* (or *non-probability*).

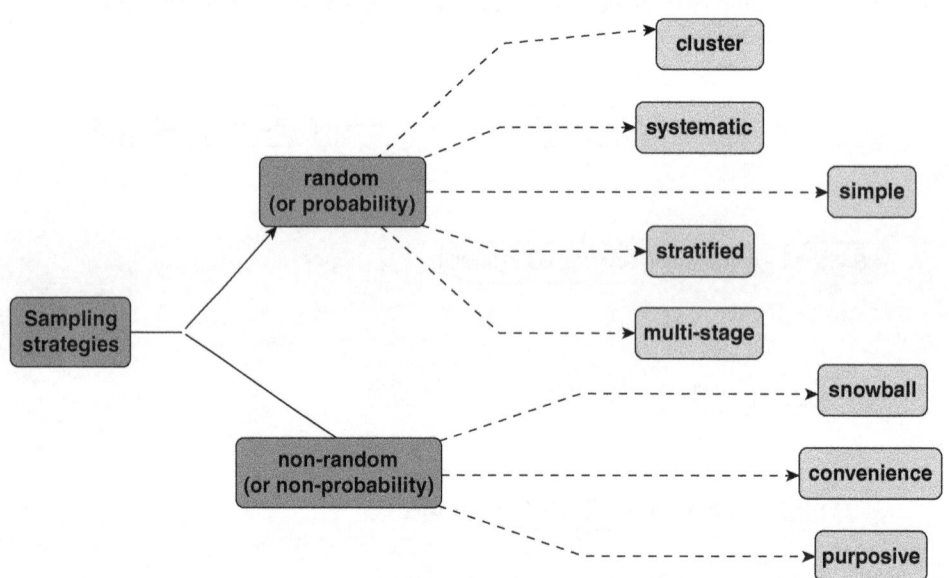

Figure 7.2 Types of sampling methods

When a random sampling strategy is used, as is often the case in an experimental study or a randomised controlled trial, every member of the population has a known chance of being selected, which increases the sample's representativeness of the population. However, using random sampling methods in educational research is not an easy task due to the difficulty of generalising the findings from a sample to the population. If, for example, a researcher concludes that a method of instruction used by a randomly selected sample in a specific content area and conditions can be transferred to the population, then the findings are said to be ecologically valid. Non-random sampling strategies are easy to use, cost- and time-effective and useful when the population size is small. However, using any non-random strategy, not every element of the population has a chance of selection in the sample, increasing the uncertainty about the representativeness of the population. Unfortunately, selecting a sample using a non-random strategy restricts generalisation, and confidence intervals and standard errors cannot be calculated because the population parameters are unknown.

7.3.1 Random sampling methods

The most common random sampling methods used in educational research are simple, stratified, cluster, multi-stage and systematic. We will take a close look at each of these strategies and give examples of how each one is used.

Simple random sampling

Simple random sampling is the process in which each member of the population has an equal chance of being selected. Drawing names from a hat is the simplest example of manually selecting a random sample. Using a printed table of random numbers is a more effective method of simple random sampling. A random number table is a series of numbers arranged randomly in rows and columns. These tables can be generated in a variety of ways, for example using two-digit numbers 01,02, ...,90 for a population of 90 items which are then randomly arranged, or using tables already created by statisticians. Nowadays, these tables have been replaced by computational random number generators. Suppose we want to select a sample of size seven from the population of 90 items. Selecting members with labels 16, 41, 87, 88, 45, 63, 82, corresponding to the first seven rows of two-digit numbers from a random number table, is an example of a simple random sample. However, these methods are fairly time-consuming. In Example 7.2, we demonstrate how to use the `sample()` function to very quickly select a random sample.

Example 7.2 Selecting a simple random sample

Let us take the population defined in Example 7.1 and imagine that it consists of 1000 dyslexic students. We create a list of all dyslexic students, with each student identified by a unique integer number. To obtain a random sample of 100, we use a table of random integer numbers, which can be easily created in R using the function `sample()`. We take the first row of two numbers as an example. The first number in the first row is 455, so in the list of students in the population the student numbered 455 will be the first one selected. The second number in the random list is 167, so the second participant is the 167th student on the population list.

Generating random numbers

```
sample(1:1000,100, replace=FALSE)
```

```
 [1]  455 167 384   10 836 161 218 130 604 422 653 646 721   71 814 608
[17]  351 778 757 687 871 401 720 245 685 240 311 654 773 197 325 611
[33]  430 699 891 798 663 624 700 994 561 671 467 257 936   59 340    8
[49]   55   42 968 895   35 393 301 950 178 306    1   67 331   40 785 694
[65]  270 918 248 549 278 893 904 915 853 702 211 990 352 998 811 976
[81]  571    3 417 812 437 426 850 517   64 491 225 392 616 787 388 363
[97]  112 866 595 334
```

In this example, the function sample() generates a sample of 100 random integers (without replacement) from 1 to 1000.

The advantages of simple random sampling are:

- it produces a representative sample;
- it is easy to do.

The disadvantages of simple random sampling are:

- the list of all members of the target population must be available;
- each member of the population must be identified;
- it cannot be used if we want to ensure that certain groups, for example, males and females, are represented in the same proportion in the sample as in the population.

Stratified random sampling

Stratified random sampling is the process in which members of each particular group, or *stratum*, are selected for the sample in the same proportion as they exist in the population.

Example 7.3 Selecting a stratified random sample

The accessible population of 1000 dyslexic students, described in Example 7.1, consists of 400 females (40%) and 600 males (60%). Suppose we decide to take a sample consisting of 30% of the accessible population (Figure 7.3). Using a table of random numbers or drawing names from a hat, we randomly select 30% from each group or stratum of the population: 120 (= 30% × 400) females, and 180 (= 30% × 600) males. Observe that the proportion of females and males is the same in both the sample and the population, 40% and 60%, respectively.

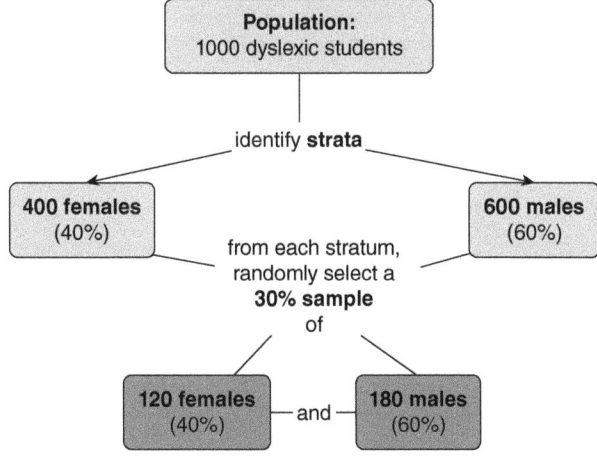

Figure 7.3   Selecting a stratified random sample

The advantages of stratified random sampling are:

- it produces a representative sample and increases the likelihood of representativeness of specific groups;
- certain groups are included in the same proportion in the sample as in the population.

The disadvantages of stratified random sampling are:

- the list of all members of the target population must be available;
- each member of the population must be identified;
- it requires more effort on the part of the researcher.

Cluster random sampling

There are often situations when a researcher does not have access to the complete list of the target population. This situation is especially true when research takes place in schools. Cluster sampling is the random selection of groups or clusters of individuals rather than the individuals.

Example 7.4 Selecting a random cluster sample

There are 33 universities in London, with many campuses distributed over a large area. The researcher does not have enough time or budget to visit all 33 universities. Instead of randomly selecting a sample of students from all universities, a certain number of universities (or clusters) is randomly selected instead. Each of the 33 universities in London constitutes a cluster (Figure 7.4), and each has a number assigned. A table of random numbers can be used to randomly select six universities. All undergraduate dyslexic students from the six randomly selected London universities will constitute the sample.

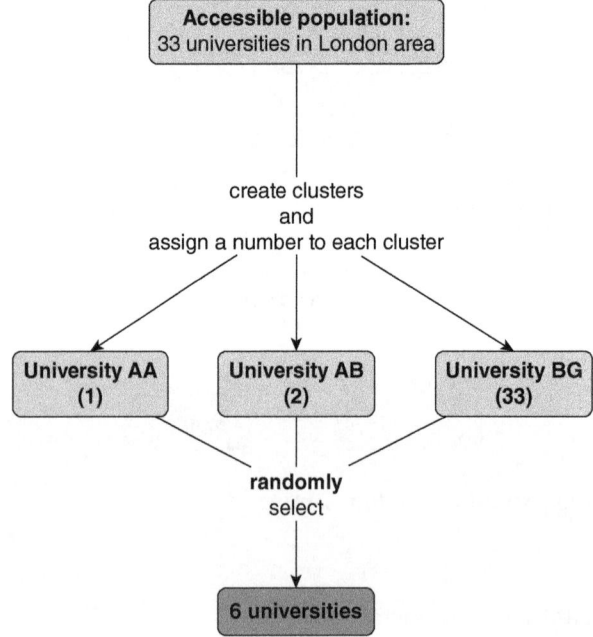

Figure 7.4   Selecting a random cluster sample

The advantages of random cluster sampling are:

- it is useful when it is difficult or impossible to select a random sample of individuals;
- it is less time-consuming;
- it is easier to implement.

The main disadvantage of random cluster sampling is:

- it reduces the chances of selecting a sample that is representative of the population.

Multi-stage random sampling

The most common multi-stage random sampling used in educational research, also known as multi-stage cluster sampling, is *two-stage random sampling*, and it is a combination of random cluster sampling and individual random sampling. Each stage must involve random sampling.

Example 7.5 Selecting a two-stage random sample

Firstly, 10 universities are randomly selected from the population of 33 universities, and then 10 students are randomly selected from each of the 10 selected universities, as illustrated in Figure 7.5.

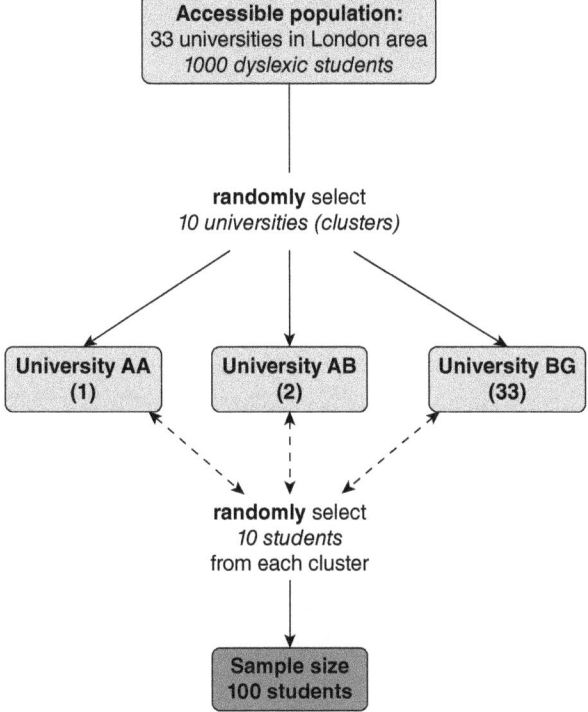

Figure 7.5   Selecting a two-stage random sample

The advantages of multi-stage random sampling are:

- it is useful for large populations;
- it is free of restrictions on how researchers divide the population into groups.

The main disadvantages of multi-stage random sampling are:

- it has a high level of subjectivity;
- it reduces the chances of getting a representative sample.

Systematic random sampling

In systematic random sampling, every nth individual of the population is selected to be included in the sample. For this method, there are two key elements to be taken into consideration: the sampling interval and the sampling ratio. The sampling interval is the distance between each of the individuals, and the following formula helps us to compute this interval:

$$sampling\ interval = \frac{population\ size}{desired\ sample\ size}$$

The sampling ratio is the proportion of individuals in the population that are selected for the sample and is determined by using the following formula:

$$sampling\ ratio = \frac{sample\ size}{population\ size}$$

Example 7.6 Selecting a systematic random sample

In our example, for a population size of 1000 and a sample size of 100, the sampling interval is 10. Every 10th student from the population list will be selected. As a starting point, the first student must be chosen randomly to avoid bias. For example, a set of ten numbers from 1 to 10 are put in a hat, and one number is drawn out at random. If, for example, the first number drawn is 4, then the fourth student on the list is selected as the starting point for selecting the next participant. Using the sampling interval, every 10th student, starting with the fourth one on the list, is selected and the sample will comprise the students on the population list numbered 4, 14, 24, 34 and so forth (Figure 7.6):

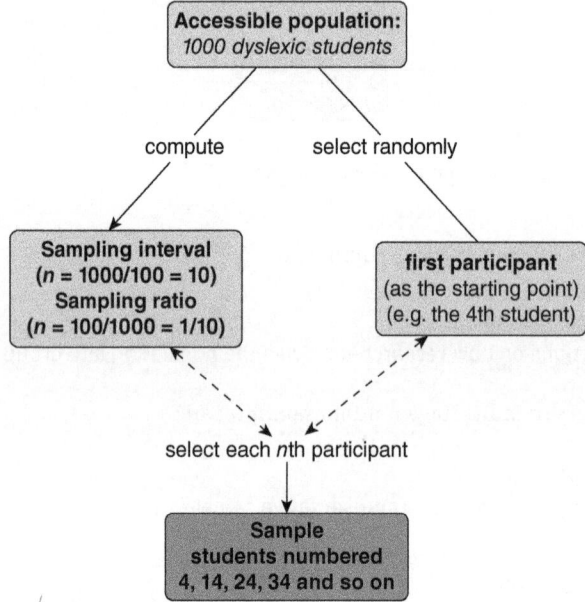

Figure 7.6   Selecting a systematic random sample

The advantages of systematic random sampling are:

- it is cost- and time-efficient;
- it is highly suitable when collecting data from geographically dispersed cases;
- it approximates the results of simple random sampling.

The main disadvantages of systematic random sampling are:

- if the population list is arranged in a specific order, and not randomly, the arrangement may create bias in the sample, which in turn could distort the results;
- it cannot be applied if a complete list of the population is not available.

7.3.2 Non-random sampling methods

Often in educational research there are situations where the selection of a random sample is infeasible or impossible, and where there is no sampling frame. These obstacles may be overcome by using non-random (also called non-probability) sampling. The term 'non-probability' refers to the idea that this type of sample selection process does not give all the individuals in the population an equal chance of being selected. Purposive, quota, convenience and snowball sampling methods are the most common non-probability sampling methods used in educational research.

Convenience sampling

In convenience sampling, a specific group of individuals is chosen for the study because they are available to be studied. For example, a teacher may select students in her class, or a researcher may interview the first 100 people who visit a museum and are willing to be interviewed.

Example 7.7 Selecting a convenience sample

The researcher might decide to select a sample of dyslexic students from his or her university. Here is an example of a convenience sample: all dyslexic students who came to an induction meeting about the support the university offers to this group of students.

The advantages of convenience sampling are:

- it is simple and easy to use;
- it is useful for conducting pilot data collection.

The main disadvantage of convenience non-random sampling is:

- the sample selected will quite likely be biased and cannot be considered as representative of any population.

Purposive sampling

Purposive sampling is used when the researcher selects a sample based on a specific purpose of the research and on his judgement that the selected participants are representative of the population. No sampling frame is identified before the selection of the sample.

Example 7.8 Selecting a purposive sample

The researcher selects 100 dyslexic students from the largest London university on the basis that they are representative of all dyslexic undergraduate students from all London universities. This criterion is based simply on the subjective judgement of the researcher.

The main advantage of purposive non-random sampling is that it is cost- and time-effective. The main disadvantage is that the sample might not be representative of the population.

Snowball sampling

Sometimes in educational research we would like to research a population either with specific characteristics or because it is rare, which implicitly makes it difficult to find. Snowball sampling is an advantageous method of selecting a sample for the purposes mentioned above, and involves either a linearly or exponential selection of participants.

Example 7.9 Selecting a snowball sample

When the researcher recruits the first dyslexic student, and then this student nominates another potential student, this is an example of linear snowball sampling (Figure 7.7(a)). Each new referral is recruited until the desired sample size is reached, or no other referrals are made. If the first student provides multiple referrals, this type of sampling is called exponential snowball sampling. If each new referral is explored, then this type of snowball sampling is called non-discriminatory exponential. However, if we select, based on the aims and objectives of the study, only one student, for example, the second student and then the fifth student, this is an example of discriminatory exponential snowball sampling (Figure 7.7(b)).

The advantages of snowball sampling are:

- it is completed in a short time;
- it is cost-effective;
- it requires very little planning for sample selection.

The main disadvantages are:

- the representativeness of samples is not guaranteed;
- it is impossible to determine the sampling error.

 **Making decisions about the population based on the information about the sample**

Suppose we want to know the average number of days a student has to wait to attend the Study Needs Assessment for the Disabled Students' Allowance process. We want to base our conclusions on students from London universities. Statistically speaking:

- the target population is all undergraduate students from England who are registered for the Study Needs Assessment for the Disabled Students' Allowance process
- the accessible population is all undergraduate students from London who are registered for the Study Needs Assessment for the Disabled Students' Allowance process
- the sample will consist of undergraduate students from London universities who are registered for the Study Needs Assessment for the Disabled Students' Allowance process
- the variable of interest is the number of days taken to attend the Study Needs Assessment for the Disabled Students' Allowance process
- the parameter of interest is the average number of days taken for all undergraduate students from London to attend the Study Needs Assessment for the Disabled Students' Allowance process
- the statistic of interest is the number of days taken for the undergraduate students from a London university to attend the Study Needs Assessment for the Disabled Students' Allowance process.

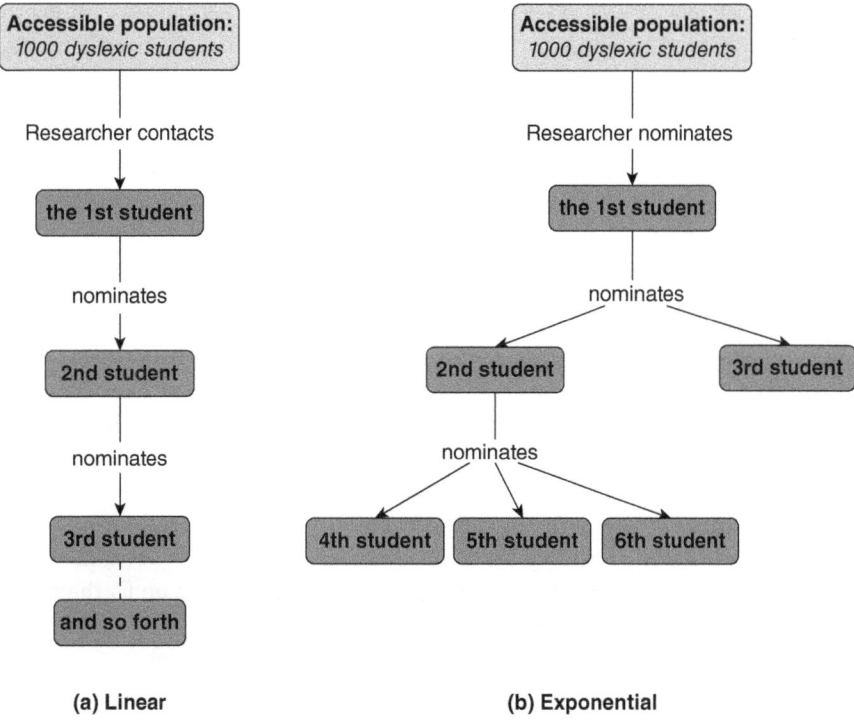

Figure 7.7 Selecting (a) a linear, (b) an exponential snowball sample

If we take more than one sample, each sample gives us a different mean for the number of days taken for the undergraduate students to attend the Study Needs Assessment for the Disabled Students' Allowance process. All possible means of the samples form a normal distribution, which is called the *sampling distribution of the means*. This distribution is different from the distribution of a variable (the number of days) because it is the distribution of a sample statistic: in our example, the sample distribution of the average number of days (or the mean) taken by undergraduate students from a London university to attend the Study Needs Assessment for the Disabled Students' Allowance process. Like all sampling distributions, the sampling distribution of the means tends to be normally distributed and has a mean equal to the mean of the population.

In conclusion, a *sampling distribution* of any statistic, for example of the means ($\bar{x}$) or of a proportion (P), is obtained by:

- drawing a large number of random samples of the same size from the defined population;
- computing the statistic for each sample;
- plotting the frequency distribution of the statistic.

 **Standard distributions**

We saw in previous chapters that if we want to compare two scores from different distributions, we need to standardise them. We can do this by calculating z-scores. There are four theoretical variables, known as the standard normal z variable, the t variable, the chi-squared (χ^2) variable and the F variable. Each of these continuous variables has its own distribution, and they are very useful when we want to make inferences or to generalise from the sample data to the larger population from which the sample is selected.

7.5.1 Standard normal distribution

When the values of a continuous (or interval) variable, which form a normal distribution, are converted to z-scores, we can create a new distribution called the standard normal distribution, shown in Figure 7.8. The mean of the z-values equals 0.00, and their standard deviation equals 1.00. Any normal variable with a mean equal to 0, and standard deviation equal to 1, is said to have a standard normal distribution. The area underneath the whole curve is 1 (or 100%), and the z-scores cut it into areas. Also, the curve is symmetrical around the mean (0.5 of the area is above the mean and 0.5 is below the mean). These proportions are linked to probabilities. Looking at the area under the curve, above or below a selected z-score, we can find the probability of finding a score from the distribution larger or smaller than the selected score. Areas under the density curve can be found using a standard normal table, as described in Section 6.6.

7.5.2 t-distributions

The t-distribution is also known as the *Student's t-distribution* because, when William Gosset published his results about this distribution, he signed his paper with the pseudonym 'Student'. He found that if two samples are selected from the same population, the shape of their distributions was close, but not identical. Gosset computed the values for each sample, called t-values, and he called the new distribution the t-distribution. The t-values are used when we do not know the population standard deviation, and we make an estimate using the sample size:

$$t\text{-}score = \frac{sample\ mean - population\ mean}{sample\ standard\ deviation\big/\sqrt{sample\ size}}$$

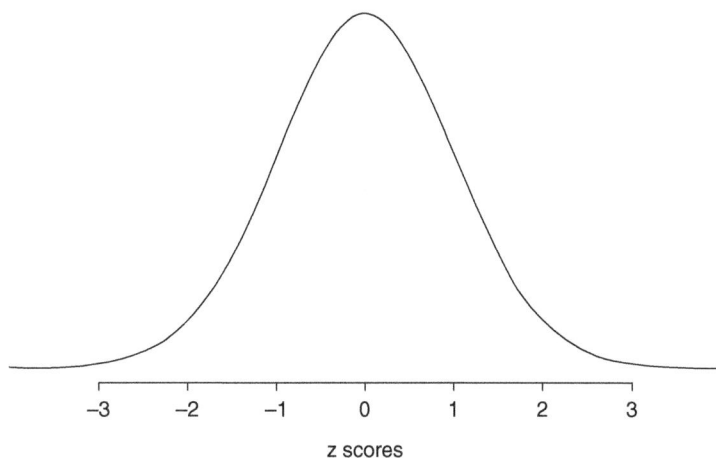

Figure 7.8 The standard normal distribution

Because we compute on sample data and we estimate population parameters through sample statistics, we use degrees of freedom (*df*) instead of sample size (*n*). The *degrees of freedom* (*df*) concept refers to the number of choices one can make in repeated random samples that constitute the distribution, and it is equal to $df = n - 1$ for each sample. The concept of degrees of freedom is important in many inferential statistics tests. For example, it refers to the number of scores in a frequency distribution that are free to vary. Suppose we had a distribution of only three scores, *a*, *b* and *c*, and the sum of these scores is 10. We can have several different values that add up to 10:

2 2 and 6
1 3 and 6
3 5 and 2

Once any two of these values are fixed, then the third one cannot vary. Hence, we say that there are two degrees of freedom in this distribution – any two of the values are free to vary.

There is a family of *t*-distributions, and there is one distribution for each number of degrees of freedom. The size of the sample indicates which *t*-distribution to use. For example, if the sample size $n = 10$, then $df = 10 - 1 = 9$, and we check the row labelled 9 in the statistical Table 7.1. We use the degrees of freedom alongside the desired confidence level (which will be presented in Chapter 8) to decide whether to reject or not a null hypothesis. For example, the critical *t*-value for 9 degrees of freedom and a probability of 95 per cent is equal to the value (1.833) found at the intersection between the ninth row and the third column ($t_{0.95}$).

Table 7.1 Critical values of the *t*-distribution. The column headers indicate the probabilities and the rows the degrees of freedom. For example, t (9, 0.95) = 1.833

df	$t_{0.80}$	$t_{0.90}$	$t_{0.95}$	$t_{0.975}$	$t_{0.99}$	$t_{0.995}$
1	1.376	3.078	6.314	12.71	31.82	63.66
2	1.061	1.886	2.920	4.303	6.965	9.925
3	0.978	1.638	2.353	3.182	4.541	5.841
4	0.941	1.533	2.132	2.776	3.747	4.604
5	0.920	1.476	2.015	2.571	3.365	4.032
6	0.906	1.440	1.943	2.447	3.143	3.707
7	0.896	1.415	1.895	2.365	2.998	3.499
8	0.889	1.397	1.860	2.306	2.896	3.355
9	0.883	1.383	1.833	2.262	2.821	3.250
10	0.879	1.372	1.812	2.228	2.764	3.169

Figure 7.9 shows the *t*-distribution with 9 degrees of freedom (dashed curve) and the normal distribution (solid curve). The area under the curve equals 1.00, the same as for the normal standard distribution, and the shape of the distribution depends on the degrees of freedom; the *t*-distribution has fatter tails than the normal distribution. When the sample size is quite large, the *t*-distribution is almost identical to the standard normal distribution.

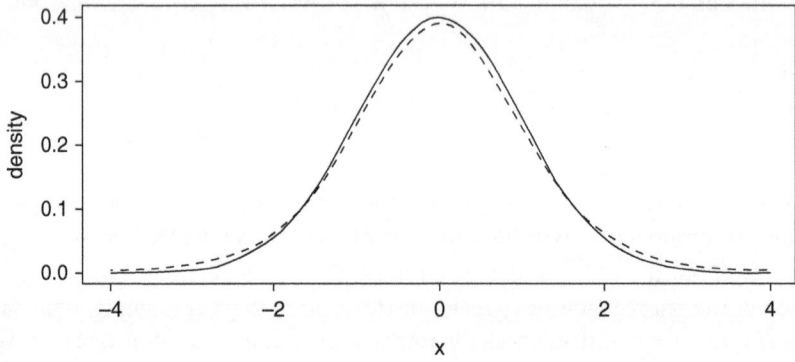

Figure 7.9 *t*-distribution (dashed curve) and standard normal distribution (solid curve)

Creating and plotting the *t*-distribution in R

We use the `dt()` function to create the *t*-distribution and the function `curve()` to plot it for 9 degrees of freedom (*df=9*) (Figure 7.9).

```
curve(dt(x, df=9), add=TRUE, lty=2)
```

The argument *lty=2* creates a dashed line.

The *t*-distribution is used when the sample size is smaller than 30, and the standard deviation of the population is not known. If the number of degrees of freedom is over 30, the curve of *t*-distribution approximates the curve of standard normal distribution.

7.5.3 Chi-squared distributions

Like the *t*-distribution, the chi-squared distribution is a family of distributions and the shape of each distribution depends on the number of degrees of freedom. Figure 7.10 shows the chi-squared distribution with 10 degrees of freedom, with the total area under the curve being equal to 1. The shape of the chi-squared distribution looks completely different from the standard normal and *t*-distribution curves; it is a right-skewed distribution because chi-squared scores have only positive values. The chi-squared statistic follows the chi-squared distribution with the corresponding degrees of freedom (*df = n – 1*) and is calculated as:

$$\text{chi-squared} = \frac{\left(sample\ size - 1\right)\left(sample\ standard\ deviation\right)^2}{\left(population\ standard\ deviation\right)^2}$$

If we sum up all the random samples squared taken from a normal distribution and also take into consideration the degrees of freedom, we will obtain a chi-squared distribution.

This distribution has many uses in statistical interference, including estimation of the confidence interval for a population standard deviation of a normal distribution from a sample standard deviation or for testing for a population variance, statistical independence, goodness of fit or homogeneity. If, for example, doing a statistical test which requires the calculation of a value of chi-squared for specific sample size, then the chi-squared distribution may be used to find the probability of getting a chi-squared value equal to or larger than the critical value. The probability of a chi-squared score higher than this value can be easily found in chi-squared distribution tables, which can be found in Table 7.2. For example, the critical chi-squared value for 11 degrees of freedom and a *p*-value of 0.05 is equal to 19.675 which is found and the intersection of the corresponding row and column, and is indicated by the black circle in Table 7.2.

Table 7.2 Value of chi-squared distribution

						P					
Df	0.995	0.975	0.20	0.10	0.05	0.025	0.02	0.01	0.005	0.002	0.001
1	0.0000393	0.000982	1.642	2.706	3.841	5.024	5.412	6.635	7.879	9.550	10.828
2	0.0100	0.0506	3.219	4.605	5.991	7.378	7.824	9.210	10.597	12.429	13.816
3	0.0717	0.216	4.642	6.251	7.815	9.348	9.837	11.345	12.838	14.796	16.266
4	0.207	0.484	5.989	7.779	9.488	11.143	11.668	13.277	14.860	16.924	18.467
5	0.412	0.831	7.289	9.236	11.070	12.833	13.388	15.086	16.750	18.907	20.515
6	0.676	1.237	8.558	10.645	12.592	14.449	15.033	16.812	18.548	20.791	22.458
7	0.989	1.690	9.803	12.017	14.067	16.013	16.622	18.475	20.278	22.601	24.322
8	1.344	2.180	11.030	13.362	15.507	17.535	18.168	20.090	21.955	24.352	26.124
9	1.735	2.700	12.242	14.684	16.919	19.023	19.679	21.666	23.589	26.056	27.877
10	2.156	3.247	13.442	15.987	18.307	20.483	21.161	23.209	25.188	27.722	29.588
11	2.603	3.816	14.631	17.275	(19.675)	21.920	22.618	24.725	26.757	29.354	31.264
12	3.074	4.404	15.812	18.549	21.026	23.337	24.054	26.217	28.300	30.957	32.909
13	3.565	5.009	16.985	19.812	22.362	24.736	25.472	27.688	29.819	32.535	34.528
14	4.075	5.629	18.151	21.064	23.685	26.119	26.873	29.141	31.319	34.091	36.123
15	4.601	6.262	19.311	22.307	24.996	27.488	28.259	30.578	32.801	35.628	37.697

Create and plot a chi-squared distribution in R

We use the function `dchisq()` to create the chi-squared probability density and the function `curve()` to plot it (Figure 7.10):

```
curve(dchisq(x, df=10), from=0, to=40)
```

Here x is a vector, df is the degrees of freedom and from= and to= indicate the minimum and maximum values on the x-axis.

Interpretation

The chi-squared distribution shown in Figure 7.10 is a probability density whose values range from zero to positive infinity. Compared to a normal distribution, the density function approaches the x-axis asymptotically only at the right-hand tail of the curve. The chi-squared distribution is a function of the number of degrees of freedom, so there is one distribution for each number of degrees of freedom.

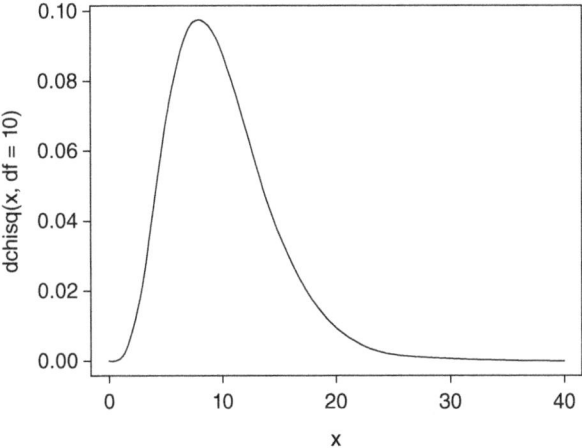

Figure 7.10 The chi-squared distribution for $df = 10$

Formulas

Sampling interval

$$sampling\ interval = \frac{N}{n}$$

Sampling ratio

$$sampling\ interval = \frac{n}{N}$$

where N is the population size and n is the sample size.

t-score

$$t = \frac{\bar{x} - m}{s/\sqrt{n}}$$

where $\bar{x}$ is the sample mean, μ is the population mean, s is the sample standard deviation and n is the sample size.

chi-squared score

$$\chi^2 = \frac{(n-1)s^2}{\sigma^2}$$

where s is the sample standard deviation, n is the sample size and σ is the population mean.

Exercises

7.1 What is the difference between a parameter and a statistic?

7.2 What is inferential statistics?

7.3 How can we get the sampling ratio if we know the sampling interval?

7.4 Name an advantage and a disadvantage of each of the sampling methods.

7.5 What is the common difficulty with all sampling procedures?

7.6 Search for an example of sample data from a journal:

    (a) Does the author clearly explain how the sample was selected?

    (b) Is the population to which the findings are generalised specified?

7.7 What factors are essential to take into consideration in selecting a sample?

7.8 A researcher wishes to find out which technological devices students use on a particular course:

    (a) What sampling strategy may we choose and why?

    (b) What possible problems might we face in selecting the random sample?

    (c) How would we solve these problems?

7.9 List the names and the properties of all types of distributions.

Further reading

Bergin, T. (2018) *An introduction to data analysis: Quantitative, qualitative and mixed methods*. London: Sage.

In Chapter 3, the author explains the differences among different methods for finding a sample of data and how to deal with issues such as sampling error, non-response and missing data.

Field, A. (2016) *An adventure in statistics: The reality enigma*. London: Sage.

Chapter 6 of the book presents raw and z-scores, how to transform a score into a z-score, and how to convert a distribution of scores into a z-score distribution.

Taherdoost, H. (2016) Sampling methods in research methodology: How to choose a sampling technique for research. *International Journal of Academic Research in Management*, 5(2), 18–27.

This paper presents different types of sampling techniques and the sampling process steps, as well as a summary of the strengths and weaknesses of sampling techniques.

8

Estimation and hypothesis testing

━━━━━━━━━ **Chapter Objectives** ━━━━━━━━━

In this chapter, we will:

- explain the role of statistical estimation and hypothesis testing
- define sampling distribution and hypothesis
- compute the sample size
- compute the confidence interval for the population mean and proportions
- learn how to do hypothesis testing and make estimations.

Population parameter values are almost always unknown, so the sample data is used to estimate the parameter values. Two steps need to be followed in the *estimation of a parameter*:

1. computing the point estimate
2. computing the interval estimate, also called the confidence interval.

For example, a value for a sample statistic like the sample mean ($\bar{x}$) may not be exactly equal to the true value of a population parameter (μ); it is only a point estimate. The confidence interval can be found in the following way:

1. Compute the sample statistic, for example the mean or standard deviation.
2. Compute the standard error.
3. Add and subtract the standard error to and from the sample statistic, which gives the length of the confidence interval.

8●1 Making estimations

In this section, we will present the steps to go through and compute from formulas the variances of statistics other than the mean. The first statistic we will discuss is the standard error, which is a statistic measuring the reliability of an estimate. We will introduce the theory of sample size in Section 8.1.2, and we will discuss the confidence interval and level and show their application to samples in Section 8.1.3.

8.1.1 Standard error

Often, the information collected from a sample will not be a complete representation of the entire population; if we have more than one sample, each will have a slightly different mean and standard deviation. To overcome this matter of representativeness, for a researcher, it is essential to consider the *standard error* (SE), which estimates the variation of a sample statistic from the population parameters. For example, the mean will vary from sample to sample, and the standard error of the mean describes the standard deviations of a distribution of means for samples of a given size n. The standard error is a theoretical concept because the population parameters are unknown, but the standard error of the mean can be quantified and expressed as the extent to which a sample mean can vary (the standard deviation of the mean) as a different sample of the same size is randomly selected from the same population (sampling distribution).

The *standard error of the sample mean* depends on both the standard deviation of the population (σ) and the sample size (n) by the following relationship:

$$SE = \frac{population\, standard\, deviation}{\sqrt{sample\, size}}$$

If the sample size increases, the standard error decreases, which means that the chance of variation is reduced.

Unfortunately, this formula involves the standard deviation of the population, which is unknown in practical situations. There are two possible solutions to this situation: either we estimate the standard deviation of the population using the standard deviation of the sample, or we replace the standard deviation of the population with the sample proportion (P) for which it is easy to get a numerical value.

To calculate the *standard error of the mean* using the standard deviation of the sample, we divide the standard deviation of the sample by the square root of the sample size minus 1:

$$SE = \frac{standard\, deviation\, of\, the\, sample}{\sqrt{n-1}}$$

Approximately 68 per cent of the sample means fall between plus and minus 1 SE, 95 per cent between plus and minus 2 SE, and 99.7 per cent between plus and minus 3 SE, as shown in Figure 8.1.

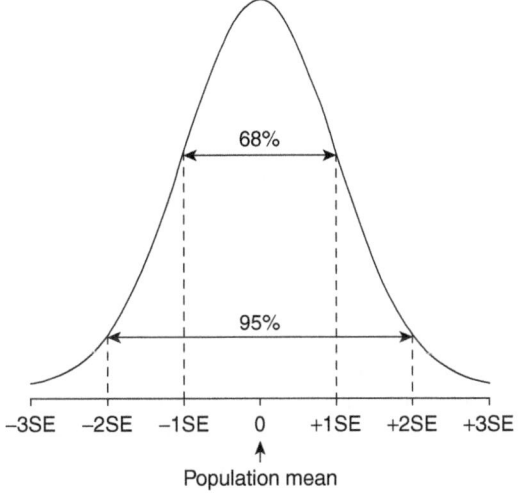

Figure 8.1 Sampling distribution of a mean

The standard deviation of the sampling distribution of a proportion is called the *standard error of a proportion* (σ_p, where σ is the lower-case Greek letter sigma) and is calculated using the following formula:

$$\sigma_P = \sqrt{\frac{P(1-P)}{n}}$$

where P is the proportion of interest and n is the sample size. In this case, the value of the standard error of a proportion, which is an indication of the amount of error in a proportion, is used to estimate the corresponding population parameter. Both the size (n) and heterogeneity (P) of the sample influence the value of the standard error of proportion. A larger sample size reduces the standard error of a proportion, while more significant heterogeneity in the sample (that is, a larger variance), for example a P-value closer to 0.5, increases its value. If the population becomes homogeneous, that is, the P-value gets closer to 0 or 1, the sampling variability will reduce.

Example 8.1 Computing the standard error of a proportion

An educational psychologist surveyed a sample of university students to investigate the university's policies and procedures for supporting dyslexic students. She found out that 40% of those asked believe that their universities are now better at supporting dyslexic students. What is the standard error of this proportion $P = 0.4$ (or 40%) when the sample size is 100?

$$SE = \sqrt{\frac{0.4(1-0.4)}{100}} = 0.049$$

What is the standard error of the same proportion if the sample size is 400?

$$SE = \sqrt{\frac{0.4(1-0.4)}{400}} = 0.024$$

A larger sample makes the standard error smaller. If the sample size is quadrupled, the standard error is halved.

8.1.2 Sample size

What constitutes an adequate or sufficient sample size? At what point is a sample defined as too small or too large? These are some of the key questions asked by novice researchers about the sample size. The answers to these questions are very diverse and disputed by various researchers and statisticians. For example, the suggested guidelines come under two categories. Firstly, the sample size should be at least 100 participants for descriptive studies, at least 50 for correlation studies, and at least 30 for experimental and causal-comparative studies. Secondly, the sample size must be a certain proportion of the population; for example, 5 per cent is often used as a cut-off value. Unfortunately, these are not reliable answers to questions regarding the sample size because they are based on different assumptions and not on sampling theory.

The size of the sample is adequately derived from sampling theory by taking into consideration the expected level of accuracy of the sample results and how significant a standard error is acceptable. To calculate the sample size by taking the standard error into consideration, recall the formula for the standard error of the mean presented in Section 8.1.1:

$$SE = \frac{population\ standard\ deviation}{\sqrt{sample\ size}}$$

Then if we raise both sides to the power of 2 to clear the square root, we obtain the formula for the squared standard error:

$$SE^2 = \frac{(population\ standard\ deviation)^2}{sample\ size}$$

Moreover, inverting this formula, we get the formula for the sample size, n:

$$n = \frac{SE^2}{(population\ standard\ deviation)^2}$$

To calculate the sample size, n, we must know the standard deviation of the population (or rather, the estimate of the population standard deviation based on the sample) and the value of standard error that can be tolerated.

Example 8.2 Computing the sample size

For example, a simple random sample is to be drawn from a population of 1000 dyslexic students with a sample squared standard deviation of $s^2 = 0.30$ and a desired standard error of $SE = 0.016$; the estimated sample size is:

$$n = \frac{0.30}{0.000256} = 1171.875$$

However, this result is too large relative to the population, because we sampled some students repeatedly. To adjust the variance of the sample distribution, a finite correction factor ($n_{correction}$) must be added:

$$n_{correction} = \frac{n}{1 + n/N}$$

In our example, for $N = 1000$, the corrected sample size is:

$$n_{correction} = \frac{1171.875}{1 + 1171.875/1000} = 539.57 \sim 540$$

This finite correction factor is appropriate to use when more than 5% of the population is being sampled and the population has a known population size. In practice, decisions regarding the sample size are more complicated and may also depend on the type of data analysis, the number of variables, and so forth.

8.1.3 Confidence interval and confidence level

A *confidence interval* (CI) is a range of uncertainty around a parameter of interest. In education, if we are trying to measure learning using test scores, these measures are imprecise estimates of learning because they can be affected by many events or factors (latent variables). Using a confidence interval is a way of quantifying how imprecise any parameter is. Confidence intervals are constructed using confidence levels. A confidence level states how confident we are that we will obtain the same results if we repeat the test or experiment. It is expressed as a percentage; 95% is the standard value in research, but other values, such as 90% or 99%, can also be used. This means that we expect that 95% of the time the results will match the population's results.

A confidence interval can be created for any significance level using z-tables or t-tables, the sample statistic and the standard error, using the following formula:

sample statistic $\pm\ t$ (or z) × standard error

where the sample statistic is usually represented by the sample mean. Whether we use z or t depends on the sample size and on whether the population standard deviation is known or unknown. For example, if the sample size is greater than or equal to 30 and the population standard deviation is known, we use z. If the population standard deviation is unknown, then we use t.

A confidence level does not say how often a confidence interval contains the value of an unknown parameter; it only refers to how many confidence intervals contain the parameter value across many samples. A 95% confidence level of all the confidence intervals contains the real value of a parameter, and 5% of all intervals do not contain the real value of the parameter. The length of the confidence interval depends on the size of the sample; for example, for larger sample size, we get a short confidence interval, and for smaller sample size, a larger confidence interval. By increasing the width of the confidence interval, a higher probability or certainty of including the population parameter is achieved. A lower confidence level, for example 90%, gives us a shorter confidence interval and a higher level (99%) gives a larger one. If many samples are selected, a confidence level can be set up for each sample. The standard error describes how samples tend to vary, and it is advantageous as a measure of calculating the confidence interval. The manual calculation of a confidence interval is illustrated in Example 8.3.

Example 8.3 The confidence interval for a population mean

The confidence interval for a population mean, when the mean of a sample is known, is specified as follows:

$$CI = sample\ mean \pm (critical\ t\text{-}value \times SE\ of\ the\ mean)$$

Here, the critical t is the value of the t-statistic, and it can be found in Table 8.1 of the t-distribution for $n - 1$ degree of freedom. For example, for a 95% CI, the critical value of t for a sample size of 20 values ($df = n - 1 = 19$) is 1.7291 (the circled value in Table 8.1), such that 95% of all t-values lie between −1.7291 and 1.7291.

Table 8.1 t-distribution table

α (1-tailed)	0.05	0.025	0.01	0.005	0.0025	0.001	0.0005
α (2-tailed)	0.1	0.05	0.02	0.01	0.005	0.002	0.001
df							
1	6.3138	12.7062	31.8205	63.6567	127.3213	318.3088	636.6192
2	2.9200	4.3027	6.9646	9.9248	14.0890	22.3271	31.5991
3	2.3534	3.1824	4.5407	5.8409	7.4533	10.2145	12.9240
4	2.1318	2.7764	3.7469	4.6041	5.5976	7.1732	8.6103
5	2.0150	2.5706	3.3649	4.0321	4.7733	5.8934	6.8688
6	1.9432	2.4469	3.1427	3.7074	4.3168	5.2076	5.9588
7	1.8946	2.3646	2.9980	3.4995	4.0293	4.7853	5.4079
8	1.8595	2.3060	2.8965	3.3554	3.8325	4.5008	5.0413
9	1.8331	2.2622	2.8214	3.2498	3.6897	4.2968	4.7809
10	1.8125	2.2281	2.7638	3.1693	3.5814	4.1437	4.5869
11	1.7959	2.2010	2.7181	3.1058	3.4966	4.0247	4.4370
12	1.7823	2.1788	2.6810	3.0545	3.4284	3.9296	4.3178
13	1.7709	2.1604	2.6503	3.0123	3.3725	3.8520	4.2208
14	1.7613	2.1448	2.6245	2.9768	3.3257	3.7874	4.1405
15	1.7531	2.1314	2.6025	2.9467	3.2860	3.7328	4.0728
16	1.7459	2.1199	2.5835	2.9208	3.2520	3.6862	4.0150
17	1.7396	2.1098	2.5669	2.8982	3.2224	3.6458	3.9651
18	1.7341	2.1009	2.5524	2.8784	3.1966	3.6105	3.9216
19	(1.7291)	2.0930	2.5395	2.8609	3.1737	3.5794	3.8834
20	1.7247	2.0860	2.5280	2.8453	3.1534	3.5518	3.8495

The confidence interval for a population mean when the mean of the population is known is specified as follows:

$$CI = sample\ mean \pm \left(critical\ z\text{-}value \times SE\ of\ the\ mean\right)$$

In this case, a z-score is used from the normal distribution instead of t because we have a normal distribution for the population mean. For a 95% confidence level, z = 1.96 and the confidence interval then is:

$$CI = sample\ mean \pm \left(1.96 \times SE\right)$$

Example 8.4 The confidence interval for a proportion from Example 8.1

The student researcher found a sample statistic for the data collected from one sample: 40% of students believe that universities' policies and procedures regarding dyslexia have increased the support for this group of students. Because this statistic is based on a sample which was selected randomly, it is subject to a standard error. The value of the standard error is computed using the formula presented in Section 8.1.1 and equals 0.049. If we use the formula for the standard error of a proportion, for the 95% confidence level, the confidence interval will be between

$$P + 1.96\sqrt{\frac{P(1-P)}{n}} \quad \text{and} \quad P + 1.96\sqrt{\frac{P(1-P)}{n}}$$

where $P = 0.40$ and $n = 100$, that is,

$$CI_{0.95} = 0.304\ to\ 0.496 \quad \text{or} \quad CI_{0.95} = 30\%\ to\ 50\%$$

Figure 8.2 shows a schematic drawing of the confidence intervals for this example, and that we are 95% certain that the percentage of students who believe that universities' policies and procedures regarding dyslexia have increased the support for this group of students, is somewhere between 30% and 50%. If the data is collected from only one sample, whether this confidence interval contains the real value of the parameter is not known. The 95% confidence level means that if we did use the same method to collect data, for a large number of randomly selected samples having the same size, in 95% of these cases the confidence interval would include the real population value.

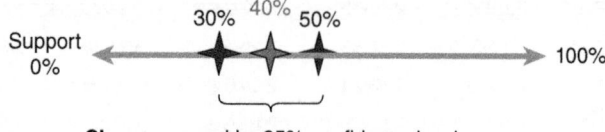

Figure 8.2 Schematic representation of a confidence interval

8 ● 2 Statistical hypothesis testing process

Now that we know how to provide a confidence interval for a parameter of interest, we are interested to know about the real value of a parameter. For example, the Student Loan Company claimed that the average number of days a student has to wait to attend the Study Needs Assessment for the Disabled Students' Allowance process is 22 working days. We select 100 students and ask them how many days they waited for the assessment. We got a mean of 24 working days from our sample, which represents the sample mean, instead of 22 days. Does this mean that we are wrong? Not necessarily. Sample results, or statistics, may match or deviate from expectations. Making an estimation, using the confidence level and interval on the selected sample, and the corresponding statistic, will provide information about the population parameter, such as the average days. To assess the probability of specific sample results under assumed population conditions, we use *hypothesis testing* to make an inference about variables, for example the average number of days undergraduate students from London's universities had to wait to attend the Study Needs Assessment for the Disabled Students' Allowance process. We can use the results from our sample to reject or fail to reject a hypothesis about the population based on sample data. Also, to determine whether a sample statistic falls within a range that occurs by an acceptable level of probability or chance, the following hypothesis testing procedures are employed:

1. Formulate a research hypothesis, which is a statement of the factors influencing the behaviour of the variable(s) under investigation.
2. Formulate a null and an alternative hypothesis and express them in mathematical terms that can be analysed with inferential statistical methods.
3. Choose a significance level (alpha, which is the probability of rejecting the null hypothesis when it is true).
4. Choose a statistical test according to the different conditions, such as the type of distribution (e.g. *z-*, *t-* or *chi-squared* distribution), the scale of measurements (e.g. nominal, ordinal or interval), the number of samples (e.g. one, two or more than two) and the relationship between the samples (e.g. unrelated or independent).
5. Specify the confidence level (1 minus alpha) and define the region of rejection.
6. Compute the statistical test and reject or retain the null hypothesis. If the statistic is not in the region of rejection, then we fail to reject the null hypothesis, which only gives us an indication of *how likely it is to be true.*

In addition to these steps, it is beneficial to plot the distribution, the confidence interval for the desired confidence level, the critical value and statistics to get a clearer understanding of the statistical results.

8.2.1 Null and alternative hypotheses

Almost all research designs include an explanation of the problem statement, which sets up the grounds for the research and the research problem. Research problems are usually stated as questions, and often as hypotheses (Figure 8.3), which are derived from theories, observations, intuition, practice, findings from previous research or a combination of all these approaches. Not all research studies in educational research will test a hypothesis, but many do, such as experimental, quasi-experimental, randomised controlled trials and observational studies.

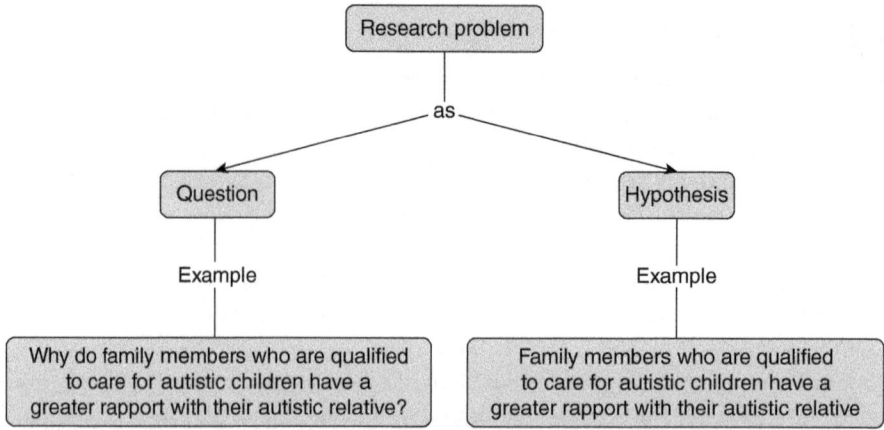

Figure 8.3 Example of research question restatement in the form of a hypothesis

A *hypothesis* is a statement, a prediction, about specific relationships between variables (factors, characteristics or conditions), which can only be verified after it has been tested empirically. There are two mutually exclusive statistical statements involved in hypothesis testing, the null and alternative hypotheses, which are always identified before any testing is done:

- The *null hypothesis*, denoted by H_0, is the testable statistical statement which postulates that there is no difference or relationship of interest. Whether this hypothesis is true or false, its rejection or failure to reject should be reported.
- The *alternative hypothesis*, denoted by H_1 or H_a, postulates that there is a difference in the relationship of interest, and that we are inclined to believe it.

A hypothesis must be stated in a declarative form, testable, logical, succinct and specific. Examples of null and alternative hypotheses are presented in Table 8.2. Both null hypotheses contain statements that two or more variables are equal or unrelated to each other, while the alternative hypotheses contain statements about inequality or relationship between variables.

Table 8.2 Example of null and alternative hypotheses

Type of hypothesis	Notation	Type of statement	Examples
Null hypothesis	H_0	There is no relationship or difference	'There is no relationship between teachers' and head teachers' attitudes towards innovation.'
			'There is no difference in achievement between students who are taught through Cooperative Integrated Reading and Composition and those taught through the traditional approach.'

Type of hypothesis	Notation	Type of statement	Examples
Alternative hypothesis	H_a or H_1	There is a relationship or difference	'There is a significant relationship between teachers' and head teachers' attitude towards innovation.'
			'There is a significant difference in achievement between students who are taught through Cooperative Integrated Reading and Composition and those taught through the traditional approach.'

A null hypothesis always suggests that there will be a 'null' or an absence of any difference or relations between the parameters of two distributions (e.g. the population mean), and is usually expressed as:

$$H_0 : \mu_1 = \mu_2$$

or as an equality statement between a population mean (μ) and a specific value (μ_0):

$$H_0 : \mu = \mu_0$$

The alternative hypothesis states that there is a difference or relationship between the means of two populations (μ_1 and μ_2) which would be written as:

$$H_1 : \mu_1 \neq \mu_2$$

or that the population mean (μ) is not equal to a specific value (μ_0):

$$H_0 : \mu \neq \mu_0$$

Both the null and alternative hypotheses are expressed in terms of the population parameters, and the null hypothesis will be the one tested directly using appropriate statistical tests.

Example 8.5 Formulating null and alternative hypotheses for Example 8.1

In hypothesis testing, we can compare a score with a population of scores, so we need to compare a sample mean with a population of sample means. To do this, we select all possible samples of size 100 of undergraduate students from the population of undergraduate students in England and calculate the sample means. Then we create a distribution of means. However, it is a non-trivial task to select so many samples. Fortunately, from sampling distribution theory, we know that with a sample size greater than 30, the distribution of sample means will be like a normal distribution. Now we can compare the two populations of sample means.

Suppose we know that one sample of students from England has waited on average more days than another sample of students from Scotland to attend the Study Needs Assessment for the Disabled Students' Allowance process. With μ_1 as the average number of days for students from England and μ_2 as the average number of days for students from Scotland, the null hypothesis would be expressed as being that there is no difference between the average number of days' wait for students in England and Scotland to attend the Study Needs Assessment for the Disabled Students' Allowance process, thus:

$$H_0 : \mu_1 = \mu_2 \text{ or } H_0 : \mu_1 - \mu_2 = 0$$

The alternative hypothesis would be written as:

$$H_1 : \mu_1 \neq \mu_2$$

8.2.2 Directional and non-directional hypotheses

There are other ways to express a research hypothesis, as shown in Table 8.3: either as a directional hypothesis, also called a one-tailed hypothesis, or as a non-directional hypothesis, also called a two-tailed hypothesis. When we state that there is a difference between two statistics and we do not have enough information to know which one is greater than the other, then we formulate a non-directional hypothesis, as in the example below:

There is a difference between girls' and boys' reading achievement

or, in symbols:

$$H_1 : \mu_1 \neq \mu_2$$

where μ_1 is the population mean for girls and μ_2 is the population mean for boys.

If we know that one group's mean is larger than the other, then we formulate a directional hypothesis:

The girls' reading achievement is greater than the boys' reading achievement

or, in symbols:

$$H_1 = \mu_1 > \mu_2$$

We will return to discuss one-and two-tailed aspects when we discuss one-and two-tailed tests later in the chapter.

Table 8.3 Mathematical symbols used to express directional and non-directional hypotheses

Directionality		Null hypothesis (H$_o$)	Alternative hypothesis (H$_1$)
Non-directional (two-tailed)		equal (=) $H_o{:}\mu = 45$	not equal ($\neq$) $H_1{:}\mu \neq 45$
Directional (one-tailed)	right-tailed	less than or equal to () $H_o{:}\mu \leq 45$	greater than (>) $H_1{:}\mu > 45$
	left-tailed	greater than or equal to (+) $H_o{:}\mu \geq 45$	less than (<) $H_1{:}\mu < 45$

8.2.3 Decisions about the null hypothesis: statistical levels, types of error and power

If we compare the null and alternative hypotheses, the result is simply a probability statement, and this can be interpreted as the likelihood of making an error when the null hypothesis is rejected, and the alternative hypothesis is accepted. *Type I error* occurs when we reject the null hypothesis when we should retain it because the statement was true. In order to decide between the acceptance or rejection of the null hypothesis, we must set up a small value, usually 5% or 1%, as the risk of making a Type I error. This value is called the *level of significance* (α). If the probability of making a Type I error is found to be as small as the significance level, we can reject the null hypothesis and accept the alternative hypothesis. Type I error can be minimised by setting a lower significance level, which will reduce the size of the region of rejection. A key idea to remember about the failure to confirm any hypothesis is that it does not constitute evidence against it, and knowing that something is not true is massively different from not knowing that it is true.

Type II error occurs when we accept the null hypothesis when we should reject it because the statement was false. The risk associated with making a Type II error is a probability statement, like the level of significance, and is designated by β. If we subtract this value from unity $(1 - \beta)$, we get the *statistical power* which indicates the probability of rejecting a false null hypothesis in favour of an alternative hypothesis. The statistical power can be controlled indirectly by modifying the sample size. For example, an increase in the sample size (n) reduces β, which, in turn, increases the statistical power. In educational research, the level of the power must be specified because it is sensitive to the differences between means and much research in education is based on comparing means of two or more variables, for example the difference between populations means.

For experimental educational research, it is essential for the researcher to decide about the risks he or she is willing to assume for both types of errors, and this decision must be taken before the experiment begins. In connection with these risks, we must choose a significance test with appropriate power, for example by drawing a large sample of participants and using precise educational measurements or tools.

The novice researcher is often confused about the difference between the level of significance (α) and the *p*-value because both values represent probabilities between 0 and 1 and the most common number used for both is 0.05 or 5%, and statistical levels are universally reported as *p*-values. However, there are differences between these two, which are listed below:

- The level of significance (α) is associated with the confidence level of a statistical test and, in general, is equal to:

$$\alpha = 1 - confidence\ interval$$

- p-values come from different sources than α and represent the probability (or how often) the sample statistic comes from the population represented by the null hypothesis. For example, every statistical test has a corresponding p-value, which is the probability that the observed statistic occurs by chance alone. A p-value of 0.05 means that there is a 5% chance of seeing these results when the null hypothesis is true. It is imperative to remember here that the p-value does not tell us if the experiment worked or not, an assumption which is made in a hurry by many researchers when looking at this value. A low p-value means that the sample statistic is unlikely to come from the population from which the sample was selected.
- p-values are used alongside α-values to determine if a result is statistically significant, for example:

  o if $\alpha = 0.05$ and $p = 0.02$ there is a significant difference
  o if $\alpha = 0.05$ and $p = 0.07$ there is no significant difference.

In general, if $p < \alpha$, there is a statistical significance, and for $p \geq \alpha$, a statistical significance is not found.

8.2.4 Regions of rejection

Any set of extreme results can be selected as a basis for rejecting a null hypothesis. The range of these results, which forms the extremity of a distribution, is called a *tail* as well as the *region of rejection*.

Example 8.4 One-tailed and two-tailed hypotheses

Suppose we have a sample of 100 ten-year-old children who had the opportunity to attend weekly science clubs and we want to compare their science test scores to those of all 10-year-old children in the Trends in International Mathematics and Science Study (TIMSS) on the same science test. The decision to locate the region of rejection in one or two tails will depend on whether or not the alternative hypothesis implies a specific direction to the predicted result and if it is a larger or smaller value than some critical value. Suppose we hypothesise that:

1. *The mean score of the science test for our sample is different from that of all 10-year-old children in the TIMSS (population mean) on the same science test.*

This hypothesis is a two-tailed hypothesis, and the region of rejection is located in the two tails (Figure 8.4). The sum of the probabilities of the extreme results included in the region of rejection is referred to as the level of significance (α), and it is customary to set it at 0.05 or 0.01. Because we have two tails, the value for α in each tail is halved, for example 0.025 on the left and 0.025 on the right. If a sample statistic falls within the region of rejection, the null hypothesis can be rejected at the corresponding α level.

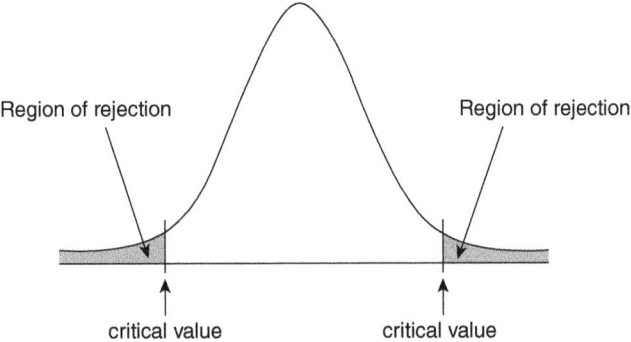

Figure 8.4 Two-tailed region of rejection

2. *The mean score of the science test for our sample will be greater than that of all 10-year-old children in the TIMSS (population mean) on the same science test.*

This hypothesis is a one-tailed hypothesis. When the alternative hypothesis predicts a larger value, as in the last example, the region of rejection will be located in the right tail of the sampling distribution (Figure 8.5(a)), and if it implies a lower value, the left tail is selected as a region of rejection (Figure 8.5(b)).

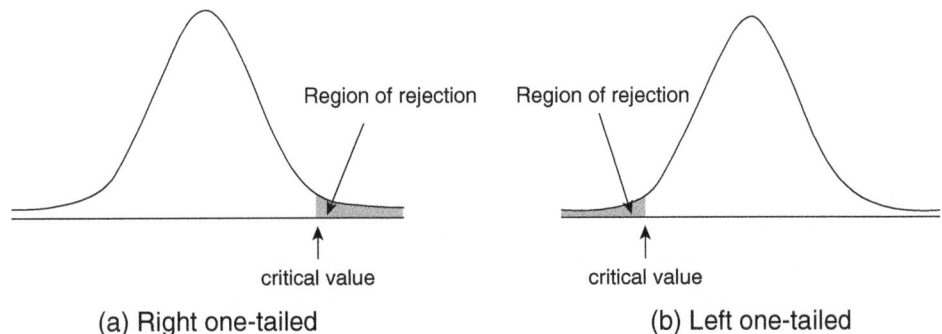

Figure 8.5 (a) right one-tailed rejection region; (b) left one-tailed rejection region

The evaluation of any statistical tests or statistical hypothesis testing and the conclusion reached on their results must be complemented by other powerful methods such as:

*   effect size – how big a difference does an intervention make and is it practically meaningful?
*   confidence intervals (CI) – what is the range of uncertainty built into any given answer?

- whether the research data can be freely accessed to verify if the data have not been manipulated pre- and post-test
- alternative techniques such as Bayesian analysis based on Bayes factors, which is another alternative to the hypothesis testing described previously.

8 3 Selection of statistical tests

The selection of statistical tests is based on several assumptions about the parameters of the populations from which the sample is drawn, for example on:

- the type of population distribution – if the distribution is normally distributed then we use a parametric test; if not, we select a nonparametric test
- scales of measurement for the variables
- number of samples
- related or unrelated samples – if we have two or more samples, then we check if these are related (or paired) or unrelated (or independent).

The decision about which statistical test to use can be seen as quite complicated and confusing. However, the selection of statistical tests is based on several assumptions:

- types of analysis (i.e. differences or similarities)
- scales of measurement (i.e. nominal, ordinal, interval or ratio)
- distribution of data (i.e. normal or skewed)
- number of samples
- sample size
- related or unrelated samples
- number of independent and dependent variables.

Based on combinations of these assumptions, the selection of the most common statistical tests used in educational research is illustrated in Table 8.4. All these inferential tests help us to answer only one question or to make a statement about the probability relating the sample data with the population characteristics and the extent to which the results may be generalisable.

The statistical tests presented in Table 8.4 for interval and ratio data can be classified into two categories: parametric and nonparametric statistical tests. *Parametric* statistical tests, such as the *t*-test, ANOVA, Pearson's product-moment correlation and linear regression, assume that the population from which the samples are drawn is normally distributed. *Nonparametric* tests, such as Spearman's (rho) rank correlation, Kendall's tau, Mann–Whitney *U*, Wilcoxon signed ranks and Kruskal–Wallis, on the other hand, make few (or no) assumptions about the population from which the samples are taken. For example, the distribution is not normally distributed, and it can be left- or right-skewed. Parametric tests are more likely to reveal an actual difference or relationship if one exists, hence they are much more powerful than nonparametric tests. On the other hand, an advantage of nonparametric tests is that they are safer to use when the assumptions for the parametric test are not satisfied. In Part Five, we will start to examine in detail the use of all these parametric and nonparametric tests for one sample, two samples and more than two samples.

Table 8.4 The most common inferential statistical tests used in educational research

Types of analysis	Number of samples/types and number of variables		Nominal	Ordinal	Interval (distribution type)	
					normal distribution	skewed distribution
Differences	One sample		Binomial test; Pearson chi-squared goodness-of-fit test	Wilcoxon signed-rank test	t-test; z-test	Sign test; Wilcoxon test
	Two samples	Independent (unpaired)	Chi-squared test	Mann-Whitney test	t-test	Mann-Whitney test
		Dependent (paired)	McNemar test	Wilcoxon signed-rank test	Paired t-test; z-test (sample size > 30)	Wilcoxon signed-rank test
	Multiple samples (one independent variable)	Independent (unpaired)	nxm Chi-squared test	Kruskal-Wallis ANOVA test	One-way ANOVA	Kruskal-Wallis test
		Paired	–	–	One-way ANOVA	
	Multiple samples (more than one independent variable)	Unpaired	–	Friedman ANOVA	Two-way ANOVA	
		Paired	Cochran's Q-test	–	Two-way ANOVA split test	
Associations/ relations	One sample		Chi-squared goodness-of-fit test (one variable); Chi-squared independence test (two independent variables); Phi coefficient; Cramér's phi or V	G-test for goodness of fit (one category); Chi-squared test (multiple categories	–	–
	Two samples		Chi-squared test of homogeneity	–	–	–
	Multiple samples		Chi-squared	–	Factor analysis; Structural equation modelling	–
Correlations	One sample		–	–	Pearson's product-moment correlation	Spearman (rho) rank correlation test; Kendall's tau
Predictions	One sample and multiple variables		–	–	Linear/multiple regression; Path analysis	

Formulas

Standard error

$$SE = \frac{s}{\sqrt{n}}$$

where σ is the population standard deviation and n is the sample size.

Standard error of a proportion

$$\sigma_P = \sqrt{\frac{P(1-P)}{n}}$$

where P is the proportion of interest and n is the sample size.

Sample size

$$n = \frac{SE^2}{\sigma^2}$$

Confidence interval of a population mean

From $CI = samplestatistics - t\ (or\ z) \times SE$ to $samplestatistics + t(or z) \times SE$

Exercises

8.1 What is the difference between a confidence interval and a confidence level?

8.2 Calculate the confidence interval for five different proportions, all containing a true value proportion of 0.60 for a confidence level of 95%.

8.3 In a study about how high-fructose corn syrup can trigger memory problems in a group of students who were put on a diet high in high-fructose corn syrup, 30 of the 125 students (24%) reported memory problems. A 95% confidence level for this group of students goes from 17% to 31%:

   (a) How do you interpret this confidence interval?
   (b) How large is the standard error in this study?

8.4 Does a p-value describe the Type I error rate?

8.5 What is probability?

8.6 What constitutes an adequate or sufficient sample size?

8.7 Think about a research area that interests you and write down a null and an alternative hypothesis.

Further reading

Altman, D. and Bland, M. (2005) Standard deviations and standard errors. *British Medical Journal*, 331, 903.

This paper is part of the 'Statistical Notes' series edited by the authors; it explains clearly the important distinction between the standard deviation and standard error.

MacInnes, J. (2019) *Little quick fix: Statistical significance*. London: Sage.

This book is an excellent source of definitions of key concepts, such as statistical significance, standard error and p-value, and practical examples, such as how to calculate confidence intervals with standard errors and how to use p-values to test a null hypothesis.

Salkind, N. J. (2010) *Encyclopedia of research design* (3 vols). Thousand Oaks, CA: Sage.

This is an excellent resource and practical and useful tool providing quick and easy access to definitions of many statistical concepts, including those presented in this chapter.

PART FIVE

From sample to population

Part Five Contents

9

One-sample tests

━━━━━━━━━━ Chapter Objectives ━━━━━━━━━━

In this chapter, we will:

- understand the use of different statistical tests for one sample, for example the z-test, t-test, sign test, chi-squared test and Wilcoxon signed-rank test
- explain what assumptions are made for the selection of one-sample statistical tests
- interpret the results from different one-sample tests based on the probability level of the null hypothesis.

In educational research, the information we obtain about a population parameter in most cases comes from a sample, instead of from a population, and we want to know how accurately the sample statistics represent the population parameter. Therefore, using inferential statistics tests, we make an inference from the sample to the population. Every statistical test produces a final numerical value, sometimes called a *test statistic*, which determines whether the null hypothesis is accepted or not. For example, the *t*-test uses the *t*-value which is the most common test statistic used in educational research in the process of hypothesis testing. The probability distribution of this test statistic is used to calculate a *p*-value which forms the basis for statistical decision-making. In general, for any statistical test, if a test statistic has a lower value compared to a critical value determined before the testing, then the null hypothesis is rejected, and if it has a higher value, the null hypothesis is not rejected. In terms of distribution, this critical probability defines and sets the limits of the rejection region of the null hypothesis, which we already discussed in Chapter 8. The reason we discuss this in terms of probabilities, as we have done in previous chapters, is because the information collected from a sample will not necessarily be an accurate representation of the entire population.

 **Parameter hypothesis testing using sample statistics**

To carry out a hypothesis test to compare a sample statistic to a population parameter, go through the following steps:

1. State the null and alternative hypotheses and specify if the alternative hypothesis is one-tailed or two-tailed by using relationships such as not equal to, less than or greater than.
2. Specify the significance level (α).
3. Determine the appropriate statistical inference test and sampling distribution based on information about the type of variable: interval/ratio, ordinal or nominal (Table 8.4).
4. Compute the test statistic (e.g. z-score or *t*-value), depending on which test was selected.
5. Compare the test statistic with the critical value(s) that divide the rejection and non-rejection regions.
6. Conclude whether the null hypothesis is rejected or not. If the *p*-value is less than α, the null hypothesis should be rejected; if it is greater than or equal to α, we should fail to reject the null hypothesis. At this step, it is also good to evaluate the risks of making Type I and II errors.

The selection of a particular statistical test (Table 9.1) for one sample is based on the following assumptions:

- the size of the sample (e.g. whether it is smaller or larger than 30)
- whether the standard deviation of the population is known or unknown
- the scale of measurement of the variable of interest (i.e. internal/ratio, ordinal or nominal)
- how the data is distributed – if the data is normally distributed, a parametric test should be selected, and if it not normally distributed, then the choice is a nonparametric test.

Table 9.1 Statistical tests for one sample under different conditions

Scale of measurement for the sample statistic	Type of tests	
	Parametric	Nonparametric
Interval		
• normal distribution	z-test (sample size > 30) t-test (sample size < 30)	
• skewed distribution	–	Sign test Wilcoxon test
Ordinal	–	Wilcoxon signed-rank test
Nominal		
• two categories	–	Binomial test
• more than two categories	–	Pearson chi-squared goodness-of-fit test

One-sample statistical tests for interval/ratio data

There are four different types of statistical tests which can be used to compare a sample statistic to a population parameter when the level of measurement (or the variables) is of interval/ratio type, as shown in Figure 9.1:

1. The one-sample z-test compares the sample mean with the population mean when the sample size is 30 or larger, and the standard deviation of the population is unknown.
2. The one-sample t-test compares the sample mean with the population mean when the sample size is less than 30.
3. The one-sample sign test compares the median of the sample with the population median, and it is used for data which follow a skewed distribution when the standard deviation of the population is unknown.
4. The Wilcoxon test is a rank-based test and is used when the one-sample t-test assumptions are not fulfilled.

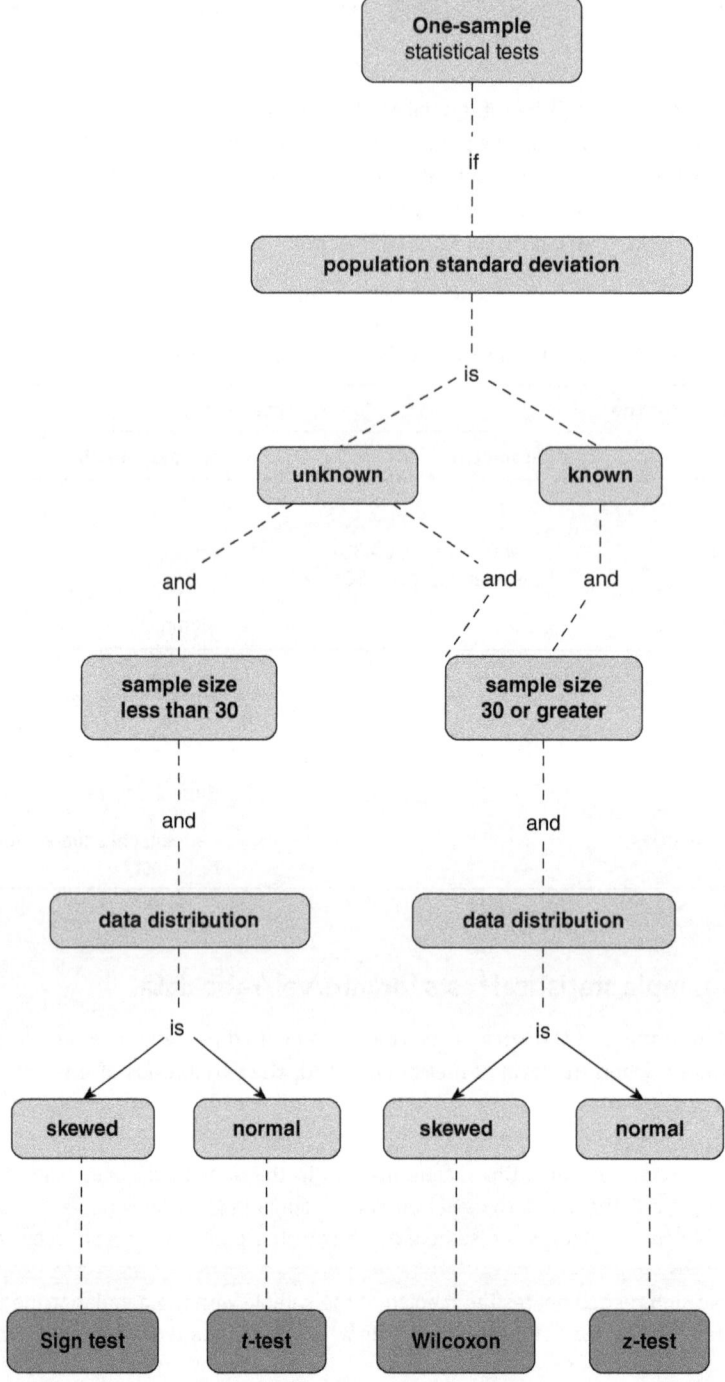

Figure 9.1 Selecting one-sample statistical tests

9.2.1 z-test

The z-test for one sample is a parametric test which can only be used if we know the standard deviation of the population from which we draw the sample and for a sample size, n, larger than 30. As stated in the previous section, the first step required for all statistical tests is the formulation of the null and alternative hypotheses. The z-test will produce a numerical value, called the z-value or z-score, which determines whether or not the null hypothesis is rejected. Before we compute the z-test, a critical probability must always be determined. This probability, called the significance level, is essential for hypothesis testing because it defines and delimits the rejection region of the null hypothesis.

Since we do not know the population mean, we select a sample consisting of n observations ($df = n - 1$), with a known value for the mean ($\bar{x}$) and standard deviation (s). Let us assume that the sample comes from the same population, and we can, therefore, refer to the sampling distribution. Remember that the sampling distribution of the mean is the distribution of the mean for repeated random samples of equal size, whose properties are known in detail. We then refer to the sampling distribution to determine the probability of getting a sample mean of $\bar{x}$, and a two-tailed null hypothesis is written as:

$$H_0 : \mu = \bar{x}$$

Secondly, we create an alternative hypothesis:

$$H_1 : \mu \neq \bar{x}$$

which states that the population mean is different from the sample mean.

We concentrate on the null hypothesis because it is easier to prove whether it is true or false. To test the null hypothesis, we must first change the sample mean into a standardised value of the observed *z-value* by the following formula, if the level of measurement is interval and data is normally distributed (parametric):

$$z = \frac{(sample\ mean - population\ mean)/sample\ standard\ deviation}{\sqrt{sample\ size}} = \frac{\bar{x} - \mu}{s/\sqrt{n}}$$

Using this z-value, the corresponding p-value can be found with statistical software or in statistical tables. If the p-value is less than the critical probability (the statistical significance), then the null hypothesis is rejected.

For a population proportion, the null hypothesis is stated as:

$$H_0 : \pi = \pi_0$$

where the population proportion (π) is equal to a certain value (π_0). Since we do not know the population proportion, we select a sample consisting of n observations ($df = n - 1$), with a known value for the proportion (p), and then we change the sample proportion to a value of standard z-variable according to the formula:

$$z = \frac{p - \pi_0}{\sqrt{\pi_0(1-\pi_0)/n}}$$

Example 9.1 The z-test for means

A mathematics teacher wants to ensure that her secondary school children are making enough progress with their financial skills. The mean performance of 50 children (aged 15) in her school on a mock financial literacy test was 498, with a standard deviation of 100. Data from the Organisation for Economic Co-operation and Development (OECD) suggest that the mean value for PISA Financial Literacy in 2015 for the OECD countries was 489, with a standard deviation of 110. Since the data collected comes from a sample larger than 30 and it is normally distributed, she carries out a z-test at the 5% level of significance to determine whether the test result in the sample is significantly different from the OECD average, as follows:

1. Formulate the null and alternative hypotheses:

$$H_0 : \mu = \bar{x}$$

$$H_1 : \mu \neq \bar{x}$$

2. Specify the significance level: $\alpha = 0.05$.
3. Calculate the standard error of the sampling distribution by dividing the population standard deviation by the square root of the sample size:

$$SE = \frac{100}{\sqrt{50}} = 14.14$$

4. Calculate the z-score by dividing the difference between the sample mean and population mean by the standard error:

$$z = \frac{498\text{-}489}{14.14} = 0.636$$

5. Find the p-value for the z-score by looking it up in the z-score table for two-tailed p-values for z-statistics. In this case, the p-value is 0.525, which can also be computed in R as described below.

Computing the one-sample z-test in R

Calculate the z-score:

```
z.score<-(498-489)/(100/sqrt(50))
z.score
[1] 0.6363961
```

Calculate the *p*-value and round it to three decimal places:

```
p<-round(2*pnorm(-abs(z.score),0,1),3)
p
[1] 0.525
```

6. Compare the *p*-value from step 5 with the α-value from step 2.

Interpretation

Since the *p*-value is greater than α, the teacher accepts the null hypothesis, which means that there is no difference between the sample mean and the population mean. The comparison shows no significant difference, the null hypothesis is true, and we conclude that the sample represents the population, and it is part of the population.

9.2.2 *t*-test

The one-sample *t*-test compares the mean of a single sample to a hypothetical population mean, which is assumed to be the population mean. This test helps us to analyse whether the difference between the sample and population means is due to random effects of chance if the sample means differ from the population mean.

Example 9.2 Exploring the difference between the sample and population means

Data file: Ex9_2.csv

Suppose that a new teaching strategy was introduced to engage primary school children in reading. A sample of 25 children was randomly selected to participate in a mock reading test. The results are displayed in Table 9.2 and saved as a .csv file in the file named Ex9_2.csv.

Table 9.2 Reading test results from a sample of 25 primary school children

Scores				
95	84	76	72	67
91	71	82	69	56
82	79	75	76	88
100	78	67	91	71
87	69	78	78	79

We want to find out if there is a significant difference between the mean of the randomly selected sample and the population mean. The population mean is 70. Before we calculate the *t*-value, we must decide on the significance level (let us say 0.05) and state the non-directional (or two-tailed) hypotheses:

- Null hypothesis: *There is no difference between the sample mean and the population mean*

$$H_0 : \mu = \bar{x}$$

where $\bar{x}$ is the sample mean and μ is the population mean (2015 PISA Reading test for the UK).

- Alternative hypothesis: There is a statistical difference between the sample mean and the population mean

$$H_1 : \mu \neq \bar{x}$$

Another possible alternative hypothesis would be the one-tailed hypothesis that the population mean is less (say) than the sample mean. The null hypothesis remains the same, while the alternative hypothesis would be:

$$H_1 : \mu < \bar{x}$$

The formula for the *t*-value is:

$$t = \frac{sample\ mean\ -\ population\ mean}{standard\ error\ of\ the\ mean}$$

where the standard error of the mean equals

$$SE = \frac{sample\ standard\ deviation}{\sqrt{sample\ size}}$$

Computing the Kolmogorov–Smirnov test in R

Import the data from the Ex9_2.csv data file into R:

```
Ex9_2<- read.csv(file.choose())
```

Print the data:

```
Ex9_2
Scores
1      95
2      91
```

3	82
4	100
5	87
6	84
7	71
8	79
9	78
10	69
11	76
12	82
13	75
14	67
15	78
16	72
17	69
18	76
19	91
20	78
21	67
22	56
23	88
24	71
25	79

Before we compute the one-sample t-test, it is important to check whether our data is normally distributed using the `ks.test()` function (the one-sample Kolmogorov–Smirnov test).

```
ks.test(Ex9_2$Scores, "pnorm", mean=mean(Ex9_2$Scores), sd=sd(Ex9_2$Scores))
      One-sample Kolmogorov-Smirnov test
data: Ex9_2$Scores
D = 0.11765, p-value = 0.8794
alternative hypothesis: two-sided
```

Interpretation

The null hypothesis of the Kolmogorov–Smirnov test is that the distribution is normal. Because the p-value of 0.8794 is larger than 0.05, we do not reject the null hypothesis and conclude that the distribution of the scores is not statistically different from a normal distribution.

Using R to calculate the t-value (two-tailed hypothesis)

In R, by default, the one-sample t-test can be performed by using the function `t.test()` to compare the mean value of a sample with a constant value for a two-tailed hypothesis.

Computing the one-sample *t*-test in R

```
t.test(dataset$sample1, mu=mean_value)
```

By default, R performs a two-tailed test:

```
t.test(Ex9_2$Scores,mu=70, conf.level = 0.05)
      One Sample t-test
data: Ex9_2$Scores
t = 4.2234, df = 24, p-value = 0.0002992
alternative hypothesis: true mean is not equal to 70
5 percent confidence interval:
 78.31337 78.56663
sample estimates:
mean of x
   78.44
```

Using R to calculate the *t*-value (one-tailed hypothesis)

We use a one-sample *t*-test for a one-tailed hypothesis if we are interested in determining whether the sample mean score is higher than the population score, or whether the high mean score for the sample is purely the result of random variation. In our example, the one-sided test is suitable because we are interested in knowing whether the mean score is higher than 70. The test has the same null hypothesis as the one for the two-tailed test, and the alternative hypothesis is that the sample mean score is higher than 70, and a 0.05 significance level is used.

To perform a one-tailed test, set the *alternative* argument to "greater", as shown below.

Computing one-tailed *t*-test in R

```
t.test(Ex9_2$Scores,mu=70, conf.level = 0.05, alternative = "greater")
```

This gives the following output:

```
      One Sample t-test
data: Ex9_2$Scores
t = 4.2234, df = 24, p-value = 0.0001496
alternative hypothesis: true mean is greater than 70
5 percent confidence interval:
 81.85903 Inf
sample estimates:
mean of x
   78.44
```

Interpretation

To interpret the results, firstly we examine the confidence interval. The lower and upper limits of the confidence interval for the two-tailed test (78.31337 and 78.56663) tell us that we are 95% confident that the true mean is between these two values. For the one-tailed test, we obtain only the lower limit of the confidence interval, which indicates that the population mean is likely to be greater than 70. Secondly, we must compare the *p*-value to the significance level to determine whether the test results are statistically significant. Since the *p*-values for both tests are less than 0.05, the decision is to reject the null hypothesis. In addition, the *t*-value of 4.2235 indicates that the mean will be in the rejection region of the right tail of the distribution.

The effect size for the one-sample *t*-test (Cohen's *d*)

In Example 9.2, we found that the average reading score in the population is significantly different from 70, but we do not know if it is a big difference because the answer is based on the sample. To determine the size of the difference, we can use an *effect size measure*, known as *Cohen's d*, which works well with the one-sample *t*-test. There are two formulae for this effect size measure: the first includes the sample mean, the expected population mean (the test value or hypothesised mean) and the standard deviation:

$$Cohen's\ d = \frac{sample\ mean - population\ mean}{sample\ standard\ deviation}$$

while the second formula uses the *t*-statistic and the sample size:

$$Cohen's\ d = \frac{t}{\sqrt{sample\ size}}$$

Computing the effect size (Cohen's *d*) in R

Calculate the sample mean:

```
meanRS<-mean(Ex9_2$Scores)
meanRS
[1] 78.44
```

Compute the sample standard deviation:

```
sdTS<-sd(Ex9_2$Scores)
sdTS
[1] 9.991997
```

(Continued)

Compute Cohen's *d*:

```
cohenDST<-(meanRS-70)/sdTS
cohenDST
[1] 0.844676
```

We can also calculate the Cohen's *d* measure by using the function `cohensD()`, which can be found in the `lsr` package:

```
install.packages("lsr")
library(lsr)
cohensD(Ex9_2$Scores, mu=70)
[1] 0.844676
```

Alternatively, we can use our second formula for Cohen's *d* measure above, which takes into consideration only two values – the *t*-value (computed previously using the `t.test()` function) and the sample size (*n*):

```
4.2234/sqrt(25)
[1] 0.84468
```

Interpretation

Cohen's *d* for the reading test results is equal to 0.844676. To interpret this effect size, we can follow Cohen's recommendations, which are summarised in Table 9.3. However, these recommendations should be seen only as a frame of reference when no other basis is available.

Table 9.3 Interpretation of Cohen's *d*

Cohen's *d*	Interpretation
$0.00 \leq d < 0.20$	negligible
$0.20 \leq d < 0.50$	small
$0.50 \leq d < 0.80$	medium
0.80 or more	large

Our result indicates a large effect size, supporting our previous finding of statistical significance of the difference between the sample mean score and the population mean. Because the sign of Cohen's *d* is positive, it indicates that our sample mean is larger than the population mean and its value of 0.84 also indicates that the sample mean is 0.84 standard deviations higher than the population mean.

9.2.3 Sign test

The sign test is used for samples smaller than 30 of interval data which are not normally distributed. This test compares the median of a sample with a population median, instead of the mean, because the median is a better measure for skewed distribution. It is also used when the population median is known. If the sample is no different from the population, half of the observations in the sample should lie above the population median and half below it. If the sample is entirely different from the population, the proportions of observations above the median will be higher or lower than half of the total observations.

Example 9.3 Computing the sign test

Data file: Ex9_3.csv

The salaries of 20 primary school teachers from a large city in the south of England are shown in Table 9.4. The median salary of primary and nursery professionals in 2018 in the UK was £35,767 (source: Office for National Statistics, 2018), and this represents the population median. Are the salaries of our sample significantly different from the population median?

Table 9.4   Primary school teachers' salaries for schools in a city in the south of England

Salaries (£)	
35,500	34,900
35,400	36,600
34,700	34,200
36,200	34,800
35,500	38,000
35,900	33,300
39,500	34,800
37,000	34,000
35,500	35,100
33,900	34,200

1.   We consider the following null and alternative hypotheses which are written in terms of the proportion of observations about the median:

H_0 : The salaries of primary school teachers from a city in the south of England come from a population with half of the observations above £35,767.

H_1: The salaries of primary school teachers from a city in the south of England do not come from a population with half of the observations above £35,767.

2.   The confidence level is set to 95%, that is, $\alpha = 0.05$.

3. Also, we checked the normality of data by creating a box and whisker plot using the function `boxplot()` (Figure 9.2), which shows that our data is skewed and has an outlier. If we use the `skewness()` function from the moments library to compute the skewness, the results is 1.12, which indicates highly skewed data (see Section 5.7).

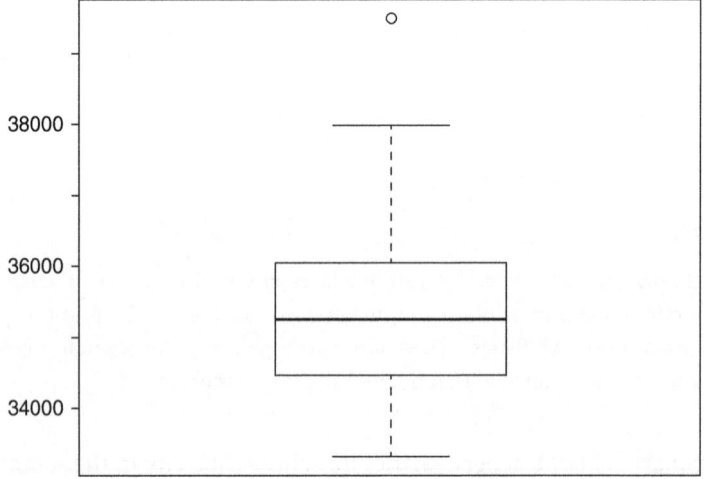

Figure 9.2 Checking the distribution of the primary school teacher salary data

Computing the two-tailed sign test in R

Install the `BSDA` package which contains the function `SIGN.test()`:

```
install.packages("BSDA")
library(BSDA)
```

Upload the file Ex9_3.csv into R and then compute the sign test (two-tailed) for a median equal to £35,767:

```
SIGN.test(Ex9_3$Salaries,md=35767)
```

where *Ex9_3$Salaries* is the numeric vector and *md=35767* represents the value of the population median specified by the null hypothesis.

The results are displayed below:

```
    One-sample Sign-Test
data: TeachersSalaries$Salaries
s = 6, p-value = 0.1153
alternative hypothesis: true median is not equal to 35767
```

```
95 percent confidence interval:
 34711.65 35853.41
sample estimates:
median of x
      35250
Achieved and Interpolated Confidence Intervals:
                   Conf.Level   L.E.pt   U.E.pt
Lower Achieved CI     0.8847 34800.00 35500.00
Interpolated CI       0.9500 34711.65 35853.41
Upper Achieved CI     0.9586 34700.00 35900.00
```

By default, the SIGN.test() function is set for a two-tailed test. If we want to carry out a one-tailed test, then we can add a third argument, *alternative= "greater"* or *alternative= "less"*, specifying the alternative hypothesis (e.g. H_1 : The median salaries of primary school teachers from a city in the south of England is less than £35,767).

Computing the one-tailed sign test in R

```
SIGN.test(Ex9_3$Salaries,md=35767, alternative = "less")
       One-sample Sign-Test
data: TeachersSalaries$Salaries
s = 6, p-value = 0.05766
alternative hypothesis: true median is less than 35767
95 percent confidence interval:
      -Inf 35582.88
sample estimates:
median of x
      35250
```

By default, the confidence level is set to 95%. To change the value of the confidence level, a fourth argument must be added; for example, to change the confidence level to 99%, add the argument *conf. level = 0.99*.

Because the *p*-values in both cases (0.1153 for a two-tailed test and 0.5766 for one-tailed) are greater than 0.05, we reject the null hypothesis and accept the alternative hypotheses: for the two-tailed test, the sample median is not equal to the population median; for the one-tailed test, the sample median is less than the population median. The median of teachers' salaries from our sample is significantly different from the population median. An essential aspect of the sign test that we must take into consideration when interpreting the results is that the test only considers whether the observation is above or below the median and not its actual value.

9●3 One-sample statistical tests for ordinal data

9.3.1 Wilcoxon signed-rank test

The one-sample Wilcoxon signed-rank test is the first nonparametric test developed to test a difference between a sample and a population median, and it will tell us whether the median of a sample is equal to a known value. Because the test takes into consideration the ranked positions of individual scores, it is suitable for ordinal data.

Example 9.4 Computing the one-sample Wilcoxon signed-rank test for ordinal data

Data file: Ex9_4.csv

A university lecturer is interested in students' perceptions regarding the difficulty of the online statistics resources developed for their statistics course. He set up a four-point Likert item on Mentimeter for undergraduate students to answer the following question:

How difficult do you find the online statistical resources?

1. *Very difficult*
2. *Somewhat difficult*
3. *Somewhat easy*
4. *Very easy*

The answers are displayed in Table 9.5, and the raw data is saved under the file name Ex9_4.csv.

Table 9.5 Results of the survey

Likert scale	Very difficult	Somewhat difficult	Somewhat easy	Very easy
Number of answers	9	12	20	11

Because these answers are based on a sample, we would like to know how these results would be in the population. To find out, we use the Wilcoxon signed-rank test, which requires the following steps:

1. Define the null and alternative hypotheses:
    If we plan to use a two-tailed test, then the null and alternative hypotheses are written as:

    $H_0 : m = 2.5$
    $H_1 : m \neq 2.5$

to find out if the median in the population is significantly different from 2.5, which is the score in the middle.

If we want to use a one-tailed test, the null and alternative hypotheses will be either:

$H_0 : m \leq 2.5$
$H_1 : m > 2.5$

or

$H_0 : m \geq 2.5$
$H_1 : m < 2.5$

2. Specify the significance level: $\alpha = 0.05$ (or 95% confidence).
3. Perform the one-sample Wilcoxon signed-rank test using the `wilcox.test()` function in R.

Computing the one-sample Wilcoxon signed-rank test in R

Download the data file Ex9_4.csv and upload the file to R.

Compute the frequency for each category using the function `table()`:

```
SR<-table(Ex9_4$Scores)
```

Display the results:

```
SR
 1  2  3  4
 9 12 20 11
```

Out of 52 students, 12 think that the statistical resources are somewhat difficult, and 20 found the resources somewhat easy.

Compute the one-sample Wilcoxon signed-rank test using the function `wilcox.test()`:

```
wilcox.test(Ex9_4$Scores,mu=2.5)
Wilcoxon signed-rank test with continuity
correction
data: Ex9_4$Scores
V = 797.5, p-value = 0.3077
alternative hypothesis: true location is not equal to 2.5
```

where the first argument represents the data, and the second one represents the mean. By default, the significance level is set to 0.05, and the test is two-tailed.

Interpretation

The one-sample Wilcoxon signed-rank test for ordinal data indicates that there is no difference between the hypothesised median (2.5) and the sample median because the *p*-value of 0.3077 is statistically higher than the significance level and the null hypothesis is not rejected.

The *V*-statistic (*V* = 797.5) does not have a direct interpretation; it is only the sum of signed ranks. We can only say that the larger the *V*-value, the larger the difference between the sample and the population median.

Because the median is based on sample data and not on the population, it is better to estimate the population median by using the confidence interval, which provides a rank of possible values for the population median. To find out the confidence interval, we use the same function `wilcox. test()` and, in addition, we add two more arguments, *conf.int=* and *conf.level=*.

Finding the confidence interval

```
wilcox.test(Ex9_4$Scores,mu=2.5, conf.int = TRUE, conf.level = 0.95)
        Wilcoxon signed-rank test with continuity
        correction
data: Ex9_4$Scores
V = 797.5, p-value = 0.3077
alternative hypothesis: true location is not equal to 2.5
95 percent confidence interval:
 2.499967 2.999914
sample estimates:
(pseudo)median
       2.500055
```

The lower value of the confidence interval (2.499997) defines the value that the population median is likely to be greater than.

 **4** One-sample statistical tests for nominal data

9.4.1 Binomial test

The binomial test is used to determine if the proportion of a nominal variable in one or two categories is different from a specified amount (0.5 is the most common value used for the proportions).

Example 9.5 Science or sports club?

Data file: Ex9_5.csv

A Year 5 teacher asked all the children in his class to choose whether they would like to attend either a science club or a sports club after school. We want to find out if the proportion of children who selected a science club is different from the proportion of children who selected a sports club. The results are displayed in Table 9.6. In this data set, the 'Clubs' variable is a nominal variable with two categories: the science club (code 1) and the sports club (code 2).

Table 9.6 Pupils' selection of after school club (science = 1, sports = 2)

Clubs			
1	2	2	1
1	2	2	2
2	1	2	2
2	2	2	2
2	2	2	2
2	2	2	2
1	2	2	2
1	2	1	2
2	1	2	1
2	2	1	2

Hypothesis testing requires the following steps:

1. Formulate the null and alternative hypotheses:

$$H_0: P=0.5$$
$$H_1: P \neq 0.5$$

where P is the proportion (or frequency) of children who selected a science club.

2. Determine if the hypothesis is one- or two-tailed. In our example, because the null hypothesis is written with an equal sign, it is a two-tailed hypothesis.
3. Specify the significance level: $\alpha = 0.05$ (or 95% confidence).
4. Perform the binomial test using the `binom.test()` function in R.

Computing the binomial one–sample test in R

Download the data file Ex9_5.csv and upload the file to R.

Compute the frequency for each category using the function `table()`:

```
freq<-table(Ex9_5$Clubs)
```

Display the results:

```
freq
 1  2
10 30
```

(Continued)

We see that 10 children selected a science club and 30 selected a sports club.

Compute the binomial test using the function `binom.test()`:

```
binom.test(10,40, p=0.5)
        Exact binomial test
data: 10 and 40
number of successes = 10, number of trials = 40, p-value = 0.002221
alternative hypothesis: true probability of success is not equal to 0.5
95 percent confidence interval:
 0.1269148 0.4119620
sample estimates:
probability of success
                0.25
```

where the first argument represents the frequencies for the first category, the second argument represents the total number of possible selections, and p is the hypothesised probability of success. The confidence level is 0.05 and is set by default for this function.

Interpretation

Because the p-value is 0.002221, which is lower than the confidence level of 0.05, we reject the null hypothesis and conclude that the two categories are significantly different from the specified value, which in our case is 0.5 (or 50%).

If we want to find out how much each of these two categories (sports club and science club) was below and above our specified value, we calculate the *effect size* using *Cohen's g coefficient*.

The effect size for one-sample binomial test (Cohen's *g*)

Install and load the package "foreign":

```
install.packages("foreign")
library(foreign)
```

Calculate the ratio of the frequencies for each category and save it as a vector, which is named 'prop':

```
prop<-freq/sum(freq)
prop
    1    2
 0.25 0.75
```

Compute the effect size, the Cohen's *g* coefficient if *p* = 0.5:

```
CohenG<-unname(prop[1]-0.5)
CohenG
[1] -0.25
```

Interpretation

Cohen's *g* can be used as an effect size measure for a one-sample binomial test if the expected proportions are 0.5 for each of the two categories. Each of the categories, the science club and the sports club, was 25% below or above 0.5.

9.4.2 Pearson chi-squared goodness-of-fit test (χ^2)

The Pearson chi-squared test, also called the goodness-of-fit test, is a nonparametric test which is suitable to use if a set of sample data represents the data we would expect to find in the actual population for a nominal variable with more than one category. In other words, the χ^2 test can be used to test if sample data collected from a nominal variable with two or more categories, for example the 'marital status' variable with the categories single, married, widowed, divorced, separated and registered partnership, fits a distribution from a particular population. The χ^2 test compares the observed frequencies for each category with a hypothesised set of frequencies for each category.

The test statistic is a chi-squared random variable (χ^2) defined by the following formula:

$$\chi^2 = \sum_i \frac{(O_i - E_i)^2}{E_i}$$

where O_i is the observed frequency count for the *i*th category of the nominal variable, and E_i is the expected frequency count for the *i*th category of the nominal variable.

The minimum requirements for this test are:

- The frequencies must be counts, rather than percentages or ratios. If we have proportions, the observed frequency counts (O_i) at each level of the categorical variable will be:

  O_i = *sample size × observed proportion*

- The data categories must be discrete.
- The expected frequencies must be different from zero.
- There should not be an expected frequency of less than 5 in more than 20 per cent of the categories.

Chi-squared testing does not provide any insight into the degree of difference between each category of the nominal variable, meaning that we are not able to compare the χ^2 statistics for each category, to see if one is greater or less than the other.

Example 9.6 Progression of children to A-level Science

Data file Ex9_6.csv

Suppose a head teacher would like to monitor and evaluate the progression of Year 11 children to A-level science. He randomly selected 40 children and asked them which one of the following subjects they might consider for their A-level exams: physics, biology or chemistry. In this case, then, we have one nominal variable, 'A-level subjects', with three categories: physics, biology, chemistry. The observed proportions and frequencies for each category are displayed in Table 9.7, and the observed frequency for each category is calculated by multiplying the sample size by the observed proportion. The observed counts tell us the observed frequencies the head teacher found out after interviewing all 40 children.

Table 9.7 The observed frequencies for each category of the nominal variable

Categories	Observed proportions	Observed frequencies (Counts)
Physics	0.20	$O_1 = 40 \times 0.20 = 8$
Biology	0.60	$O_2 = 40 \times 0.60 = 24$
Chemistry	0.20	$O_3 = 40 \times 0.20 = 8$

We will perform the following steps in the hypothesis testing:

1. Formulate the hypotheses:

   H_0 : There is no difference between the observed and expected frequencies.
   H_1: There is a difference between the observed and expected frequencies.

2. Specify the significance level: $\alpha = 0.05$ (or 95% confidence).
3. Calculate the degrees of freedom:

We had three categories, so there are $3 - 1 = 2$ degrees of freedom. This will determine our critical value later, which is an important value to know when we look at the chi-squared test table.

4. Calculate the χ^2 statistic:

For the χ^2 test, we need to calculate a table of expected values (E). Suppose that the teacher expects that 13 children will choose physics, 14 biology and 13 chemistry for their future A-level exams (Table 9.8).

Table 9.8 Step-by-step calculation of the χ^2 value

Categories	Observed frequencies (O)	Expected frequencies (E)	O - E	$(O - E)^2$	$(O - E)^2/E$
Physics	8	13	-5	25	25/13=1.92
Biology	24	14	10	100	100/14=7.14
Chemistry	8	13	-5	25	25/13=1.92
Total					= 10.98

Computing the χ^2 statistic in R

The R function `chisq.test()` can be used as follows:

```
chisq.test(x, p)
```

where *x* is a numeric vector (i.e. the observed frequencies) and *p* is a vector of probabilities of the same length as *x*.

Create the numeric vector 'observed' for the observed frequencies and the *p*-vector 'p' of probabilities for the expected frequencies:

```
observed<-c(8,24,8)
p<-c(13/40, 14/40, 13/40)
```

Run the test:

```
chisq.test(observed, p=c(13/40,14/40,13/40))
        Chi-squared test for given probabilities
data: observed
X-squared = 10.989, df = 2, p-value = 0.004109
```

If we use the raw data (data file Ex9_6.csv) which is displayed in Table 9.9, a table of frequencies must be created before running the test using the function `table()`:

```
myfreq<-table(Ex9_6$Subjects)
myfreq
   Biology Chemistry Physics
        24         8       8
```

Table 9.9   Raw data

Subjects			
Physics	Biology	Biology	Biology
Physics	Biology	Biology	Biology
Physics	Biology	Biology	Chemistry
Physics	Biology	Biology	Chemistry
Physics	Biology	Biology	Chemistry
Physics	Biology	Biology	Chemistry
Physics	Biology	Biology	Chemistry
Physics	Biology	Biology	Chemistry
Biology	Biology	Biology	Chemistry
Biology	Biology	Biology	Chemistry

(Continued)

To compute the chi-squared test using the table of frequencies, the first argument of the function `chisq.test()` will be the table of frequencies, saved as an object under the name `myfreq`:

```
chisq.test(myfreq, p=c(14/40,13/40,13/40))
        Chi-squared test for given probabilities
data: myfreq
X-squared = 10.989, df = 2, p-value = 0.004109
```

Interpretation

When reporting a one-sample chi-squared test, the x^2 statistic and *p*-value are reported as:

$$\chi^2(2) = 10.989, p = 0.004109$$

The *p*-value of the test is 0.004109, which is lower than the significance level $\alpha = 0.05$, and we reject the null hypothesis and conclude that the observed frequencies are significantly different from the expected frequencies.

The x^2 statistic indicates how significant the difference is between the observed and expected values; for example, if it is a large number, the difference widens. Also, the greater the number of categories in the variables, the larger the chi-squared statistic should be. Plotting the observed values alongside the expected values for each category in a barplot is a useful method to determine whether there is a difference in a particular category.

Formulas

z-score for a sample mean

$$z = \frac{\bar{x} - \mu_0}{s/\sqrt{n}}$$

where $\bar{x}$ is the sample mean, μ_0 is the population mean, s is the sample standard deviation, and n is the sample size.

z-score for a sample proportion

$$z = \frac{p - \pi_0}{\sqrt{\pi_0(1 - \pi_0)/n}}$$

where p is the sample proportion, π_0 is the population proportion, and n is the sample size.

t-value

$$t = \frac{\bar{x} - \mu}{SE}$$

where $\bar{x}$ is the sample mean, μ is the population mean, and SE is the standard error of the mean:

$$SE = \frac{s}{\sqrt{n}}$$

Cohen's d measure of effect size

$$d = \frac{\bar{x} - \mu}{s} \text{ or } d = \frac{t}{\sqrt{n}}$$

where s is the sample standard deviation and t is the t-statistic.

Exercises

9.1 According to the Child Poverty Action Group in 2019, in the UK the mean weekly cost of living per week in 2018 for a lone parent with at least one dependent child of 17 months old was £157.11. A researcher interviewed 17 lone parents at a local nursery and found out that they spent on average £149 per week for one child of 17 months old, with a standard deviation of £33. Is there enough evidence at the 5% significance level that the group of lone parents at the local nursery is different from the national average?

9.2 List all the essential conditions a researcher must take into consideration for selecting a statistical test for one sample.

9.3 What is the difference between the null and alternative hypotheses?

9.4 Which of the two types of hypothesis is tested using statistical inference?

9.5 Why is the effect size vital to compute alongside the t-statistic? Give examples of effect size measures.

9.6. A group of students would like to run for the second time an annual sponsored 'Bake for Students' charity event. Last year the median amount raised per student was £60. This year they would like to raise more money for the charity, and they tested their bakery products at 15 farmers' markets in the local area. The results are displayed in Table 9.10. Use a sign test to find out if the amount of money raised by the group of students has changed significantly since their first charity event.

Table 9.10 Money raised by a group of students at 15 farmers' markets for their bakery products (£)

23	38	101
52	68	61
73	69	65
45	76	59
100	50	58

Further reading

Cohen, J. (1988) *Statistical power analysis for the behavioral sciences* (2nd ed.). Hillsdale, NJ: Lawrence Erlbaum Associates.

This book discusses the use of the *t*-test for means, the sign test, and the chi-squared tests for goodness of fit and contingency tables. The updated content is well suited for researchers interested in analysing quantitative data in the social and behavioural sciences.

Fogarty, B. (2019) *Quantitative social science data with R*. London: Sage.

In Chapter 9, the author introduces the key concepts of hypothesis testing and statistical significance, and gives examples of hypothesis testing, for example through using the Wilcoxon rank-sum test.

Terrell, S. R. (2012) *Statistics translated*: *A step-by-step guide to analyzing and interpreting data*. New York: Guilford Press.

Chapter 6 is dedicated to the one-sample *t*-test, alongside a lot of examples and the six-step process to ensure we know when and how to use the test.

10

Differences between two independent or dependent samples

━━━━━━━ **Chapter Objectives** ━━━━━━━

In this chapter, we will:

- distinguish between dependent (matched or paired) and independent (unmatched or unpaired) samples
- present the selection criteria for a statistical test for finding the difference between two samples
- compute different tests to test a hypothesis about statistic difference, such as the chi-squared, Mann-Whitney, McNemar and Wilcoxon tests
- report and interpret the results of various two-sample parametric and nonparametric tests.

As we have seen in Chapter 9, the *z*-test or *t*-test is used when we have one sample, and we wish to check whether the sample is likely to come from the population or a different one. However, there are situations when we have more than one sample, and we would like to find the differences between them. In this chapter, we are interested in the differences between two samples. It is crucial to consider whether the two samples are independent or dependent. If we are interested in measuring, for example, the variable 'SAT score' for two different groups, such as boys and girls, then we have two samples which are independent (also referred to as unrelated or unpaired samples). However, if we take a group of boys and we collect the SAT scores on two occasions, for example at the beginning and the end of an intervention programme, we have two dependent groups (matched or paired). Our choice of statistical test, as shown in Table 10.1, is made depending on the type of samples (independent or dependent) and on the scale of measurement of the variable (interval/ratio, ordinal or nominal).

Table 10.1 Selection criteria for a statistical test for finding the difference between two samples

Type of samples	Type of variable			
	Nominal	Ordinal	Interval/ratio	
			parametric	nonparametric
Independent (or unpaired)	chi-squared test	Mann-Whitney test	independent *t*-test	Mann-Whitney test
Dependent (or paired)	McNemar test	Wilcoxon signed-ranked test	paired *t*-test	Wilcoxon signed-rank test

10●1 Differences between two independent samples

Several inferential statistical techniques have been developed for analysing the difference between two independent samples. In this section, we demonstrate how to use three statistical tests: the Mann–Whitney test, the independent *t*-test and the chi-squared test, which are designed for certain scales of measurement and types of distribution of data. Each test is introduced by an example from the field of education.

10.1.1 Mann–Whitney test (or Wilcoxon rank-sum test)

The Mann–Whitney test, also called the Wilcoxon–Mann–Whitney test or Wilcoxon rank-sum test, was first designed in 1945–1947 for ordinal data collected from two independent samples in which the data can be ranked, and the median was used as the measure of central tendency. If the observations are of interval/ratio type and come from skewed distributions with equal variances or they are of ordinal type, the Mann–Whitney test is the right test to examine the differences between two independent samples. The Mann–Whitney test is often described as a nonparametric analogue of the independent t-test when the assumptions of the normal distribution of interval data is not satisfied. One of the advantages of this test is that it is suitable for small as well as large sample sizes. However, with samples smaller than 20 cases, a continuity correction should be used, and most statistical software will apply such a correction, including R. In addition, this test has a great feature regarding the size of the two independent samples, and this is that the samples do not have to be of the same size. However, in terms of statistical power (the ability to avoid Type II error), the Mann–Whitney test is described as a less powerful test than its parametric counterpart.

Example 10.1 Finding the difference between two unpaired groups (ordinal data)

Data file: Ex10_1.csv

A growth mindset intervention is being implemented in 20 secondary schools in an urban area in England. A marketing company wishes to find the level of agreement among teachers on the effectiveness of the intervention. It asks teachers for their level of agreement with 20 statements about the intervention, each on a five-point Likert scale (1 = strongly disagree, 2 = disagree, 3 = neutral, 4 = agree, 5 = strongly agree). The scores across the statements are summed for each teacher, and the results are shown in Table 10.2. Notice that there are unequal numbers of responses when these are separated into two groups according to the gender of the teachers.

To determine whether the difference between the median agreement score of male and female teachers is statistically ($\alpha = 0.05$) significant or not, the Mann–Whitney test is applied. This works with equal or unequal sample sizes.

Table 10.2 Total agreement scores by gender

Female (n = 19)				Male (n = 15)		
69	60	83	80	63	73	97
56	76	71	56	76	88	73
64	73	55	85	65	55	57
59	95	85	84	94	78	84
85	86	76		58	83	54

The null and alternative hypotheses are:

H_0 : There is no difference in agreement between male and female teachers.

H_1 : There is a difference in agreement between male and female teachers.

The alternative hypothesis is non-directional (two-tailed).

Computing the Mann–Whitney test in R (ordinal level of measurement)

Upload the Ex10_1.csv data file into R and name it 'GrowthMindset':

```
GrowthMindset <- read.csv(file.choose())
```

```
GrowthMindset
```

	Female	Male
1	69	63
2	56	76
3	64	65
4	59	94
5	85	58
6	60	73
7	76	88
8	73	55
9	95	78
10	86	83
11	83	97
12	71	73
13	55	57
14	85	84
15	76	54
16	80	NA
17	56	NA
18	85	NA
19	84	NA

Create a simple multi-panelled plot (Figure 10.1) using the function `par(mfrow())`:

```
par(mfrow = c(1, 2))
```

Visualise the GrowthMindset data set using two boxplots:

```
boxplot(GrowthMindset$Female, xlab="Female")
boxplot(GrowthMindset$Male, xlab="Male")
```

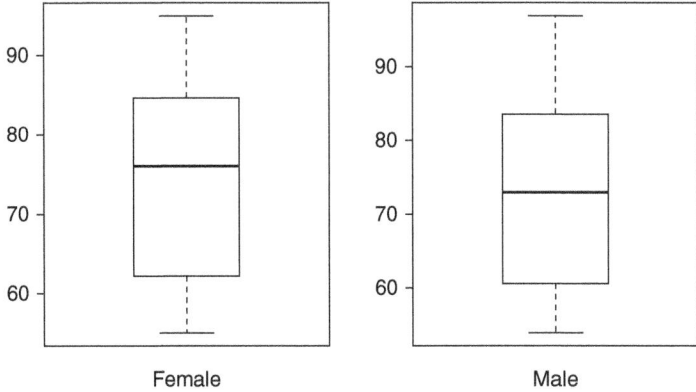

Figure 10.1 Agreement scores by group

Calculate the median for both groups using the function `median()`. The argument `na.rm` was set to TRUE to ignore the NA (introduced because we have different samples size):

```
median(GrowthMindset$Male, na.rm=TRUE)

 [1] 73

median(GrowthMindset$Female)

[1] 76
```

Compute the Mann-Whitney test:

```
wilcox.test(GrowthMindset$Female, GrowthMindset$Male)
    Wilcoxon rank-sum test with continuity correction
data: GrowthMindset$Female and GrowthMindset$Male
W = 148.5, p-value = 0.8485
alternative hypothesis: true location shift is not equal to 0
```

Interpretation

In this example, because we have an ordinal variable, it is better to compare the medians because they are less sensitive to outliers and skewness of distributions. The two distributions have similar shape and dispersions, which are shown in Figure 10.1, and, from the calculations, comparable medians for the male and female groups (73 for the male sample and 76 for the female sample). The Mann–Whitney test is effectively a test of differences in medians between the two groups. Our results, from a two-sided test with a p-value = 0.8485, indicate that we should accept the null hypothesis that there is no difference in agreement between male and female teachers regarding the effectiveness of a growth mindset intervention that was being implemented in 20 secondary schools in an urban area in England.

10.1.2 Independent samples *t*-test

The two independent samples *t*-test is often used in experimental and survey methodologies, when, for example, a teacher or a researcher wishes to know which of two teaching strategies is more helpful in improving children's achievements. With the two independent samples *t*-test, the researcher or the teacher is testing the differences between the sample means to estimate the parameters of the unknown population. The *t*-statistic is an estimate of the differences between the population means and it can only be used if the data is measured on an interval scale or level.

The *t*-test is conducted to determine if there are differences between two independent samples and requires the following conditions:

- The data is interval and follows a normal distribution. This assumption can be tested using the Kolmogorov–Smirnov test for a sample of size $n > 100$ or the Shapiro–Wilk test for smaller sample sizes.
- The variances of the two groups are equal (homogeneous). This assumption of homogeneity of variance can be tested using the *F*-test for two independent groups. If there are more than two independent groups, Bartlett's test can be used to test the variance, as long as the data is normally distributed. An alternative to this test is the Fligner–Killeen test, which is a nonparametric test that is less sensitive to the normality of data condition.

Another alternative to the *t*-test is a modification of this test known as the Welch test, which does not assume that both populations have the same variance. Because the standard deviations for the two samples are not the same, the degrees of freedom for this test tend to be smaller than the degrees of freedom for the *t*-test. Thus, a correction to the degrees of freedom is included to adjust the degrees of freedom. However, if we use the Welch test and apply the correction, the *p*-value changes.

Example 10.2 Finding the difference between two unpaired groups (interval data)

Data file Ex10_2.csv

Dog-assisted programmes were introduced in 2001 in a variety of educational settings. A group of researchers conducted quasi-experimental research to find out if there are differences in children's reading skills in group work when interacting with dogs, compared to a control group. Once a week, children in the group work tried the new dog-assisted reading programme with highly structured sessions; the control group was not exposed to the programme. At the end of the programme, the reading ability of the children in both groups was assessed using the York Assessment of Reading for Comprehension: Early Reading and Passage Reading Primary (YARC Primary), which is a one-to-one, diagnostic reading assessment of pupils' reading and comprehension skills from an early age through to the end of secondary school. The YARC scores for the two independent groups are shown in Table 10.3.

Table 10.3 York Assessment of Reading for Comprehension scores for the experimental (dog group work) and control groups

Experimental group			Control group		
107	82	85	69	62	74
97	100	113	84	98	85
83	111	112	67	81	88
94	91	93	83	73	80
123	91	113	79	105	100
89	116	115	55	68	79
65	96	109	78	85	69
112	98	130	98	99	88
92	91	71	90	89	47
92	114	83	82	75	86

Before we compute the independent *t*-test, we must first test the two conditions about the distribution of data and the homogeneity of variances.

Testing for normality

Using the function `shapiro.test()`, we test whether data in the control and experimental groups are normally distributed. Upload the Ex10_2.csv data file into R and name it Ex10_2:

```
Ex10_2 <- read.csv(file.choose())

Ex10_2
    Experimental Control
1            107      69
2             97      84
3             83      67
4             94      83
5            123      79
6             89      55
7             65      78
8            112      98
9             92      90
10            92      82
11            82      62
12           100      98
13           111      81
14            91      73
15            91     105
16           116      68
```

(Continued)

17	96	85
18	98	99
19	91	89
20	114	75
21	85	74
22	113	85
23	112	88
24	93	80
25	113	100
26	115	79
27	109	69
28	130	88
29	71	47
30	83	86

```
shapiro.test(Ex10_2$Control)
   Shapiro-Wilk normality test
data: Ex10_2$Control
W = 0.97649, p-value = 0.7264
shapiro.test(Ex10_2$Experimental)
   Shapiro-Wilk normality test
data: Ex10_2$Experimental
W = 0.97033, p-value = 0.5484
```

Interpretation

In both cases, the p-value is $p > 0.05$, so we accept the null hypothesis that the distributions of scores for the experimental and control groups are normally distributed. The first condition on the distribution of data is fulfilled.

Test for the homogeneity of variances

```
var((Ex10_2$Control))
[1] 177.9126
var((Ex10_2$Experimental))
[1] 232.6851
```

Interpretation

If the two independent groups had the same variance, we would use the t-test. But since they have different variances, we will use Welch's t-test, which computes the difference between the two groups by adding a correction to the degrees of freedom due to an inequality of variances because the estimate of the variance of the difference in means is no longer precisely a chi-squared distribution.

Computing the t-test (interval scale of measurement)

```
t.test(Ex10_2$Control,Ex10_2$Experimental)
   Welch Two Sample t-test
data: Ex10_2$Control and Ex10_2$Experimental
t = -4.9736, df = 56.986, p-value = 6.379e-06
alternative hypothesis: true difference in means is not equal to 0
95 percent confidence interval:
 -25.80824 -10.99176
sample estimates:
mean of x mean of y
 80.53333 98.93333
```

In a situation where the variances are equal, we set to TRUE the argument *var.equal=* in the
`t.test()` function

```
t.test(data, var.equal=TRUE)
```

Interpretation

Since the assumption about the homogeneity of variance is not fulfilled, the Welch t-test, also known as the Welch–Satterthwaite or Welch–Aspin test, is used instead of the t-test. The Welch test is an adaptation of the t-test which includes a correction to the degrees of freedom (df) which increases the test power for samples with unequal variance. Using this test, a non-integer value for the degrees of freedom is obtained ($df = 56.986$), which can be reported as 57. If we run the t-test without taking into consideration the Welch correction, the resulting value for the degrees of freedom is larger ($df = n_1 + n_2 - 2 = 30 + 30 - 2 = 58$), but the power of the test will decrease. In conclusion, at a significance level of 0.05, the dog-assisted programme makes a different impact on the result since the p-value is much less than 0.05 ($p = 0.000006379$) and the null hypothesis is rejected. The difference between the sample mean correct score was –18.40 with a 95 per cent confidence interval from –25.81 to –10.99.

10.1.3 Chi-squared test

The chi-squared (χ^2) test for one sample and nominal data has already been introduced in Section 9.4.2, and there are some similarities and differences when it is used for two independent or unpaired samples. For example, in terms of hypotheses, the chi-squared test for two unpaired samples tests the hypothesis of a difference between the statistics of two samples, rather than between a sample statistic and a population statistic. To compute the chi-squared test, the data (on a nominal scale of measurement) must first be organised as a two-way table, where the frequencies of each category of the nominal data is appropriately displayed. For example, in a 2 × 2 contingency table, in the columns we may represent the independent groups, and in the rows we may represent the nominal categories. The degrees of freedom are determined by reference to the number of rows and columns so that:

$$degrees\ of\ freedom = (number\ of\ columns - 1)(number\ of\ rows - 1)$$

Moreover, df will always be equal to 1 for a 2 × 2 contingency table.

Example 10.3 Finding the difference between two unpaired groups (nominal data)

Data file Ex10_3.csv

Suppose we have carried out a survey of pet preferences (cat or dog) in a sample of 30 male and female children. The results are shown in Table 10.4 which show that there are differences between the two unpaired samples. However, are such differences large enough to be considered significant?

The null and alternative hypotheses are:

H_0: There is no difference in pet preferences between male and female children.
H_1: There is a difference in pet preferences between male and female children.

The significance level is set to 0.05.

Table 10.4 Sample survey of male and female children's pet preferences

	Independent groups	
Pet preferences	Male	Female
Cat	8	11
Dog	7	4

The column variable in the 2 × 2 contingency table shown in Table 10.4 shows the two independent (or unpaired) groups of children and the rows show the frequencies of the response variable by category.

Computing the chi-squared test in R (nominal data)

Upload the Ex10_3.csv data file into R:

```
Ex10_3 <- read.csv(file.choose())
Ex10_3

    Gender Pet
1     Male Dog
2   Female Dog
```

```
3   Female Cat
4   Female Cat
5     Male Cat
6     Male Cat
7   Female Dog
8   Female Dog
9     Male Cat
10  Female Cat
11  Female Cat
12  Female Cat
13    Male Dog
14    Male Cat
15    Male Cat
16  Female Cat
17    Male Cat
18    Male Cat
19  Female Dog
20    Male Cat
21    Male Cat
22    Male Cat
23    Male Dog
24  Female Dog
25  Female Dog
26  Female Cat
27    Male Dog
28    Male Cat
29  Female Dog
30  Female Cat
```

Create a two-way table and save it as an object; let us call it 'tbGP':

```
tbGP<-table(Ex10_3)
```

```
tbGP
```

```
        Pet
Gender  Cat Dog
  Female  8   7
  Male   11   4
```

Compute the chi-squared test using the function `chisq.test()`:

```
chisq.test(tbGP)
    Pearson's chi-squared test with Yates' continuity
    correction
data: tbGP
X-squared = 0.57416, df = 1, p-value = 0.4486
```

Interpretation

Looking at the frequencies presented in Table 10.4, we expect children's preferences for pet dogs or cats to be mainly determined by their sex because we see some differences in these frequencies, for example the female children (just) prefer cats and the male children (strongly) prefer dogs. Using a 0.05 statistical level, and taking into consideration the test's assumption that preferences will be equal (7.5 in all categories), from the p-value of 0.4486 obtained from the chi-squared test, we conclude that there is no difference between the two independent samples, despite the initial assessment that there might be a difference.

10.2 Differences between two dependent samples

For two dependent samples and different levels of measurement, there are statistical tests that are the same as or analogous to those for independent samples. For example, the t-test can be used in both situations, either for dependent or independent samples. For nominal data, the McNemar test for paired samples is analogous to the chi-squared test for independent samples. This section presents tests that are applied for paired samples for different scales of measurement (nominal, ordinal or interval/ratio) and, in the case of interval data, whether the data is normally or non-normally distributed.

10.2.1 Wilcoxon signed-rank test

The first thing to say about the Wilcoxon signed-rank test is that it is not the same test as the Wilcoxon rank-sum test (or Mann–Whitney test), which was presented in Section 10.1.1. The Wilcoxon rank-sum test is used to test the difference between two dependent samples, while the Wilcoxon signed-rank test is used to test the difference between two independent samples. The Wilcoxon signed-rank test is more powerful than the sign test because it uses the information about both the magnitude and direction of the differences between the paired groups, and under certain conditions, for example given an exponential distribution, it is statistically more powerful than the parametric t-test.

The Wilcoxon signed-rank test assumptions are:

- the pairs of observations consist of interval/ratio or ordinal data;
- the data can be ranked, as well as the differences between two measures;
- the distribution of the data is non-normal.

Example 10.4 Finding the difference between two paired groups (non-normally distributed interval data)

Data file Ex10_4.csv

A group of researchers developed a new growth mindset development programme for children aged 10–11 to help them to improve their maths SAT score results. A sample of 100 children was tested before and after the implementation of the programme, and the results of a mock SAT are shown in Table 10.5.

Table 10.5 Maths SAT scores before and after the implementation of a new mindset programme

Pre-test	77	73	58	73	77	65	63	71	73	68
	60	78	62	67	62	68	70	78	91	87
	64	90	58	63	63	78	79	71	62	63
	66	64	66	74	60	62	69	61	69	72
	73	57	59	61	65	59	77	61	65	58
	63	68	63	68	68	61	72	71	64	58
	61	57	64	76	60	76	63	65	80	63
	73	60	62	69	91	67	76	87	72	71
	69	74	63	72	80	63	81	97	69	66
	65	77	61	72	98	63	74	67	91	89
Post-test	90	87	77	81	85	76	73	73	83	84
	49	75	86	77	71	90	78	88	77	89
	91	88	81	92	64	90	70	83	82	90
	74	91	81	88	78	72	85	78	79	82
	82	71	71	75	83	86	90	87	76	77
	76	72	78	56	75	90	91	90	70	89
	72	69	85	85	91	92	91	90	69	78
	89	93	88	82	76	84	83	86	92	88
	91	71	84	53	60	84	64	91	86	88
	73	82	83	81	79	73	65	80	90	79

The null and alternative hypotheses are:

H_0 : There is no difference between the pre- and post-maths SAT scores.
H_1 : There is a difference between the pre- and post-maths SAT scores.

Summary of data and testing for normality

Import the Ex10_4.csv file into R and name it Ex10_4.

To get a summary of the data for both groups, first install and load the `dplyr` package:

```
install.packages("dplyr")
library("dplyr")
group_by(Ex10_4, Groups) %>%
+     summarise(
+         count = n(),
+         median = median(Scores, na.rm = TRUE),
+         IQR = IQR(Scores, na.rm = TRUE)
+     )
```

The results are displayed below:

```
# A tibble: 2 x 4
Groups count median IQR
<fct> <int> <dbl> <dbl>
1 posttest 100 82 13
2 pretest  100 68 11
```

Visualize the data using boxplots

Install and load the `devtools` and `ggpubr` packages and load the `ggpubr` library:

```
install.packages("devtools")
install.packages("ggpubr")
library(ggpubr)
```

Plot the data using boxplots (Figure 10.2):

```
ggboxplot(Ex10_4, x = "Groups", y = "Scores", order = c("pretest",
"posttest"), ylab = "Scores", xlab = "Groups")
```

Interpretation

The summary of our data shows differences between the groups' means and the interquartile ranges. Furthermore, the box and whisker plots (Figure 10.2) for the dependent groups confirm that the scores in each group are not normally distributed.

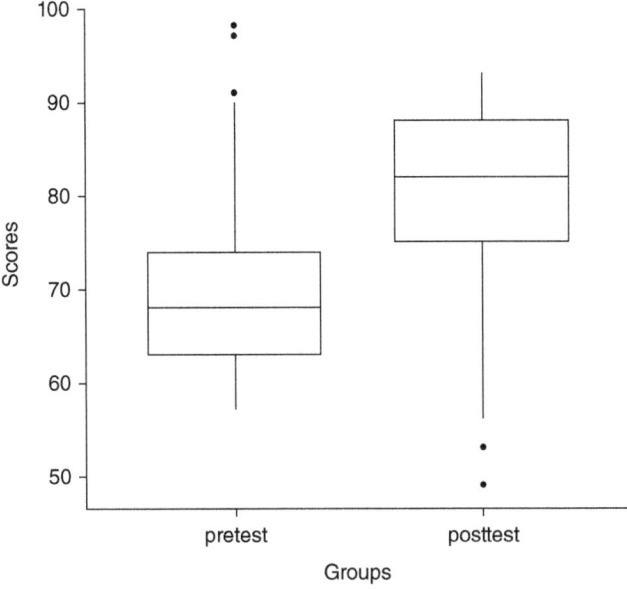

Figure 10.2 Boxplots from maths SAT results before (pre-test) and after (post-test) the implementation of the new growth mindset programme

Computing the Wilcoxon signed-rank test in R

```
wilcox.test(Scores ~ Groups, data = Ex10_4, paired = TRUE)
    Wilcoxon signed-rank test with continuity
    correction
data: Scores by Groups
V = 4428, p-value = 6.021e-11
alternative hypothesis: true location shift is not equal to 0
```

Interpretation

To determine whether the difference between the medians of two dependent groups of interval (not normally distributed) data is statistically ($\alpha = 0.05$) significant or not, the Wilcoxon signed-rank test was applied. The p-value of the test is 0.00000000006, which is much less than the significance level of 0.05. We can conclude that the median maths SAT score after introducing the new growth mindset programme is significantly different from the median maths SAT scores before implementing the programme. The group of researchers believed that the mindset is a factor influencing mathematics learning and performance in school. If the p-value associated with the Wilcoxon signed-rank test had been greater than the significance level, we could not have rejected the null hypothesis and would have concluded that there is no difference between the medians of the two paired groups.

10.2.2 Paired samples *t*-test

A paired *t*-test is often used to analyse the results of a before-and-after experimental or quasi-experimental research design and to test if there is a difference between the means of two dependent groups. Before running the *t*-test, preliminary tests must be carried out to check the following paired *t*-test assumptions:

1. The interval/ratio data is normally distributed. If the sample size is less than 30, then the Shapiro-Wilk normality test can be used; otherwise, the Kolmogorov-Smirnov test is used.
2. The variances between the groups are equal.

Example 10.5 Finding the difference between two paired groups (normally distributed interval data)

Data file: Ex10_5.csv

Suppose that a researcher conducted quasi-experimental research using the same programme as described in Example 10.2, but this time he would like to find out if there are differences in a randomly selected group of children's reading skills before and after interacting with dogs. Once a week, the same group of 30 children tried the new dog-assisted reading programme with highly structured sessions. In this situation, we have two dependent or paired groups. The children's reading ability was tested using the same YARC Primary method before and after introducing the dog-assisted reading programmes. If the results are saved in a data frame format, then the first column, which can be labelled 'Before', will show the YARC results before the experiment, and the second column, which is labelled 'After', will show the YARC results after the experiment.

The null hypothesis can be written as:

$$H_0 : YARC\ mean_{before} = YARC\ mean_{after}$$

For the alternative hypothesis, there are three alternatives:

$$H_1 : YARC\ mean_{before} \neq YARC\ mean_{after}$$

$$H_1 : YARC\ mean_{before} - YARC\ mean_{after} > 0$$

$$H_1 : YARC\ mean_{before} - YARC\ mean_{after} < 0$$

Computing the paired *t*-test in R

Import the Ex10_5.csv file into R and name it Ex10_5.

We use the same function `t.test()` as the one presented in Section 10.2 by adding a logical value, specifying that we want to compute a paired *t*-test, `paired = TRUE`.

```
t.test(Ex10_5$Before,Ex10_5$After, paired=TRUE)
Paired t-test
data:  Ex10_5$Before and Ex10_5$After
t = -7.003, df = 29, p-value = 1.062e-07
alternative hypothesis: true difference in means is not equal to 0
95 percent confidence interval:
 -23.98909 -13.14424
sample estimates:
mean of the differences
            -18.56667
```

Interpretation

Because the observed *p*-value is less than 0.05, we reject the null hypothesis and accept the alternative hypothesis that there is a mean difference in YARC test scores before and after the dog therapy programme was implemented. We are also 95% certain that the true mean difference in the test scores before and after the intervention falls between –23.99 and –13.14, and that the average of the differences between scores is –18.57.

10.2.3 McNemar's test

McNemar's test is used to determine if there are differences between the two dependent samples when the variable is nominal. The outcome for each case in one sample is compared with the outcome for its corresponding pair in the other sample. McNemar's test can only be used for a 2 × 2 contingency table.

Example 10.6 Finding the difference between two paired groups (nominal data)

Data file Ex10_6.csv

A special educational needs coordinator (SENCo) would like to investigate whether newly qualified teachers are prepared and confident to teach inclusively following a new inclusion enhancement programme. The coordinator randomly selected 120 newly qualified teachers from a group of schools maintained by a local education authority, and asked them, before and after the inclusion programme, whether they are more confident and prepared to teach inclusively. Teachers responded before and after the inclusion programme with agreement or disagreement statements about their preparedness to teach inclusively. There are thus four possibilities, which are illustrated in Table 10.6 with the corresponding distribution of responses. For 47 teachers (24 + 23) there is no change in their perception regarding the preparedness to teach inclusively before and after the inclusion programme, however for 73 (50 + 23) teachers there is a change in their perception.

Table 10.6 Teachers' responses before and after the inclusion programme regarding the change in their preparedness to teach inclusively

Before	After	
	Agree	Disagree
Agree	23 (no change)	23 (change)
Disagree	50 (change)	24 (no change)

The null and alternative hypotheses are:

H_0 : The inclusion programme does not change teachers' perceptions about their preparedness to teach inclusively.

H_1 : The inclusion programme does change teachers' perceptions about their preparedness to teach inclusively.

Creating a two-dimensional contingency table for nominal data

If we want to know if the teachers' responses change after the inclusion programme, then we have to create a two-dimensional contingency table using the function `table()`, which is then analysed using the function `mcnemar.test()`.

Import the Ex10_6.csv file into R and name it 'Inclusion':

```
Inclusion <- read.csv(file.choose())
```

Create a two-dimensional contingency table as an object and name it, for example, 'incl':

```
incl<-table(Inclusion$Before, Inclusion$After)
incl

          Agree Disagree
   Agree    23      23
   Disagree 50      24
```

Computing the McNemar test in R

```
mcnemar.test(incl)
   McNemar's chi-squared test with continuity correction
data:  incl
McNemar's chi-squared = 9.2603, df = 1, p-value = 0.002342
```

Interpretation

The McNemar test only considers those pairs for which a change has occurred and analyses whether any change tends to occur in one direction, for example if the newly qualified teachers have changed in their preparedness to teach inclusively after attending the inclusion programme. The *p*-value is less than 0.05 and leads us to reject the null hypothesis. The inclusion programme does affect teachers' perceptions of their preparedness to teach inclusively.

Exercises

10.1 What are the selection criteria for a statistical test for finding the difference between two samples?

10.2 What are the assumptions we must take into consideration when we run a *t*-test for two independent samples?

10.3 Find an example of the *t*-test from the literature and investigate if all the assumptions are met.

10.4 Create in R two samples of 1000 numbers each which are normally distributed using the following function:

```
rnorm(1000)
```

    (a) Plot the histogram for this sample.
    (b) Check if the sample is normally distributed using the appropriate statistical test.
    (c) Which statistical test can be used to check for a difference between samples?
    (d) Compute the statistics for the difference between samples and interpret the results.

10.5 What can be done when the assumption of homogeneity of variance is not met?

Further reading

Argyrous, G. (2014) *Statistics for research: With a guide to SPSS*. London: Sage.

This book concentrates on the most popular inferential statistical tests, and the entire book is devoted to two-sample tests for independent or dependent samples, taking into consideration different levels of measurement or variables. The interpretation of statistical results is accompanied by a 'five-step hypothesis testing procedure' and by explanations of how to report findings.

Nussbaum, M. (2015) *Categorical and nonparametric data analysis: Choosing the best statistical technique*. New York: Routledge.

In Chapter 6 of this book, the meaning of the term 'nonparametric' is discussed first, and then the author addresses how to conduct nonparametric statistical tests when one or more of the variables are ordinal.

Redelmeier, D. (2017) A simple method for analyzing matched designs with double controls: McNemar's test can be extended. *Journal of Clinical Epidemiology*, 81, 51–55.

This article presents a new approach to McNemar's test for matched studies, where precisely two controls are linked to each case when evaluating binary predictors and outcomes.

11

Differences between more than two independent samples

Chapter Objectives

In this chapter, we will:

- introduce various statistical tests to analyse the difference between more than two independent samples for different scales of measurement – one-way and two-way ANOVA, and Kruskal-Wallis tests
- assess various assumptions for these statistical tests
- compute the corresponding statistical tests using R
- understand how the analysis of these tests is reported and interpreted.

Depending on the type of samples (dependent or independent), we consider various types of statistical tests, as shown in Table 11.1, which are also differentiated depending on the scale of measurement (interval/ratio, ordinal or nominal) and several other factors. Special terminology is used with ANOVA when we refer to the independent variable. The word *factor* is used instead of the term *independent variable,* and the term *level* is used for different values of the factor, which is synonymous with conditions or groups within each factor. We talk about 'one factor' when we have one independent variable and one dependent variable, and 'two factors' when we have two independent variables and one dependent variable.

Table 11.1 Selection criteria for a statistical test for finding the difference between more than two independent samples

Samples type	Data type			
	Nominal	**Ordinal**	**Interval/ratio**	
			One factor	**Two factors**
Statistical test	$n \times m$ chi-squared test	Kruskal-Wallis ANOVA test	One-way ANOVA F- test	Two-way ANOVA test

In this chapter, we will present the manual and computational calculations in R for the differences between more than two independent samples when the levels of measurement are interval or ordinal.

 ## 11.1 The analysis of variance (ANOVA)

A statistical test closely related to the *t*-test is the *analysis of variance* (ANOVA), which is used to infer whether there are *differences* between two or more independent groups' values when there are one or more independent variables and one dependent variable, by analysing the overall variance in the samples. There are different forms of this test, depending on the number of independent variables we have:

- *One-way ANOVA*, also known as *single-factor ANOVA*, is applied if we have one independent variable and one dependent variable. Rather than finding the difference between two means as in a *t*-test, in one-way ANOVA we find the average difference between the groups' means relative to the average amount of variation within each group.
- *Two-way ANOVA*, known as *two-factor ANOVA*, is used if we have two independent variables and one dependent variable.
- *Three-way ANOVA* is used when we have three independent variables and one dependent variable.
- *n*-way ANOVA is used when we have *n* independent variables and one dependent variable.

The analysis of the overall variance depends on comparing the two components of the variability:

- The *within*-samples variance, which indicates the deviation of each data value within a sample from the corresponding sample mean. This kind of variability may come from individual differences or experimental error. The within-sample variance measures uncontrolled and unexplained variability, and it is called the *error term* or *residual*.
- The *between*-samples variance, which indicates how much each sample mean deviates from the overall mean of all samples. This kind of variability may come from the groups' conditions, individual differences or experimental error. The *between*-samples variance contains the same variability of the error term plus the variability from groups' conditions.

Once these two components of total variance are calculated, they are used in calculating the ANOVA test statistic, the mean score for each group, and the *p*-values. However, the *p*-values only tell us that there is some significant difference between groups, and not which of the groups differ from each other. Performing a post-hoc analysis will help us to find out more information about the differences between groups.

Prior to the ANOVA test, we need to test the following assumptions:

1. The dependent variable should be of interval/ratio type.
2. The dependent variable is normally distributed within each group. The Shapiro–Wilk test is commonly used to test the normality of data if the sample size is less than 50, or D'Agostino's modification is used instead for larger samples.
3. The variance in the dependent variable is equal in each of the samples being compared; in other words, the samples have similar dispersion. The homogeneity of variance within each group is tested using Levene's test.
4. The groups are independent, which is ensured by employing random assignment to groups (random sampling). Mauchly's test of sphericity is commonly employed to test this assumption. Sphericity appears when participants in the study are exposed to all levels of an independent variable, and its effects can persist and impact the response to subsequent interventions.
5. There are no outliers.

There are often situations in educational research when normality and the homogeneity of equal variance (assumptions 2 and 3) are violated, which is problematic for running ANOVA tests. However, the ANOVA test can handle moderate violations of these assumptions if there is a large enough sample size or by deleting the outliers from the data. Removal of outliers needs to be justified and explained.

After we run the ANOVA test, it is essential to do an analysis of residuals and evaluate the following assumptions about them:

- The residuals are normally distributed. If this assumption is not met, the dependent variable can be transformed using bootstrapping so that they follow a normal distribution. Alternatively, we can use a nonparametric test, the Kruskal-Wallis test.
- The variances of the residuals of each group need to be roughly equal. If this homoscedasticity assumption is not fulfilled, one solution is to use Welch's ANOVA test which does not assume unequal variances.

Once the two components of total variance are calculated, they are used in calculating the ANOVA test statistic, which is called the *F-ratio* or *F-score* and is calculated as the ratio between the mean squares between groups and the mean squares within groups:

$$F = \frac{mean\ squares\ between\ groups}{mean\ squares\ within\ groups} = \frac{explained\ variance}{unexplained\ variance}$$

The mean squares (MS) are the average deviations of individual scores from their respective mean and are calculated by dividing the sum of squares (SS) by their corresponding degree of freedom (*df*). There are two forms of the sum of squares. The first form is called the *between-groups sum of squares* (SS_b) and it is the sum of all squared differences between each score and the mean of all scores in all groups (called the grand mean). The second form is called *within-groups sum of squares* (SS_w) which is the sum of squared differences between the individual data scores and their respective group means. There are also two types of mean squares – the *mean squares between groups* (MS_b) which indirectly measure the differences in group means:

$$MS_b = \frac{SS_b}{df_b}$$

and the *mean squares within groups* (MS_w) which represent the unexplained variance due to the effect of the independent variable on the dependent variable (also called 'error variance'):

$$MS_w = \frac{SS_w}{df_w}$$

The ratio between the two:

$$F = \frac{MS_b}{MS_w}$$

provides our *F*-score, which is always positive. When the numerator and the denominator are the same, $F = 1$, which means that the variance between the groups is the same as the variance within groups. If $F > 1$, then the sum of squares between groups is larger than the sum of squares within groups, which means that the group means diverge from each other and there is more variance between group scores in relation to the grand mean. If there is more variation within group means, quantified by the sum of squares within means, this will reduce the *F*-score. If $F > 1$, we look at a set of *F*-distributions, depending upon the degrees of freedom in our samples, to see if the difference between the groups is statistically significant. The *p*-value yielded by the ANOVA is influenced by the sample size, and the number of groups tested, and larger *F*-scores equate to lower *p*-values.

11 2 One-way ANOVA

Example 11.1 Testing the differences between more than two independent samples with one dependent and one independent variable

Data file: Ex11_1.csv

A researcher wanted to examine whether augmented reality teaching is more effective for medical students than the virtual reality and simulation-assisted teaching methods currently used. He randomly selected 45 medical students and divided them into three groups, corresponding to each form of e-learning. All participants in each group completed a knowledge and skill test at the end of the programme; the maximum possible score is 45. The test results are displayed in Table 11.2. The independent variable is the e-learning strategy (the factor) with multiple groups or categories (levels: augmented, virtual and simulation), while the dependent variable is the skill test score. Using one-way ANOVA, we will compare the means of the test scores (the dependent variable) for the three types of e-learning (the independent variable), and we will check if the differences are statistically significant.

Table 11.2 The knowledge and skill test results for three groups exposed to different types of e-learning: augmented, virtual reality and simulation assisted

TypesLearning	Scores	TypesLearning	Scores	TypesLearning	Scores
Augmented	33	Virtual	34	Simulation	34
Augmented	36	Virtual	32	Simulation	33
Augmented	33	Virtual	35	Simulation	33
Augmented	38	Virtual	28	Simulation	37
Augmented	36	Virtual	31	Simulation	37
Augmented	30	Virtual	31	Simulation	35
Augmented	35	Virtual	35	Simulation	35
Augmented	32	Virtual	34	Simulation	33

(Continued)

Table 11.2 (Continued)

TypesLearning	Scores	TypesLearning	Scores	TypesLearning	Scores
Augmented	34	Virtual	33	Simulation	30
Augmented	36	Virtual	31	Simulation	36
Augmented	36	Virtual	28	Simulation	35
Augmented	35	Virtual	29	Simulation	36
Augmented	38	Virtual	33	Simulation	38
Augmented	31	Virtual	32	Simulation	32
Augmented	33	Virtual	31	Simulation	33

11.2.1 Calculating one-way ANOVA by hand

1. Formulate the null and alternative hypotheses:

$H_0 : mean_{Augmented} = mean_{Virtual} = mean_{Simulation}$

$H_1 : mean_{Augmented} \neq mean_{Virtual} \neq mean_{Simulation}$

2. Determine the degrees of freedom between and within groups:

$$df_b = number\ of\ groups - 1 = 3 - 1 = 2$$

$$df_w = df_1 + df_2 + df_3 = (n_1 - 1) + (n_2 - 1) + (n_3 - 1)$$

where n_1, n_2 and n_3 are the sizes of each group. In our example:

$$df_w = df_{Augmented} + df_{Virtual} + df_{Simulation} = (15 - 1) + (15 - 1) + (15 - 1)$$

$$= 14 + 14 + 14 = 42$$

3. Calculate the mean of each group:

$$mean_{Augmented} = \frac{33 + 36 + ... + 33}{15} = 34.4$$

$$mean_{Virtual} = \frac{34 + 32 + ... + 31}{15} = 31.8$$

$$mean_{simulation} = \frac{34 + 33 + ... + 33}{15} = 34.46667$$

4. Compute the grand mean (G) which is the sum of all the individual group means, divided by the total number of groups:

$$G = \frac{mean_{Augmented} + mean_{Virtual} + mean_{Simulation}}{3} = 33.56$$

5. Calculate the sum of squared deviations between groups (SS_b):

$$SS_b = n_1 (mean_{Augmented} - G)^2 + n_2 (mean_{Virtual} - G)^2 + n_3 (mean_{Simulation} - G)^2$$

$$= 15 \times [(mean_{Augmented} - G)^2 + (mean_{Virtual} - G)^2 \times (mean_{Simulation} - G)^2]$$

$$= 69.38$$

6. Calculate the mean squares between groups (MS_b) or the variance between groups:

$$MS_b = \frac{SS_b}{df_b} = \frac{69.38}{2} = 34.69$$

If the sizes of the groups are different, we use the average size of the groups.

7. Calculate the sum of squared deviations within groups (SS_w):

    (a) Subtract the group mean from each score in each group, which gives the deviations of each score from the corresponding group mean. For example, the first score in the augmented group is 33, and the mean score for this group is 34.4. The difference between these two values is –1.4 (Table 11.3, column B).

    (b) Square each deviation score for each group. For example, the square of the deviation score for the first score in the augmented group is $(-1.4)^2 = 1.96$ (Table 11.3, column C).

Table 11.3 Sum of squares within groups for the augmented group

Type of Learning	Deviations	Square of the deviation
A	B	C
Augmented	33 - 34.4 = -1.4	1.96
Augmented	36 - 34.4 = 1.6	2.56
Augmented	33 - 34.4 = -1.4	1.96
Augmented	38 - 34.4 = 3.6	12.96
Augmented	36 - 34.4 = 1.6	2.56
Augmented	30 - 34.4 = -4.4	19.36
Augmented	35 - 34.4 = 0.6	0.36
Augmented	32 - 34.4 = -2.4	5.76

(Continued)

Table 11.3 (Continued)

Type of Learning	Deviations	Square of the deviation
Augmented	34 - 34.4 = -0.4	0.16
Augmented	36 - 34.4 = 1.6	2.56
Augmented	36 - 34.4 = 1.6	2.56
Augmented	35 - 34.4 = 0.6	0.36
Augmented	38 - 34.4 = 3.6	12.96
Augmented	31 - 34.4 = -3.4	11.56
Augmented	33 - 34.4 = -1.4	1.96
Total		79.6

(c) Add all the deviation scores for each group. For the augmented group, the sum of these deviations is 79.6, for the virtual group is 72.4 and for the simulation group is 65.73.

(d) Finally, add up the sums of squares for all the groups, which gives the sum of squares within groups:

$$SS_W = 79.6 + 72.4 + 65.73 = 217.73$$

8. Calculate the mean squares within groups (MS_w) or the variance within the groups:

$$MS_W = \frac{SS_W}{df_W} = \frac{217.73}{42} = 5.18$$

The mean squares within the group can also be calculated using the variance within each group:

$$MS_w \quad \frac{variance_{Augmented} + variance_{Virtual} + variance_{Simulation}}{3} \quad \frac{5.68 + 5.17 + 4.69}{3} = 5.18$$

9. Calculate the F-ratio (F-statistic) as the ratio of the variance between the groups (among e-learning strategies in our case) and the variance within the groups (within e-learning strategies):

$$F = \frac{MS_b}{MS_w} = \frac{34.69}{5.18} = 6.691$$

The one-way ANOVA test has helped us to find out if the variations between the e-learning means are due to true differences about the populations means or just due to sampling variability. Through the F-score, we can see whether or not the variation among sample means is larger than the variation within groups. Since $F = 6.69$ is greater than 1, the variation of test score means among different types of e-learning is much larger than the variation of test scores within each group (the type of e-learning). This manual calculation of the one-way ANOVA generates only the F-statistic. In order to interpret this F-statistic, we also need the p-value, and the easiest way to find that is to compute the test in R.

11.2.2 Computing one-way ANOVA in R

Import the Ex11_1.csv data file into R and save it as the object 'eLearning':

```
eLearning <- read.csv(file.choose())

attach(eLearning)
```

The function `attach()` allows us to attach the eLearning object to the R search path and we can refer to the variables in the object by their names alone, rather than as components, for example `Scores` rather than `eLearning$Scores`. However, using the `attach()` function in R means that all further calculations depend on the most recent data attached. To remove the attachment of a previously attached data set, we can use the `detach()` function.

Before performing a one-way ANOVA, it is essential to verify the assumptions of this test. Firstly, let us test whether the dependent variable is normally distributed using the Shapiro–Wilk test. The null and alternative hypotheses are:

H_0 : The samples come from a normal distribution.
H_1 : The samples come from a non-normal distribution.

Performing a grouped Shapiro–Wilk test on the data frame

```
with(eLearning, tapply(Scores, list(TypesLearning), function(x)
if(length(unique(x))==1) NA else shapiro.test(x)))
$Augmented

    Shapiro-Wilk normality test
data: x
W = 0.9531, p-value = 0.5745


$Simulation
    Shapiro-Wilk normality test
data: x
W = 0.96395, p-value = 0.7606
```

(Continued)

```
$Virtual
    Shapiro-Wilk normality test
data: x
W = 0.93336, p-value = 0.3061
```

Since all the *p*-values are greater than 0.05 for each sample, we cannot reject the null hypothesis, and we conclude that the data is normally distributed.

Next, we test the homogeneity of variance. This can be done using Levene's or Bartlett's tests. The null and alternative hypotheses are:

H_0 : The variances are equal across the groups.
H_1 : Not all variances are equal across the groups; at least one is different from the others.

Performing Bartlett's test in R

```
bartlett.test(Scores~TypesLearning, data=eLearning)
    Bartlett test of homogeneity of variances
data: Scores by TypesLearning
Bartlett's K-squared = 0.12416, df = 2, p-value = 0.9398
```

Performing Levene's test in R

To compute the Levene test in R, we use the function `leveneTest()` which is part of the `car` package:

```
install.packages("car")
library(car)
leveneTest(Scores~TypesLearning)
Levene's Test for Homogeneity of Variance (center = median)
      Df F value Pr(>F)
group  2 0.0835 0.9201
      42
```

Now we compute the statistics necessary for producing boxplots:

```
boxplot.stats(Scores[TypesLearning=="Augmented"])
$stats
[1] 30 33 35 36 38
$n
[1] 15
$conf
[1] 33.77614 36.22386
$out
```

```
integer(0)
boxplot.stats(Scores[TypesLearning=="Virtual"])
$stats
[1] 28.0 31.0 32.0 33.5 35.0
$n
[1] 15
$conf
[1] 30.98011 33.01989
$out
integer(0)
boxplot.stats(Scores[TypesLearning=="Simulation"])
$stats
[1] 30 33 35 36 38
$n
[1] 15
$conf
[1] 33.77614 36.22386
$out
integer(0)
```

The first two lines ($stats) give us the information about the minimum and the maximum test scores using an e-learning strategy, followed by the information about the sample size ($n), then the confidence intervals ($conf), and the values of any outliers ($out) are indicated in the last line. In our examples, there are no outliers. However, there are situations where we might have one or more outliers. There are two possibilities: either we keep the outliers or remove them from the analysis. If we keep them and compute the ANOVA test, and if, at a later stage of data analysis, we discover that these two outliers create problems of estimation, we can consider removing them from the data set.

Finally, we carry out the one-way ANOVA and compute the F-score. The one-way ANOVA compares the skill test scores of three different e-learning techniques (augmented, virtual and simulation); there is only one factor or criterion (Scores) for classifying the sample observations. The null and alternative hypotheses are:

H_0 : $mean_{Augemented}$ = $mean_{Virtual}$ = $mean_{Simulation}$.
H_1 : Not all means are equal; at least one is different from the others.

One-way ANOVA analysis is done using the aov() function.

Computing one-way ANOVA in R

```
anova1<-aov(Scores~TypesLearning)
```

Note that the dependent variable, Scores, is placed in front of the independent variable TypesLearning.

(Continued)

To display the results of the one-way ANOVA, we use the `summary()` function:

```
summary(anova1)
               Df  Sum Sq  Mean Sq  F value  Pr(>F)
TypesLearning   2   69.38    34.69    6.691   0.003 **
Residuals      42  217.73     5.18
---
Signif. codes:  0 '***' 0.001 '**' 0.01 '*' 0.05 '.' 0.1 ' ' 1
```

or

```
aov_count<-aov(eLearning$Scores~eLearning$TypesLearning)
summary(aov_count)
                          Df  Sum Sq  Mean Sq  F value  Pr(>F)
eLearning2$TypesLearning   2   69.38    34.69    6.691   0.003 **
Residuals                 42  217.73     5.18
---
Signif. codes:  0 '***' 0.001 '**' 0.01 '*' 0.05 '.' 0.1 ' ' 1
```

Interpretation

The first row in the ANOVA table represents the variation that can be explained by the model, while 'Residuals' is the portion of the variability unexplained by the model. 'Sum Sq' represents the sum of squares calculation for each source of variation. The 'Df' column displays information about the degrees of freedom for between- and within-group variances.

'F value' is the F statistic, and the value obtained in our example is 6.691. Because this value is greater than 1, it indicates that the variability between groups is larger than the variability within groups. This result indicates a strong effect from e-learning strategies and could or could not be expected by chance, depending on the p-value. There are two ways to find out whether this result is statistically significant: either we compare the F value with the cut-off value for the F-ratio from an F-distribution table; or we compare the 'Pr(>F)', which is just the p-value, with the level of significance ($\alpha = 0.05$). If our p-value is greater than the level of significance, we fail to reject the null hypothesis that there is no significant relationship between e-learning strategies and skill test scores; if it is less than the level of significance, we reject the null hypothesis and accept the alternative hypothesis that there is a significant relationship between e-learning strategies and skill test scores.

Let us compare our F-value with the critical value for the F-distribution with the appropriate degrees of freedom (Table 11.4), which are $df_b = 2$ and $df_w = 42$. We select the value at the intersection of $df_b = 2$ and $df_w = 40$ (which is the closest value to 42), which is $F(2, 40) = 3.23$. Because our computed F-value (6.691) is greater than the cut-off F value (3.23), there is enough evidence to conclude that the e-learning types do have a statistically significant effect on skill test scores overall and that different categories of e-learning will change the scores significantly.

Table 11.4 Critical values of the *F*-distribution ($\alpha = 0.05$)

df$_w$ \ df$_b$	1	2	3	4	5	6	7	8	9	10
1	161.4	199.5	215.7	224.6	230.2	234.0	236.8	238.9	240.5	241.9
10	4.96	4.10	3.71	3.48	3.33	3.22	3.14	3.07	3.02	2.98
20	4.35	3.49	3.10	2.87	2.71	2.60	2.51	2.45	2.39	2.35
30	4.17	3.32	2.92	2.69	2.53	2.42	2.33	2.27	2.21	2.16
40	4.08	(3.23)	2.84	2.61	2.45	2.34	2.25	2.18	2.12	2.08
60	4.00	3.15	2.76	2.53	2.37	2.25	2.17	2.10	2.04	1.99

11.2.3 Post-hoc tests for one-way ANOVA

The null hypothesis (which we have rejected) states that there are no differences between the skill test score means using the three e-learning strategies, while the alternative hypothesis states that there are differences between the skill test score means. However, the one-way ANOVA test statistic does not tell us which specific groups were different from each other, and we do not know between which e-learning groups the significant differences exist. In order to find out which specific group or groups differ from the others and to compare multiple group means, we can perform post-hoc testing. There are numerous post-hoc tests, such as Scheffé's test, Duncan's test and Tukey's honestly significant differences (HSD) test, which are all based on the same principle: modification of the significance level for each comparison or modification of the probability distribution.

To find out how the three different types of e-learning differ, we use Tukey's HSD test, which is used for a single factor significance and to control Type I errors. In R, there are two functions, `TukeyHSD()` and `HSD.test()`, which can be used to determine which groups significantly differ.

The Tukey HSD test

Performing the Tukey HSD test in R

```
TukeyHSD(anova1, conf.level = 0.95)
   Tukey multiple comparisons of means
     95% family-wise confidence level
Fit: aov(formula = Scores ~ TypesLearning)
$TypesLearning
                           diff        lwr        upr       p adj
Simulation-Augmented  0.06666667 -1.953201  2.0865346 0.9964616
Virtual-Augmented    -2.60000000 -4.619868 -0.5801321 0.0087994
Virtual-Simulation   -2.66666667 -4.686535 -0.6467987 0.0070866
```

Interpretation

The `TukeyHSD()` function shows us whether the two compared means are significantly different from each other ('p adj' in the output). The 'lwr' and 'upr' columns provide lower and upper 95% confidence limits, respectively. For example, the 95% confidence interval of the difference between simulation and augmented scores is between –1.95 and 2.08. The 'diff' column provides the difference in the observed means. The 'p adj' column provides the p-values adjusted for the number of pairwise comparisons made (three in this case). As we have three types of e-learning, there are three possible pairwise comparisons: simulation–augmented, virtual–augmented and virtual–simulation. There is no significant difference in test scores between the first pair, the simulation and augmented groups ($p = 0.99 > 0.05$), while there is a significant difference in test scores between the other two pairs: virtual and augmented ($p = 0.009 < 0.05$) and virtual and simulation ($p = 0.007 < 0.05$). More specifically, for example, the pairwise difference between virtual and simulation learning is –2.67 which means that the group assigned with simulation learning had higher skill test scores than the group assigned virtual learning, and this difference is statistically significant. The Tukey's HSD test results are plotted using the function `plot()`, as shown in Figure 11.1. Each horizontal line represents the mean difference between paired groups. Those pairs that do not include zero are significantly different. In our example, the mean differences between the virtual and simulation groups and between the virtual and augmented groups are significant.

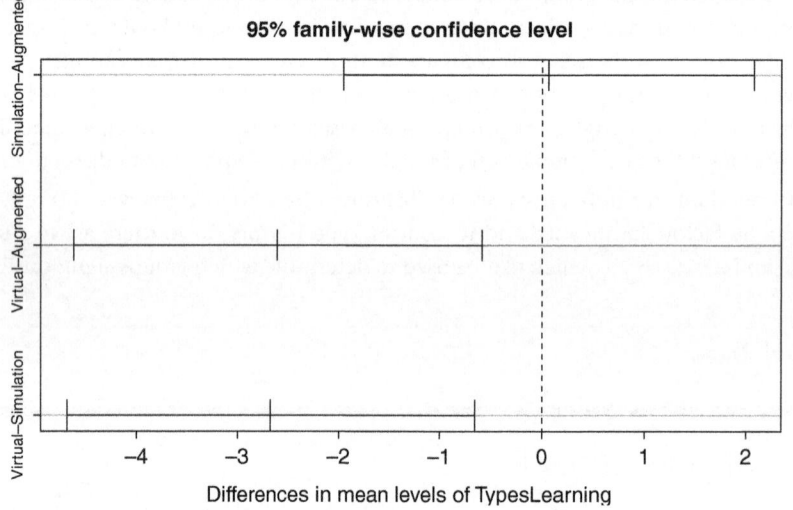

Figure 11.1 Tukey's test results

Plotting the Tukey's HSD test results

The graph in Figure 11.1 is obtained as follows:

```
plot(TukeyHSD(anova1, conf.level = 0.95))
```

Computing the post-hoc test in R

Install and load the `agricolae` package:

```
install.packages("agricolae")
library(agricolae)

HSD.test(anova1, "TypesLearning", console = TRUE)
Study: anova ~ "TypesLearning"
HSD Test for Scores
Mean Square Error:  5.184127
TypesLearning,  means
              Scores       std   r Min Max
Augmented   34.40000 2.384474 15   30  38
Simulation 34.46667 2.166850 15   30  38
Virtual     31.80000 2.274078 15   28  35
Alpha: 0.05 ; DF Error: 42
Critical Value of Studentized Range: 3.435823
Minimun Significant Difference: 2.019868
Treatments with the same letter are not significantly different.
             Scores groups
Simulation 34.46667      a
Augmented   34.40000      a
Virtual     31.80000      b
```

Interpretation

The final three lines of the output from the `HSD.test()` function indicate the mean scores for each group, and the letters in the 'groups' column show which groups are different. Both the simulation and augmented groups belong to the same group, marked 'a', so they are not different from each other, but the virtual group is different from the other two and belongs to group 'b'.

11.2.4 Measuring the effect size in a one-way ANOVA

The effect size for an ANOVA is measured through two types of effect size index:

1. *eta-squared* (η^2), *partial* η^2 and *omega-squared* (ω^2), which are based on proportions of the sum of squares. These indices explain the percentage of variance in the dependent variable that is explained by the independent variable.
2. *Cohen's F*, which is based on a standardised difference between two group means. This effect size index is useful for power analysis.

When using effect size with ANOVA, we use η^2 rather than Cohen's F, but note that Cohen's F can easily be obtained from η^2 using the following formula:

$$F = \sqrt{\frac{\eta^2}{1-\eta^2}}$$

Because the scale of measurement for the independent variable is always categorical, the η^2 effect size index measures how much of the variable is explained by group differences:

$$\eta^2 = \frac{between - groups\ sum\ of\ squares}{total\ sum\ of\ squares} = \frac{SS_b}{SS_{total}}$$

and ranges in value from 0 (no effect) to 1 (maximum) effect. Partial η^2 is calculated as:

$$partial\ \eta^2 = \frac{SS_b}{SS_b + SS_{error}}$$

For the manual calculation of η^2 we use the results produced by R for the one-way ANOVA test:

$$\eta^2 = \frac{SS_b}{SS_{total}} = \frac{69.38}{69.38 + 217.73} = 0.242$$

ω^2 is calculated as:

$$\omega^2 = \frac{df_b\left(MS_b - MS_w\right)}{SS_{total} + MS_w} = \frac{2\left(34.69 - 5.18\right)}{69.38 + 217.73 + 5.18} = 0.20$$

Cohen's F normalises the difference between two means with the pooled standard deviation:

$$F = \frac{\bar{x}_2 - \bar{x}_1}{pooled\ standard\ deviation} = \frac{\bar{x}_2 - \bar{x}_1}{\sqrt{\left(s_1^2 + s_2^2\right)/2}}$$

One-way ANOVA summary statistics

```
summary(anova1)
              Df Sum Sq Mean Sq F value Pr(>F)
TypesLearning  2  69.38   34.69   6.691  0.003 **
Residuals     42 217.73    5.18
---
Signif. codes:  0 '***' 0.001 '**' 0.01 '*' 0.05 '.' 0.1 ' ' 1
```

The function `summary()` gives us the immediate information about both the sum of squares between groups and the sum of squares of the residuals, which allow us to calculate SS_{total}.

Compute the effect size indices in R

```
install.packages("sjstats")
library(sjstats)
```

Eta squared

```
eta_sq(anova1)
            term etasq
1 TypesLearning 0.242
```

Partial eta squared

```
eta_sq(anova1, partial=TRUE)
            term partial.etasq
1 TypesLearning 0.242
```

Omega squared

```
omega_sq(anova1)
            term omegasq
1 TypesLearning 0.202
```

Cohen's F

```
effectsize::cohens_f(anova1)
effectsize::cohens_f(anova1)
Parameter     | Cohen's f (partial) |       90% CI
-------------------------------------------------
TypesLearning |                0.56 | [0.26, 0.82]
```

Interpretation

η^2 is either equal or less than partial η^2. In our example, eta-squared equals 0.242, which means that 24.2% of the variation in the independent variable (TypesLearning) is explained by the differences between the three groups. This effect size index tends to be biased in certain situations, for example when the sample size is small, or the independent variables have many group levels. The η^2 effect size index estimates are corrected for these biases. Finally, Cohen's F effect size represents a number of standard deviation units, and a value of 0.2 is considered a small effect size, while 0.5 represents a medium effect size and 0.8 a large effect size. There is a wide range of effect sizes reported across disciplines and there is no straightforward way to interpret these measures.

These values are standardised and, regardless of what is being measured, for example education levels or types of learning, the effects are all put onto the same scale. When reporting these values, it is also useful to present the unstandardised measures of effect size in original units and put the findings into context.

11.3 Two-way ANOVA

A two-way ANOVA test is a hypothesis-based test like the one-way ANOVA test. One of the main differences between these two tests is that the two-way ANOVA examines the effect of two independent variables or factors, rather than one, on one dependent variable. A major strength of this analysis is that it enables us to examine whether there is an *interaction* between different levels (categories) of the factors and to test the effects of two factors simultaneously. For example, if the mean score of a category of one factor (independent variable) varies according to the categories of the other factor, then an interaction exists.

A two-way ANOVA has three distinct hypotheses:

(a) The null hypothesis states that there are no statistically significant mean differences between levels or categories of the first independent variable.
(b) The null hypothesis states that there are no statistically significant mean differences between levels of the second independent variable.
(c) The null hypothesis states that there is no statistically significant interaction between the first and second independent variables.

The assumptions of a two-way ANOVA are:

1. The dependent variable should be an interval variable and normally distributed.
2. The two independent variables should be nominal.
3. Each sample has been drawn randomly and independently of the other samples.
4. The variance of data in each sample or group should be the same (homogeneity of variance).

Example 11.2 Testing the differences between more than two independent samples with two factors

Data file: Ex11_2.csv

A key aspect of any medical student's education is the level of realism or fidelity, both visually and to physical touch, that is required in practical training situations. Suppose that the skill test scores from the Example 11.1 results might also depend on two levels of realism, low and high, respectively, under the same different e-learning strategies. In this situation, we have one dependent variable, the skill test scores ('Scores'), and two independent variables (factors), the e-learning teaching strategies ('TypesLearning') and the level of realism ('Realism'). The 'TypesLearning' factor has three categories (augmented, virtual and simulation) and the 'Realism' factor has two categories (low and high). The sources of variability are shown in Figure 11.2.

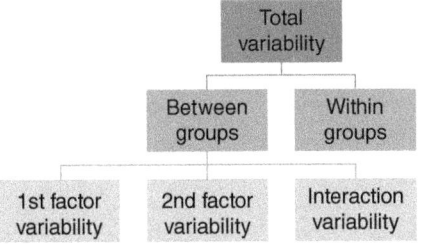

Figure 11.2 Sources of variability

The hypotheses of a two-way ANOVA are as follows:

H_{01} : The mean test score is the same for each of the e-learning strategies.
H_{11} : The mean test score is not the same for all e-learning strategies.
H_{02} : There is no main effect due to realism levels.
H_{12} : There is a main effect due to realism levels.
H_{03} : There is no interaction between the e-learning strategy and realism levels.
H_{13} : There is an interaction between the e-learning strategy and realism levels.

Two-way ANOVA allows an evaluation of the two main effects, one for each independent variable, on the dependent variable and whether there is an interaction between different levels of the independent variables. The interaction describes how two or more independent variables interact such that different levels of the independent variable have non-additive effects on the dependent variable.

11.3.1 Computing a two-way ANOVA in R

The first step is to check the assumption about the homogeneity of variance using Levene's test of equality of variances. Import the data into R and save it as the object Ex11_2:

```
Ex11_2 <- read.csv(file.choose())
```

Computing the Levene test

To compute the Levene test in R, we use the function `leveneTest()` which is part of the `car` package. If you have worked through Example 11.1, you will already have the `car` package installed and just need to call it using `library()`:

```
install.packages("car")
library(car)
```

(Continued)

```
leveneTest(Scores~as.factor(TypesLearning)*as.factor(Realism),
+ data=Ex11_2)
Levene's Test for Homogeneity of Variance (center = median)
      Df F value Pr(>F)
group  5  1.2625 0.2995
      39
```

The *p*-value is 0.2995, which is greater than 0.05, so equal variances can be assumed.

To compute a two-way ANOVA with an interaction, firstly we use the str() function to display the internal structure of the Ex11_2 object:

Displaying the internal structure of an object in R

```
str(Ex11_2)
'data.frame': 45 obs. of  3 variables:
 $ TypesLearning: chr  "Augmented" "Augmented" "Augmented" "Augmented" ...
 $ Scores       : int  33 36 33 38 36 30 35 32 34 36 ...
 $ Realism      : chr  "high" "low" "high" "low" ...
```

These results confirm that we have three variables: 'TypesLearning' is an independent variable (or factor) with three categories (or levels), 'Realism' is the second independent variable with two levels, and 'Scores' is the dependent variable which is an interval variable.

Because the sample sizes within each group are equal ($n = 15$), we have a so-called *balanced design*. In this case, the standard two-way ANOVA test can be applied using the function aov(), and a summary of the analysis is displayed using the function summary():

Computing two-way ANOVA in R

```
anova2<-aov(Scores~TypesLearning*Realism, data = Ex11_2)
summary(anova2)
                      Df Sum Sq Mean Sq F value   Pr(>F)
TypesLearning          2  69.38   34.69  15.323 1.23e-05 ***
Realism                1 129.13  129.13  57.040 3.78e-09 ***
TypesLearning:Realism  2   0.32    0.16   0.071    0.932
Residuals             39  88.29    2.26
---
```

or we can use different arguments for the same function:

```
anova3<-aov(Scores~as.factor(TypesLearning)*as.factor(Realism), data=Ex11_2)
summary(anova3)
                                        Df Sum Sq Mean Sq F value Pr(>F)
as.factor(TypesLearning)                 2  69.38   34.69  15.323 1.23e-05 ***
as.factor(Realism)                       1 129.13  129.13  57.040 3.78e-09 ***
as.factor(TypesLearning):as.factor(Realism)  2   0.32    0.16   0.071    0.932
Residuals                               39  88.29    2.26
                                ---
    Signif. codes:  0 '***' 0.001 '**' 0.01 '*' 0.05 '.' 0.1 ' ' 1
```

where the `as.factor()` function tells R that the two independents are categorical.

Interpretation

The results of the two-way ANOVA test are reported in the same way as for one-way ANOVA for the main effects and the interaction. The variance is divided into four components:

1. the variation explained by factor 'TypesLearning';
2. the variation explained by factor 'Realism';
3. the variation explained by the interaction of 'TypesLearning' and 'Realism';
4. the variation explained by randomness (Residuals).

From the ANOVA table, which includes the F values and Pr(>F) corresponding to the p-value of the test for both factors, we conclude that both factors, TypesLearning and Realism, are statistically significant; and Realism is the most significant factor variable.

There are three different values of F, and these correspond to the three different hypotheses. The evidence for the hypothesis on e-learning strategies is significant, and we reject the null hypothesis, H_{01} ($F = 15.323$, $df_1 = 2$, $df_2 = 39$, $p = 0.0000123$). The evidence for the hypothesis on realism levels is significant, and we reject the null hypothesis, H_{02} ($F = 57.040$, $df_1 = 2$, $df_2 = 39$, $p = 0.00000000375$). Finally, the evidence for the interaction hypothesis is not significant, and we fail to reject the null hypothesis, H_{03} ($F = 0.071$, $df_1 = 2$, $df_2 = 39$, $p = 0.932$).

These results lead us to believe that both independent variables, the e-learning strategy and the level of realism of training, will impact the mean skill test score (dependent variable) significantly. The F-value (0.071) and the p-value (Pr(>F) = 0.932) indicate that the interaction between the two factors is not statistically significant and the test scores do not depend on the relationships between the participants' level of realism of training and the e-learning strategy. The residuals, which are the difference between each individual and their TypesLearning–Realism combination mean, allow us to check the assumption that the residuals should be normally distributed by creating a histogram (Figure 11.3) using the function `hist()`.

Saving residuals as a separate object and plotting them using a histogram

Let us save the residuals as the object 'res':

```
res<-anova3$residuals
hist(res,main="Histogram of residuals",xlab="Residuals")
```

The graph is shown in Figure 11.3.

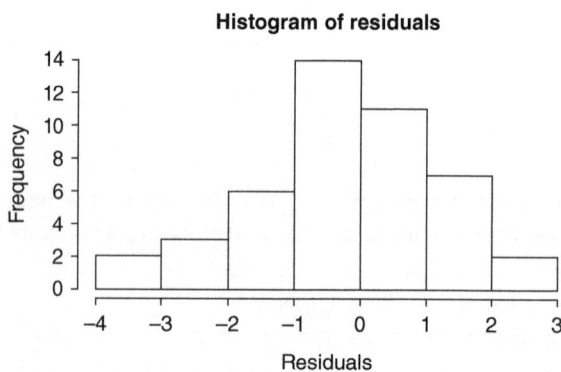

Figure 11.3 The distribution of residuals

The histogram shown in Figure 11.3 shows a normal distribution of residuals.

11.3.2 Interaction plot for two-way ANOVA test results

An interaction plot shows the relationship between the factors and the independent variables. This type of plot displays the means for the levels of one factor on the x-axis and a separate line for each level of another factor. The plotted lines help us evaluate the interactions; for example, if the lines are parallel, no interaction has occurred. The more non-parallel the lines are, the greater the strength of the interaction. The interaction.plot() function can be used to create a simple interaction plot for two-way ANOVA test results (Figure 11.4).

Creating an interaction plot

```
interaction.plot(x.factor     = Ex11_2$TypesLearning,
+ trace.factor = Ex11_2$Realism,
+ response     = Ex11_2$Scores,
+ fun = mean,
+ type="b",              # to draw both lines and points
```

```
+ pch=c(19, 17, 15),    # to plot symbols for levels of trace variable
+ fixed=TRUE,           # to have the legend in the order of the levels
+ leg.bty = "o")        # to pass arguments to the legend
```

The options available for this function indicate that we used the independent variable 'TypesLearning' for the x-axis, 'Realism' for the trace factor (second independent variable), and 'Scores' for the response variable (dependent variable). The fourth option, *fun=mean*, indicates that the mean for each group will be plotted. The graph is shown in Figure 11.4.

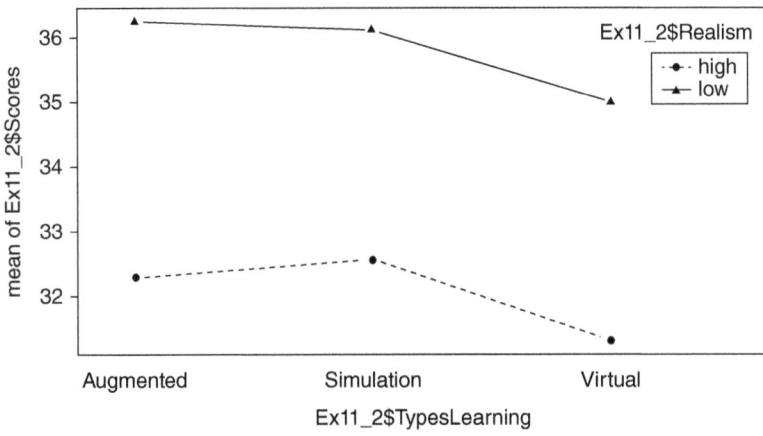

Figure 11.4   Interaction plot for two-way ANOVA

Interpretation

Figure 11.4 shows that the mean test score for each gender was lower for the virtual e-learning than for the other two types of e-learning. These differences were relatively constant for each level of realism, which is shown by the parallel lines on the plot. This result also suggests that there is no significant interaction effect, that the difference among levels of realism is consistent across e-learning strategies, and that the differences in e-learning strategies are consistent across levels of realism.

11.3.3 Post-hoc analysis in two-way ANOVA

The TukeyHSD() function will produce a post-hoc test for the main effects and the interactions.

Computing a post-hoc analysis

```
TukeyHSD(anova3)
   Tukey multiple comparisons of means
```

(Continued)

```
    95% family-wise confidence level


Fit: aov(formula = Scores ~ as.factor(TypesLearning) * as.factor(Realism),
data = Ex11_2)


$'as.factor(TypesLearning)'
                           diff       lwr       upr     p adj
Simulation-Augmented 0.06666667 -1.271832  1.405165 0.9919167
Virtual-Augmented    -2.60000000 -3.938498 -1.261502 0.0000847
Virtual-Simulation   -2.66666667 -4.005165 -1.328168 0.0000580


$'as.factor(Realism)'
             diff      lwr      upr p adj
low-high 3.191358 2.265309 4.117407     0


$'as.factor(TypesLearning):as.factor(Realism)'
                                  diff        lwr       upr     p adj
Simulation:high-Augmented:high  0.2857143 -2.1237602 2.6951888 0.9991961
Virtual:high-Augmented:high    -0.9780220 -3.0912709 1.1352269 0.7346052
Augmented:low-Augmented:high    3.9642857  1.6313221 6.2972493 0.0001299
Simulation:low-Augmented:high   3.8392857  1.5063221 6.1722493 0.0002138
Virtual:low-Augmented:high      2.7142857 -0.8999260 6.3284974 0.2390956
Virtual:high-Simulation:high   -1.2637363 -3.3769852 0.8495126 0.4826941
Augmented:low-Simulation:high   3.6785714  1.3456078 6.0115351 0.0004035
Simulation:low-Simulation:high  3.5535714  1.2206078 5.8865351 0.0006577
Virtual:low-Simulation:high     2.4285714 -1.1856403 6.0427831 0.3536130
Augmented:low-Virtual:high      4.9423077  2.9167280 6.9678874 0.0000001
Simulation:low-Virtual:high     4.8173077  2.7917280 6.8428874 0.0000002
Virtual:low-Virtual:high        3.6923077  0.2684531 7.1161622 0.0280775
Simulation:low-Augmented:low   -0.1250000 -2.3788570 2.1288570 0.9999809
Virtual:low-Augmented:low      -1.2500000 -4.8136608 2.3136608 0.8973954
Virtual:low-Simulation:low     -1.1250000 -4.6886608 2.4386608 0.9318266
```

Interpretation

The post-hoc analysis provides greater insight into the differences and similarities between the means of each factor (TypesLearning and Realism), as well as between the means of the interaction effect which indicate how the effect of one-factor changes across the different levels of the other factor (TypesLearning: Gender). When the interaction effects are statistically significant, it is important to interpret the main effects while taking into consideration the interaction effects. We compare the adjusted p-values to our significance level ($\alpha = 0.05$), and if these values are less than α, the difference between the corresponding group means is statistically significant. In this example, the differences between the virtual and augmented and virtual–simulation are statistically significant, as well as the differences between high and low levels of realism. There are also

15 interactions, and the p-values for eight of the interaction terms are not even close to significant. Note that the non-significant main effect for simulation–augmented ($p = 0.9919$) does not mean that the type of e-learning strategy is unimportant because it appears in a significant interaction with level of realism.

11.3.4 Measuring the effect size in two-way ANOVA

The effect size (η^2) is defined as the proportion of variance accounted for by each of the main effects, interactions, and error in the study. It is computed in the same way as the one described in section 11.1.4.

Computing η^2 in R

We use the function `etaSquared()` which is part of the `lsr` package:

```
install.packages("lsr")
library(lsr)
etaSquared(anova3)
                        eta.sq eta.sq.part
TypesLearning          0.038322789 0.110815793
Realism                0.449739198 0.593918444
TypesLearning:Realism  0.001118468 0.003624096
```

The results can be interpreted as proportions of variance associated with each of the main effects, the interaction, and error.

The effect size for a two-way ANOVA is measured through the same two categories of effect size indices (η^2 and Cohen's F) described in Section 11.1.4. η^2 tends to be smaller in two-way ANOVA than in one-way ANOVA because the SS_{total} grows larger due to it including the sums of squares arising from the second factor.

Computing the effect size statistics

We use the function `eta_sq()` to calculate η^2 and `omega_sq()` to calculate ω^2:

```
eta_sq(anova3)
                    term etasq
1         TypesLearning 0.242
2                Gender 0.450
3 TypesLearning:Gender 0.001
```

(Continued)

```
omega_sq(anova3)

                    term omegasq
1           TypesLearning   0.224
2                  Gender   0.438
3 TypesLearning:Gender   -0.015
```

Interpretation

The difference between the three types of learning explains 24.2% of the variation in the first independent variable (TypesLearning), and the difference between the high and low groups explains 45% of the variation in the second variable (Realism). Omega-squared has the same basic interpretation as eta-squared, but because it is using the unbiased estimate of population variances, it is always smaller than eta-squared.

 Kruskal–Wallis ANOVA test

When assumptions of the analysis of variance (ANOVA) are not fulfilled, for example a non-normal interval data distribution and heterogeneity of variance, the Kruskal–Wallis test can be used to test the differences between two or more independent samples. This test is also used for ordinal data that may be displayed in a contingency table which is more powerful than the traditionally chi-squared test that is often used for this type of data.

The assumptions of the Kruskal–Wallis test are as follows:

- It is preferable to have at least four or five subjects in each independent sample.
- It is not necessary to have an equal number of subjects in each independent group.
- The dependent variable is ordinal or non-normal distributed interval data.

The null hypothesis is that the independent samples come from the same population and from populations which have the same median. The alternative hypothesis is that at least one sample has a different median from the others. A significant value of the test statistic (H) leads to the rejection of the null hypothesis. To compute the H-value, the individual scores in each group are pooled together and then ranked as if they all come from the same group. The sums of the ranks for each group are then compared, and the H-value is computed. The probability of occurrence of the H-value is then checked in the appropriate statistical table.

Example 11.3 Finding the difference between more than two independent samples with an ordinal dependent variable

Data file: Ex11_3.csv

In Example 11.2 we investigated the difference in skill test scores between independent groups corresponding to different forms of e-learning strategies: augmented, virtual and simulation.

In this example, we are interested in describing the effectiveness of these three forms of e-learning strategies. The effectiveness of the e-learning strategies is the dependent variable, and it is measured by using the following items, which were formulated in the form of statements containing the use of each learning technique:

Augmented e-learning helped me to make associations between the knowledge presented in the new content and my prior knowledge.

Virtual e-learning helped me to make associations between the knowledge presented in the new content and my prior knowledge.

Simulation e-learning helped me to make associations between the knowledge presented in the new content and my prior knowledge.

These three items are on the four-point Likert scale, graded as 'excellent' (=1), 'good' (=2), 'fair' (=3) and 'poor' (=4). The independent variable is the e-learning strategy with three levels, and the dependent variable is the effectiveness of the e-learning strategy measured on a four-point Likert scale from 'Excellent' to 'Poor'.

The medical students were asked to respond to the statements described above, and the results are displayed in Table 11.5.

Table 11.5 Medical students' answers to three statements regarding the effectiveness of each learning strategy. The three statements are on a four-point Likert scale, graded as 'Excellent' (=1), 'Good' (=2), 'Fair' (=3) and 'Poor' (=4)

TypesLearning	Effectiveness	TypesLearning	Effectiveness	TypesLearning	Effectiveness
Augmented	2	Virtual	2	Simulation	2
Augmented	1	Virtual	2	Simulation	2
Augmented	2	Virtual	1	Simulation	2
Augmented	1	Virtual	4	Simulation	1
Augmented	1	Virtual	3	Simulation	1
Augmented	3	Virtual	3	Simulation	2
Augmented	1	Virtual	2	Simulation	1
Augmented	2	Virtual	2	Simulation	2
Augmented	2	Virtual	3	Simulation	3
Augmented	1	Virtual	2	Simulation	1
Augmented	1	Virtual	2	Simulation	2
Augmented	1	Virtual	4	Simulation	1
Augmented	1	Virtual	2	Simulation	1
Augmented	3	Virtual	2	Simulation	3
Augmented	2	Virtual	3	Simulation	3

The null and alternative hypotheses are:

H_0: There are no differences in effectiveness between the three types of e-learning.
H_i: There are differences in effectiveness between the three types of e-learning.

Computing the Kruskal–Wallis test in R

To perform the test, we use the `kruskal.test()` function:

```
Ex11_3 <- read.csv(file.choose())
attach(Ex11_3)
kruskal.test(Effectiveness~TypesLearning)
        Kruskal-Wallis rank-sum test
data:  Effectiveness by TypesLearning
Kruskal-Wallis chi-squared = 8.1894, df = 2, p-value = 0.01666
```

Interpretation

Our Kruskal–Wallis chi-squared test statistic is 8.1894. We compare this value with the critical chi-squared value for $df = 2$ degrees of freedom and $\alpha = 0.05$, which is 5.9915. Since the critical chi-squared value is less than the computed chi-squared statistic, we reject the null hypothesis. Note also that the p-value of 0.01666 is stated in the output. We conclude that there is a statistically significant difference in the effectiveness of e-learning strategies.

11.4.1 Post-hoc analysis for the Kruskal–Wallis test

The results of the Kruskal–Wallis test do not provide an indication as to which groups are different in terms of effectiveness. In R, the function `dunnTest()` in the FSA package performs Dunn's multiple comparison test to identify which pairs of groups significantly differ; this is an alternative to the Tukey test described in the previous section.

Computing Dunn's multiple comparison test

```
install.packages("FSA")
library(FSA)
## FSA v0.8.25. See citation('FSA') if used in publication.
## Run fishR() for related website and fishR('IFAR') for related book.
dunnTest(Effectiveness~TypesLearning)
Dunn (1964) Kruskal-Wallis multiple comparison
```

```
    p-values adjusted with the Holm method.
                 Comparison        Z     P.unadj      P.adj
1 Augmented - Simulation -0.7112708 0.476916451 0.47691645
2     Augmented - Virtual -2.7561743 0.005848182 0.01754455
3    Simulation - Virtual -2.0449035 0.040864372 0.08172874


tmp<-dunnTest(Effectiveness~TypesLearning)
print(tmp,dunn.test.results = TRUE) # generic printing of an object
   Kruskal-Wallis rank sum test

 data: x and g
 Kruskal-Wallis chi-squared = 8.1894, df = 2, p-value = 0.02
                      Comparison of x by g
                           (Holm)

 Col Mean-|
 Row Mean | Augmente Simulati
 ---------+---------------------
 Simulati | -0.711270
          |  0.4769
          |
  Virtual | -2.756174 -2.044903
          |  0.0175*    0.0817

 alpha = 0.05
 Reject Ho if p <= alpha
```

Interpretation

The 'Comparison' column identifies the paired comparison that is being performed, the Z column gives the z-score corresponding to the paired comparison, the P.unadj column is the unadjusted p-value corresponding to the paired comparison, and the P.adj column displays the adjusted p-value using Holm's method corresponding to the paired comparison.

Since the p-values for the pair simulation and augmented ($p = 0.476$) and the pair simulation and virtual ($p = 0.0817$) are greater than 0.02 (= $\alpha/3 = 0.016667$), there is no significant difference between the effectiveness of simulation and augmented strategy and between the effectiveness of simulation and virtual. However, there is a significant difference between the effectiveness of virtual and augmented reality. To visualise the differences between these three independent groups, we can use the function boxplot(). The key information is obtained by comparing the boxes, the middle lines and the whiskers. For example, if two boxes do not overlap with each other, there is a difference between the groups. In our example, we see that there is no overlap between the box for the virtual group and the other two groups, which indicates the existence of a difference in test scores between the virtual and simulation groups (Figure 11.5).

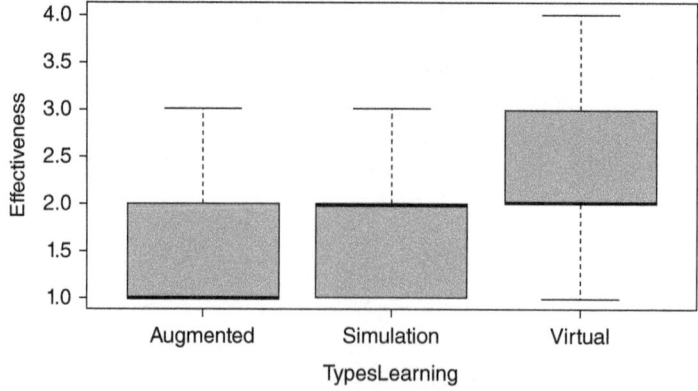

Figure 11.5 Box and whisker plots for the three types of e-learning

━━━━━━━━━━ Exercises ━━━━━━━━━━

11.1 Explain when you would use a nonparametric test to compare two or more independent samples.

11.2 What are the assumptions for one-way analysis of variance?

11.3 What is the difference between one-way ANOVA and two-way ANOVA?

11.4 What test is appropriate in the following situations?

(a) Two independent groups, one independent variable and one dependent variable

(b) Two independent groups, two independent variables and one dependent variable

(c) The dependent variable is non-normally distributed

(d) The dependent variable is ordinal

11.5 State the null and alternative hypotheses for a one-way ANOVA test if there are four groups.

11.6 What is the F statistic?

11.7 When can the Kruskal-Wallis test be used?

11.8 A psychologist was interested in whether a memory drug improves students' exam scores. An undergraduate class of students was split into two groups. One group tried the memory drug and the other group a placebo drug. The exam scores are shown in Table 11.5. Carry out a one-way ANOVA manually and using R to test the hypothesis that the treatments will give different effects.

Table 11.6 Exam scores for the memory drug group and the placebo group

Memory drug	Placebo
70	55
77	69
83	56

Memory drug	Placebo
90	45
97	60
92	55
80	56
76	63
75	62
78	54

Further reading

Olejnik, S. (2003) Generalized eta and omega squared statistics: Measures of effect size for some common research designs. *Physiological Methods*, 8(4), 434–447.

This article provides formulas for computing generalised eta-squared and omega-squared statistics and their two significant advantages.

Pek, J. and Flora, D. (2018) Reporting effect sizes in original psychological research: A discussion and tutorial. *Physiological Methods*, 23(2), 208–225.

This paper presents general principles and recommendations for correct effect size reporting, elucidating common misconceptions.

Wiley, J. and Pace, L. (2015) *Beginning R: An introduction to statistical programming* (2nd ed.). Berkeley, CA: Apress.

Chapter 12 provides useful information on one-way and two-way analysis of variance and detailed information about the functions used to compute the corresponding tests in R.

12

Differences between more than two dependent samples

━━━━━━ Chapter Objectives ━━━━━━

In this chapter, we will:

- introduce various statistical tests to assess the difference between more than two dependent groups, different levels of measurement and different numbers of variables: repeated measures ANOVA, Friedman's test and Cochran's Q-test
- understand how the analysis of these tests is reported and interpreted
- assess various assumptions for these statistical tests
- compute the corresponding statistical tests using R.

In this chapter, we will present the statistical tests performed on variables with different scales of measurement (nominal, ordinal and interval) and with one or two factors to test the differences between more than two dependent samples (Table 12.1). Cochran's Q-test is a nonparametric test that is performed to verify whether there are differences on a nominal dependent variable when there are two or more paired groups. Friedman's test is also a nonparametric test which is performed on ordinal data. With repeated measures ANOVA, also known as factor ANOVA, we can examine differences on a dependent variable that has been measured repeatedly over time and it is based on the same general principles as all ANOVA tests. For example, as with one-way ANOVA, the one-way repeated measures ANOVA also takes the variance into consideration, but the difference consists in dividing up the variance in the dependent variable. The purpose of a two-way repeated measures ANOVA is to determine the effect of different conditions on a dependent variable.

Table 12.1 Selection criteria for a statistical test for finding the difference between more than two dependent samples

| | Type of variable | | | |
| | Nominal | Ordinal | Interval/ratio | |
			One factor	Two factors
Statistical test	Cochran's Q-test	Friedman ANOVA test	One-way repeated measures ANOVA	Two-way repeated measures ANOVA

12 ● 1 Repeated measures ANOVA

Research in education often involves repeated measurements for the dependent variable which has categories called levels or related (paired) groups, involving the same sample of subjects participating in each condition of the experiment or test. So, the term *repeated measures* means that each research participant is assigned in turn to all treatments of an experiment. The repeated measures ANOVA is also named *within-subjects ANOVA* because the comparison of the effects of the independent variable on the dependent variable is within subjects. The independent variable more commonly is referred to as the *within-subjects factor*.

The procedures behind repeated measures ANOVA are very similar to those of the between-subjects ANOVA described in Chapter 11. Recall that in one-way ANOVA there are only two sources of variance: the between-groups variability (SS_b) and within-groups variability (SS_w). With repeated-measures ANOVA, there are three sources of variability: between treatments (or conditions), between participants, and random (or residual). In a one-way related measures ANOVA, there is a separate source of variance, called *subjects variance* (SS_{subj}) because the same subjects take part in each of the experimental or test conditions. The general formula to calculate an appropriate *F*-value is:

$$F = \frac{between\text{-}conditions\ variance}{within\text{-}conditions\ variance\ -\ individual\ differences}$$

The *F*-test of the significance of the *F*-ratio is equal to:

$$F = \frac{MS_b}{MS_w}$$

where MS_b is the mean sum of squares between groups and MS_w is the mean sum of squares within groups, which is also called the *error term*. These means squares are computed using the following formulas:

$$MS_b = \frac{SS_b}{df_b} \text{ and } MS_w = \frac{SS_w}{df_w}$$

where df_b and df_w are the corresponding degrees of freedom.

The error term is reduced in comparison to what it would be for one-way ANOVA because part of the variation within subjects is attributable to the different conditions, and part is due to individual differences. Since we are interested in differences among conditions and not differences among subjects, the *F*-statistic is calculated as the ratio of MS_b (or $MS_{conditions}$) and MS_w (or MS_{error}) because we assume that there are no interactions between subjects and conditions or treatments.

The assumptions for repeated measures ANOVA are the same as those described in Section 11.1, with the additional requirements of homogeneity of covariance among population error terms for the different treatments/conditions and independence of errors for different treatment conditions. This additional assumption is of little concern in a practical setting. However, in a repeated measures design we expect a consistent covariation between the results in the different conditions; for example, if a participant had a high score in the first test or treatment condition, we would expect her to score highly in the second test. This is named *sphericity*. The assumption of sphericity is met when we have the same variances across each pair of conditions. Mauchly's test, like the normality test, can be used to test that the data is significantly different from sphericity.

12 ● 2 One-way repeated measures ANOVA

The one-way repeated measures ANOVA is similar to the one-way unrelated ANOVA described in Section 11.1, but it is used to identify the differences between dependent or paired group means on one dependent and one independent variable which is measured in either of the situations described below:

1. differences in means of the dependent variable on two occasions, for example before and after an intervention, with the same participants;
2. differences in means of the dependent variable under three or more conditions, with the same participants.

There are three main assumptions for this test:

- The dependent variable is normally distributed in each group that is being compared.
- Variances are homogeneous. This means that the population variances in each group are equal.
- There is an independence of observations.

Example 12.1 Finding the difference between dependent samples

Data file: Ex12_1.csv

A teacher sets up an intervention to evaluate the Maths Recovery Programme, a long-established international intervention programme for pupils aged 7–11 years who are struggling with their mathematics. A total of 20 pupils aged between 10 and 11 were randomly selected to be part of this intervention programme. All pupils were tested using the Progress Test in Maths (PTM) test series on three occasions, when they entered the programme (Phase1), three months after entry (Phase2) and six months after entry (Phase3). The data is shown in Table 12.2.

Table 12.2   Progress scores for the group of pupils for three levels of the independent variable (Maths Recovery Programme)

Phase1	Phase2	Phase3
101	131	140
88	118	124
89	93	98
92	114	120
79	88	95
88	99	103
96	113	128
105	108	130
110	106	140
100	105	132

Phase1	Phase2	Phase3
81	104	122
103	102	135
85	101	128
103	98	126
105	98	119
79	98	123
86	96	133
91	95	137
77	92	129
79	88	118

The independent variable is the Maths Recovery Programme, and each phase of the intervention is a level or related (dependent) group. For the Maths Recovery Programme intervention, the three test occasions or phases resulted in three related groups. This is a clear example of a repeated measures ANOVA because the independent variable has three categories called levels or related groups, and the dependent variable is the PTM score.

The null and alternative hypotheses for ANOVA are:

H_0: The means of the three groups are identical.
H_i: At least one of the means is different.

12.2.1 Checking assumptions for one-way repeated measures ANOVA

Firstly, we import the Ex12_1.csv data file into R:

```
Ex12_1 <- read.csv(file.choose())
```

and print the first three rows of data:

```
head(Ex12_1,3)
```

```
  Phase1 Phase2 Phase3

1     92    116    125

2     88    118    124

3     89     93    117
```

Before performing a repeated one-way ANOVA, it is essential to verify the following assumptions of this test:

Assumption 1. The independent variable is measured on a categorical scale and the dependent variable on the interval scale.

The independent variable (Maths Recovery Programme) is categorical and has three levels (Phase 1, Phase 2, Phase 3), and the dependent variable is interval data (PTM score).

Assumption 2. There are no outliers in the data set.

The outliers can be easily identified using box and whisker plots, as shown in Figure 12.2, which can be easily created using the R function `boxplot()` or tested using the function `boxplot.stats()`.

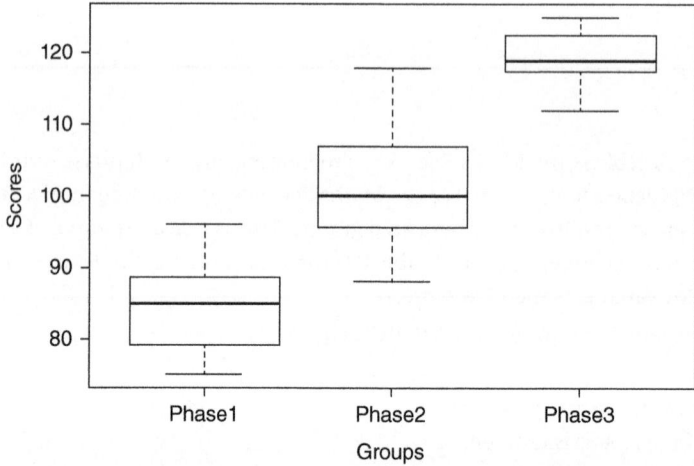

Figure 12.1   Box and whisker plots for each level of the independent variable

Testing the presence of outliers in R using the function `boxplot.stats()`

```
boxplot.stats(Ex12_1$Phase1)
$stats
[1] 75.0 79.0 85.0 88.5 96.0
$n
[1] 20
$conf
[1] 81.64366 88.35634
$out
integer(0)
boxplot.stats(Ex12_1$Phase2)
$stats
[1] 88.0 95.5 100.0 107.0 118.0
$n
```

```
[1] 20
$conf
[1] 95.93706 104.06294
$out
integer(0)
boxplot.stats(Ex12_1$Phase3)
$stats
[1] 112.0 117.5 119.0 122.5 125.0
$n
[1] 20
$conf
[1] 117.2335 120.7665
$out
integer(0)
```

The box and whisker plots displayed in Figure 12.1 show the absence of outliers in all three groups, and the outlier value ($out) for each group equals zero, which confirms that there are no outliers in each group.

Assumption 3. The dependent variable is normally distributed.

The null and alternative hypotheses are:

H_0 : The samples come from a population which has a normal distribution.
H_1 : The samples come from a population which has a non-normal distribution.

Performing a grouped Shapiro–Wilk normality test

```
shapiro.test(Ex12_1$Phase1)
        Shapiro-Wilk normality test
data: Ex12_1$Phase1
W = 0.95572, p-value = 0.4623
shapiro.test(Ex12_1$Phase2)
        Shapiro-Wilk normality test
data: Ex12_1$Phase2
W = 0.95911, p-value = 0.5263
shapiro.test(Ex12_1$Phase3)
        Shapiro-Wilk normality test
data: Ex12_1$Phase3
W = 0.94641, p-value = 0.3158
```

Interpretation

Since the *p*-values (0.4623, 0.5263, 0.3158) are greater than 0.05 for each condition (or group or phase), we cannot reject the null hypothesis and conclude that the data is normally distributed in all three groups.

We can also visualise if the data is normal distribution for each group by creating the QQ plots for each phase, using the function ggqqplot() from the ggpubr package.

Visualising the distribution of data from Example 12.1

```
install.packages("ggpubr")
library(ggpubr)
ggqqplot(Ex12_1$Phase1)
ggqqplot(Ex12_1$Phase2)
ggqqplot(Ex12_1$Phase3)
```

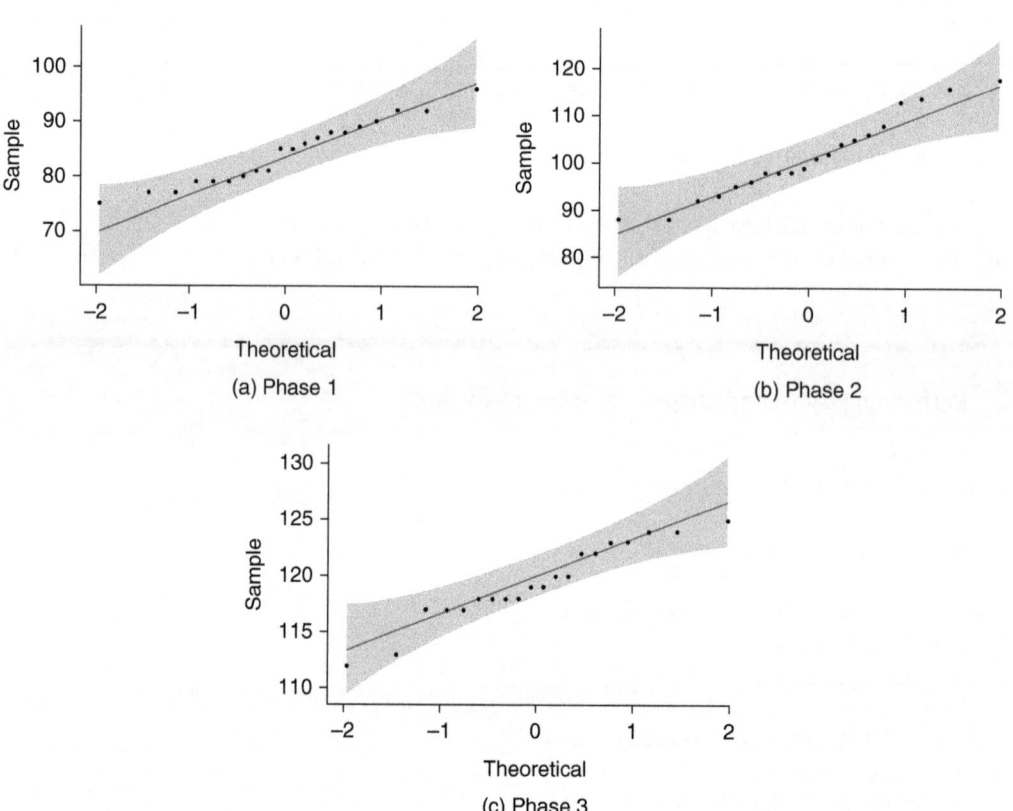

Figure 12.2 QQ plots for all three phases

Interpretation

Figure 12.2 shows that, for the most part, the data points for all three conditions fall alongside the straight line, and that all the points fall within the 95% confidence limits (grey areas), which suggest that our data come from a population that is normally distributed. Because the data points are close to these reference lines, and within the confidence bands (grey areas), the normality assumption is met. The progress scores of all pupils lie within the confidence limits on all three occasions of the intervention programme, when they entered the programme (Phase 1), three months after entry (Phase 2) and six months after entry (Phase 3).

> *Assumption 4.* The variances of the group differences are equal (also called the sphericity assumption).

The assumption of sphericity will be automatically checked during the computation of the ANOVA test. The null hypothesis for sphericity is that the variances of the group differences are equal.

12.2.2 Computing one-way repeated measures ANOVA and Mauchly's test of sphericity

Using the R function `anova_test()` from the rstatix package, we can easily compute the one-way repeated measures ANOVA alongside Mauchly's test of sphericity. Before we compute the test, for our Example 12.1, we must convert the three levels 'Phase1', 'Phase2' and 'Phase3' into factors (or long format). This can be done by using the `convert_as_factor()` function (from the rstatix package) alongside the `gather()` function (from the tidyr package) that takes multiple columns and collapses them into key–value pairs:

```
library(rstatix)
library(tidyr)
fEx12_1<-Ex12_1 %>%
gather(key = "phase", value = "score", Phase1, Phase2, Phase3) %>%
convert_as_factor(id, phase)
```

Computing one-way repeated measures ANOVA

The key arguments for the `anova_test()` function are:

- *data*: data frame
- *dv*: the dependent (or outcome) variable name (numeric)
- *wid*: variable name specifying the case/sample identifier
- *within*: within-subjects factor or grouping variable.

```
res.aov<-anova_test(data= fEx12_1, dv=score, wid=id, within= phase)
res.aov
```

(Continued)

```
ANOVA Table (type III tests)
$ANOVA
    Effect DFn DFd            F         p p<.05   ges
1   phase   2  38     238.319 3.14e-22      * 0.838
$`Mauchly's Test for Sphericity`
    Effect     W      p p<.05
1   phase 0.953 0.646
'Sphericity Corrections'
    Effect   GGe      DF[GG]    p[GG] p[GG]<.05  HFe      DF[HF]     p[HF]    p[HF]<.05
1   phase 0.955 1.91, 36.28 2.53e-21           * 1.059 2.12, 40.23 3.14e-22      *
```

Interpretation

The output is a list including three tables.

- The first table, which is labelled $ANOVA, shows the p-value and the effect size in the column labelled 'ges' (generalised eta-squared), which will be discussed at the end of this section.

In our example, the F-ratio obtained is 238.319, and this is compared to an F-distribution with numerator degrees of freedom (DFn) 2 and denominator degrees of freedom (DFd) 18 ($\alpha = 0.05$). The critical value for this F-distribution (3.55) can be found at the intersection of $df_1 = 2$ with $df_2 = 18$ in Table 12.3. Because the computed F-value (238.319) is much greater than the critical F-value (3.55; note the p-value given in the output, which is much less than 0.05), we reject the null hypothesis and conclude that the PTM score is statistically different at different phases due to the Maths Recovery Programme.

Table 12.3 F-distribution for $\alpha = 0.05$

/	$df_1 = 1$	2	3	4	5	6	7	8	9	10
$df_2 = 2$	18.51	19.00	19.16	19.25	19.30	19.33	19.35	19.37	19.38	19.40
3	10.13	9.55	9.28	9.12	9.01	8.94	8.89	8.85	8.81	8.79
4	7.71	6.94	6.59	6.39	6.26	6.16	6.09	6.04	6.00	5.96
5	6.61	5.79	5.41	5.19	5.05	4.95	4.88	4.82	4.77	4.74
6	5.99	5.14	4.76	4.53	4.39	4.28	4.21	4.15	4.10	4.06
7	5.59	4.74	4.35	4.12	3.97	3.87	3.79	3.73	3.68	3.64
8	5.32	4.46	4.07	3.84	3.69	3.58	3.50	3.44	3.39	3.35
9	5.12	4.26	3.86	3.63	3.48	3.37	3.29	3.23	3.18	3.14
10	4.96	4.10	3.71	3.48	3.33	3.22	3.14	3.07	3.02	2.98
11	4.84	3.98	3.59	3.36	3.20	3.09	3.01	2.95	2.90	2.85
12	4.75	3.89	3.49	3.26	3.11	3.00	2.91	2.85	2.80	2.75
13	4.67	3.81	3.41	3.18	3.03	2.92	2.83	2.77	2.71	2.67

/	$df_1 = 1$	2	3	4	5	6	7	8	9	10
14	4.60	3.74	3.34	3.11	2.96	2.85	2.76	2.70	2.65	2.60
15	4.54	3.68	3.29	3.06	2.90	2.79	2.71	2.64	2.59	2.54
16	4.49	3.63	3.24	3.01	2.85	2.74	2.66	2.59	2.54	2.49
17	4.45	3.59	3.20	2.96	2.81	2.70	2.61	2.55	2.49	2.45
18	4.41	(3.55)	3.16	2.93	2.77	2.66	2.58	2.51	2.46	2.41
19	4.38	3.52	3.13	2.90	2.74	2.63	2.54	2.48	2.42	2.38
20	4.35	3.49	3.10	2.87	2.71	2.60	2.51	2.45	2.39	2.35
21	4.32	3.47	3.07	2.84	2.68	2.57	2.49	2.42	2.37	2.32
22	4.30	3.44	3.05	2.82	2.66	2.55	2.46	2.40	2.34	2.30
23	4.28	3.42	3.03	2.80	2.64	2.53	2.44	2.37	2.32	2.27
24	4.26	3.40	3.01	2.78	2.62	2.51	2.42	2.36	2.30	2.25
25	4.24	3.39	2.99	2.76	2.60	2.49	2.40	2.34	2.28	2.24

- In the second section of the results table, which provides Mauchly's test of sphericity, only the variables or effects with more than two levels are listed because sphericity necessarily holds for effects with only two levels. A significant p-value ($p < 0.05$) indicates that the variances of group differences are not equal.
- The third section of the results table displays the sphericity corrections results, which are needed if the sphericity assumption is not fulfilled, that is, if the p-value from Mauchly's test is less than 0.05. Two corrections are provided: the Greenhouse-Geisser epsilon ('GGe') and the Huynh–Feldt epsilon ('HFe'), with their corresponding p-values; these are the corrections most commonly applied when the sphericity assumption is not met. These corrections are made by adjusting the degrees of freedom, by multiplying DFn and DFd by the correction estimate (Greenhouse-Geisser or Huynh–Feldt epsilon), which leads to a strong impact on the statistical significance (i.e. p-value) of the test. We have no need for these corrections in our example, because Mauchly's test provided a non-significant value.

12.2.3 Post-hoc analysis for one-way repeated measures ANOVA

The one-way repeated measures ANOVA test does not tell us which group has a different mean. Instead, we can perform a pairwise paired t-test between the levels of the within-subjects factor – in our example, the factor 'phase', with three levels (Phase1, Phase2, Phase3).

```
pwc <- fEx12_1 %>% pairwise_t_test(score ~ phase, paired = TRUE,p.adjust.
method = "bonferroni")

pwc
```

(Continued)

```
# A tibble: 3 x 10
  .y. group1 group2 n1 n2 statistic df p p.adj p.adj.signif
* <chr> <chr> <chr> <int> <int> <dbl> <dbl> <dbl> <dbl> <chr>

1 score Phase1 Phase2 20 20 -10.1 19 4.53e- 9 1.36e- 8 ****

2 score Phase1 Phase3 20 20 -24.7 19 6.90e-16 2.07e-15 ****

3 score Phase2 Phase3 20 20 -10.7 19 1.88e- 9 5.64e- 9 ****
```

Interpretation

We know already from running the ANOVA test that the PTM score was statistically significantly different at the three phase points. The post-hoc pairwise *t*-tests, for which all the *p*-values are adjusted using the Bonferroni multiple testing correction method, revealed that all the differences between the three conditions (Phase1, Phase2 and Phase3) were statistically significantly different (both the *p* and p.adj < 0.05). The adjusted *p*-value (p.adj) is calculated by dividing the alpha level by the number of pairs:

$$p_{adj} = \frac{\textit{target overall alpha level (usually 0.05)}}{\textit{number of paired tests}}$$

This adjusted *p*-value is called the *Bonferroni correction*, which sets up a new adjusted value for the alpha level to reduce the possibility of getting a Type I error. In Example 12.1, the new alpha is set to $p_{adj} = 0.05/3 = 0.017$.

12.2.4 Measuring the effect size in a one-way repeated measures ANOVA

The effect size is essentially the amount of variability due to the within-subjects factor, ignoring the effect of the subjects, and its size is shown on the column labelled 'ges' (generalised eta-squared).

Measuring the effect size

To extract the ANOVA table, which contains the information about the effect size, we use the function `get_anova_table()` from the `rstatix` package:

```
get_anova_table(res.aov)
ANOVA Table (type III tests)
    Effect DFn DFd      F        p p<.05    ges
1   phase   2  38 238.319 3.14e-22     * 0.838
```

Interpretation

The value of the generalised eta-squared is 0.838, which indicates that 83.8% of the variance in the dependent variable is due to the independent variable.

 **Two-way repeated measures ANOVA**

In this section, we will deal with the two-factor repeated measures ANOVA where both factors are repeated measures. In Section 11.3, we presented the two-factor independent ANOVA, and the key difference between these two types of parametric statistical tests is in calculating the error terms for the variances' ratios.

Example 12.2 Finding if there is an interaction between two factors of a dependent variable

Data file: Ex12_2.csv.

We will use the same example as the one described in Section 12.1.1, containing the PTM scores of 20 randomly selected pupils. Each participant took the test at three time intervals, and the PTM scores were recorded on three occasions, when they entered the programme (Time 1), three months after entry (Time 2) and six months after entry (Time 3). The data is shown in Table 12.4. However, some of the pupils received private tuition, while others did not, so we introduce a second independent variable, 'PrivateTuition', with two levels, 'yes' and 'no'.

Table 12.4   PTM scores for the group of pupils (Example 12.2)

id	PrivateTuition	Time1	Time2	Time3
1	yes	92	116	125
2	yes	88	118	124
3	no	89	93	117
4	no	92	114	120
5	yes	79	88	118
6	no	88	99	113
7	no	96	113	120
8	no	87	108	118
9	yes	80	106	124
10	yes	77	105	122
11	yes	81	104	122
12	no	75	102	117

(Continued)

Table 12.4   (Continued)

id	PrivateTuition	Time1	Time2	Time3
13	yes	85	101	119
14	no	81	98	118
15	yes	90	98	119
16	yes	79	98	123
17	no	86	96	123
18	no	85	95	117
19	no	77	92	112
20	yes	79	88	118

Does private tuition induce a significant increase in maths scores over time? In other words, we would like to find out if there is a significant interaction between the two independent variables, 'PrivateTuition' and 'time' on the maths scores. The two-way repeated measures ANOVA will be performed in order to determine whether there is a significant interaction between these two nominal independent variables (paired conditions) and one interval dependent variable.

12.3.1 Checking assumptions for two-way repeated measures ANOVA

Before we start checking the assumptions for two-way repeated measures ANOVA, we will convert the data set columns ('Time1', 'Time2' and 'Time3') into factor variables:

```
library(rstatix)
fEx12_2<-Ex12_2 %>%
        gather(key = "time", value = "score", Time1, Time2, Time3) %>%
        convert_as_factor(id, time)
```

Then we will inspect some random rows of the data by groups:

```
fEx12_2 %>% sample_n_by(PrivateTuition, time, size = 1)
# A tibble: 6 x 4
  id    PrivateTuition time  score
  <fct> <fct>          <fct> <int>
1 6     no             Time1    88
2 19    no             Time2    99
3 4     no             Time3   120
4 11    yes            Time1    81
5 10    yes            Time2   105
6 9     yes            Time3   124
```

Assumption 1. There are no outliers in the data set.

Visualising the data using box and whisker plots

```
library(ggpubr)
ggboxplot(fEx12_2, x = "time", y = "score", color = "PrivateTuition",
palette = "grey")
```

The results are displayed in Figure 12.3:

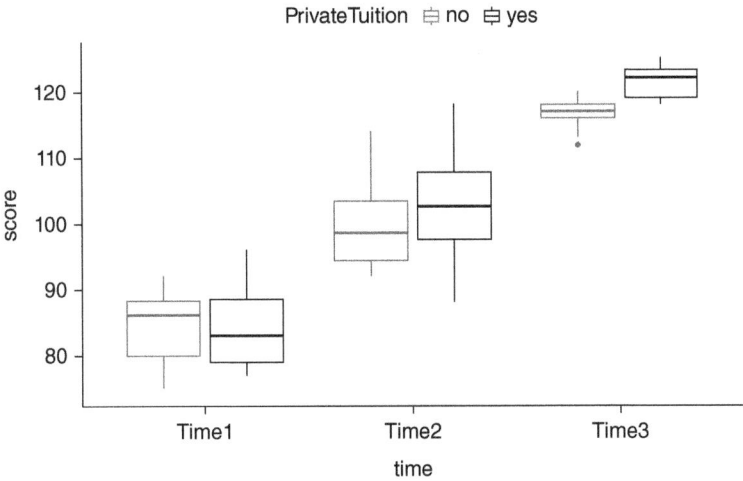

Figure 12.3 Box and whisker plots coloured by private tuition groups

Checking for outliers using the function `identify_outliers()`

```
fEx12_2%>% group_by(PrivateTuition, time) %>% identify_outliers(score)
# A tibble: 1 x 6
  PrivateTuition time id score is.outlier is.extreme
  <fct>          <fct> <fct> <int> <lgl>      <lgl>
1 no             Time3 19    112 TRUE        FALSE
```

The results in the last column indicate that there are no outliers.

Assumption 2. The dependent variable is normally distributed.

Computing the Shapiro–Wilk test for each combination of factor levels:

```
fEx12_2%>% group_by(PrivateTuition, time) %>% shapiro_test(score)
# A tibble: 6 x 5
  PrivateTuition time  variable statistic     p
```

(Continued)

	<fct>	<fct>	<chr>	<dbl>	<dbl>
1	no	Time1	score	0.938	0.592
2	no	Time2	score	0.919	0.423
3	no	Time3	score	0.870	0.152
4	yes	Time1	score	0.913	0.233
5	yes	Time2	score	0.951	0.649
6	yes	Time3	score	0.909	0.204

The results displayed in the last column indicate that the maths scores are normally distributed at each time point ($p > 0.05$).

Assumption 3. Each pair of data is normally distributed.

Creating a QQ plot for each pair

```
ggqqplot(fEx12_2, "score", ggtheme = theme_bw()) +
+ facet_grid(time ~ PrivateTuition, labeller = "label_both")
```

The results are displayed in Figure 12.4.

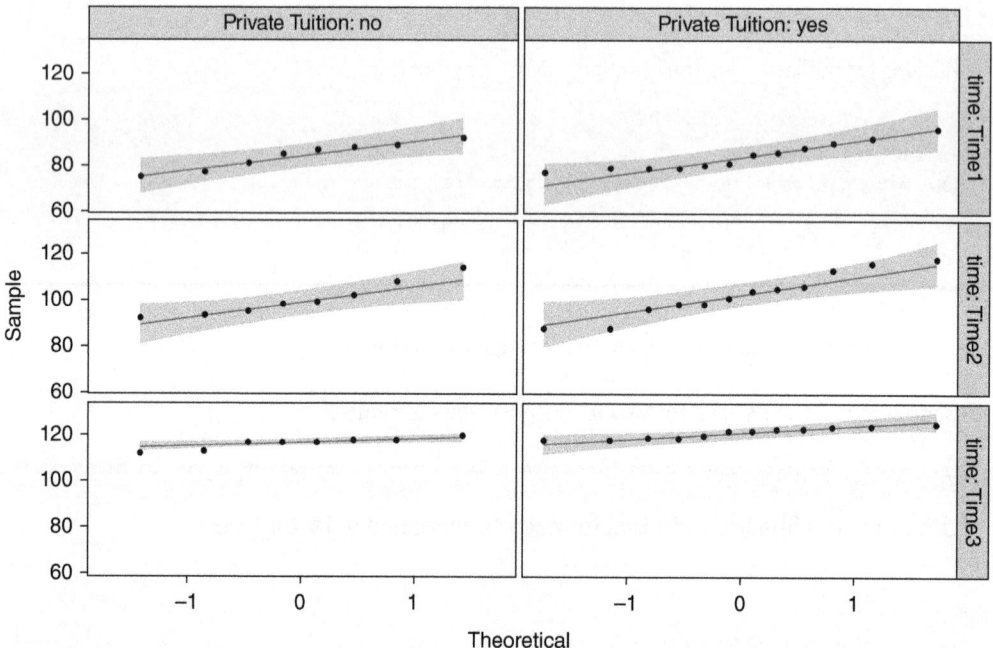

Figure 12.4 QQ plots by time and private tuition groups

From Figure 12.4, we can assume the normality of data because all the points fall approximately along the reference line and the majority of them are within the confidence bands.

12.3.2 Computing two-way repeated measures ANOVA in R

To compute the two-way repeated measures ANOVA in R, we use the same function `anova_test()` as for one-way repeated measures ANOVA, but with a different format for the first argument which is shown in the box below.

Computing two-way repeated measures ANOVA in R

```
fEx12_2 %>% anova_test(score~time*PrivateTuition)
Coefficient covariances computed by hccm()
ANOVA Table (type II tests)

              Effect DFn DFd        F        p p<.05   ges
1               time   2  54  148.217 1.18e-22     * 0.846
2      PrivateTuition   1  54    2.135 1.50e-01       0.038
3 time:PrivateTuition   2  54    0.673 5.15e-01       0.024
```

Interpretation

The asterisk in the `anova_test` function's argument (*score~time*PrivateTuition*) specifies that we want to look at the interaction between the two independent variables (time and PrivateTuition) as well. There are no statistically significant two-way interactions between the two independent variables, PrivateTuition and time, with $F(2, 54) = 1.263$ and $p < 0.05$. The computed F value (1.263) is smaller than the critical F value (3.17; see Table 12.5), and there is enough evidence to conclude that the PrivateTuition factor has no impact on the dependent variable, time. In this case, there is no need for a post-hoc analysis to decompose the two-way interaction into two components: the main effect and the pairwise comparisons.

Table 12.5 Critical values of the F-distribution ($\alpha = 0.05$)

df_w \ df_b	1	2	3	4	5	6	7	8	9	10
50	4.03	3.18	2.79	2.56	2.40	2.29	2.20	2.13	2.07	2.03
51	4.03	3.18	2.79	2.55	2.40	2.28	2.20	2.13	2.07	2.02
52	4.03	3.18	2.78	2.55	2.39	2.28	2.19	2.12	2.07	2.02
53	4.02	3.17	2.78	2.55	2.39	2.28	2.19	2.12	2.06	2.02
54	4.02	3.17	2.78	2.54	2.39	2.27	2.19	2.12	2.06	2.01
55	4.02	3.17	2.78	2.54	2.38	2.27	2.18	2.11	2.06	2.01

12.4 Friedman's test

Friedman's test is an alternative to repeated measures ANOVA. It is a nonparametric test used to determine if there are differences within subjects from two or more dependent samples or groups, and it requires the following assumptions:

- The dependent variable consists of ordinal or non-normally distributed interval data.
- The independent variable is considered nominal.
- The test requires at least a minimum sample size of 12.

The test statistic for Friedman's test is chi-squared.

12.4.1 Computing Friedman's test in R

Example 12.3 Testing the differences between several dependent samples when the dependent variable is ordinal

Data file: Ex12_3.csv

A teacher designed a study to examine whether differences existed in students' engagement level using different forms of conversations online, such as chat, discussion forums, and email. Twenty undergraduate students enrolled on an online course completed a questionnaire revised from a 19-item Online Student Engagement (OSE) questionnaire. To ascertain engagement, the teacher used the following item from this questionnaire:

'Engaging in the following conversations online: chat, discussion forums, email'

and asked students to rate their level of engagement in these three different online conversations on a 1–5 scale (where 1 = 'not at all characteristic of me', 2 = 'not really characteristic of me', 3 = 'moderately characteristic of me', 4 = 'characteristic of me', and 5 = 'very characteristic of me'). The results from the questionnaire are displayed in Table 12.6.

Table 12.6 Students' ratings of three forms of online conversation

Student ID	Chat rating	Discussion forums rating	Email rating
a1	2	4	3
a2	3	3	2
a3	2	4	3
a4	3	4	3
a5	3	4	4
a6	3	3	5
a7	5	5	4

	Chat	Discussion forums	Email
a8	5	5	3
a9	5	5	3
a10	4	5	4
a11	2	4	3
a12	3	4	3
a13	3	4	4
a14	3	3	5
a15	5	4	4
a16	3	4	5
a17	4	4	4
a18	3	3	3
a19	2	5	3
a20	3	4	4

The null and alternative hypotheses are:

H_0: Different forms of online conversations do not affect the engagement level.
H_1: At least one pair of repeated measurements (conditions) has a different median.

Computing Friedman's test in R

Import data file Ex12_3.csv into R:

```
Ex12_3 <- read.csv(file.choose())
```

'Online' is the name of the online conversation variable, and 'Engagement' is the variable for the level of engagement with different forms of online conversation.

Summarise the data, treating the Engagement scores as factors:

```
xtabs ( ~ Online + Engagement, data = Ex12_3)
   Engagement
Online      2  3  4  5
  chat       4 10  2  4
  discussion 0  4 11  5
  email      1  9  7  3
```

(Continued)

Compute the Friedman test statistic using the `friedman.test()` function:

```
friedman.test(Engagement ~ Online | Student, data = Ex12_3)
        Friedman rank sum test
data:   Engagement and Online and Student
Friedman chi-squared = 9.4576, df = 2, p-value = 0.008837
```

Interpretation

The arguments of the `friedman.test()` function indicate that 'Engagement' is the dependent variable, 'Online' is the independent variable, and 'Student' is the factor which contains information about students' IDs. The option *data=* indicates the data frame that contains the variables. For the meaning of other options, type `?friedman.test` in the RStudio Console.

The results provide the Friedman test statistic value ('chi-squared'), degree of freedom ('df') and the significance level ('*p*-value'). We can report the result of this test as follows:

> There was a statistically significant difference in engagement levels for different forms of online conversations, χ_2 = 9.4576, *p* = 0.008837.

Since *p* = 0.009 or 0.9%, we reject the null hypothesis and find that there is a significant difference between our three forms of online discussion in terms of engagement. The differences in our example have a small chance of occurring, and we can conclude that the medians for the three groups or conditions differ significantly.

The Friedman test tells us only if there are overall differences; however, it does not tell us which conditions differ from each other. To find the differences between these three conditions, we will run a post-hoc test, as we have done for its parametric alternative, the Kruskal–Wallis test.

12.4.2 Post-hoc analysis for Friedman's test

The post-hoc analysis should only be run if the Friedman's test results are statistically significant. One of the following post-hoc tests may be used if this assumption is fulfilled, and to detect which pairwise conditions have a significant difference:

- Nemenyi test;
- Conover test;
- pairwise signed-rank tests which are then followed up with one of the multiple tests, such as Bonferroni test.

The Nemenyi post-hoc test, also called the Wilcoxon–Nemenyi–McDonald–Thomson test, is an adaptation of the Tukey HSD test which was described in Section 11.2.3.

Computing the Nemenyi test

To compute the Nemenyi test, we will use the function `posthoc.friedman.nemenyi.test()` which can be found in the `PMCMRplus` package:

```
install.packages("PMCMRplus")
library(PMCMRplus)
posthoc.friedman.nemenyi.test(Engagement ~ Online|Student, data = Ex12_3)
        Pairwise comparisons using Nemenyi multiple comparison test
            with q approximation for unreplicated blocked data
data:   Engagement and Online and Student
            chat discussion
discussion 0.025 -
email      0.609 0.221
P value adjustment method: none
```

Interpretation

According to the Nemenyi post-hoc test for multiple joint samples, there is a significant difference ($p < 0.05$) between the online discussion forums and online chat, but not between other forms of online conversation ($p > 0.05$).

12.4.3 Measuring the effect size in Friedman's test

The effect size is a measure of association, specifically Kendall's W (the coefficient of concordance), and it must be reported alongside the results of the Friedman test.

The null and alternative hypotheses are:

H_0 : There is no agreement among the rankers.
H_1 : There is an agreement among the rankers.

Kendall's W for concordance tries to quantify if the two sets of data are the same, and it is a non-parametric statistic that ranges from 0 to 1 and measures the level of agreement between multiple variables. When the number of observations $n > 10$, its significance can be determined by using a χ^2 distribution with $df = n - 1$.

Computing Kendall's coefficient

You will need to install the `DescTools` package if you have not already done so:

```
install.packages("DescTools")
```

(Continued)

```
library(DescTools)
KendallW(Ex12_3, test=TRUE, correct = TRUE )
        Kendall's coefficient of concordance Wt
data: Ex12_3
Kendall chi-squared = 70.578, df = 59, subjects = 60, raters = 3,
p-value = 0.1438
alternative hypothesis: Wt is greater 0
sample estimates:
     Wt
0.398743
```

The results show that Kendall's coefficient of concordance Wt equals 0.40, which indicates some level of agreement between the categories of independent variables. We see also that the p-value = 0.143, which is larger than $\alpha = 0.05$, thereby allowing us to accept the null hypothesis that 'There is no agreement among the rankers'.

12.5 Cochran's Q-test

Cochran's Q-test is an extension of McNemar's test, and it is used to detect the differences between three or more related or dependent samples in longitudinal or experimental designs where the participants have undergone multiple different treatments or conditions, while the dependent variable is nominal. For example, a typical research scenario involves n subjects or participants, and each subject responds to three or more training conditions (independent variable) with either 'yes' or 'no' or numeric values of 1 or 0 (dichotomous dependent variable).

Before running Cochran's Q-test, the following assumptions must be met:

- There is one dependent variable where the responses are dichotomous.
- There is one independent variable with three or more categorical, related groups or levels.
- The participants are independent of one another, and they have been randomly selected from a population.
- The sample size is sufficiently large that it allows us to have an accurate interpretation of the p-value produced by Cochran's Q-test. For example, as a rule of thumb, the number of participants (n) should be at least 4. In addition, if the number of participants is multiplied by the number of levels in the independent variable (k), the results should be greater than or equal to 24 ($nK \geq 24$).

Once these assumptions have been checked, Cochran's test can be run. If the result is statistically significant, it indicates that there are differences in the proportions between three or more related groups, but it does not tell us which specific groups differ from each other. To investigate further the differences between conditions, a post-hoc analysis can be done.

Example 12.4 Testing the difference between three or more dependent samples when the dependent variable is nominal

Data file Ex12_4.csv

During a training course for a group of 12 newly qualified teachers (NQTs), a special educational needs (SEN) coordinator has introduced three new multi-sensory teaching methods approaches, named MS1, MS2 and MS3, that will help them develop their teaching approaches for pupils with SEN and/or disabilities. After the course, the SEN coordinator surveys the NQTs about their willingness to adopt these three multi-sensory teaching methods. The results are shown in Table 12.7, where each column contains all responses for each multisensory teaching method (condition), and each row corresponds to a single subject.

Table 12.7 NQTs' responses to the SEN coordinator's survey about their willingness to adopt the multi-sensory teaching methods, with dichotomous response (Yes = 1, No = 0)

NQT ID	Multi-sensory teaching methods		
	MS1	MS2	MS3
a1	1	0	1
a2	0	0	0
a3	1	1	1
a4	1	0	1
a5	0	1	1
a6	1	0	1
a7	1	0	1
a8	1	1	1
a9	0	0	1
a10	1	1	1
a11	1	0	1
a12	1	0	0

The null and alternative hypotheses are:

H_0 : The frequencies (or proportions) of responses to the categories of the dependent variable (three different multi-sensory teaching methods) are the same across the categories for the population of NQTs represented by the sample.

H_1 : Within this population, the subjects respond differently across the categories (the NQTs do not equally prefer the three multi-sensory teaching methods).

The probability level (p-value) is compared to alpha ($\alpha = 0.05$) to determine whether to reject the null hypothesis.

12.5.1 Manual calculation of Q-statistic

The calculation of Cochran's Q is carried out as follows:

1. Compute the column and row totals (ΣC and ΣR) and the square of the column and row totals (ΣC^2 and ΣR^2). The results are displayed in the last two columns and the last three rows in Table 12.8.

Table 12.8   Manual calculation of R, C, R^2 and C^2

NQT ID	Multi-sensory teaching methods			Totals	
	MS1	MS2	MS3	R	R²
a1	1	0	1	2	4
a2	0	0	0	0	0
a3	1	1	1	3	9
a4	1	0	1	2	4
a5	0	1	1	2	4
a6	1	0	1	2	4
a7	1	0	1	2	4
a8	1	1	1	3	9
a9	0	0	1	1	1
a10	1	1	1	3	9
a11	1	0	1	2	4
a12	1	0	0	1	1
Totals				$\Sigma R = 23$	$\Sigma R^2 = 53$
C	9	4	10	$\Sigma C = 23$	
C²	81	16	100	$\Sigma C^2 = 197$	

2. The formula for the test statistic Q is:

$$Q = (k-1)\frac{k\sum C^2 - \left(\sum C\right)^2}{k\sum R - \sum R^2}$$

where k is the number of conditions. Note that the column totals are always equal to row totals ($\Sigma C = \Sigma R$).

In Example 12.3, the Q value is equal to:

$$Q = (3-1)\frac{3 \times 197 - 23^2}{3 \times 23 - 53} = 2 \times \frac{62}{16} = 7.75$$

3. Compare the Q-value obtained to the *critical value of χ^2*.

To find the critical chi-squared value, we look in a chi-squared distribution table (Table 12.9) at the intersection of the row corresponding to 2 degrees of freedom ($df = 3 - 1 = 2$) and $\alpha = 0.05$ and the result is 5.99.

Table 12.9 Chi-squared distribution table

df	0.995	0.99	0.975	0.95	0.9	0.1	0.05	0.025	0.01
1	0.00	0.00	0.00	0.00	0.02	2.71	3.84	5.02	6.63
2	0.01	0.02	0.05	0.10	0.21	4.61	5.99	7.38	9.21
3	0.07	0.11	0.22	0.35	0.58	6.25	7.81	9.35	11.34
4	0.21	0.30	0.48	0.71	1.06	7.78	9.49	11.14	13.28
5	0.41	0.55	0.83	1.15	1.61	9.24	11.07	12.83	15.09
6	0.68	0.87	1.24	1.64	2.20	10.64	12.59	14.45	16.81
7	0.99	1.24	1.69	2.17	2.83	12.02	14.07	16.01	18.48
8	1.34	1.65	2.18	2.73	3.49	13.36	15.51	17.53	20.09
9	1.73	2.09	2.70	3.33	4.17	14.68	16.92	19.02	21.67
10	2.16	2.56	3.25	3.94	4.87	15.99	18.31	20.48	23.21

If the Q-value obtained is less than the critical chi-squared value, we retain the null hypothesis, and if it is higher than the critical chi-squared value, then we accept the alternative hypothesis.

12.5.2 Computing Cochran's Q-test in R

To compute Cochran's Q-test, we will use the function `CochranQTest()`, which is included in the DescTools package. There is another function, `cochran.qtest()`, in the RVAideMemoire package, which can also be used.

Computing Cochran Q-test in R

```
library(DescTools)
```

Import data file Ex12_4.csv into R:

```
Ex12_4 <- read.csv(file.choose())
```

Compute Cochrane's Q-test using the `CochranQTest()` function:
```
CochranQTest(Answers~Method | NQT, data=Ex12_4)
        Cochran's Q test
data:  Answers and Method and NQT
Q = 7.75, df = 2, p-value = 0.02075
```

Interpretation

For our example, we reject the null hypothesis because the Q-value of 7.75 obtained is larger than the critical chi-squared value of 5.99 and the Q-statistic is significant at the 5 per cent level (indeed we have $p = 0.02075$). This means that the probabilities of adopting a multi-sensory teaching strategy (1 scores) are different under the three teaching approaches. There are some significant differences between the conditions and at least one of the multi-sensory teaching methods is preferred to the others. Having rejected the null hypothesis, we should perform a post-hoc analysis in order to look further into these differences.

12.5.3 Post-hoc analysis for Cochran's Q-test

A post-hoc analysis is carried out by performing pairwise McNemar's tests; this is the most common statistical procedure for analysing cross-tabulation or contingency tables on nominal variables and for providing evidence of significant differences across observations. For our Example 12.4, we will conduct three pairwise McNemar's tests for the three conditions MS1, MS2, MS3 (three different multi-sensory teaching methods approaches), that is, pairwise tests of MS1 versus MS2, MS1 versus MS3, and MS2 versus MS3. These multiple comparisons require the application of different corrections to adjust the p-value to reduce the possibility of different errors, for example Type I error. Performing the McNemar's tests with Bonferroni, Holm or Benjamini–Hochberg corrections will determine the number of pairs that may or may not be significantly different. The Bonferroni correction reduces the possibility of getting a Type I error (i.e. a statistically significant result when performing multiple tests). It sets up a new adjusted value for the alpha level, which is simple to calculate using the formula described in Section 12.1.1. In Example 12.4, the new alpha is set to $\alpha_{adj} = 0.05/3 = 0.017$.

Computing the pairwise McNemar test with Bonferroni correction

The `rstatix` package has the function `pairwise_mcnemar_test()`, which will conduct the post-hoc analysis. Install this package if you have not already done so:

```
install.packages("rstatix")
library(rstatix)
```

The McNemar's test with the Bonferroni correction:

```
pairwise_mcnemar_test(Ex12_4, Answers~Method|NQT, p.adjust.
method="bonferroni")
# A tibble: 3 x 6
  group1 group2      p p.adj p.adj.signif method
* <chr>  <chr>   <dbl> <dbl> <chr>        <chr>
1 MS1    MS2    0.131  0.393 ns           McNemar test
2 MS1    MS3    1      1     ns           McNemar test
3 MS2    MS3    0.0412 0.124 ns           McNemar test
```

Interpretation

Notice that for each pair of conditions, we get, alongside the *p*-value, an adjusted *p*-value (p.adj) based on the Bonferroni correction method. The *p*.adj is simply the *p*-value multiplied by the total number of pairs. For instance, the *p*-value of 0.0412 is adjusted by multiplying it by 3, which gives a Bonferroni p.adj of 0.124. If we compare this *p*-value directly with α, the result will indicate that the second and third teaching methods (MS2 and MS3) are significantly different from each other because the $p < 0.05$. However, the adjusted *p*-value of 0.124 for this pair is larger than 0.017, which indicates a non-significant result in the dichotomous outcome within the two conditions. Examining the p.adj values for all three pairs, we see that their values are all larger than the adjusted alpha level (0.017), which indicates a non-significant result in the dichotomous outcome within the three conditions.

Although the Bonferroni correction is straightforward to calculate, it lacks statistical power. A modification of the Bonferroni correction, called the *Holm–Bonferroni method*, increases the statistical power, and it is simple to calculate. The formula for the Holm–Bonferroni correction is:

$$a_{adj} = \frac{target\ alpha\ level\ (usually\ 0.05)}{number\ of\ tests - rank\ number\ of\ pairs\ (by\ degree\ of\ significance) - 1}$$

The next example shows how the formula works:

1. We already know the *p*-values associated with each hypothesis:

    H_1: 0.131
    H_2: 1
    H_3: 0.0412

2. We order the *p*-values from smallest to largest:

    H_3: 0.0412
    H_1: 0.131
    H_2: 1

3. We then calculate the Holm-Bonferroni formula for the first rank:

    HB = target α / (*n* - rank + 1)
    HB = 0.05 / (3 - 1 + 1) = 0.05 / 3 = 0.0167

4. Compare the first-ranked (smallest) *p*-value (0.0412) from step 2 to the alpha level calculated in step 3 (HB = 0.0167).

    If the adjusted *p*-value is smaller, reject the null hypothesis for this individual test and repeat the Holm-Bonferroni formula for the second rank.

    The *p*-value of 0.0412 is larger than 0.0167, so the null hypothesis for H_3 is accepted.

    The testing stops when we reach the first non-rejected hypothesis. All subsequent hypotheses are non-significant. In our example, the testing stops at the first rank because it is a non-significant result, and the two other subsequent hypotheses are also non-significant.

Computing the pairwise McNemar test with Holm–Bonferroni correction

We will use the function `pairwise_mcnemar_test()` to compute McNemar's test with the Holm correction:

```
pairwise_mcnemar_test(Ex12_4,Answers~Method|NQT, p.adjust.method="holm")
# A tibble: 3 x 6
  group1 group2     p p.adj p.adj.signif method
* <chr>  <chr>  <dbl> <dbl> <chr>        <chr>
1 MS1    MS2    0.131 0.262 ns           McNemar test
2 MS1    MS3    1     1     ns           McNemar test
3 MS2    MS3    0.0412 0.124 ns          McNemar test
```

Interpretation

Notice that for each pair of conditions, except for MS1–MS2, we get the same results as in the previous example, where we use the Bonferroni correction. These can even be reported without a *p*-value, with only an explanation required of how the pairs of group means differed.

12.5.4 Effect size for Cochran's *Q*-test

There are two measures for the effect size for Cochran's *Q*-test:

- The *maximum-corrected measure of effect size* (η_Q^2), which is given by the following formula:

$$\eta_Q^2 = \frac{Q}{n(c-1)}$$

  where Q is the Cochran's Q-value, n is the sample size (number of participants) and c is the number of conditions (or treatments). The η_Q^2 values lie between 0 and +1 ($0 \leq \eta_Q^2 \leq +1$). However, it possesses no meaningful interpretation except for the values of 0 and 1 because its value relies on an idealised set of data for its maximum value.

- The *chance-corrected measure of effect size* (R), which was developed by Berry et al. (2007), has several advantages in interpretation over η_Q^2. Firstly, R is completely data-dependent. Secondly, R can achieve an effect size of unity for the observed data, an important property which is usually impossible for η_Q^2. Furthermore, R has a clear interpretation of its values, for example, $R = 0$ under chance conditions, $R = 1$ when agreement among the n subjects is perfect, and $R = -1$ under conditions of disagreement.

Unfortunately, there are no packages or functions in R to calculate the maximum-corrected measure of effect size (η_Q^2) and the chance-corrected measure of effect size (R). For η_Q^2 we can follow the calculations below.

Computing the effect size in R

```
Q = 7.75                    # Cochran's Q value
b=12                        # Number of participants
k=3                         # Number of conditions
etasq=Q/(b*(k-1))           # The effect size eta-squared
etasq
[1] 0.3229167
```

For R, there is an instructional video produced by Peter Statistics at www.youtube.com/watch?
v=JGx2YfrceYk.

The η_Q^2 statistic is useful for finding out about the contribution to an effect (a factor or an interaction) of a dependent variable and for comparing effect sizes within a study. However, there is some risk in comparing η_Q^2 values across studies which have different designs because these risks might appear due to the differences in total variability that arise from controlling variables.

Formulas

Test statistic Q

$$Q = \left(k-1\right)\frac{k\Sigma C^2 - \Sigma\left(R \text{ or } C\right)^2}{k\Sigma\left(R \text{ or } C\right) - \Sigma\left(R^2\right)}$$

where k is the number of conditions, C is the column total, and R is the row total.

Bonferroni correction

$$a_{adj} = \frac{target\ overall\ alpha\ level\ (usually\ 0.05)}{number\ of\ paired\ tests}$$

Holm-Bonferroni correction

$$a_{adj} = \frac{overall\ alpha\ level\ (usually\ 0.05)}{number\ of\ tests\text{-}rank\ number\ of\ pairs\ (by\ degree\ of\ significance)\text{-}1}$$

(Continued)

Maximum-corrected measure of effect size

$$\eta_Q^2 = \frac{Q}{n(c-1)}$$

where Q is the Cochran's Q-value, n is the sample size (number of participants), and c is the number of conditions (or treatments).

Exercises

12.1 A teacher gives a group of secondary school children a reading test at the beginning of the school year and again at the end of the year. The teacher wants to use the data to estimate how much reading scores change during the year. Which test should the teacher use for her estimate?

12.2 If the null hypothesis is true, what is the expected value for the F-ratio for ANOVA?

12.3 How are the results of the following tests reported?

    (a) One-way ANOVA

    (b) Two-way ANOVA

12.4 What is the main difference between the within-groups sum of squares and the between-groups sum of squares?

12.5 When is post-hoc analysis required?

12.6 What are the assumptions for repeated one-way ANOVA?

12.7 Which test can we use for paired samples when the dependent variable is nominal? What scale of measurement is permitted for the independent variable?

12.8 Do we have to rank the factors before we use Friedman's test?

Further reading

Berry, K. J., Johnston, J. E., and Mielke, P. W., Jr (2007) An alternative measure of effect size for Cochran's Q-test for related proportions. *Perceptual and Motor Skills*, 104, 1236–1242.

This paper introduces an alternative measure of the effect size called the chance-corrected measure of effect size (R) for Cochran's Q-test.

Nussbaum, E. M. (2015) *Categorical and nonparametric data analysis: Choosing the best statistical technique.* New York: Routledge.

Chapter 7 presents a detailed description of nonparametric tests, including formulas, calculations and examples, for comparing two or more dependent samples.

Serlin, R. C., Carr, J. and Marascuillo, L. A. (1982) A measure of association for selected nonparametric procedures. *Psychological Bulletin*, 92, 786–790.

This article introduces the maximum-corrected measure of effect size (η^2) for Cochran's Q-test.

PART SIX

Relationships and predictions

Part Six Contents

13

Relationships between variables

━━━━━━━━━━ Chapter Objectives ━━━━━━━━━━

In this chapter, we will:

- define covariance and correlation
- describe the relationship between two variables using a scatterplot
- compute the covariance to measure the direction of the relationship between two variables
- compute the correlation coefficient to measure the direction and strength of the relationship between two variables
- compute different types of coefficients to measure the correlation between nominal data (Cramér's *V* correlation), ordinal data (Spearman's correlation) and interval data (Pearson's correlation)
- interpret the value of the correlation and determination coefficients.

Educationalists and researchers in education are often interested in knowing how several variables are related to each other. The analysis of relationships between two or more variables, which is often depicted using a scatterplot, involves getting answers to questions about the direction (positive or negative) and strength of the relationship (or variation) between the variables, and whether the relationship exists in both the sample and the population. For example, we may ask relationship-based questions when the ideas of relationships between variables are of interest:

> Is there a relationship between children's gender and activity preference during school time? If this relationship exists, is it strong or weak?

> Does a child's gender in any way influence how the child chooses a specific type of activity?

To get a better understanding of the data and the relationship between variables, we usually go through the following steps:

1. The data should be arranged as a correlation table or plotted as a scatter graph. The table or scatterplot should be carefully examined to compare the variables and to see whether the paired data points follow a straight line which indicates that the value of one variable is linearly associated with the value of the other variable.
2. If an association or a relationship exists between variables, the strength and direction of the relationship will be measured by a *coefficient of correlation*.
3. To see if the relationship occurs by chance, a null hypothesis is formulated, and then the *p*-value is computed from the data.
4. We cannot go directly from statistical correlation to causation, and further investigations are required.

 Covariance and correlation between two variables

Covariance and correlation describe the association (relationship) between two variables, and they are closely related statistics to each other, but not the same. The *covariance* measures only the directional relationship between the two variables and reflects how they change together. A direct or positive covariance means that paired values of the two variables move in the same direction, while an indirect or negative covariance means they move in the opposite direction.

The formula for covariance is:

$$\text{cov}(X,Y) = \frac{\Sigma(x_i - \bar{x})(y_i - \bar{y})}{n-1}$$

where x_i is the ith x-value in the data set, $\bar{x}$ is the mean of the x values, y_i is the ith y-value in the data set, $\bar{y}$ is the mean of the y-values and n is the number of data values in each data set.

If $\text{cov}(X, Y) > 0$ there is a positive relationship between the dependent and independent variables, and if $\text{cov}(X, Y) < 0$ the relationship is negative.

Example 13.1 Computing the covariance

Data file: Ex13_1.csv

Suppose that a physics teacher would like to convince her students that the amount of time they spend studying for a written test is related to their test score. She asks seven of her students to study for 0.5, 1, ..., 3.5 hours and records their test scores, which are displayed in Table 13.1.

Table 13.1 Test scores recorded by seven students in preparation for their physics test, together with time spent studying

Study time (hours)	Physics scores (%)
0.5	60
1	70
1.5	80
2	83
2.5	86
3	90
3.5	96

The x-variable is the study time, with a mean value of 2, and the y-variable is the test score with a mean value of 80.71. The manual calculation of covariance yields:

$$Covariance = [(0.5-2)\times(60-80.71)+(1-2)\times(70-80.71)+(1.5-2)\times$$
$$(80-80.71)+(2-2)(83-80.71)+(2.5-2)\times(86-80.71)+$$
$$(3-2)\times(90-80.71)+(3.5-2)\times(96-80.71)]/(7-1)=12.83$$

Computing covariance in R

Import the Ex13_1.csv file into R and save it as an object with the same name:

```
x13_1 <- read.csv(file.choose())
```

Compute the covariance between the independent variable 'Time' and the dependent variable 'Scores' using the function `cov()`:

```
cov(Ex13_1$Time,Ex13_1$Score)
[1] 12.83333
```

Interpretation

The covariance of the data set is 12.83. Because this number is positive, we can state that the two variables, study time and test score, are in a positive relationship, or we can say that as study time increases, the test score also increases. The more time students spend studying, the higher their physics test score will be. This value does not tell us how strong this relationship is, and to find its strength, we must compute the correlation coefficient.

The analysis of *correlation* is concerned with two characteristics of the relationship between variables that are measured based on a number or index, which is called the *correlation coefficient*:

- the *direction* of the correlation coefficient, which can be either positive, negative or null;
- the *strength* or *magnitude* of the correlation coefficient, which can be anywhere between –1 and +1. If the correlation equals zero, it does not mean that the dependent and independent variables are not related, only that their relationship is not linear.

Measuring the strength of the relationship between two variables, irrespective of their units and removing the influence of scaling, can be done by standardising the variables. The correlation coefficient, r, is an example of a standardised statistic. It is calculated by dividing the covariance of the two variables (x and y) by the product of their standard deviations (s_x and s_y) which are measures of dispersion around the mean of each variable:

$$r = \frac{\text{cov}(x, y)}{s_x s_y}$$

The correlation coefficient between the two variables presented in Example 13.1 is:

$$r = \frac{12.83}{1.08 \times 12.23} = 0.97$$

Computing the correlation coefficient in R

```
cor(Ex13_1$Time,Ex13_1$Score)
[1] 0.9714977
```

The symbol *r* is used to represent the *Pearson correlation coefficient* or the *product-moment correlation coefficient* for a sample, and this is the statistic most widely used to measure the relationship between two interval variables, while the Greek letter rho (ρ) is used for a population. A value of the correlation coefficient of −1 indicates a perfect negative (or indirect) relationship between variables and a value of +1 indicates a perfect positive (or direct) correlation between variables, while a value of 0 shows no linear relationship at all. The values of *r* cannot be interpreted as proportions; for example, 0.5 is not equivalent to 50% (see Section 13.1.3). Also, the correlation coefficient describes the relationship between two variables, but it is not a sufficient condition to determine or prove cause and effect. However, the correlation forms the basis for regression analysis that determines the nature of the relationship, which will be discussed in Chapter 14.

13.1.1 Visual representation of the correlation

The scatterplot is the most straightforward visual aid to quickly identify the direction and pattern between a pair of variables. Each dot on all five scatter diagrams presented in Figure 13.1 represents the paired values of two variables distributed along the horizontal and vertical axes. Figure 13.1(a) shows a perfect positive correlation between two variables when the correlation coefficient equals +1, meaning that there is a perfect positive rate of change between the variables: as the value of one variable increases, the other variable value increases. In other words, all points are aligned along a line which has a positive slope. If all points appear scattered randomly on the scatterplot, it implies that no correlation exists between the variables. In Figure 13.1(b) we can see that the data points align themselves along a positive slope, which indicates a positive, though not perfect, relationship (*r* = 0.86). A negative correlation indicates that as one variable increases, the other variable decreases (Figure 11.3(c) and (d)) and the data points group themselves in clusters from the upper left-hand corner to the lower right-hand corner of the graph following a negative slope. The two variables in Figure 13.1(e) appear not to be linear related (*r* = 0).

The relationships in Figure 13.1 are summarised by straight lines. The position of the straight line may be determined by the method of least squares best fit which will be described in Chapter 14. However, the correlation is not always an appropriate measure of the relationship between two variables. The relationship may be curvilinear, with the pattern of data points (or rate of change) changing in a non-linear fashion, for example first increasing and then decreasing. The correlation coefficient should be used to show the relationship only after displaying the data using a scatterplot.

In conclusion, the value and sign of the correlation coefficient help us to interpret the linear association between two variables. The higher the value of the correlation coefficient, regardless of its sign, the stronger the association is (Table 13.2).

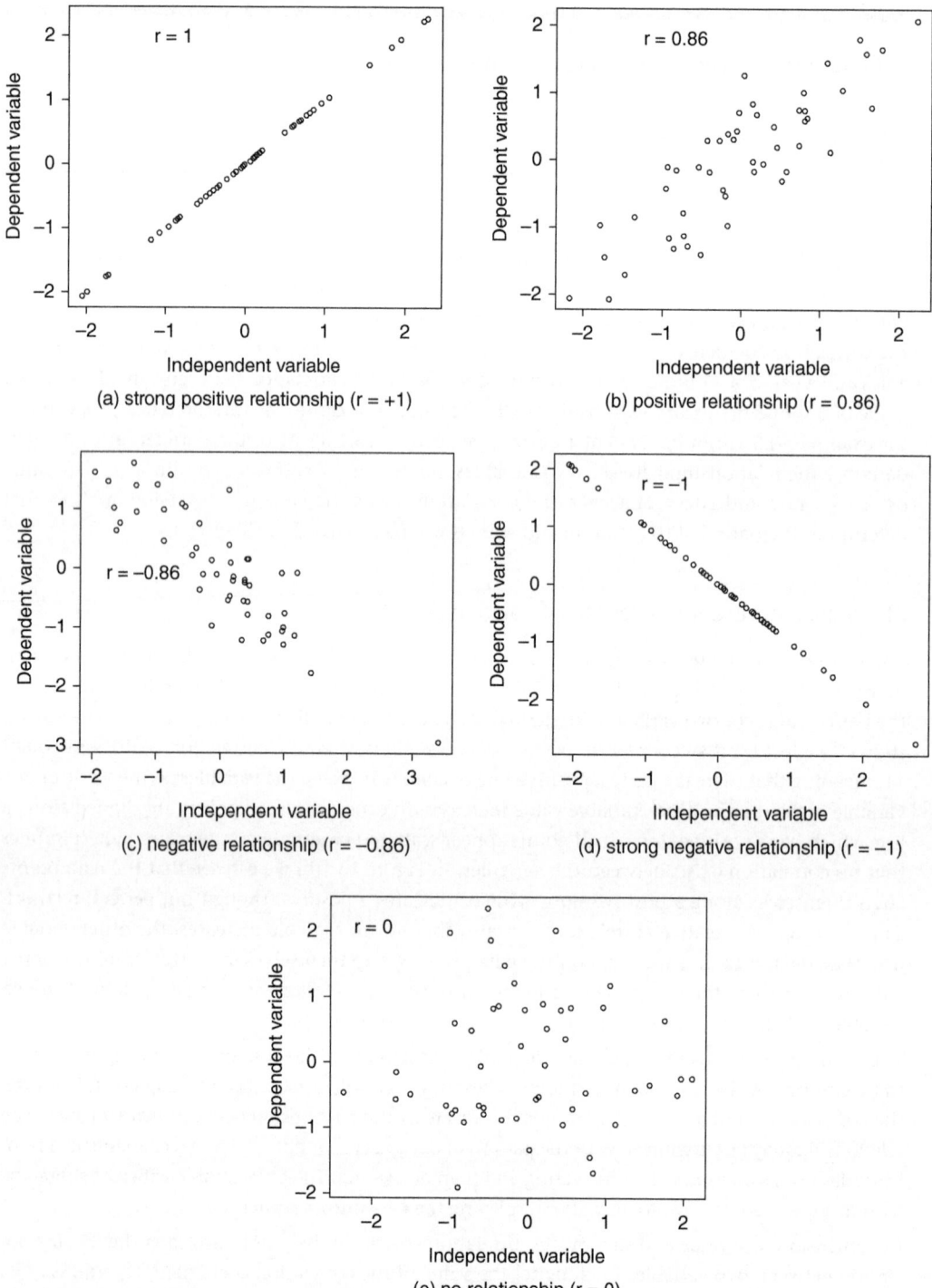

Figure 13.1 Relationships between two variables: (a) perfect positive, (b) positive, (c) negative, (d) perfect negative, and (e) no relationship

Table 13.2   Interpreting the correlation coefficient

Size of r	Interpretation of the relationship
0.00-0.19	No relation or weak
0.20-0.39	Weak
0.40-0.59	Moderate
0.60-0.79	Strong
0.80-1.00	Very strong or perfect

13.1.2 Coefficient of determination

The coefficient of determination estimates the strength of the relationship between two variables and is used to interpret the correlation coefficient more precisely. To compute the coefficient of determination, we square the correlation coefficient, r:

$$coefficient\ of\ determination = r^2$$

r^2 is the proportion of the variation in a dependent variable (Y) accounted for by the variation in the independent variable (X) in a sample, and it is an estimate of the population coefficient of determination (ρ^2). To be specific, the coefficient of determination is the proportion of the variance in one variable that is explained by the variance in the other variable.

The value of r^2 lies between 0 and 1, and it will always be smaller in magnitude than the correlation coefficient unless both are equal to 0 or 1. If $r^2 = 0$, it means that the independent variable can explain none of the variation in the dependent variable. If $r^2 = 1$, it means that the independent variable can explain all the variation (or 100%) in the dependent variable. And, for example, if $r = 0.4$, it means that the independent variable can explain $r^2 = 0.4^2 = 0.16$ or 16% of the variation in the dependent variable. In Example 13.1, we compared the study time with the test scores and found the correlation coefficient to be 0.97. The coefficient of determination is $r^2 = 0.97^2 = 0.94$, which means that 94% of the variation in test scores (dependent variable) can be explained by the variation in study time (independent variable), and the independent variable cannot explain 6% of the variation. The amount of unexplained variance, $1 - r^2$, is called the *coefficient of non-determination* (or *alienation*).

13.1.3 Errors of the correlation coefficient

The calculation, use and interpretation of the correlation coefficient are subject to error. The most common error concerns the interpretation of the correlation coefficient as a decimal fraction or percentage. This interpretation is misleading since the strength of the association between variables does not vary directly with the size of the correlation coefficient, but with the coefficient of determination. We should interpret the size of the correlation coefficient as an indication of the proportion of common elements in the two variables and as an indicator in determining the error in predicting or estimating one variable from another. The correlation coefficient is only a mathematical expression for the degree of association between two variables, not a measure of a causal relationship.

The size of the correlation coefficient depends very much on the sampling errors introduced due to small sample size or by the failure to select a random sample. These two types of errors may, for example, increase the standard deviation and consequently reduce the size of the correlation coefficient, which, in turn, does not give us the right information to estimate the amount of association that exists between variables in a population.

From research in psychology, it is well known that the presence of random errors due to measurement error or test construction attenuates the correlation between two tests, and the computed correlation coefficient between tests which contains an error component is less than the error-free (or 'true') correlation coefficient. Spearman introduced a correction for attenuation to estimate the true correlation coefficient. The formula for the correction of attenuation is:

$$r_{XY} = \frac{correlation(X,Y)}{\sqrt{reliability_X \times reliability_Y}}$$

where r_{XY} is the true correlation, $correlation(X, Y)$ is the computed correlation, $reliability_X$ measures the reliability of the variable X, and $reliability_Y$ measures the reliability of the variable Y. The failure to take into consideration the correction for attenuation will lead to errors of incomplete analysis of the correlation coefficient.

13.2 Correlations for more than two variables

In education research, the calculation and analysis of the relationship between more than two variables are not unusual. For example, the relationships between the ability to solve arithmetic problems and the general intellectual ability and teaching strategies are multiple variables which can be found in many research papers in education and psychology. If there are more than two variables, for each pair of variables, there is a correlation coefficient, and it is calculated using the same formula for the correlation coefficient described in Section 13.1. Each multiple correlation coefficient has its corresponding regression equation, which will be discussed in Chapter 14.

Example 13.2 Multiple correlation coefficients

The physics teacher got the same seven students to prepare for a maths test by spending the same amount of time revising as they did for the physics test. We expand the data from Example 13.1 and include a third variable, called the 'Maths scores', in addition to the other two variables, 'Study time' and 'Physics scores'. The data set is shown in Table 13.3.

Table 13.3 The amount of study time recorded by students in preparation for their physics and maths tests and their tests scores

Study time (hours)	Physics scores (%)	Maths scores (%)
0.5	60	58
1	70	68
1.5	80	75
2	83	78
2.5	86	80
3	90	85
3.5	96	90

To compute in R the correlation coefficients between each pair of variables, we use the same function *cor()* which returns a table that is called a *correlation matrix*, as shown in the box below.

Computing the correlation matrix in R

Import the Ex13_2.csv file into R and save it as an object with the same name:

```
x13_2 <- read.csv(file.choose())
cor(Ex13_2)
             Time     Physics      Maths
Time     1.0000000 0.9714977 0.9744816
Physics 0.9714977 1.0000000 0.9977987
Maths    0.9744816 0.9977987 1.0000000
```

Interpretation

The correlation matrix is symmetrical, which means the values above the diagonal have the same values as those below. The diagonal of a correlation matrix always consists of 1s because these are the correlations between each variable and itself. To locate the correlation for any pair of variables, for example between physics and maths test scores, we look at the value in the correlation matrix where the physics row and maths column (or the physics column and maths row) intersect for those two variables. The correlation coefficient for these two paired variables is 0.9977987, which indicates a positive and almost perfect relationship between maths and physics test scores.

13.2.1 Visual representation of the correlation matrix

The basic plot for a correlation matrix is the heat map. A heat map is a two-dimensional representation of data in the form of a map in which data values are represented using different colours or shades of the same colour. This type of graph is well suited for the graphical display of the correlation coefficients between more than two variables because it provides an immediate visual summary of strength of the relationship between variables. One colour indicates a positive correlation, and another colour indicates a negative correlation. The shade of each colour indicates the strength of correlation: darker shades indicate a stronger relationship between variables, while lighter shades indicate a weaker relationship. The absence of a relationship between variables is shown in white. Heat maps can be created in R using the `ggcorr()` function from the `GGally` library.

Visual representation of the correlation matrix in R

```
install.packages("GGally")
library(GGally)
ggcorr(Ex13_2, nbreaks = 12, low = "grey", mid="white", high="black")
```

where *low="grey"* indicates the colours for negative correlation, *mid="white"* for mid-range correlation and *high="black"* indicates the colours for positive correlation. The argument *nbreaks=12* specifies the number of breaks or colour levels contained in the colour scale. The results are shown in Figure 13.2.

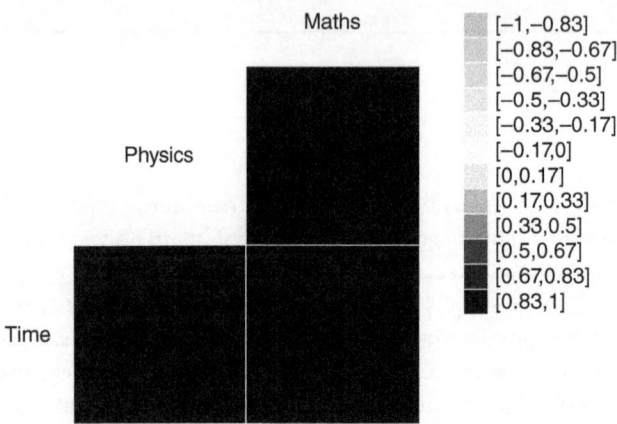

Figure 13.2 The heat map for the correlation matrix

In Figure 13.2, the intensity of the background colour of all three squared areas is the same, which indicates that there are strong positive correlations between maths and physics, between time and physics, and between time and maths. It is important to remember that correlations express only an associative relationship between variables and not a causal relationship.

13 ● 3   Correlations and scales of measurement

So far we have discussed how to manually calculate Pearson's correlation coefficient, which is used if both variables are measured on interval/ratio measurement scales. This does not mean we cannot compute correlations for other measurement scales (ordinal or nominal). If the variables are measured on other scales of measurement, other kinds of correlation are available. These are summarised in Table 13.4. In this section, we will describe in detail one parametric correlation coefficient (Pearson's r_p) and three nonparametric correlation coefficients (Spearman's rho, Cramér's phi and lambda), used when the scales of measurement for each variable are the same; these are highlighted in Table 13.4.

Table 13.4   Types of correlation as a function of levels of measurement

Variable B Scales of measurement	Variable A Scales of measurement		
	Interval/ratio	Ordinal	Nominal
Interval/ratio	Pearson	Biserial	Point biserial
Ordinal	Biserial	Spearman	Rank point biserial
Nominal	Point biserial	Rank point biserial	Cramér's phi (or V), lambda

13.3.1 Pearson's correlation coefficient

The most widely used correlation coefficient is *Pearson's product-moment correlation coefficient*, usually shortened to Pearson's correlation coefficient. The assumptions of Pearson's correlation are:

- the relationship between variables is linear, which means that it is meaningful to fit a straight line through the scatter of points when the two variables are plotted;
- the variables are measured at the interval/ratio scales;
- the interval/ratio data is normally distributed (note that Pearson's correlation coefficient is very sensitive to the presence of outliers);
- the variables are independent of each other.

When data is collected from a sample, and the correlation coefficient is computed, it is necessary to calculate the probability of the sample showing a relationship occurring by chance or not. The null hypothesis of no relationship between variables, which is represented by the correlation coefficient, is usually rejected when this probability is less than 0.05.

Pearson's product-moment correlation coefficient (r_p) is used to estimate the population correlation coefficient and is defined as:

$$r_p = \frac{\Sigma (x_i - \bar{x})(y_i - \bar{y})}{\sqrt{\Sigma (x_i - \bar{x})^2 \, \Sigma (y_i - \bar{y})^2}}$$

where:

- $x_1, ..., x_i$ and $y, ..., y_i$ are the i observations for variable x and variable y;
- $\bar{x}$ and $\bar{y}$ are the mean values.

This equation describes Pearson's correlation coefficient as the centred and standardised sum of cross-products of two variables because in the numerator the data values are centred by subtracting out the mean of each variable and the sum of cross-products of the centred variables. The denominator adjusts the scales of the variables to have equal units.

Example 13.3 Pearson's correlation

Data file: Ex13_3.csv

A lecturer is interested in finding out what is the relationship between the average number of hours spent by students each week doing homework and their assignment grades. A random sample of 30 students is considered, the assignment grades are recorded as the dependent variable and the average number of hours spent doing homework as the independent variable. The data is given in Table 13.5, and a scatterplot of these data is shown in Figure 13.3.

Table 13.5 Average time per week spent on homework and assignment grades

Time	Grades	Time	Grades
8.2	97.25	9.6	97.74
9.6	98.18	9.9	98.38
8.9	97.24	10.2	96.89
10.1	98.16	9.1	98.55
10.1	97.59	11.3	99.93
9.9	97.58	10.3	97.63
10	97.47	10.6	99.38
10.8	98.63	7.6	95.55
9.5	98.48	10.6	99.41
11.6	99.03	11.2	98.61

Time	Grades	Time	Grades
8.4	96.56	9.4	97.87
10.1	98.57	10	97.37
11.6	99.72	11.7	98.35
9.3	96.64	9.9	98.17
9.6	96.71	11	98.38

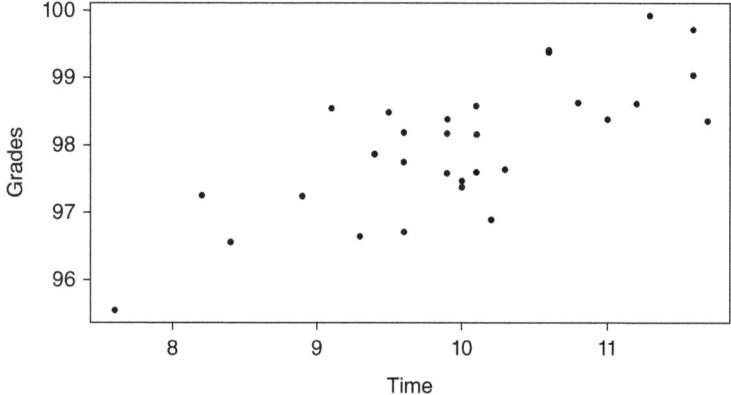

Figure 13.3   Scatterplot of assignment grades against time spent on homework

The assumption of normality of data is tested by using the Shapiro–Wilk test, as shown below. The output *p*-value (0.9123) is higher than the significance level 0.05, which implies that the distribution of data is normal.

Testing for normality of data

Load the data (Ex13_3.csv) into R and name it 'Ex13_3'. Now carry out the Shapiro-Wilk test:

```
shapiro.test(Ex13_3$Grades)
        Shapiro-Wilk normality test
data: Ex13_3$Grades
W = 0.98366, p-value = 0.9123
```

Pearson's correlation coefficient can be computed using the function `cor()`, which only returns the correlation coefficient, or `cor.test()`, which returns both the correlation coefficient and the significance level (or *p*-value) of the correlation. We will demonstrate below the use of both functions.

Computing Pearson's correlation coefficient in R

```
cor(Ex13_3$Time, Ex13_3$Grades,, method = "pearson")
[1] 0.7504007
cor.test(Ex13_3$Time, Ex13_3$Grades, method = "pearson")
          Pearson's product-moment correlation
data:  Ex13_3$Time and Ex13_3$Grades
t = 6.0073, df = 28, p-value = 1.794e-06
alternative hypothesis: true correlation is not equal to 0
95 percent confidence interval:
 0.5346803 0.8743049
sample estimates:
     cor
0.7504007
```

Interpretation

In the results above, t is the test statistic, df is the degrees of freedom ($df = n - 2 = 30 - 2 = 28$), and the *p-value* is compared to the significance level of the t-test to determine whether the correlation coefficient is significant. These are followed by the 95% confidence interval (0.53, 0.87) for the correlation coefficient and the sample estimate of the correlation coefficient. The computed value of the Pearson's correlation coefficient ($r = 0.75$) helps only to quantify the correlation, and in our case indicates a strong positive correlation between the time spent on homework and the assignment grades. However, we also need to consider whether the correlation is statistically significant. To assess the statistical significance of the correlation, we perform a hypothesis test to decide whether the value of the correlation coefficient is zero or significantly different from zero.

We consider the 0.05 value for the significance level and the following null (H_0) and alternative (H_1) hypotheses:

$$H_0 : r = 0.$$

$$H_1 : r \neq 0.$$

In order to reject the null hypothesis, our computed correlation coefficient must exceed the critical value for the correlation coefficient for a certain number of degrees of freedom (df) and significance level (α). From Table 13.6 we obtain a critical value of the correlation coefficient of 0.361007 which corresponds to a $df = n - 2 = 30 - 2 = 28$, $\alpha = 0.05$ and a two-tailed test. Our observed $r = 0.7504007$ exceeds the critical value, and we reject the null hypothesis of zero correlation. Also, because the *p*-value is less than 0.05, the correlation is significant, and the correlation coefficient equals 0.75 in the population from which the sample was drawn.

Table 13.6 Critical values of Pearson's correlation coefficient

df\α	0.2	0.1	0.05	0.02	0.01	0.001
1	0.951057	0.987688	0.996917	0.999507	0.999877	0.999999
2	0.800000	0.900000	0.950000	0.980000	0.990000	0.999000
3	0.687049	0.805384	0.878339	0.934333	0.958735	0.991139
4	0.608400	0.729299	0.811401	0.882194	0.917200	0.974068
5	0.550863	0.669439	0.754492	0.832874	0.874526	0.950883
6	0.506727	0.621487	0.706734	0.788720	0.834342	0.924904
7	0.471589	0.582206	0.666384	0.749776	0.797681	0.898260
8	0.442796	0.549357	0.631897	0.715459	0.764592	0.872115
9	0.418662	0.521404	0.602069	0.685095	0.734786	0.847047
10	0.398062	0.497265	0.575983	0.658070	0.707888	0.823305
11	0.380216	0.476156	0.552943	0.633863	0.683528	0.800962
12	0.364562	0.457500	0.532413	0.612047	0.661376	0.779998
13	0.350688	0.440861	0.513977	0.592270	0.641145	0.760351
14	0.338282	0.425902	0.497309	0.574245	0.622591	0.741934
15	0.327101	0.412360	0.482146	0.557737	0.605506	0.724657
16	0.316958	0.400027	0.468277	0.542548	0.589714	0.708429
17	0.307702	0.388733	0.455531	0.528517	0.575067	0.693163
18	0.299210	0.378341	0.443763	0.515505	0.561435	0.678781
19	0.291384	0.368737	0.432858	0.503397	0.548711	0.665208
20	0.284140	0.359827	0.422714	0.492094	0.536800	0.652378
21	0.277411	0.351531	0.413247	0.481512	0.525620	0.640230
22	0.271137	0.343783	0.404386	0.471579	0.515101	0.628710
23	0.265270	0.336524	0.396070	0.462231	0.505182	0.617768
24	0.259768	0.329705	0.388244	0.453413	0.495808	0.607360
25	0.254594	0.323283	0.380863	0.445078	0.486932	0.597446
26	0.249717	0.317223	0.373886	0.437184	0.478511	0.587988
27	0.245110	0.311490	0.367278	0.429693	0.470509	0.578956
28	0.240749	0.306057	(0.361007)	0.422575	0.462892	0.570317
29	0.236612	0.300898	0.355046	0.415792	0.455631	0.562047
30	0.232681	0.295991	0.34370	0.409327	0.448699	0.554119

13.3.2 Spearman's correlation coefficient

Charles Spearman, the British psychologist and statistician, did pioneering work in the area of the strength of the relationship between two ordinal variables which is quantified by a coefficient called the Spearman rank-order correlation coefficient, also known as Spearman's rho and denoted r_s.

Spearman's rho is a nonparametric application of Pearson's correlation and it is used to measure the strength of association between two ordinal variables or between two interval variables which are not normally distributed. The correlation coefficient lies between –1 and +1, where $r_s = +1$ indicates a perfect positive correlation between ranks, $r_s = -1$ a perfect negative correlation between ranks, and $r_s = 0$ no linear association between ranks.

The formula for the Spearman's rho rank correlation coefficient is:

$$r_S = 1 - \frac{6\Sigma d_i^2}{n(n^2 - 1)}$$

where n is the number of pairs of ordinal data and d_i is the difference between paired ranks. Spearman's rho is a popular correlation coefficient in survey research for correlating Likert-type questionnaire responses.

Example 13.4 Spearman's rho

Data file Ex13_4.csv

A lecturer asked a group of 10 students to rate, on a scale from 1 to 10, their self and peer contributions to a university project. The results are listed as paired data in the first two columns of Table 13.7.

Table 13.7 Students' rating results of their own and peer contribution to a university project

Self-rated	Peer-rated	Rank Self-rated	Rank Peer-rated	d	d²
9	8	1.5	2	2 - 1.5 = 0.5	0.25
9	9	1.5	1	-0.5	0.25
7	5	4	5.5	1.5	2.25
6	4	5	7.5	2.5	6.25
4	4	7.5	7.5	0	0
2	3	9.5	9	-0.5	0.25
2	6	9.5	4	-5.5	30.25
4	2	7.5	10	2.5	6.25
5	5	6	5.5	-0.5	0.25
8	7	3	3	0	0
					Total: 46

Spearman's rank correlation coefficient is very easy to compute manually, and therefore we will demonstrate how to calculate by hand following the next steps:

1. Rank the data for the first and the second columns.

    Give the highest number a rank of 1, the next highest number a rank of 2, and so forth. If two or more values in one column are the same, find the mean of the ranks and use the mean value to rank the data. In our example, there are two 9s in the first column (self-rated) that would otherwise have ranks of 1 and 2. Since there are two 9s, we will take the mean of their ranks. The mean of 1 and 2 is 1.5, so we assign the rank 1.5.

2. In the d column, calculate the difference between the two ranks for each pair of ranks. That is, if one is ranked 2 and the other 1.5, the difference would be 0.5.

3. In the d^2 column, square each value in the d column. Then add all these values together. In Table 13.7 we have $d^2 = 46$.

4. With $n = 10$ pairs of data and the d^2 value calculated above, we can calculate Spearman's correlation coefficient: .

$$r_s = 1 - \frac{6 \times 46}{10 \, (10^2 - 1)} = 0.72$$

To compute Spearman's correlation coefficient in R, we use the same function `cor.test()` as we used to compute Pearson's correlation coefficient, with the difference that we replace the name in the 'method' argument.

Computing Spearman's correlation coefficient in R

Load the Ex13_4.csv file into R and name it 'Ex13_4'. Then compute Spearman's correlation coefficient:

```
cor.test(Ex13_4$SelfRated, Ex13_4$PeerRated, method = "spearman")
        Spearman's rank correlation rho
data: Ex13_4_v1$SelfRated and Ex13_4_v1$PeerRated
S = 46.707, p-value = 0.01963
alternative hypothesis: true rho is not equal to 0
sample estimates:
      rho
0.7169265
```

If we round this result to two decimal places, we obtain the same result as we previously obtained manually (0.72).

Interpretation

Both Spearman's rho results (manual calculation and R computation) indicate a strong positive correlation ($r_s = 0.72$) between self- and peer-rated evaluation; however, we do not know if this value is statistically significant. To find out if the computed value of the correlation coefficient is strong enough, we compare this value to a critical value (Table 13.8) and we are looking for this value to be higher than the critical value.

Table 13.8 Critical values of Spearman's ranked correlation coefficient

n\α	0.2	0.1	0.05	0.02	0.01	0.002
4	1.000	1.000	-	-	-	-
5	0.800	0.900	1.000	1.000	-	-
6	0.657	0.829	0.886	0.943	1.000	-
7	0.571	0.714	0.786	0.893	0.929	1.000
8	0.524	0.643	0.738	0.833	0.881	0.952
9	0.483	0.600	0.700	0.783	0.833	0.917
10	0.455	0.564	(0.648)	0.745	0.794	0.879
11	0.427	0.536	0.618	0.709	0.755	0.845
12	0.406	0.503	0.587	0.678	0.727	0.818
13	0.385	0.484	0.560	0.648	0.703	0.791
14	0.367	0.464	0.538	0.626	0.679	0.771
15	0.354	0.446	0.521	0.604	0.654	0.750
16	0.341	0.429	0.503	0.582	0.635	0.729
17	0.328	0.414	0.488	0.566	0.618	0.711

To find the critical value, we go through the following steps:

- Choose the third column which corresponds to our 0.05 value of α.
- Read down until we get to the row matching our score for $n = 10$.
- The critical value is 0.648.

In conclusion, our correlation coefficient value (0.72) is higher than the critical value (0.648) for a two-tailed test, and it is significant at $p < 0.05$.

13.3.3 Lambda, phi and Cramér's V correlation coefficients

The lambda and phi correlation coefficients are the two most commonly used measures to examine the relationship between two variables measured on a nominal scale. *Lambda* (λ) is a statistic used to measure the strength of association between two nominal variables, and it is an asymmetric statistic, in the sense that the value of λ varies depending on which variable is considered the dependent variable and which variables are considered the independent variable. Lambda can take any value from 0 to 1 (Table 13.9), with 0 representing no association between the two nominal variables and 1 representing a perfect association. Lambda is also called the proportional reduction in error, because if the two variables are related, then we should be able to predict the value of one variable based on the value of the other variable.

Table 13.9 Interpreting values of lambda

Range	The relative strength of the association between variables
0	No relationship
0.01–0.19	Very weak
0.20–0.39	Weak
0.40–0.69	Moderate
0.70–0.89	Strong
0.90–0.99	Very strong
1.00	Perfect relationship

The *phi correlation coefficient* (ϕ) is a measure of association for nominal variables in a 2 × 2 contingency table, as shown in Table 13.10. It is a symmetric statistic because the independent and dependent variables are interchangeable.

Table 13.10 A general example of a 2 × 2 contingency table. X is one variable with two levels X' and X'', and Y is the second variable with two levels Y' and Y''. a, b, c and d represent the frequencies, e and f are the sums of frequencies for each row, and g and h are the sums of frequencies for each column. t is the sum of all frequencies

	X'	X''	Total
Y'	a	b	e
Y''	c	d	f
	g	h	t

The formula for the phi coefficient is:

$$\phi = \frac{ad - bc}{\sqrt{efgh}}$$

and its value varies between 0 and 1; it cannot take negative values.

Cramér's V correlation coefficient is a measure of association for nominal variables in contingency tables larger than 2 × 2. Like the other two nonparametric coefficients, Cramér's V varies between 0 and 1 and cannot take negative values.

Example 13.5 Phi correlation coefficient

Data file: Ex13_5.csv

A teacher wants to know if gender is related to the science discipline students are going to choose for their A-level exams. He asks 10 students to choose between two subjects, biology and physics, and the results are displayed in Table 13.11.

Table 13.11 Subject chosen by a group of students for their A-level exam

Gender	Subject
Male	Physics
Male	Biology
Female	Biology
Male	Physics
Female	Physics
Male	Physics
Male	Biology
Female	Biology
Female	Physics
Male	Biology

To test the correlation between the two nominal variables, 'Gender' and 'Subject', we use the phi() function in the psych package. The phi() function requires the 2 × 2 matrix of frequencies to calculate the phi coefficient. Cramér's *V* correlation coefficient can be computed in R by using the function cramersV() which can be found in the lsr package.

Computing the phi correlation coefficient

Create a contingency table in R named 'GenderSubject' using the function table():

```
Ex13_5 <- read.csv("C:/Users/Ex13_5.csv") # Import data file into R
View(Ex13_5)
GenderSubject<-table(EX13_5$Gender, EX13_5$Subject)
GenderSubject
          Biology Physics
Female         2       2
Male           3       3
```

Computing the phi correlation coefficient

To use the `phi()` function, first we must install the `psych` package:

```
install.packages("psych")
library(psych)
```

Now compute the phi coefficient using the function `phi()`:

```
phi(GenderSubject)
[1] 0
```

We can check this result by calculating the phi correlation coefficient by hand:

$$\phi = \frac{ad - bc}{\sqrt{efgh}} = \frac{2 \times 3 - 2 \times 3}{\sqrt{4 \times 6 \times 5 \times 5}} = 0$$

Interpretation

The phi coefficient was calculated between all possible pairs of categories (female–physics, female–biology, male–physics and male–biology) as a measure of the correlation between the two variables, Gender and Subject. The value of the phi correlation coefficient for the data shown in Table 13.10 is 0, which means that there is no association between the two nominal variables. In general, dichotomous variables mostly lead to weaker correlation compared to interval/ratio variables.

Formulas

Covariance

$$\text{cov}(x, y) = \frac{\sum (x_i - \bar{x})(y_i - \bar{y})}{n - 1}$$

Correlation coefficient (r)

$$r = \frac{\text{cov}(x, y)}{s_x s_y}$$

Coefficient of determination

$$\text{coefficient of determination} = r^2$$

(Continued)

Pearson's product-moment correlation coefficient (r_p)

$$r_p = \frac{\sum(x_i - \bar{x})(y_i - \bar{y})}{\sqrt{\sum(x_i - \bar{x})^2 \sum(y_i - \bar{y})^2}}$$

Spearman's rank correlation coefficient (r_s)

$$r_s = 1 - \frac{6\sum d^2}{n(n^2 - 1)}$$

Exercises

13.1 What does a correlation coefficient of -1 indicate?

13.2 Is it possible to have a positive and weak relationship between two variables?

13.3 What is the difference between covariance and correlation?

13.4 Use the data presented in Table 13.12 to answer the following questions:

Table 13.12 Data values for two variables: VarA and VarB

VarA	VarB	VarA	VarB
7.7	48.3	11.2	51.4
11.1	50.5	11	50.4
9.3	48.7	10.5	51.3
9.4	49.6	10.5	51
9.3	49.8	9.6	49.9
9.3	49.3	10.5	49.6
9.8	49.1	10.3	50.6
9.8	48.8	9.2	49.3
10.9	50.4	12	50.8
9.5	51.1	10.2	50.3
10.5	50	9.3	50.1
7.8	48.2	9.2	49.6
9.1	51.6	10.2	50.9
9.7	48.5	10.8	48.8
12	51.5	10.2	50.8

    (a)   Construct a scatterplot.
    (b)   Compute the correlation coefficient using R.
    (c)   Compute the coefficients of determination and non-determination.
    (d)   What are the direction and strength of the relationship between variables?
    (e)   How much of the variance in the relationship between the variables is unaccounted for?

13.5   List all types of correlation as a function of scales of measurement.

13.6   What are the critical steps to find the critical values of the Spearman's rank correlation coefficient?

13.7   Write down the names of the functions to compute Spearman's correlation coefficient and Pearson's correlation coefficient in R.

Further reading

Akoglu, H. (2018) User's guide to correlation coefficients. *Turkish Journal of Emergency Medicine*, 18, 91–93.

The author of this article presents Pearson's *r*, Spearman's rho and Kendall's tau bivariate correlation coefficients to clarify misconceptions when reporting them in medical manuscripts, and summarises the naming practices for the strength of these correlation coefficients.

Holcomb, Z. (2017) *Fundamentals of descriptive statistics*. London: Routledge.

In Chapter 9, the author describes the relationship between two sets of scores using the scatterplot and Pearson's r coefficient.

Krehbiel, T. (2004) Correlation coefficient rule of thumb. *Decision Sciences Journal of Innovative Education*, 2(1), 97–100.

This paper presents an alternative version of the 'rule of thumb' general mechanism for deciding if the observed value of the correlation coefficient is significant.

14

Predictions for independent and dependent variables

━━━━━━━━━━ **Chapter Objectives** ━━━━━━━━━━

In this chapter, we will:

- present the simple and multiple linear regression models, taking into consideration the number of independent and dependent variables and scales of measurement
- discuss the differences between simple linear regression and multiple regression
- determine the simple and multiple linear regression equations
- test the assumptions for linear and multiple regression analysis
- understand how to report and interpret the results of linear regression analysis.

The existence of an association between two variables, which was discussed in detail in Chapter 13, is closely connected to prediction because the presence of a relationship means that information on the value of one variable can be used to predict the value of the other variable. For example, if there is a strong relationship between a person's age and the time spent on online games, then we can predict how much time a person will spend online. While correlation is concerned with the magnitude and direction of a relationship between two variables, prediction is concerned with estimation based on covariance, that is, on how the two variables covary. Thus, correlation analysis, which measures the strength of the relationship between variables, is complementary to *regression analysis*, which is a method to investigate the relationship between a dependent variable and one or more independent variables. In education research, there are three main goals for regression analysis:

1. To find out if variables are associated with each other - for example, as an independent variable increases, the dependent variable increases or decreases. The *p*-value summarises the measure of the association between variables.
2. To estimate the strength of the relationship between the dependent and independent variables. The coefficient of determination, r^2 (or R^2), measures the strength of the association.
3. To model the relationship between variables, and to determine the regression equation, which is used for predicting the dependent variable values (or a line that best fits the data points).

There are different types of regression models, and the classification of these models depends on various factors. For example, if the classification is made on the type of distribution of the dependent variable, we have the following types of regression models:

- linear regression - if the distribution is continuous and approximately normal;
- logistic regression - if the independent variable is dichotomous;
- log-linear regression - if the distribution is multi-modal or Poisson.

If the classification of regression models is based on the type of *parameter* (such as the regression coefficients, which are unknown constants to be estimated from the data) there are two forms of regression models, *linear* and *nonlinear regression* models, and each type of regression model is represented by an equation, which contains information about the relationship between variables and parameters (Figure 14.1).

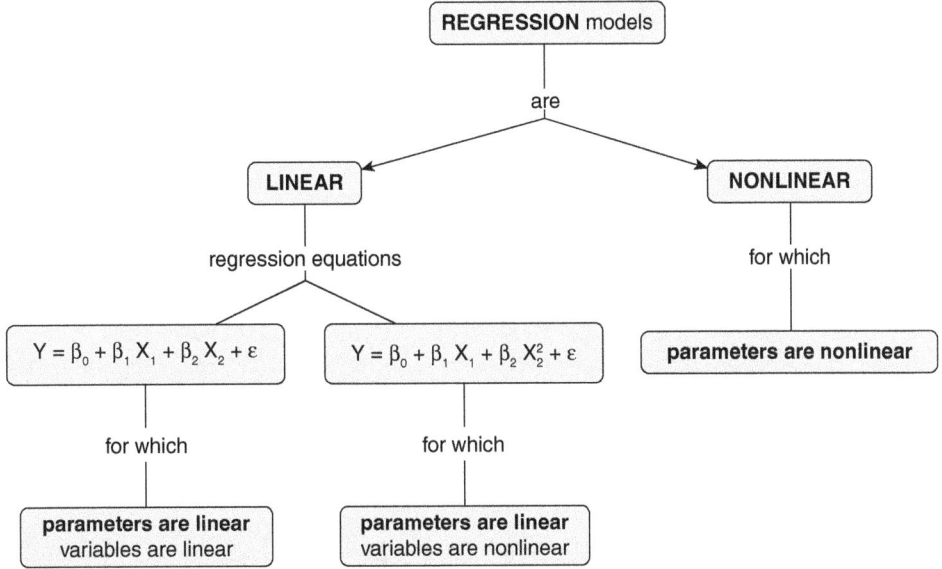

Figure 14.1 Types of regression models

14 ● 1 Linear regression models

There are various types of linear regression models, and the classification of these models is based on the number of independent variables and the scale of measurement of the dependent variable (Figure 14.2). For example, *ordinary least squares regression* gives a regression line that minimises the sums of squared differences between the observed values from one interval independent variable and the expected values as predicted by the regression line, and *multiple linear regression* analysis, which is an extension of the simple linear regression model, predicts the value of an interval dependent variable based on the value of two or more other independent variables.

A linear relationship between two variables is described by a *linear regression*, which models the relationship between two variables by fitting a linear equation to observed data. The general linear regression model is represented by the following equation:

$$\hat{Y} = \beta_0 + \beta_1 X_1$$

where:

- $\hat{Y}$ denotes the predicted dependent variable (often termed the fitted value);
- X_1 denotes the independent variable (or the explanatory or predictor variable);
- β_0 is a regression coefficient, often called the y-intercept;
- β_1 is a regression coefficient, also called the regression slope.

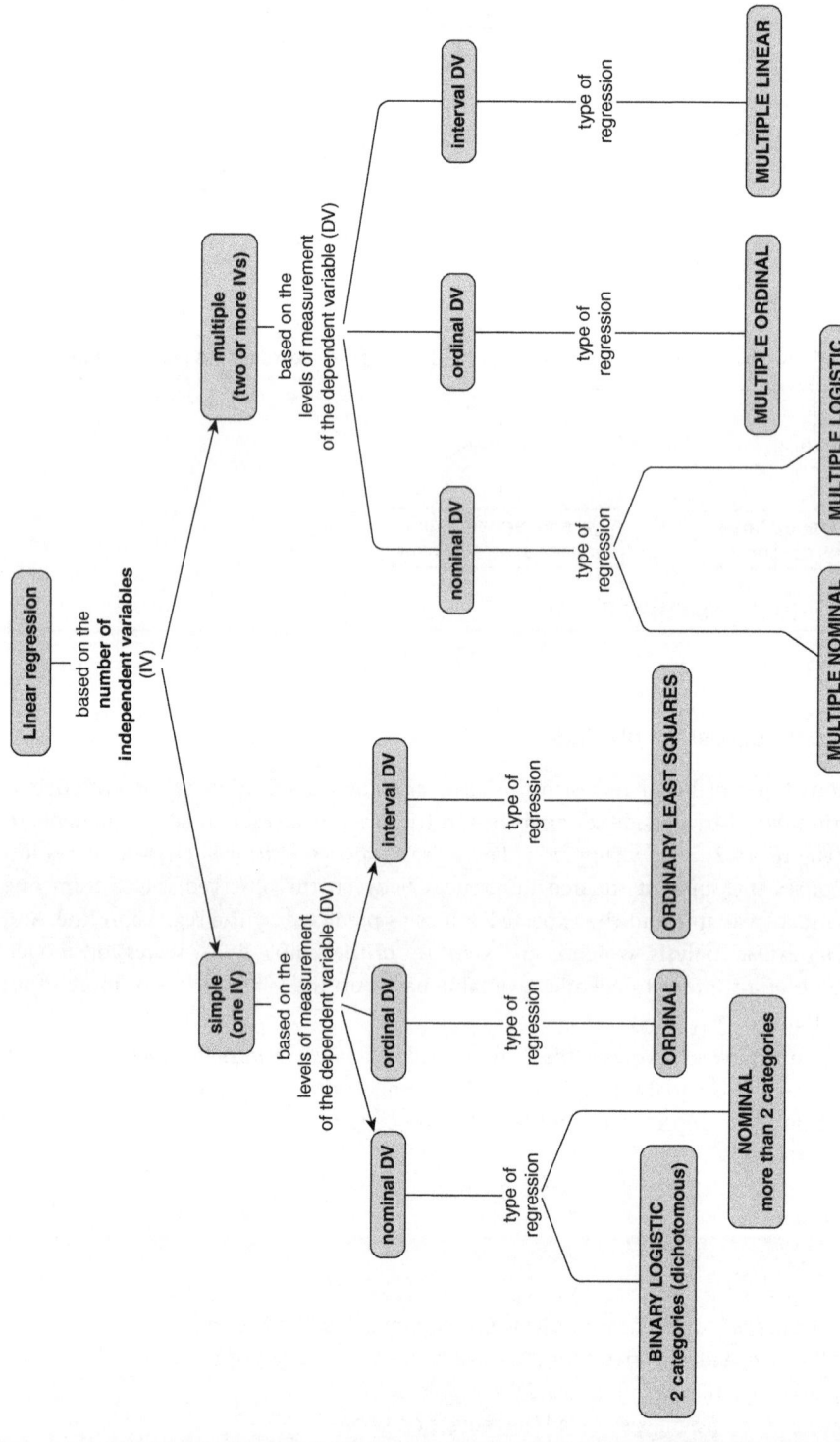

Figure 14.2 Linear regression models

Multiple linear regression analysis is used to find a relationship between one dependent variable and two or more independent variables with the following form of the regression line:

$$\hat{Y} = \beta_0 + \beta_1 X_1 + \beta_2 X_2 + \beta_3 X_3 + \dots + \beta_n X_n$$

There are several types of multiple regression analysis, for example:

- *Standard* or *simultaneous* regression is used when all the independent variables are treated simultaneously and equally and all are entered into the regression equation at once.
- *Hierarchical* regression is used when the independent variables are entered cumulatively according to a specified hierarchy.
- *Sequential* regression is used when not all independent variables are entered into the regression equation, and three different procedures can be used to enter the variables:
  - the *forward procedure* selects from a group of independent variables the one which makes the most significant contribution to the regression coefficient at each stage;
  - the *backward procedure* selects the variable which makes the smallest contribution to the regression coefficient, which is then dropped;
  - the *stepwise procedure* is a forward procedure but with an added condition from the backward procedure that, at each stage, the possibility of deleting an independent variable is considered.

Once the data have been collected, the next steps are as follows:

1. Start to investigate the linear relationships between the dependent and independent variables.
2. Measure the direction and strength of the linear relationships based on the covariance and correlation coefficients.
3. Formulate the linear regression model.
4. Estimate the regression coefficients of the model, referred to as parameter estimation or model fitting.

In previous chapters, we emphasised the importance of testing all the assumptions associated with a model because it is essential to be sure that we do not over- or underestimate the test significance or effect size and that the results are trustworthy (acceptable Type I and Type II error). The underlying assumptions in regression analysis are about the form of the model, the errors, the independent variables and observations. All these assumptions will be discussed later in the next sections.

In the next two sections, we will present ordinary least squares and multiple linear regression methods where the variables used are measured on an interval/ratio scale. Ordinary least squares is a simple linear regression method that models the best-fit value for each observation in our data. We will also demonstrate how to compute the associated statistics and their corresponding assumptions.

14●2 Ordinary least squares regression

Let us assume there is a linear relationship between one interval dependent variable (Y) and one interval independent variable (X_1). When we use the linear regression equation to find the predicted values of the independent variable ($\hat{Y}$) for different values of the independent variable, we are only making predictions about the values of the dependent variable, we are not calculating the actual values of Y. The formula for predicting the value of the dependent variable is:

$$\hat{Y} = \beta_0 + \beta_1 X_1$$

However, when we make such predictions, they will be subject to errors. These *errors* (ε), also known as *residuals,* are defined as the difference between the actual value (Y) and predicted value ($\hat{Y}$) of the dependent variable:

$$\varepsilon = \hat{Y} - Y$$

The formula for the linear regression for the actual value of the dependent variable will be:

$$Y = \beta_0 + \beta_1 X_1 + \varepsilon$$

The slope (β_1) is a geometrical interpretation of the correlation coefficient between the two variables, which is also known as the standardised regression coefficient. There are some general rules which apply to any regression line; for example, if β_1 is positive, Y increases as X_1 increases and if β_1 is negative, Y decreases as X_1 increases. When $\beta_1 = 0$, there is no linear relationship between the two variables and the regression line will be horizontal. The intercept (β_0) is the value of dependent variable Y when the independent variable X is zero (i.e. the y-intercept), which is also called the 'constant' (Figure 14.3). Often, there are situations when we must go outside the range of observed values or dependent variable values to find the intercept. The intercept must be interpreted with caution because of the uncertainty regarding the relationship between the two variables when we are outside the observed values.

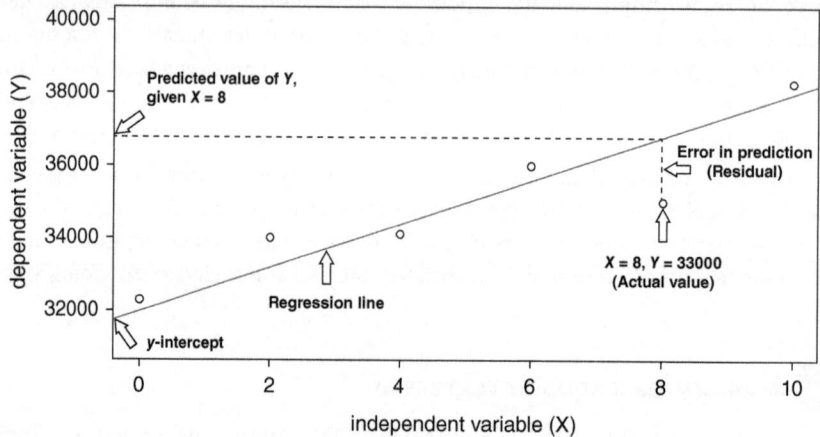

Figure 14.3 The main characteristics of the regression line

Ordinary least squares regression (OLS) creates a regression line that 'best' fits the data values, and this line is calculated mathematically to ensure that the *sum of all squared deviations* of the actual points from the expected values, as predicted by the regression line, is as small as possible. This criterion is known as the *least squares solution*, hence the name of this type of linear regression. The estimated regression line for the OLS model is determined to minimise the standard deviation of the residuals.

The main goal of OLS regression analysis is to make predictions about the values of the dependent variable given specific values of the independent variable, along with the description of the association (relationship) between the variables, usually described by the coefficient of determination (r^2), finding the equation of the line that 'best fits' the data values, validating the required assumptions, and evaluating the model.

Example 14.1 Making predictions using OLS regression

Data set: Ex14_1.csv

(Source: https://cpb-us-w2.wpmucdn.com/sites.lufkinisd.org/dist/c/2/files/2019/08/Teacher-Salary-Schedule-for-2019-2020-for-Sheila.pdf)

In the USA, in May 2018, the median annual wage of the 1.4 million population of elementary school teachers (not including special education teachers) was $58,230 (www.bls.gov/opub/ted/2019/elementary-school-teachers-had-median-annual-wage-of-58230-in-2018.htm). A public school teacher's salary depends on many factors such as education, qualifications, additional skills and length of teaching experience. If we take the example data set shown in Table 14.1, where the years of teaching experience, labelled 'Years', represent the values of the independent variable, and the teachers' salaries, labelled 'Salary', represent the values of the dependent variable, using the linear regression we can predict teachers' salaries based on years of experience.

Table 14.1 Lufkin ISD 2019–20 Teacher Pay Scale ($) in East Texas (US) as a function of years of teaching experience (Source: www.lufkinisd.org)

Years	Salary
0	45,510
2	46,304
4	47,146
6	48,569
8	49,494
10	50,725
12	52,424
14	54,274
16	55,269
18	57,169
20	59,474

We would like to find out how well the independent variable X ('Years') can predict the dependent variable Y ('Salary') by establishing a statistically significant linear relationship between these two variables as accurately as possible. Specific procedures must be followed, which allow us to find the linear regression model. In order to determine which regression model to use, it is essential to start by investigating the relationship between the variables by plotting the dependent variable against the independent variable using a scatterplot.

Import the data set Ex14_1.csv into R and attach it to the R search path using the `attach()` function, which allows us to access the variables by simply giving their names.

```
Ex14_1 <- read.csv(file.choose())
attach(Ex14_1)
```

Create a scatterplot (Figure 14.4) using the `plot()` function:

```
plot(Salary~Years, data=Ex14_1, pch=16, xlab="Years", ylab="Salary ($)")
```

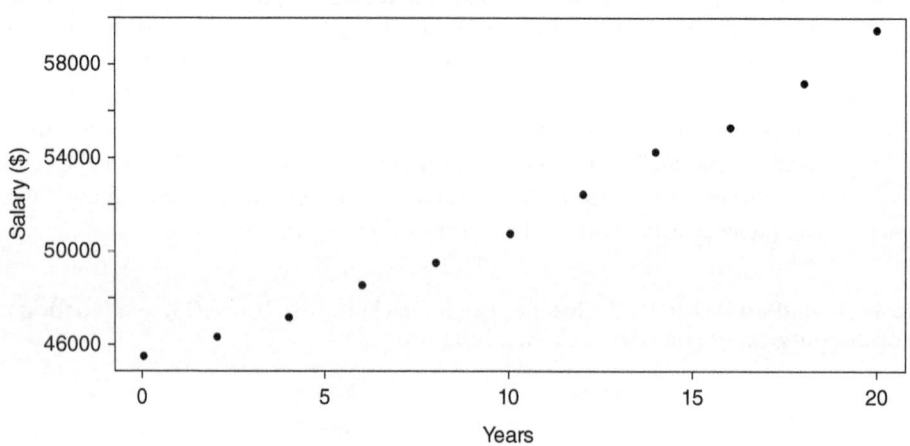

Figure 14.4 Scatterplot for the Ex14_1.csv data set

Interpretation

The scatterplot shown in Figure 14.4 suggests that there is a linear relationship between the two variables, 'Salary' and 'Years', so a simple linear regression model can be used. At every instance, when the independent variable 'Years' increases, the dependent variable 'Salary' also increases along with it, which indicates a positive correlation between the variables. Besides, we can use the function `cor()` to compute the correlation between these two variables to confirm our observation:

```
cor(Salary,Years)
[1] 0.9917234
```

In addition, the correlation is a good indicator of the accuracy of the prediction. If the correlation between the two variables is high, the prediction will be more accurate. Our result, which is a value very close to 1, suggests a strong positive correlation between the two variables, and we expect to obtain accurate prediction values for the 'Salary' variable.

If the variables are not linearly related, we can either use a nonlinear model or transform the data set by using a logarithmic transformation of one or more variables or by replacing the variable by its square root. Such transformations change the shape of a distribution (making it closer to normal) and thus change the relationship between the variables.

14.2.1 Creating the OLS regression model

The primary function in R to compute a linear regression is `lm()` with the following format:

```
lm(formula, data)
```

where *formula* indicates the model to be used, and *data* is the data frame.

Performing linear regression in R

```
lm(Salary~Years)
Call:
lm(formula = Salary ~ Years)
Coefficients:
(Intercept) Years
    44578.5 690.9
```

where the symbol ~ separates the dependent variable labelled 'Salary' from the independent variable labelled 'Years'.

The results help us to establish the relationship between the dependent and independent variables in the form of the following formula:

$$Y = \beta_0 + \beta_1 X_1$$

Salary = Intercept + Slope × Years

The intercept (β_0) is the value of Y when $X = 0$. In our example, the average salary of the teacher with 0 years of teaching experience equals \$44,578.5. In graphical terms, the intercept is the point where the regression line intersects the y-axis (i.e. when $X = 0$). The slope (β_1) is the measure of the steepness (or gradient) of the line. A positive value for the slope suggests a positive relationship between the independent and dependent variables. In our example, the slope value is 690.9, meaning that teachers with more years of teaching have a higher salary. We can also calculate the slope and the intercept individually by using the following formulas in R.

Compute the slope and intercept

```
int = lm(Salary~Years)$coefficient["(Intercept)"]
#This is the coefficient β₀
int
(Intercept)
    44578.5
slope = lm(Salary~Years)$coefficient["Years"]
#This is the parameter β₁
slope
    Years
690.8591
```

If we substitute the regression coefficients into the regression equation, the estimated teacher's salary will be:

$$Salary = 44{,}578.5 + 690.86 \times Years$$

This equation can be used to generate a predicted value of 'Salary' for any given value of 'Years', even if we do not have a specific data point that covers the value. Predicting Y values inside the range of X values (e.g. 3 or 11 years) is called *interpolation*, and if it is outside (e.g. 25 years), it is called *extrapolation*.

The least-squares regression for our independent ('Years') and dependent variables ('Salary') is a method of *fitting a best straight line* that predicts the values of the dependent variable by using the *least-squares* method which minimises the sum of the squares of the deviations of the data from the line. The slope of the regression line tells us the strength and direction of the relationship between variables. For example, a steep regression line means that the rate of change in Y as X changes is bigger; a nearly flat regression line means that while the two variables vary together, the rate of change in one is very slow as the other changes. The intercept of the regression line is the expected mean value of Y when $X = 0$ and tells us the elevation above (or below) the zero point on the vertical axis.

Adding the regression line to the scatterplot

We can add the regression line to our scatterplot (the grey line in Figure 14.5) as follows:

```
abline(int, slope,lty=1, lwd=2, col="grey") #style and colour of line
```

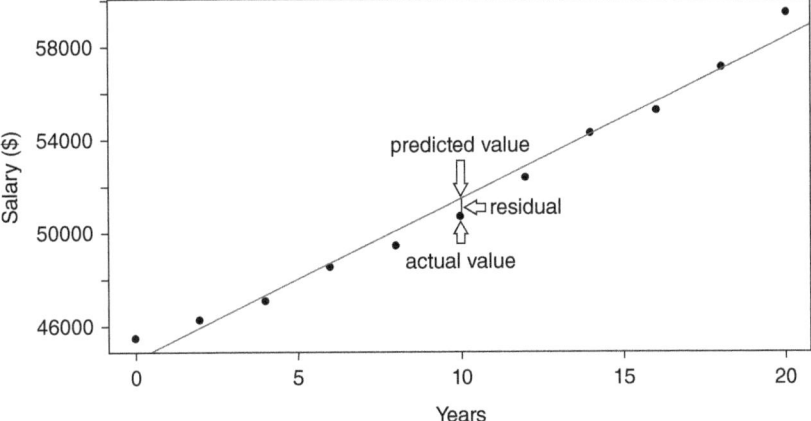

Figure 14.5 Scatterplot and regression line for the Ex14_1.csv data set

The least-squares method states that the regression line always minimises the differences between the actual values (shown as black circles in Figure 14.5) and the predicted values from the regression line (the vertical line). If, for example, a point lies exactly on the fitted line (the eighth point in Figure 14.5), then its vertical deviation is 0. The *error* term is the population value of this deviation which we will never know. Instead, we will use the *residuals*, which are the sample estimate of the error for each observation and are the differences between the actual values (Y) and the predicted values ($\hat{Y}$) of the dependent variable:

$$Residuals = Y - \hat{Y}$$

The vertical distances from each data point to the regression line (Figure 14.3) represent the residuals. In this type of regression, the 'best fit' is defined as the line that minimises the squared vertical distances between the data points and the regression line. The residual standard deviation characterises the variability around the regression line and is defined as:

$$S_{res} = \sqrt{\frac{\Sigma\left(\hat{Y}_i - Y_i\right)^2}{n-2}}$$

The smaller the standard deviation of the residuals, the better the regression line fits the data.

14.2.2 Checking for statistical significance

Now it is essential to establish that the regression model is statistically significant. To do this, we first define the null and alternative hypotheses and then check the statistical significance (*p*-value). The null hypothesis for linear regression is:

$$H_0 : \beta_1 = 0$$

We can express this as 'there is no relationship between the dependent and independent variables'. The alternative hypothesis for linear regression is:

$$H_1 : \beta_1 \neq 0$$

We can express this as 'there is a relationship between the dependent and independent variables'. To generate more information on the regression, for example to get the p-values which are essential for checking statistical significance, we use the `summary()` function to display the detailed output.

Generating more information on the regression

```
summary(lm(Salary~Years)
Call:
lm(formula = Salary ~ Years)
Residuals:
    Min    1Q Median    3Q    Max
-762.1 -404.0 -154.7 249.4 1078.3
Coefficients:
              Estimate Std.  Error  t value  Pr(>|t|)
(Intercept)  44578.50    352.76  126.37  6.18e-16 ***
Years          690.86     29.81   23.17  2.47e-09 ***
---
Signif. codes: 0 '***' 0.001 '**' 0.01 '*' 0.05 '.' 0.1 ' ' 1
Residual standard error: 625.4 on 9 degrees of freedom
Multiple R-squared: 0.9835,  Adjusted R-squared: 0.9817
F-statistic: 537 on 1 and 9 DF, p-value: 2.469e-09
```

Interpretation

The first part of the information listed in the summary output is entitled 'Call:' and shows what function and parameters were used to create the regression model. In this example, the variable labelled 'Salary' is the dependent variable and 'Years' is the independent variable'.

The second part of the information listed is the five-number summary of the 'Residuals' of the regression (minimum, first quartile, median, third quartile, maximum). These descriptive statistics help us to do a quick check of the distribution assumptions of the residuals (the difference between what the model predicted and the actual value of 'Salary' (Y-variable)).

The 'Coefficients' are the weights that minimise the sum of squares of the errors and give the regression coefficient (slope) and the intercept term, accompanied by the standard error ('Std. Error'), t-values and p-values. The Std. Error is the residual standard error divided by the square root of the sum of the square of the dependent variable X.

By dividing the estimated regression coefficient (β_1) by the Std. Error, we can calculate the *t-statistic* as follows:

$$t = \frac{\beta_1}{Std.\ Error}$$

It is good if we get a larger *t*-value because it indicates that it is less likely that the coefficient is not equal to zero purely by chance.

Pr(>|t|), or the *p*-value, is the probability of getting a *t*-value as high as or higher than the observed value when the null hypothesis (that $\beta_1 = 0$) is true. Because Pr(>|t|) is low, the coefficients are significant (significantly different from zero), and the null hypothesis is rejected.

The *residual standard error* expresses the variation in the data set values around the regression line, and it is the average error in predicting 'Salary' from 'Years' using the linear regression model.

The *Multiple R-squared* coefficient, also called the *coefficient of determination* (r^2 or R^2), represents the correlation between the actual and predicted values and indicates how well our model fits the data. In our example, the model accounts for 98.35% (0.9835) of the variance in Years. The formula for *R*-squared does not include the number of the independent variables, and it will always increase or remain the same when a new explanatory variable is added. The coefficient of determination estimates the strength of the relationship between the two variables and it is the square of the correlation coefficient. In other words, it estimates how close the data points on the graph are to the regression line because it is the proportion of the variation of the dependent variable that is explained by the variation in the independent variable.

r^2 may be defined either as a ratio or a percentage, and it can vary from 0 to 1 if we use the ratio form. An r^2 value near 0 indicates a minimal relationship between the variables, with the values falling far away from the regression line, while a value near 1 means that the *Y* values fall very close to the regression line.

The *adjusted R-squared* is used when there are multiple independent variables to add to the model and includes the number of independent variables in its formula. As a result, it normalises the multiple *R*-squared by considering the number of variables, which allows more variance to be explained. And its value is always less than or equal to R^2. For the simple linear regression model, when there is only one independent variable, the adjusted R^2 gives the best estimate of the degree of relationship between the independent and dependent variables, and it increases only when the independent variable is significant and the dependent variable changes because of that.

Also for simple linear regression, the *F-statistic* result is simply the square of *t*-test value ($23.17^2 = 536.8489$), and it is the overall test that checks if at least one of the regression coefficients is non-zero (or we can say that the *F*-statistic tests the null hypothesis that the regression coefficient is zero). The *p*-value is well below the significance level (< 0.05) and it is safe to reject the null hypothesis that the regression coefficient (β_1) is zero.

The linear regression results can be reported in the following format:

> A least squares linear regression was carried out to test how well the number of years of teaching practice predicted the teachers' salaries. The results of the regression indicate that the model explained 98.35% of the variance and that it is significant: $F(1,9) = 537$, $p < 0.005$.

14.2.3 Assessing the assumptions of the linear regression model

There are several assumptions for the OLS regression model that must hold in order to produce the best estimates. The next steps will show how to use R to check these assumptions, using the analysis of residuals:

1. *Linear assumption.* The regression model is assumed to be linear in the regression parameters.

Checking the linearity assumption for a linear regression model can be easily done by examining the linear relationship between the dependent and independent variables by means of the regression line, and the easiest way to evaluate this type of relationship is using scatterplots. For example, this assumption has already been assessed by creating Figures 14.4 and 14.5, which show a positive correlation.

2. *Assumption about residuals.* The residuals are assumed to be normally distributed.

We can assess the normality of the residuals using several approaches, for example the Shapiro–Wilk test and/or a quantile–quantile (QQ) plot.

Checking the normality of the residuals using the Shapiro–Wilk test

We use the function `shapiro.test()` from the `stats` package:

```
shapiro.test(residuals(lm(Salary~Years)))
        Shapiro-Wilk normality test
data:  residuals(lm(Salary~Years))
W = 0.93067, p-value = 0.4177
```

Checking the normality of the residuals using a QQ plot:

```
qqnorm(lm(Salary~Years)$resid) # create the QQ plot
qqline(lm(Salary~Years)$resid) # create the reference line
```

The QQ plot is shown in Figure 14.6.

Interpretation

Because the p-value (0.4177) > 0.05 and the statistic $W = 0.93067 > W_{critical} = 0.842$ for a sample of size $n = 10$ (Table 14.2), we cannot reject the hypothesis that the sample comes from a population which has a normal distribution. The QQ plot (Figure 14.6) has most points on or very near the line, which confirms that the residuals are normally distributed.

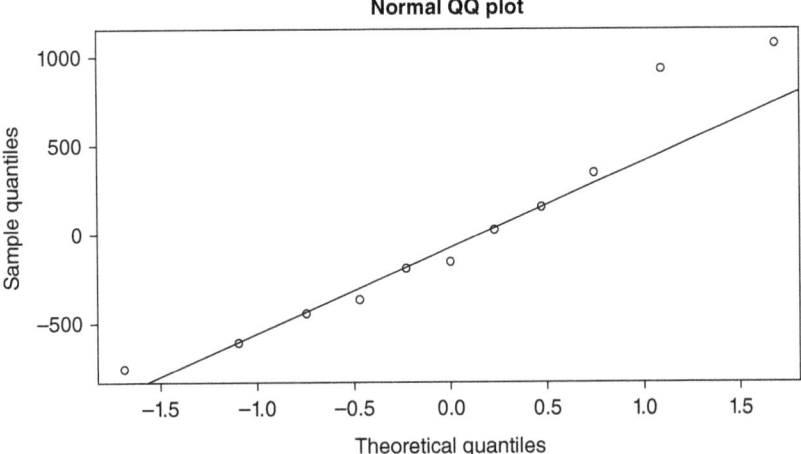

Figure 14.6 QQ plot for residuals

Table 14.2 Critical *p*-values for the Shapiro–Wilk test

n\p	0.01	0.02	0.05	0.1	0.5	0.9	0.95	0.98	0.99
3	0.753	0.756	0.767	0.789	0.959	0.998	0.999	1.000	1.000
4	0.687	0.707	0.748	0.792	0.935	0.987	0.992	0.996	0.997
5	0.686	0.715	0.762	0.806	0.927	0.979	0.986	0.991	0.993
6	0.713	0.743	0.788	0.826	0.927	0.974	0.981	0.986	0.989
7	0.730	0.760	0.803	0.838	0.928	0.972	0.979	0.985	0.988
8	0.749	0.778	0.818	0.851	0.932	0.972	0.978	0.984	0.987
9	0.764	0.791	0.829	0.859	0.935	0.972	0.978	0.984	0.986
10	0.781	0.806	0.842	0.869	0.938	0.972	0.978	0.983	0.986
11	0.792	0.817	0.850	0.876	0.940	0.973	0.979	0.984	0.986
12	0.805	0.828	0.859	0.883	0.943	0.973	0.979	0.984	0.986
13	0.814	0.837	0.866	0.889	0.945	0.974	0.979	0.984	0.986
14	0.825	0.846	0.874	0.895	0.947	0.975	0.980	0.984	0.986
15	0.835	0.855	0.881	0.901	0.950	0.975	0.980	0.984	0.987

3.   *Homoscedasticity assumption.* The residuals have the same variance.

This assumption is about the amount of error in the model, which checks if the variation in the residuals is similar at each data point of the model. To test the homoscedasticity, we can use the non-constant variance score test or the Breusch–Pagan test, alongside a plot of the standardised values of the regression model against the standardised residuals obtained.

Testing the homoscedasticity through the non–constant variance score test

Install and load the `car` package which contains the function `ncvTest(model)` to compute the score test for non-constant error variance:

```
ncvTest(lm(Salary~Years)
Non-constant Variance Score Test
Variance formula: ~ fitted.values
Chisquare = 0.05940456, Df = 1, p = 0.80744
```

Testing the homoscedasticity graphically

Plotting the standardised residuals obtained (y-axis) against the standardised values our model would predict (fitted values, on the x-axis) reveals if there is a nonlinear relationship between the variables (Figure 14.7):

```
plot(fitted(lm(Salary~Years),residuals(lm(Salary~Years))
abline(0,0)          # Add a horizontal line to the plot
```

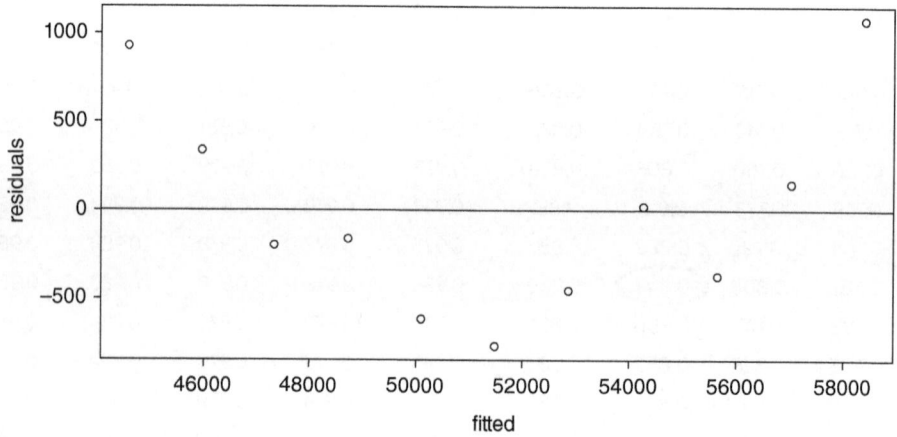

Figure 14.7   A plot of residuals against predicted values; the residuals are unbiased and homoscedastic

Interpretation

The probability value (0.80744) is greater than 0.05, which suggests that the assumption of constant variance has been met. Besides, the residuals versus predicted values plot (Figure 14.7) shows no systematic patterns of these points around the horizontal line representing the residual error of zero, which indicates that the dependent variable is linearly related to the independent variable.

14 ● 3 Multiple linear regression

The *multiple linear regression* model is used for a multivariate data set, which contains a single interval dependent variable (Y) and multiple independent interval variables ($X_1, X_2, ..., X_n$). The general formula for multiple linear regression lines is:

$$Y = \beta_0 + \beta_1 X_1 + \beta_2 X_2 + \beta_3 X_3 + ... + \beta_n X_n + \varepsilon$$

where $\beta_1, \beta_2, ..., \beta_n$ are the regression coefficients, β_0 is the intercept, and ε is the error term or residual. There are two types of multiple regression, depending on the number of dependent variables included in the model. For example, if there are only two independent variables in the model, the multiple regression is called *direct regression* and the model is given by the following equation:

$$\hat{Y} = \beta_0 + \beta_1 X_1 + \beta_2 X_2$$

In this book, we only consider the direct regression case, because the other cases are rather complex and beyond the scope of the book.

Example 14.2 Making predictions using multiple direct regression

Data set Ex14_2.csv

A group of university lecturers who teach first-year education students would like to identify the factors that could affect the performance of students in the undergraduate programme. The primary data were collected from 15 randomly selected first-year students using a questionnaire. The questionnaire contained closed questions about the following three variables related to different aspects of the students' performance at university at the end of the first semester:

- the students' weighted average mark during the semester (the dependent variable, called 'Marks');
- the preparation time for a total of four assignments and/or exams (the first independent variable, called 'Preparation');
- the students' attendance at seminars and lectures (the second independent variable, called 'Attendance').

The results are displayed in Table 14.3.

Table 14.3 Questionnaire results: the attendance (in hours) at seminars and lectures ('Attendance'), the preparation time (in hours) for exams ('Preparation') and the weighted average mark of students' academic performance ('Marks'). All data refers to the first semester

Attendance	Preparation	Marks
100	40	58
112	43	63
78	18	41

(Continued)

Table 14.3 (Continued)

Attendance	Preparation	Marks
60	10	30
85	25	46
93	33	54
88	27	50
74	17	38
90	30	53
118	47	69
120	48	70
115	45	66
70	15	35
80	20	43
95	35	55
116	40	70
100	48	70
115	45	68
70	20	35
80	25	43
95	30	55
93	35	56
80	30	50
75	27	48
100	40	60

We will now look at how to carry out a multiple linear regression and how to assess the relationship between variables and the assumptions about the model.

14.3.1 Creating the multiple linear regression model

To compute a multiple linear regression in R, we use the same function, `lm(formula, data)`, as described in Section 14.2.1 for the simple linear regression, the only difference being that two independent variables are included in the format, separated by a '+' symbol (see below).

Computing multiple regression in R

Import the Ex14_2.csv data set into R and attach it to the R search path using the `attach()` function, which allows us to access the variables by simply giving their names:

```
Ex14_2 <- read.csv(file.choose())
attach(Ex14_2)
```

Perform the multiple linear regression model:

```
lm(formula = Marks~Attendance+Preparation)
Coefficients:
(Intercept)     Attendance     Preparation
     7.4901         0.2585          0.6856
```

Interpretation

The results help us to establish the relationship between the dependent and the two independent variables in the form of the following multiple regression equation:

$$Marks = 7.49008 + 0.25849 \times Attendance + 0.68562 \times Preparation$$

The intercept (7.49008) is the value of the dependent variable when both independent variables are set to zero. In our example, the students' weighted average mark during the semester with no course attendance and preparation time equals 7.49. The regression coefficient of the independent variable 'Attendance' suggests that each unit of attendance adds 0.26 to the mark when the preparation time is held fixed. The regression coefficient of the second independent variable suggests that each unit of preparation adds 0.69 to the mark when the attendance time is held fixed.

14.3.2 Checking statistical significance

To get the *p*-values which are essential for checking statistical significance, we use the `summary()` function to display the detailed output.

Generating more information on the regression

Get the summary output using the `summary()` function:

```
MR<-lm(formula = Marks~Attendance+Preparation)
summary(MR)
```

(Continued)

```
Call:
lm(formula = Marks ~ Attendance + Preparation)
Residuals:
Min         1Q    Median     3Q     Max
-4.2970 -1.2164  -0.1554 1.2508  5.0999
Coefficients:
             Estimate Std. Error t value Pr(>|t|)
(Intercept)   7.49008    3.87170   1.935  0.06601 .
Attendance    0.25849    0.07702   3.356  0.00286 **
Preparation   0.68562    0.11681   5.870  6.61e-06 ***
---
Signif. codes: 0 '***' 0.001 '**' 0.01 '*' 0.05 '.' 0.1 ' ' 1
Residual standard error: 2.253 on 22 degrees of freedom
Multiple R-squared: 0.9685, Adjusted R-squared: 0.9656
F-statistic: 338.2 on 2 and 22 DF, p-value: < 2.2e-16
```

Interpretation

The multiple regression is highly statistically significant ($F = 338.2$, p-value < 0.0001), indicating that the model fits the data very well; that is, the relationship between attendance at seminars and lectures and exam preparation time, on the one hand, and exam marks, on the other hand, is statistically significant. The two regression coefficients (the slopes 0.25849 and 0.68562) show that each adds different values to the dependent variable when the value of the other independent variable is held fixed. The value of the second regression coefficient is much bigger than the first, which suggests that a 1% increase in the preparation time for exams brings a roughly 0.69% increase in exam marks, keeping all other factors constant. The t- and p-values allow us to determine whether preparation time and attendance are statistically significantly related to marks. Both p-values (0.002 and 0.0000) are less than 0.05, which indicates that each independent variable is a significant predictor of the dependent variable. The t-test tells us that the slope of each independent variable is significantly different from zero.

Furthermore, the multiple R-squared value equals 0.9685, which means that the multiple linear regression model can explain 96.85% of the variance in the dependent variable, leaving 3.15% unexplained variance. The adjusted R-squared (0.9656) adjusts the R-squared value by taking into consideration the number of the independent variables included in the model.

We can summarise the results of the multiple regression in the following way:

A multiple regression analysis was conducted to examine the association between two independent variables (Attendance and Preparation) and a dependent variable (Marks). The independent variables were simultaneously entered into the model, and together they accounted for 96.56% of the variation in the dependent variable. These variables were significant predictors of the exam marks ($\beta_1 = 0.25849$, $p < 0.005$ and $\beta_2 = 0.68562$, $p < 0.005$).

14.3.3 Assessing the assumptions of the multiple linear regression model

Each data point has an associated residual, which is the vertical distance between the model and the data point, and these residuals play crucial roles in assessing the assumptions of the multiple regression model. The assumptions of multiple linear regression that must be met for results to be valid are as follows:

Assumption 1. The dependent and independent variables should be measured on an interval/ratio scale.

Assumption 2. There is a linear relationship between the two independent variables and the dependent variable.

A simple way to check if the relationship between the dependent variable and each of the independent variables (Marks and Attendance, and Marks and Preparation) is linear is by producing a scatterplot using the function `plot()`. If any plot shows a nonlinearity, we may use a transformation of the data, such as log, to obtain linearity.

Showing the relationship between the dependent variable 'Marks' and the independent variable 'Attendance'

```
plot(Marks~Attendance, pch=16, xlab="Attendance(hours)", ylab="Average
Mark(%)")
```

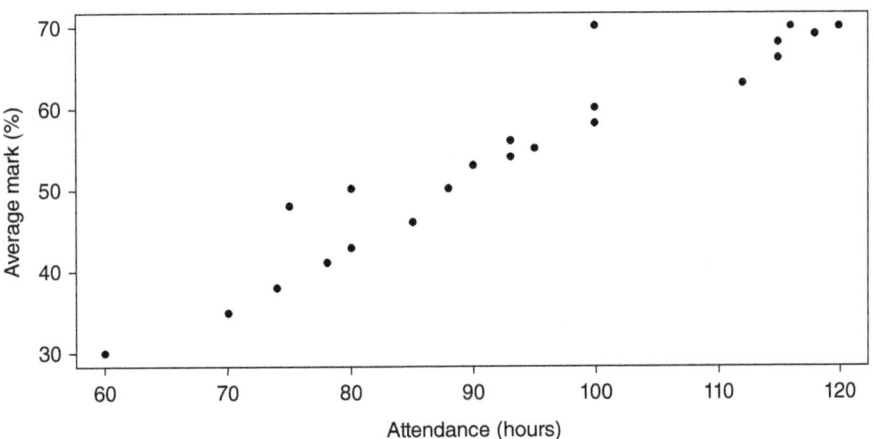

Figure 14.8 Scatterplot of the dependent variable 'Marks' against the independent variable 'Attendance'

(Continued)

Showing the relationship between the dependent variable 'Marks' and the independent variable 'Preparation'

```
plot(Marks~Preparation, pch=16, xlab="Preparation time(hours)",
+ ylab="Average Mark(%)")
```

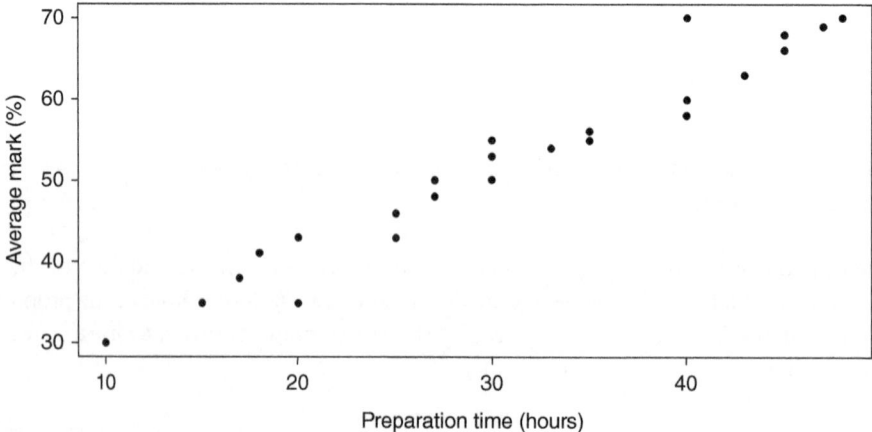

Figure 14.9 Scatterplot of the dependent variable 'Marks' against the independent variable 'Preparation'

Looking at the two scatterplots in Figures 14.8 and 14.9, we can see that the data have linear patterns in both cases, suggesting that the relationships between the dependent variable and each of the independent variables are linear.

Two or more independent variables might be correlated with each other, and this situation is called *collinearity*. In the presence of collinearity, one independent variable gives similar information to another independent variable, and the regression model becomes unstable, and it will be challenging to identify the unique relationship between each independent variable and the dependent variable. There are two well-known measures which can be used to measure collinearity:

(1)   the coefficient of multiple determination for each independent variable, and
(2)   the *variance inflation factor* (VIF) for each independent variable.

The coefficient of multiple determination (R^2) measures the proportion of variance in the dependent variable that is explained by all the independent variables. The VIF measures how much the variance of a regression coefficient is amplified due to collinearity. The smallest possible value of VIF is 1 (absence of collinearity), and it is always positive. If the VIF value is:

•   less than 5, it indicates a low correlation between independent variables;

- between 5 and 10, it indicates a moderate correlation;
- greater than 10, it indicates a high correlation which is not suitable for the model - values of VIF greater than 10 are often regarded as indicating collinearity.

To compute the variance inflation factors, we can use either the function `vif()` (from the `car` package), or the function `check_collinearity()` (from the `performance` package).

Computing the variance inflation factors

```
vif(MR)
  Attendance   Preparation
    8.187317      8.187317
check_collinearity(MR)
# Check for Multicollinearity

Moderate Correlation

    Parameter    VIF Increased SE
   Attendance   8.19         2.86
   Preparation  8.19         2.86
```

In both cases, the results for both independent variables are less than 10, which suggests moderate collinearity.

Collinearity may lead to severely biased regression coefficients and standard errors. The 'Increased SE' column in the output indicates how much larger the standard error is due to the correlation with other predictors. This assumption can be assessed by looking at the distribution of residuals using the Shapiro–Wilk test for normality or by looking at the QQ plot.

Computing the Shapiro–Wilk test

```
shapiro.test(residuals(MR))
        Shapiro-Wilk normality test
data:   residuals(MR2)
W = 0.98861, p-value = 0.9907
```

Creating the QQ plot with reference line

```
qqnorm(MR$resid)
qqline(MR$resid)
```

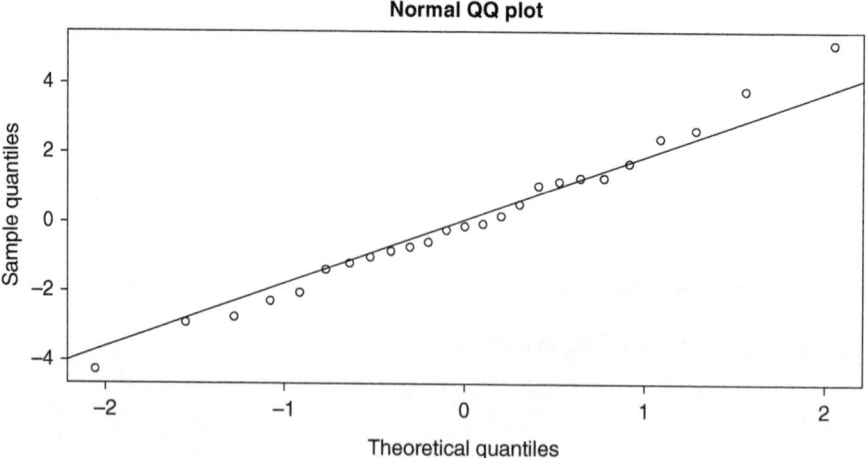

Figure 14.10 QQ plot for residuals

Because the *p*-value (0.9907) is greater than 0.05 and the QQ plot (Figure 14.10) shows that most points lie on or very near the line, we conclude that the residuals are normally distributed. This result means that this assumption is fulfilled. If the residuals are not normally distributed, we first check if there are outlier observations and then delete them.

Assumption 3. The residuals have the same variance (homoscedasticity).

The assumption that the variation in the residuals is similar at each point of the model, which is the assumption of *homoscedasticity*, can be tested using the ncvTest() function from the car package, and we will test the null hypothesis of constant error variance. Alongside this test result, we can easily evaluate the homoscedasticity by plotting the standardised residuals obtained against the standardised values our model would predict (Figure 14.11).

Checking homoscedasticity in R

```
ncvTest(MR)
Non-constant Variance Score Test
Variance formula: ~ fitted.values
Chisquare = 1.089505, Df = 1, p = 0.29658
```

Plotting the standardised residuals obtained against the predicted standardised values:
```
plot(fitted(MR), residuals(MR))
abline(0,0)
```

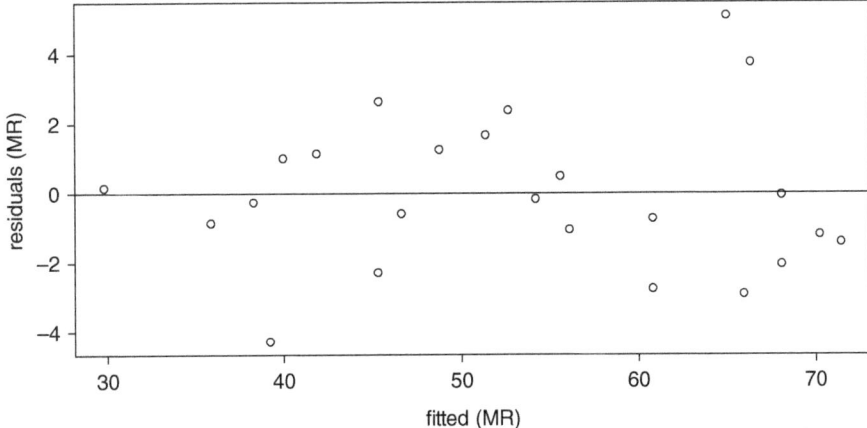

Figure 14.11 Plot of standardised residuals obtained against predicted standardised values

The probability value of the test (*p*-value = 0.29658) is more than 0.05, which suggests that the assumption of homoscedasticity (or constant variance of residuals) is met. This result is also confirmed by the scatterplot shown in Figure 14.11, where the plotted residuals appear randomly distributed around zero (the horizontal line), which is an indication that we have constant variance and our multiple linear regression model fits the data well. A systematic pattern, such as a funnel shape, would indicate a non-constant variance, which might be due to the sampling methods and sample size used or the presence of outliers. This situation must be corrected, for example, by increasing the sample size (at least 30 cases) or removing the outliers.

Assumption 4. The values of the residuals are uncorrelated.

For a multiple linear regression model, the residuals (errors) of the independent variables should be uncorrelated (or independent), and this aspect can be verified if we assess the independence of residuals, which implies the independence of the independent variables. The Durbin–Watson (DW) statistic can be used to test this assumption.

Checking if residuals are uncorrelated

```
durbinWatsonTest(MR)
lag    Autocorrelation D-W Statistic p-value
  1          0.2494206      1.427535   0.096
Alternative hypothesis: rho != 0
```

The 'lag = 1' value indicates that each observation is being compared with the one next to it in the data set.

Based on the results (DW statistic = 1.42, and $p = 0.096 > 0.05$), we can accept the null hypothesis that the errors are independent; therefore, the independent variables are not correlated.

The uses of simple and multiple linear regressions

Firstly, in regression analysis, the focus is on predicting one variable from another, taking the correlation to the next level. Secondly, if we wish to know whether changes in the independent variable cause the variation in a dependent variable, we might refer to this study as the study of causation. However, we must be cautious when making claims about causation because there may well be other factors affecting the dependent variable. In conclusion, to obtain regression results that we can trust, we need to test the assumptions associated with each model and be sure that the chosen model fits the data adequately.

Formulas

Linear regression model

$$\hat{Y} = \beta_0 + \beta_1 X_1$$

where $\hat{Y}$ is the predicted dependent variable, X_1 is the independent variable, β_0 is the intercept and β_0 is the slope or y-intercept.

If we add the residuals (ε), the regression formula for the dependent variable (Y) is:

$$Y = \beta_0 + \beta_1 X_1$$

where:

$$\varepsilon = \hat{Y} - Y$$

Multiple linear regression model

$$\hat{Y} = \beta_0 + \beta_1 X_1 + \beta_2 X_2$$

where $\hat{Y}$ is the predicted dependent variable, X_1 and X_2 are the independent variables, β_0 is the intercept and β_1, β_2 are the slopes.

Exercises

14.1   What are the difficulties of interpreting the results of any hypothesis test for normality?
14.2   Why is it essential to verify that a regression model has met the statistical assumptions?

14.3   List the assumptions of:

(a)   a linear regression model

(b)   a multiple regression model

14.4   Explain the difference between Y and $\hat{Y}$ in a linear regression model.

14.5   Define the slope and intercept.

14.6   Can we use the regression analysis if we have a dichotomous variable?

14.7   What is the difference between R-squared and adjusted R-squared?

14.8   Calculate the linear regression line for the data in Table 14.4 and test the assumptions of the model:

Table 14.4   Teachers' annual pay scale as a function of teaching experience

Teaching experience (years)	Salary (£)
0	32,275
2	34,000
4	34,126
6	36,000
8	35,000
10	38,266

Further reading

Ciaburro, G. (2018) *Regression analysis with R: Design and develop statistical nodes to identify unique relationships within data at scale.* Birmingham: Packt Publishing.

This book introduces simple linear, multiple linear and logistic regression and provides an overview of the packages and functions used in R to create various types of regression models.

James, G., Witten, D., Hastie, T. and Tibshirani, R. (2013) Linear regression. In *An introduction to statistical learning.* New York: Springer.

This book chapter deals with regression models, and the authors explain the term 'random error'.

Weisberg, S. (2005) *Applied linear regression* (3rd ed.). Hoboken, NJ: Wiley-Interscience.

This book focuses on the use of least squares regression analysis, helping the student to master the theory and application of linear modelling, from building the model to drawing conclusions. In the third edition, graphical methods and practical examples are integrated to explore the use of linear regression analyses to solve real-life problems.

BIBLIOGRAPHY

Ackoff, R. (1989) From data to wisdom. *Journal of Applied Systems Analysis*, 16, 3–9.

Akoglu, H. (2018) User's guide to correlation coefficients. *Turkish Journal of Emergency Medicine*, 18, 91–93.

Almer, E. (2017) *Statistical tricks and traps: An illustrated guide to the misuses of statistics*. London: Routledge.

Altman, D. and Bland, M. (2005) Standard deviations and standard errors. *British Medical Journal*, 331, 903.

Argyrous, G. (2014) *Statistics for research: With a guide to SPSS*. London: Sage.

Arnold, T. and Tilton, L. (2015) *Humanities data in R*. Cham: Springer.

Balnaves, M. and Caputi, P. (2001) *Introduction to quantitative research methods: An investigative approach*. London: Sage.

Bergin, T. (2018) *An introduction to data analysis: Quantitative, qualitative and mixed methods*. London: Sage.

Berry, K. J., Johnston, J. E. and Mielke, P. W., Jr (2007) An alternative measure of effect size for Cochran's Q-test for related proportions. *Perceptual and Motor Skills*, 104, 1236–1242.

Black, T. (1999) *Doing quantitative research in the social sciences: An integrated approach to research design, measurement and statistics*. London: Sage.

Boslaugh, S. (2013) *Statistics in a nutshell* (2nd ed.). Farnham: O'Reilly.

Burns, R. (2000) *Introduction to research methods* (4th ed.). London: Sage.

Ciaburro, G. (2018) *Regression analysis with R: Design and develop statistical nodes to identify unique relationships within data at scale*. Birmingham: Packt Publishing.

Cohen, J. (1988) *Statistical power analysis for the behavioral sciences* (2nd ed.). Hillsdale, NJ: Lawrence Erlbaum Associates.

Connolly, P. (2007) *Quantitative data analysis in education: A critical introduction using SPSS*. London: Routledge.

Coolican, H. (2019) *Research methods and statistics in psychology* (7th ed.). London: Routledge.

Cramer, D. (2003) *Advanced quantitative data analysis*. Maidenhead: Open University Press.

Cramer, D. and Howitt, D. (2004) *The Sage dictionary of statistics: A practical resource for students in the social sciences*. London: Sage.

Crawley, M. (2013) *The R book* (2nd ed.). Chichester: John Wiley & Sons.

Crawley, M. (2014) *Statistics: An introduction using R* (2nd ed.). Chichester: John Wiley & Sons.

Creswell, J. (2012) *Educational research: Planning, conducting, and evaluating quantitative and qualitative research* (4th ed.). Boston: Pearson.

Davies, T. (2018) *The book of R: A first course in programming and statistics*. San Francisco: No Starch Press.

Derryberry, D. (2014) *Basic data analysis for time series with r*. Hoboken, NJ: John Wiley & Sons.

Doane, D. and Seward, L. (2011) Measuring skewness: A forgotten statistic? *Journal of Statistics Education*, 19(2).

Egbert, J. and Sanden, S. (2020) *Foundations of education research: Understanding theoretical components* (2nd ed.). New York: Routledge.

Field, A. (2016) *An adventure in statistics: The reality enigma*. London: Sage.

Fielding, J. and Gilbert, G. (2006) *Understanding social statistics* (2nd ed.). London: Sage.

Fogarty, B. (2019) *Quantitative social science data with R*. London: Sage.

Fraenkel, J. and Wallen, N. (1993) *How to design and evaluate research in education* (2nd ed.). New York: McGraw-Hill.

Frey, B. (2006) *Statistics hacks*. Sebastopol, CA: O'Reilly.

Gardener, M. (2017) *Statistics for ecologists using R and Excel: Data collection, exploration, analysis and presentation* (2nd ed., Data in the Wild series). Exeter: Pelagic Publishing.

Goodwin, W. and Goodwin, L. (1996) *Understanding quantitative and qualitative research in early childhood education*. New York: Teachers College Press.

Gorard, S. (2001) *Quantitative methods in educational research: The role of numbers made easy*. London: Continuum.

Gorard, S. (2015) Introducing the mean absolute deviation 'effect' size. *International Journal of Research & Method in Education*, 38(2): 105–114.

Grant, R. (2019) *Data visualization: Charts, maps, and interactive graphics*. Boca Raton, FL: CRC Press.

Harlow, L., Mulaik, S. and Steiger, J. (eds) (2016) *What if there were no significance tests?* New York: Routledge.

Hinton, P. (2014) *Statistics explained* (3rd ed.). London: Routledge.

Holcomb, Z. (2017) *Fundamentals of descriptive statistics*. London: Routledge.

Holcomb, Z. and Cox, K. (2018) *Interpreting basic statistics: A workbook based on excerpts from journal articles* (8th ed.). New York: Routledge.

Huck, S. (2016) *Statistical misconceptions*. New York: Routledge.

James, G., Witten, D., Hastie, T. and Tibshirani, R. (2013) Linear regression. In *An introduction to statistical learning*. New York: Springer.

Krehbiel, T. (2004) Correlation coefficient rule of thumb. *Decision Sciences Journal of Innovative Education*, 2(1), 97–100.

Landers, R. (2019) *A step-by-step introduction to statistics for business* (2nd ed.). London: Sage.

Linneman, T. (2018) *Social statistics: Managing data, conducting analyses, presenting results* (3rd ed.). New York: Routledge

MacInnes, J. (2019) *Little quick fix: Statistical significance*. London: Sage.

McGrath, M. (2018) *R for data analysis in easy steps – R programming*. Leamington Spa: Easy Steps.

Nachmias, C. and Nachmias, D. (1992) *Research methods in the social sciences* (4th ed.). London: Edward Arnold.

Nussbaum, E. (2015) *Categorical and nonparametric data analysis: Choosing the best statistical technique*. New York: Routledge.

OECD (1995) *OECD education statistics 1985-1992: Statistiques de l'enseignement de l'OCDE*. Paris: OECD.

Office for National Statistics (2018) Employee earnings in the UK: 2018. London: ONS.

Olejnik, S. (2003) Generalized eta and omega squared statistics: Measures of effect size for some common research designs. *Physiological Methods*, 8(4), 434–447.

Pandya, K., Joshi, P. and Bulsari, S. (2018) *Statistical analysis in simple steps using R*. New Delhi: Sage.

Pathak, R. (2011) *Statistics in education and psychology*. New Delhi: Dorling Kindersley.

Pearson, R. (2018) *Exploratory data analysis using R*. Boca Raton, FL: CRC Press/Taylor & Francis Group.

Peers, I. (1996) *Statistical analysis for education and psychology researchers*. London: Falmer Press.

Pek, J. and Flora, D. (2018) Reporting effect sizes in original psychological research: A discussion and tutorial. *Physiological Methods*, 23(2), 208–225.

Pyrczak, F. and Oh, D. (2018) *Making sense of statistics: A conceptual overview* (7th ed.). New York: Routledge.

Rahlf, T. (2019) *Data visualisation with R: 111 examples* (2nd ed.). Cham: Springer.

Redelmeier, D. (2017) A simple method for analyzing matched designs with double controls: McNemar's test can be extended. *Journal of Clinical Epidemiology*, 81, 51–55.

Rowntree, D. (2018) *Statistics without tears: An introduction for non-mathematicians*. London: Penguin.

Salkind, N. J. (2010) *Encyclopedia of research design* (3 vols.). Thousand Oaks, CA: Sage.

Salkind, N. J. (2011) *Statistics for people who (think they) hate statistics*. London: Sage.

Serlin, R. C., Carr, J. and Marascuillo, L. A. (1982) A measure of association for selected nonparametric procedures. *Psychological Bulletin*, 92, 786–790.

Stevens, S. (1946) On the theory of scales of measurement. *Science*, 103(2684), 677–680.

Stinerock, R. (2018) *Statistics with R: A beginner's guide*. London: Sage.

Swires-Hennessy, E. (2014) *Presenting data: How to communicate your message effectively*. Chichester: John Wiley & Sons.

Taherdoost, H. (2016) Sampling methods in research methodology: How to choose a sampling technique for research. *International Journal of Academic Research in Management*, 5(2), 18–27.

Tanner, D. (2012) *Using statistics to make educational decisions*. London: Sage.

Terrell, S. R. (2012) *Statistics translated: A step-by-step guide to analyzing and interpreting data* (1st ed.). New York: Guilford Press.

Tufte, E. (2004) *The visual display of quantitative information*. Cheshire, CT: Graphics Press.

UNESCO Institute for Statistics (2010) *Global education digest 2010: Comparing education statistics across the world*. Montreal: UNESCO Institute for Statistics.

Urdan, T. (2017) *Statistics in plain English* (4th ed.). New York: Routledge.

Van Blerkom, M. (2009) *Measurement and statistics for teachers*. New York: Routledge.

Weisberg, S. (2005) *Applied linear regression* (3rd ed.). Hoboken, NJ: Wiley-Interscience.

Wiley, J. and Pace, L. (2015) *Beginning R: An introduction to statistical programming* (2nd ed.). Berkeley, CA: Apress.

Zins, C. (2007) Conceptual approaches for defining data, information and knowledge. *Journal of the American Society for Information Science and Technology*, 58(4), 479–493.

INDEX